"This weave of neurobiology, contemporary psychology, and deep wisdom offers the most fascinating and helpful framework for understanding personality that I've encountered! Professionals and lay people alike will find a fresh perspective on how humans develop, and the compassion that allows us to relate to ourselves and others in a truly healing way."

—**Tara Brach**, author of *Radical Compassion*

"Daniel Siegel and the PDP Group have done something extraordinary. For many years, people in the Enneagram field have sought to find a neurological basis for the Enneagram types as we have come to understand them, and those within the healing professions have looked for ways to meaningfully integrate the Enneagram's powerful insights into their work. This wonderful book accomplishes both goals. It opens a new conversation about the nature of personality and looks at how we can best work with it as professionals. The authors do a marvelous job of bringing many powerful new perspectives to the field of Enneagram studies while maintaining a respect for the integrity of its core teachings. This is no small feat. I suspect this book is destined to be a classic in the field of personality studies, and highly recommend it for serious Enneagram students and professionals in psychology alike."

—**Russ Hudson**, coauthor of *The Wisdom of the Enneagram*

"At the heart of the fascinating approach presented in this book is what the authors call *patterns of developmental pathways*. They root these pathways in an ancient model of individual differences called the Enneagram, which suggested nine dimensions for personality. Dr. Siegel and the PDP Group collapse these into three domains of agency, bonding, and certainty, linking them to evolved motivational systems and neurobiological infrastructures. These three domains are subject to various genetic and social-contextual influences, giving rise to nine different patterns of personality and, importantly, different ways of helping people. As with so much of Siegel's writing, here we are provided with scholarly and fascinating new insights, as well as wisdoms to consider when empathically engaging with clients and seeking to help them. Much to savor and learn from."

—**Paul Gilbert**, PhD, author of *The Compassionate Mind* and *Living Like Crazy*

"Daniel Siegel and his colleagues have created a brand-new dimension of theoretical and clinical understanding by combining science and the enneagram. There is much to learn here."

—**Jack Kornfield**, PhD, author of *A Path With Heart*

PERSONALITY *and* WHOLENESS *in* THERAPY

The Norton Series on Interpersonal Neurobiology

Louis Cozolino, PhD, Series Editor
Allan N. Schore, PhD, Series Editor, 2007–2014
Daniel J. Siegel, MD, Founding Editor

The field of mental health is in a tremendously exciting period of growth and conceptual reorganization. Independent findings from a variety of scientific endeavors are converging in an interdisciplinary view of the mind and mental well-being. An interpersonal neurobiology of human development enables us to understand that the structure and function of the mind and brain are shaped by experiences, especially those involving emotional relationships.

The Norton Series on Interpersonal Neurobiology provides cutting-edge, multidisciplinary views that further our understanding of the complex neurobiology of the human mind. By drawing on a wide range of traditionally independent fields of research—such as neurobiology, genetics, memory, attachment, complex systems, anthropology, and evolutionary psychology—these texts offer mental health professionals a review and synthesis of scientific findings often inaccessible to clinicians. The books advance our understanding of human experience by finding the unity of knowledge, or consilience, that emerges with the translation of findings from numerous domains of study into a common language and conceptual framework.

The PDP group: Laura A. Baker, PhD,
David N. Daniels, MD, Denise Daniels, PhD,
and Jack Killen, MD

PERSONALITY

and WHOLENESS

in THERAPY

INTEGRATING 9 PATTERNS
OF DEVELOPMENTAL PATHWAYS
IN CLINICAL PRACTICE

DANIEL J. SIEGEL, MD

AND THE PDP GROUP

Norton Professional Books

An Imprint of W. W. Norton & Company
Independent Publishers Since 1923

Note to Readers: This book is intended as a general information resource for professionals practicing in the field of psychotherapy and mental health. It is not a substitute for appropriate training or clinical supervision. Standards of clinical practice and protocol vary in different practice settings and change over time. No technique or recommendation is guaranteed to be safe or effective in all circumstances, and neither the publisher nor the authors can guarantee the complete accuracy, efficacy, or appropriateness of any particular recommendation in every respect or in all settings or circumstances.

Any URLs displayed in this book link or refer to websites that existed as of press time. The publisher is not responsible for, and should not be deemed to endorse or recommend, any website other than its own or any content that it did not create. The author, also, is not responsible for any third-party material.

For information about special discounts for bulk purchases, please contact
W. W. Norton Special Sales at specialsales@wwnorton.com or 800-233-4830

Manufacturing by Lake Book Manufacturing
Production manager: Gwen Cullen

ISBN: 978-1-324-01629-8 (pbk)

W. W. Norton & Company, Inc., 500 Fifth Avenue, New York, N.Y. 10110
www.wwnorton.com

W. W. Norton & Company Ltd., 15 Carlisle Street, London W1D 3BS

1 2 3 4 5 6 7 8 9 0

To the legacy, life, and love of David Daniels, MD

Contents

Acknowledgments

It is with deep gratitude and love that we acknowledge the support and insights of a range of individuals in the care, conception, and construction of this book. We would like to begin by recognizing the collaborative journey of David and Denise Daniels, Laura Baker, Jack Killen, and myself, Dan Siegel, in these last twenty years of working together as a team. David's passing in 2017 inspired the remaining four of us to work diligently to communicate this framework for clinicians of many disciplines, so they can learn this intricate scientific view of human development and what might underlie the Enneagram of personality perspective on our inner mental lives.

As a group we obtained input from a wide range of individuals in workshops, conferences, and even the privacy of psychotherapeutic sessions. This input has informed how we came to understand the PDP framework and how best to communicate these ideas to the mental health professionals for whom this book is intended. We interviewed several clinicians who were already using the Enneagram in their practices and who offered fascinating insights into clinical applications of the traditional approach, including Matt Ahrens, Fred Boykin, and Barbara Jaquette. Heather Coros, Suzanne Dion, Gabriele Hillberg, Joan Rosenberg Ryan, Mario Sikoro, and Jerry Wagner also offered important input on the Enneagram and its relationship to other clinical approaches for understanding personality. We thank Gina Thomas, Anke Thiele, Kara Scanlon, Jessica Mingus, Travis Marchman, Sally Maslansky, Nichol Chase, Lori Baudino, Dan Attias, and Marky Asseily for providing detailed and insightful feedback on the manuscript that helped guide its unfolding from earlier iterations to the final draft.

Core teachers in the field of the Enneagram also provided important feedback in formulating our ideas over the years to help the PDP framework be as clear as possible. These leaders include Beatrice Chestnut, Helen Palmer, Terry Saracino, Renée Rosario, Peter O'Hanrahan, and Russ Hudson. The members of the Bergamo and Vallombrosa Narrative Enneagram learning communities have also offered helpful input in the shaping of this approach, as have The Narrative Enneagram workshop and panel participants over the course of over three decades of deep exploration. David Daniels's and my own patients have been a key source of deep experiential learning in how to use the PDP view in clinical practice. Over the years, numerous immersions and conferences through the Mindsight Institute have provided exciting opportunities, in-person and online, to discuss these insights about older views of personality formation and how to apply these ideas to help free the mind from past prisons. Our team of Kristi Morelli and Emily Rigby have provided key support and helpful feedback on this and our other exciting projects. Caroline Welch, our chief executive officer, has been instrumental in organizing and leading our institute as we strive to make the broader field of interpersonal neurobiology accessible to a professional and public audience of international participants.

Scientific insights over the years have provided important perspectives on how the brain develops in response to experience. My teacher of neuroscience, David Hubel, taught me early on that energy flow and the neuronal firing it entails within the nervous system can change both the brain's activation and its growth of connections. Marian Sigman was my academic mentor during a National Institute of Mental Health research training fellowship, and guided me to the fundamental principle of keeping an open mind about the overlap between inherent features of the nervous system and the importance of relationships in our growth. The affective neuroscience pioneer, Jaak Panksepp, was a guiding light in our field and also a colleague, contributing his final books in this interpersonal neurobiology series. His insights into the subcortical nature of motivation and affect are key to the PDP framework. Combining these neural insights with the subjective experience of individuals as expressed through narratives was a wonderful challenge in my initial work as a research trainee under the guidance of the attachment pioneer, Mary Main. Learning to be a narrative scientist under her tutelage is a gift that has had direct applications in helping to envision the PDP approach to personality and think about the power of narrative to reveal deep truths about the mind and mental health. At a moment of doubt and questioning about the scientific basis of our hypothesis (of the attendency feature of the PDP framework being a part of temperament that was emerging from a deep analysis of these collected narrative reports), at a memorable birthday celebration in Vancouver, our colleague and friend, Mary Helen Immordino-Yang, offered timely and important empirical support from her exciting brain research findings.

As has been true throughout my role as the founding editor of the Norton Series on Interpersonal Neurobiology, being an author for this next book has again revealed the greatly appreciated support and professional attention to this manuscript's copyediting and production provided by Sarah Johnson and Mariah Eppes, and the support of Olivia Guarnieri and Jamie Vincent. Kevin Olsen and Natalie Argentina are great teammates in getting the word out about this book and our whole IPNB series. Madeleine Welch Siegel has again provided important visual images to help bring the ideas to light in this book, and I honor her talents and her wisdom, both as her father and her colleague. I am also deeply grateful for this now quarter-of-a-century collaboration with the wise and kind vice president of Norton, Deborah Malmud, for both our relationship and for her openness to thinking outside the box in the creation of the IPNB series, and in the offering of this book on personality in therapy.

The emergence of these ideas was a deep collaboration among the five of us—David and Denise Daniels, Laura Baker, Jack Killen, and this body called Dan. Working with these four individuals in varying intensities over decades has been powerfully stimulating and deeply rewarding. I treasure the gifts that each of my colleagues on this PDP journey has brought to our mission. Denise and her brother, J.D., have been generous in making David's literary estate available to us in the creation of this book. David's teachings, published in the works cited here with permission from their original source, were also key in having David's own words represented, as this book project was initiated after his passing. We are grateful for these generous permissions granted by Suzanne Dion (coauthor with David of *The Enneagram, Relationships, and Intimacy*), Denise Daniels, PhD, and J.D. Daniels, PhD, for The

David N. Daniels Enneagram Archives, writings on the drdaviddaniels.com website, and *The Enneagram, Relationships, and Intimacy* (originally published in 2018, with a forthcoming edition from Morgan James Publishing). We also thank The Narrative Enneagram institution and its leadership for giving us access to David's teachings from *The Enneagram for Therapists, Counselors and Coaches* (2014).

David himself was a mentor, friend, and inspiration for each of us in the PDP group with him. His wisdom, insights, and laughter have illuminated the journey to let the Enneagram of personality find a developmental neuroscience foundation through the lens of the consilient approach of interpersonal neurobiology. We hope David would have been as excited and grateful as the four of us are in bringing these ideas out into the world. David, we miss you and cherish you. May this book be an offering that helps clinicians support people in freeing their minds as they enable their personality to move from being a prison to serving as a playground in their lives.

Introduction

Welcome to an exploration of how we can understand the deep mechanisms of the mind within personality and use this perspective to promote
therapeutic growth. As the first-named author of this book, I, Dan, want
to invite you to come along with me and my coauthors, Laura Baker, PhD,
David Daniels, MD, Denise Daniels, PhD, and Jack Killen, MD, as we journey into an interpersonal neurobiology (IPNB) framework of the patterns
of feeling, thought, and behavior that are the characteristics collectively
known as "personality." We'll be exploring how personality develops within
the networks of the brain and our interpersonal relationships and offer an
in-depth approach in using this view in psychotherapy.

Our Scientific Approach

This book is our attempt, as five scientists—two trained as empirical personality researchers and three as physician-scientists, with two of us being
psychotherapists—to offer you a scientifically informed framework of personality and its application in psychotherapy.

There is a tremendous amount of empirical scientific study needed to
validate or disprove the framework we are proposing. IPNB is a transdisciplinary framework with insights into the mind and mental health based on
the approach of consilience—seeking a common ground discovered independently by different disciplines about the nature of reality. We begin with a
data set from what are called "first-person" reports from a popular view of personality known as the Enneagram, autobiographical reflections accumulated
with systematic, semistructured interviews that David and Helen Palmer

oversaw for decades and that resulted in nearly 50,000 narrative accounts he obtained in his professional career.

The Enneagram of personality system describes nine fundamental or "core" patterns of personality that each have unique ways of processing emotion, directing thought, and driving behavior. Becoming aware of these patterns is often described as being liberating and supportive of personal growth and interpersonal relationships. The Enneagram system is used by millions of individuals, as well as numerous therapists, coaches, and business leaders from around the world. Each of the core nine Enneagram patterns is designated with a number, 1 to 9, and each has three subtypes as well, making a collection of 27 patterns of these fundamental features of personality. In this book, we'll be focusing on the core nine personality patterns described in the Enneagram system and attempting to find a scientifically consilient way of understanding the development and experience of each of these patterns that shape our lives.

While there are various historical views on how and when this system originated and was first described—with suggestions that elements have been articulated in religious, mathematical, and philosophical writings for many centuries—its most recent formalization was in the middle of the last century through the teachings of a Bolivian-born Chilean mystic, Oscar Ichazo, and a Chilean American psychiatrist, Claudio Naranjo (Christlieb, 2016). Naranjo directly taught a number of students in Berkeley, California, in the 1970s, including Helen Palmer. The exploration of this system of viewing personality that David Daniels carried out with Helen Palmer in an organization and approach they cofounded, now known as The Narrative Enneagram, has led to the accumulation of inner reflections on these patterns of feeling, thinking, and behaving that serve as our starting place of a "data set."

The gathering of these first-person or "subjective" reports into an assembled set is what we in science call "second-person" data. This means we've listened closely to what individuals have stated about their lived experience. And rather than just having a singular case report, something that has at times been called "mesearch" and not research, we have thousands of these reports. Now our task is to look at "third-person" data, meaning "objective" findings from other ways of studying reality, such as through neural structure and function. By examining patterns of personality and how these develop along certain pathways, we come to an exciting and useful view that we formally call Patterns of Developmental Pathways, or PDP. This is a clinically useful, scientifically informed framework. We propose a possible developmental trajectory for personality; but even without that lifespan view, the ideas here are still useful for working with clients in the present moment of their lives.

While the PDP is useful, at this moment in the development of this PDP framework, we do not yet have direct studies of whole population distributions, statistical analyses of the various factors distinguishing one pathway from another, or structural and functional studies of the human brain revealing neural correlates for the various propensities of personality we'll be exploring. Even with more academically established Big Five traits of personality, specific characteristics do not yet have fully accepted, clear associations with different brain structures and functions (Avinun et al., 2020).

Why go further, you might be wondering, if we don't have that direct set of findings empirically validated with third-person approaches? As a clinician, my use of consilient approaches in IPNB has been profoundly helpful in creating new approaches to psychotherapy that offer creative and effective means of helping individuals with a range of challenges. In taking that same consilient approach here in examining personality, I hope you will find for your work, and your life, that the IPNB-based PDP framework that we have assembled is also something that is both useful and based on a cross-disciplinary truth.

Here in *Personality and Wholeness in Therapy*, we have been devoted to balancing what we've learned from the cumulated narratives and what we are correlating with neural mechanisms of empirical science. We acknowledge that this is a proposal for a theoretical perspective, one in need of empirical research to validate its accuracy and details. But as clinicians, David and I have found this consilient view quite useful in our therapeutic practices, and we hope you will too.

Please keep in mind that this is a scientifically informed, consilient, practical, and effective way of considering how the inner process of early temperament moves ahead in our lives to shape personality. It also is a framework that reveals how attachment and other key experiences in our lives shape how temperament influences our personality across the lifespan.

Yet, while these developmental aspects of the PDP framework are plausible and testable, the usefulness of this approach is independent of what ultimately is shown to be the valid trajectory leading to the emergence of personality in adult life. The reason we are offering this hypothetical developmental account of the PDP is to provide a plausible and testable view for both science-based clinical practice and the research community. We hope that this effort will bolster the case that understanding these nine patterns of personality deserves mainstream attention and study. Very importantly, the claim that the patterns are useful does not rest on the validity of this particular account of its lifespan development.

We correlate brain research on the nature of attention, motivation, and emotion with the autobiographical reports and offer a framework that is a *hypothesis*, not in any way proven. What this means is that it might be accurate, it might be partially true, or it might be wholly false. The reason we are offering this hypothetical framework is that, as scientists and clinicians, we see the potential for this perspective to inspire new and direct applications that can help people's lives. As individuals, too, we certainly have found this to be quite helpful—but that does not make this scientifically proven. Now that you know the context and limitations of this framework, please take in whatever you find useful for your own work and life and see how it all sits with you as we go forward into the exciting details of the developmental, affective, and social neuroscience insights into personality.

Challenges in life, including nonsecure attachment relationships early on, can intensify how a given personality pathway ingrains itself in the individual's way of living. In this manner, under some developmental circumstances, your clients may present with a pathway of a certain cohesion of traits—in how they feel, think, and act—that may have become more like a prison that, with liberation and integration, can be transformed into a playground in their lives. The goal of therapy is then *not* to eliminate a pathway but to make that particular set of proclivities more flexible and functional, and to enable access to other strategies of living to allow differentiation and linkage—the process of integration—to be freed. Integration enables a life of harmony to emerge, one characterized by flexibility, adaptability, coherence, energy, and stability. This FACES flow is what opening up the patterns of developmental pathways entails.

As we'll soon see, the experience of feeling "whole" that emerges from such integration is part of what the lifelong journey of one's developmental pathways may in fact be all about. It is our hope—Laura's, David's, Denise's, Jack's, and mine—that your experience reading this book summarizing our two-decades-long work together (intermittently over these years in the intensity of our focus), will bring a sense of wholeness to your life and to the lives of those with whom you work. We actually decided to publish an outline of the PDP framework back in 2010, in a chapter on traits in *The Mindful Therapist*, which I wrote for the Norton IPNB series. In that chapter were the essentials of this approach. Since then, David and I have used this PDP framework in both therapy and lectures; Jack has been offering PDP-focused workshops since then as well. Jack published a paper at that time, too, for the *The Enneagram Journal* (Killen, 2009). This book elaborates on those prior publications and offers the first comprehensive deep dive into the Patterns of Developmental Pathways framework for clinicians.

Laura and Jack contributed in important ways to the final explorations and expressions of these ideas in book form—Laura offering her wisdom as both a personality researcher and certified teacher of Iyengar yoga, and Jack bringing his scientific rigor from years of overseeing research projects at the National Institutes of Health (NIH). Each provided inspiration in having us all take in the latest empirical findings from a range of fields with both curiosity and precision. Laura has brought to the team a deep scientific background and a wisdom in maintaining a powerful conceptual clarity in our discussions and keeping us all organized and goal directed. All of this was on top of an active academic career studying personality and behavioral genetics as a tenured professor actively pursuing research in these areas. Jack brought more than two decades of NIH experience organizing and managing multidisciplinary research programs, most recently focused on unconventional medical and behavioral interventions that might have merit and deserve rigorous study. Jack also brought to the team a deep Narrative Enneagram–grounded understanding of the Enneagram system and practice, a scientific precision and curiosity honed in his NIH career, and a relentless and inspiring push for creative, out-of-the-box thinking about traditional Enneagram teaching and what might be going on beneath these patterns from a biological perspective. Jack and Laura were instrumental in the development of our thinking about the underlying dynamics of these fascinating patterns in action.

We worked together as a group of five for over a dozen years until David's passing in 2017. Since then, the now-four-member PDP group has worked diligently to articulate what we hope is an accurate and useful model that will have utility for personal growth, clinical strategies for lifespan applications, and future research design. Denise, with her training at the interface of environment and genetics and her deep transpersonal focus, kept us all attentive to the important bridge between the psychological and spiritual aspects of traditional Narrative Enneagram teaching. As David's daughter, Denise has been a powerful source of access to all of David's literary estate, providing important input honoring her father's lifelong achievements and the narrative approach to the Enneagram. Denise has played an essential role in keeping us all attentive to the traditional Enneagram system and David's teachings about it, while at the same time serving as a deep inspiration for us all to blend scientific rigor with the important ways in which classical empirical science has limitations that should not be ignored. Denise may have been the first one of us to articulate the idea that we work together as a group to formulate this new understanding of the Enneagram. With Denise's essential role, we hope that this summary of our years of collaboration will honor these many dimensions of Enneagram teachings and David's legacy.

Naturally, the intricate and historical teachings of the Enneagram of personality have many features that interest practitioners to various degrees, and this is true for the individuals of our PDP group as well. We have collectively chosen to use the consilient science-informed approach of IPNB in order to begin the important and, we feel, useful effort to find the common ground between rigorous empirical findings, in attachment research and neuroscience studies, for example, and traditional Enneagram teachings. In this text, unless otherwise specified, when we use the term *Enneagram*, we will be referring to this particular view of forms of personality, not the broader spiritual, philosophical, and even mathematical concepts also associated with the term. This consilient effort to explore personality has meant that at this moment in the PDP framework, we very intentionally focus on what can be illuminated with existing science—and that has necessitated that we focus on the developmental origins and present-moment experiences of personality, as they can illuminate the narratives of the core nine types in the Enneagram system. With work in psychotherapy and workshops, we also have extensive experience of how the PDP approach has been useful in helping cultivate personal growth. There is much, much more in the Enneagram system than we are currently able to address in this book, so for a deep dive into those areas, please see some of the existing literature on that perspective.

While David was not alive at the initiation of this book's formal writing, we have chosen to include his own words directly in places in this text to honor his membership in the creation of the PDP model. We dedicate this book to his life and legacy. We know that he would be as excited as we are to share our common love of understanding the mind and bringing well-being to people's lives.

Why Focus on Personality in Psychotherapy?

Our hope is to add to the extensive field of personality theorizing and offer what we hope you'll find to be a novel, accessible, and practical interpersonal neurobiology approach to both understanding and working with personality in psychotherapy. While mainstream psychiatry, in which I was initially trained, focuses on "personality disorders" and generally not on personality itself, the broader field of mental health has a robust set of theories about personality that offers a range of models from which to draw ideas about our enduring ways of feeling, thinking, and behaving. You may be a therapist grounded in what is known as "personality dynamics" and already draw your insights from that interdisciplinary view of personality in your practice of psychotherapy. What we will explore here can complement that important work you are already doing. In personality dynamics, many frameworks are explored from a wide sampling of theorists, such as Allport, Cattell, McAdams, Mischel, and Shoda, and of approaches such as cognitive affective personality systems, knowledge-and-appraisal personality architecture framework, nonlinear interaction of person and situation model, whole trait theory, and narrative identity. (See Hall & Lindzey, 1997, for an overview of theorists, and Jayawickreme et al., 2021, and Kuper et al., 2021, as well for an overview of approaches.)

With all of this existing theory, why would we need yet another model of personality? The developmental affective neuroscience foundations included in this PDP model, we hope you'll find, offer a unique and powerful way of understanding personality. And we also hope that you will discover that its practical applications for psychotherapy will provide useful ways of helping people experience more fulfilling lives as they work with you on their therapeutic journeys.

If you have ever wondered how personality shapes our perceptions and interactions with the world and nudges us to perceive the world and act in certain ways, this book will offer some new inroads into how that may develop through the lens of how the embodied brain and our relational lives intersect to shape who we are. If you are like me, you may sometimes bristle at the notion of categories of personality that limit us rather than liberate us. As the neuroscience and adolescent brain researcher Sarah Blakemore has commented on her studies: "One conclusion is that individual differences are just as significant as—perhaps even more important than—averages. . . . After all, there's no average teenager" (Blakemore, 2018, p. 139). Balancing this individual approach to "who we are" and the pattern-detection effort to seek common ground across individuals will be at the heart of our efforts. The narratives that David acquired focusing on the Enneagram give us insight into both what is shared by and what is unique for individuals.

How does personality correlate with brain systems as they grow from our earliest days? How might these neural networks of personality actually be helping us or sometimes getting in the way of our leading a more fulfilling life? Does personality reveal our "true selves" or does it cover something up, making us "fall asleep" to some fundamental essence of who we really are? We all may have questions about how personality is formed and also how it might be changed, and to what extent, in the journeys of our personal and professional lives. This book will offer responses to each of these questions.

Over 20 years ago, I was introduced to a popular personality system that described nine specific patterns of the mind that tend to repeat in somewhat predictable ways, both over time and across a range of situations. What was particularly fascinating, and in many ways unique, was the inside reflection of that view and the ways people seemed to find that the perspective illuminated deep truths about their inner lives that were quite helpful to them. These inner patterns were also matched with tendencies of outer behaviors. In meeting as five science-trained individuals sharing an interest in that system, we decided to spend what has now become two decades focusing our collective study of this Enneagram personality system and "translating" some of that view into what we came to call patterns of developmental pathways (PDPs).

If you are familiar with the details of the Enneagram system, you'll find here that we will focus on only some of its foundational features, especially those regarding the core nine types of personality you are likely well aware of from other sources and books on this topic. To explore a neuroscience basis for these nine patterns, we have examined many aspects of science, from attachment research to developmental neurobiology, in an effort to find a common ground between "traditional" Enneagram teachings and empirically validated data. This effort to find consilience—how separately discovered truths from disparate approaches to reality share discoveries in common—has led to a hypothesis about how these nine patterns form, what neural pathways are involved, and how they might be cultivated in psychotherapy.

Even though in this book we will not be directly focusing on some of the details of the Enneagram, such as wings, connecting points, or "instinctual subtypes," the PDP framework offers insights and explanations regarding those areas as well, and they are being pursued by some of the PDP group. Resources exploring those features are abundant in the contemporary literature and include writings by our coauthor David Daniels (*The Essential Enneagram*, 2000, 2009, forthcoming 2025), Don Riso and Russ Hudson (*The Wisdom of the Enneagram*, 1999), Helen Palmer (*The Enneagram*, 1988; *The Enneagram in Love and Work*, 1993; and, with Paul Brown, *The Enneagram Advantage: Putting the 9 Personality Types to Work in the Office*, 1998), and Beatrice Chestnut (*The Complete Enneagram*, 2013), as well as other classic Enneagram texts offering a comprehensive discussion of these issues.

Why would we—as five trained scientists—be attempting to uncover the possible scientifically based mechanisms that might be the foundations of these distinct patterns of personality? In our own personal and professional lives, these nine pathways our development can follow seem to have robust influences on our lives. Not only do they correlate with scientifically discovered neural networks in the brain, but understanding them greatly facilitates the process of change and growth in psychotherapy. Could these correlations with neural development we've uncovered actually be accurate? Might the conceptual and scientific foundations we'll explore here hold up to careful future empirical studies that might use these proposals in their design and implementation? We certainly hope so. But as we await such controlled research projects, the practical utility of this new view of personality can be attained in your own life and work as a clinician.

In this book, I'd like your experience of reading to be as direct and useful as possible. As I don't know the name you were given, I will refer to you with the open term "you," just as I'll use the terms "I" for me, Dan, and "we" for the whole PDP group of Laura, David, Denise, Jack, and me. Since we are five authors for one reader, it has naturally been challenging in the writing to find a common, singular voice for us to connect with you. For that reason, I've been asked to take the helm and have been given the privilege, and challenge, of having the five of us bring these ideas together over many years, then taking that group effort and attempting to carefully articulate our experiences and perspectives in the form of a final manuscript. Our goal has been to synthesize this exciting new perspective on who we human beings are and offer you a way to make this both understandable and useful to your life and work.

An Intriguing Invitation

I wrote a book exploring the overlap between innate and experiential aspects of neural development and how they shape the emergence of the mind (The Developing Mind) that also proposed the framework of interpersonal neurobiology, IPNB—an interdisciplinary framework for understanding the mind and mental health. After that book was out in the world, I received a call from Drs. David and Denise Daniels, a father–daughter pair; David was a clinical professor of psychiatry at Stanford working with a popular personality system known as the Enneagram, Denise a scientist who had received her PhD on the gene-environment interplay in the development of personality. They came to a workshop I was offering, and we were having lunch when they suggested that I had not paid enough attention to how child temperament might shape how we develop into our personality as adults. I agreed that as an attachment researcher I was focused on the relational aspects of parent-child pairs and knew that research revealed how temperament did not predict future outcomes with much statistical power. Yes, they agreed, but they were both interested in a system of personality that might offer some new insights from the "inside out"—looking inward at personality rather than merely at its outward manifestations, which were what current approaches to temperament primarily assessed. They wanted to know if I was interested in learning more. I had also already published another book, *Parenting from the Inside Out* (with Mary Hartzell), with the subtitle *How a Deeper Self-Understanding Can Help You Raise Children Who Thrive*, so this invitation made my ears perk up.

What was it in me that was open to learning about this system of personality? Perhaps I had an elevated score on the Openness of my Big Five personality traits, high on wanting to be Conscientious too, to help IPNB be as comprehensive as possible in taking in the consilient perspectives—the findings that reveal a common ground across different pursuits of knowledge. I didn't think of myself as an extravert, and not really an introvert, so maybe I was the mixture of the two as an "ambivert," but I was open to David and Denise's invitation to come spend a week—as a scientist—with 50 others who would gather to explore the Narrative Enneagram together at a retreat center in Northern California. I imagine my trait of being Agreeable must have been high for David and Denise to extend that kind invitation, and yet my certainly high Neuroticism trait made me immediately doubt the value of going, question why I agreed to attend, and then fret about how I might fit in with the group as a scientist in a gathering focusing on such a popularized view of personality as the Enneagram. I was a scientist, after all, so what could such a view provide? Should I go or should I call and say I was too busy?

Research in the field of personality had already assessed the Big Five factors (McAdams, 1992) that at the time were one of the most academically established sets of features that currently dominated our research-based understanding of personality. They also form a memorable acronym: OCEAN. This mnemonic device helps us easily recall the traits of being open (versus closed), conscientious (versus not thoughtful), extraverted (versus introverted), agreeable (versus disagreeable), and neurotic (versus clear minded and calm). Could my hesitancy to try out a new system, the Enneagram, be some reflection of my characteristics of the Big Five? Was it my possibly high Neuroticism trait that left me with anything but being calm and clear minded? Well, my OCEAN traits were simply what they were, however they may have formed. Studies show that about 40% of such personality traits are heritable—we inherit them from our parents' genetic makeup—and the rest of the variance is often explained by what are called non-shared or individual environmental factors. Classically this is known as our nature (genetics) and our nurture (experience). However they came about, what could I do about them anyway?

What intrigued me about the Enneagram system was something about its postulating that there was something you might do to gain inner wisdom about how to move from lower states of functioning to more adaptive, higher states. From the more academically established view of personality of the Big Five, what would that system offer as an understanding of how I got to be who I tend to be? And what would these OCEAN characteristics, as accurate as they might be, offer as a way to guide my personal development, or my work as a psychotherapist?

With all these questions in mind, and with these particular characteristics of my "personality" in my awareness from mainstream personality studies, with both apprehension and determination, I got on an airplane and headed north to see if I might expand my experiential understanding of our lives.

A Loyal Skeptic

When I arrived at the Vallombrosa retreat center for that weeklong workshop, I was a bit late and was greeted by David Daniels and Helen Palmer, his cofounder of the educational program The Narrative Enneagram. They asked which of the nine types I resonated with and I said that I had read David's book *The Essential Enneagram* and that I only knew which type I was certainly not. They each asked me some brief questions, following up responses I gave them with more detailed inquiries, and then conferred with each other briefly and proclaimed, you might be a 6, like us! I thought, inside my inner mind, how ridiculous, and how biased of them. But I was loyal to trying to find a possible consilience amid what seemed to me on first take to be unfounded views, or at least confusing divisions into types. Then I remembered that the name of a 6 in David's terminology was a "loyal skeptic."

The workshop was organized in a panel structure. Of the 50 people from around the world who had flown in to study their own and others' Enneagram types, those who were of a given type would all be together up on a panel and interviewed with open-ended questions organized by the approach of the Enneagram in the narrative tradition. Stories were evoked—hence the "narrative" name of their approach—and in those autobiographical reflections on the inner life would be revealed fascinating patterns of where attention would tend to go, what had inner meaning to the individual, characteristic ways of responding to emotionally distressing events, and how an inner focus of attention, emotion, and meaning would emerge as outwardly manifest, observable behaviors. I was extremely doubtful of the whole process. A cult, I thought; a sham of something that had any meaning; perhaps just a "groupthink" coalescence of opinions seeking some kind of false internal validation. And certainly, something with no scientific backing, nor any seemingly useful clinical applications.

Then my type was called up for the panel. There I was, sitting with half a dozen or so others who had self-assessed as belonging to this type, this "6" grouping. As people responded to the interviewer's questions, it was as if the others were reading my mind. Every response they gave I could resonate with, and sometimes it was an uncanny tip-of-the-tongue sense that they took the words right out of my mouth before I could say them. I was a bit in shock. As I listened later to the other panels, very few of their responses resonated with me. And even the observable ways people tended to act, their nonverbal behaviors, seemed to have similarities as I watched their interactions on the panels.

I was given the informal research opportunity to offer the whole group the Adult Attachment Interview (AAI), a research instrument I had been trained to use during my National Institute of Mental Health research training fellowship, and then I had discussions with the participants afterward about their responses. It did not seem that the "state of mind with respect to attachment" that the AAI reveals correlated with a particular type or another—but rather that the degree to which a type was "intense" or "imprisoning," the way that type's characteristics were trapping a person in unhelpful patterns of feeling, thought, and behavior, seemed, in my informal initial impression, to be what correlated to the AAI findings of secure or nonsecure states of mind. In other words, when people shared their AAI reflections with me during the week, the four possible groupings of the AAI did not correlate with the nine groupings of the Enneagram.

If future research could be conducted, we could explore the validity of the following impressionistic notion: Attachment security or nonsecurity did not determine the personality features themselves, but rather may influence how those features exerted an influence in the individual's life. This view is consilient with the findings that attachment could shape the external manifestation of behavioral inhibition later in life—perhaps by cortical growth in response to experience—even as that attachment did not create that inhibition earlier in life in the first place (Kagan, 1997). In other words, it might be that one's temperament derived from subcortical innate proclivities, but attachment patterns might be cortically mediated strategies learned as a skill of adaptation. That was the hypothesis emerging in my mind during that initial workshop.

Could Science Illuminate the Inner Nature of Personality and the Enneagram?

At that workshop I was also given the opportunity to interview whole groups of individuals of a given Enneagram type. That system involves nine distinct types—each with a number designation and a name, each an equally valid way of experiencing life and the world, simply different from one another. One type is not better or worse than another; each type is simply distinct in ways that seem to endure over time. For example, a dining table full of those in the 8 category, "the protector," shared with me that their "journey to being an enlightened 8" involved coming to address two important features in their lives: One was that each of them at the table said they "could not stand" to be vulnerable or acknowledge their dependence on others; the second common experience was that they were challenged in the skills of empathy and insight, two components of a process I had named in earlier writings as "mindsight" (see Siegel, 2001b, 2010b, 2020). These were very caring people, it seemed, but caring about others was different from understanding others, or themselves. What this revealed is that while those of a "type" might share a common ground, there was a developmental pathway of self-understanding and personal growth that could be facilitated by addressing the particular challenges of an "unactualized" stance. With intention and knowledge, that challenge could be addressed, and then a shift in how a person could live their life could be cultivated. That made sense to me as an outsider to the Enneagram world, was fascinating to me as a scientist imagining what the mechanisms might be of the types' patterns, and was useful to me as a psychotherapist always seeking new ways to offer helpful skills to those with whom I worked. And as a person, a parent, and a partner, knowing about these types and their features was profoundly illuminating.

Hanging out at a dining room table with those of my own grouping—6, the loyal skeptics—I found it amazing how similar we were in various ways of having worst-case-scenario thinking and always checking for danger, even though on the surface we were such different people. When I called my wife to tell her about what I was learning about myself, she wasn't surprised at all, given that we had been living together for two decades. The recurrent challenge of finding calmness amid a deep sense of mistrust and fear was rewarding and relieving to discuss with that group of like-minded individuals. These intriguing findings, along with the Adult Attachment Interview impressions that attachment did *not* create type but could shape one's personality as either a prison or a playground, felt deeply compelling to me. I was skeptical—naturally, it turns out, given the possible validity of this personality pattern I seemed to be in—but I still wanted to know more.

At a different dining table, I found another common "type" grouping in which I fit: The other scientists present at the workshop had gathered for a meal. There I met up with David and Denise Daniels, and two other workshop participants, Laura Baker and Jack Killen. Laura had trained with Denise and was a professor of psychology at the University of Southern California, studying personality. Jack was a medical scientist working at the National Institutes of Health Center for Complementary and Integrative Health. Each of them was personally interested in the Enneagram; David applied his personal insights into this personality system as a practicing psychiatrist.

As scientists, we shared our interest in the possible underlying mechanisms that might be revealed if we were to study individuals in the various Enneagram type groupings. David had numerous narrative reports, thousands of them; I was trained as a narrative scientist; Laura and Denise were personality scientists; and Jack was adept at analyzing research on nontraditional approaches to Western science that might just have merit and be effective in helping others. And we shared a similar sense of humor. We each felt that there was "something there" in this approach to understanding human beings; we also felt that while the popular discussions of the Enneagram system itself were not based in science, there might be new ways we could discover a satisfying and accurate developmental approach to understanding how temperament might persist, from the inside, as adult personality (see Lemery et al., 1999; Loehlin, 1992; McCrae & Costa, 1994). That developmental question was intriguing to each of us. And my background in focusing on IPNB as a cross-disciplinary framework for understanding the mind and mental health, as well as reality itself, might serve as a useful scientific and conceptual foundation to explore our shared interests further.

I imagine that we each had the OCEAN features that would enable us to begin a collaboration back in 2004 that now, 20 years later, has come to fruition in the creation of this book. Laura, David, Denise, Jack, and I would meet a few times each year to explore our common interests. We tried out all sorts of ways of understanding the Enneagram through a variety of scientific frameworks. The initial forays were fun yet hit frustrating dead ends. We'd abandon our various early attempts to correlate existing empirical scientific views with the narratives of Enneagram types. We then came upon some work by a number of authors, especially that of Jaak Panksepp (*Affective Neuroscience: The Foundations of Human and Animal Emotions*, 1998; and, with Kenneth Davis, *The Emotional Foundations of Personality*, 2018), which provided a view of the subcortical motivational drives that, in our view, overlapped in fascinating and exciting ways with the Enneagram system.

The Structure of the Book

In the first five chapters, the book focuses on scientific and conceptual foundations of this model, and then in the last six chapters it explores therapeutic applications of the model in the process of psychotherapy. Although the Enneagram view of personality from which our narrative data source is derived is already being used by a fair number of therapists and counselors around the world, we are introducing a new, science-based, developmental and neurobiological framework for understanding and working with personality called Patterns of Developmental Pathways, or PDP. This is a whole-person, inner perspective of personality, with a coherent developmental foundation in terms of its origins and its applications. The PDP framework helps clinicians and clients get "underneath the hood" of personality and behavior to identify the motivations driving these patterns, and it provides a model of growth and change of personality in psychotherapy.

We will approach the journey of this book by building the conceptual foundations of temperament, attachment, and personality step by step, and then we will explore the specifics of each of the patterns of developmental pathways—diving deeply into each pathway and highlighting the strengths, challenges, and growth-edges that can be utilized in the course of psychotherapy.

The first three chapters cover "Big Idea #1"—the notion that understanding and working with personality can indeed be **clinically useful** using the PDP framework, since the system goes beyond the surface traits to reveal what is inside and underneath the external manifestations of personality.

In Chapter 1, we will introduce the PDP framework of personality and why we think it is useful for clients, to help them foster their inner development, enhance their relationships with others, and cultivate a more flexible and fulfilling way of life; and for therapists, to help them be better attuned to themselves and their clients on cognitive, emotional, and somatic levels. Chapter 2 outlines the specific components (or processes) that make up the scaffolding of the patterns, while Chapter 3 fills in the details of each of the nine personality patterns—the PDPs—in terms of these components.

We will be using the terms "PDP," "pattern," and "pathway" somewhat interchangeably to indicate aspects of this set of characteristics that cluster together and shape our lives in what we broadly call our personality. The term "pattern" highlights what is happening now, while "pathway" refers more to what occurs across time and contexts. And by "personality" we do not mean the energy or charisma a person has, such as "Oh, they have such personality"—but rather the very specific finding that we have enduring patterns of emotion, thought, and behavior that stay with us across settings and stages of our lives.

"Big Idea #2"—our **developmental hypothesis** of how the patterns might emerge from infancy and develop across the lifespan to become adaptive strategies that make up personality—is presented in Chapter 4. In Chapter 5, we'll explore in more depth our "Big Idea #3" on the importance of **wholeness** as a driving force beneath personality patterns, and how the PDP framework can be used to help clients integrate, restore, and experience the benefits of growth through the process of psychotherapy.

Once you are familiar with the nine personality patterns and their working components explored in Chapter 3, getting a feeling for them and even reflecting on how they may correspond with your own personal life experience, you will be ready for the deep dive in later chapters. Here we'll explore the patterns in more depth, offering some of the direct words regarding the Enneagram of our late coauthor, David Daniels, as well as my own insights into how the PDP framework can provide new opportunities to lead clients toward greater integration and wholeness.

Beginning with Chapters 6, 7, and 8, and their subchapters, we'll explore concepts perhaps familiar to those who know the implications of developmental neurobiology in the helping and healing professions, but here we'll focus on how they relate to integrating the pathways *in* therapy and how this framework can become integrated *into* the process of psychotherapy. We'll review some basic IPNB notions about integration itself and how these may relate to the Enneagram as approaches to growth. I then bring the Enneagram and the PDP frameworks to you through David's words and my reflections. We will dive deeply into the specific patterns in these chapters, one section exploring each of the nine pathways, including a focus on individual and relationship development, and growth of more integrative ways of living our lives with freedom. In the final synthesizing Chapters, 9, 10, and 11, we conclude by revisiting the importance of "Therapist, Know Thyself" and the theme of working toward wholeness in psychotherapy using the PDP framework.

Here in *Personality and Wholeness in Therapy*, you will find a detailed explanation of what we hope you'll come to experience as a highly accessible and clinically useful framework of personality and its development across the lifespan. Utilizing the PDP model can help clients promote inner development, enhance their interpersonal relationships, and adopt a freer, more flexible and fulfilling way of life. We also hope that loosening the sometimes-tight grip of personality can help individuals realize our deep connections with one another in our human family, and our fundamental belonging to all of nature. Yes, our work as therapists is to support the well-being of individuals and families. And yes, when that therapeutic journey supports people thriving, it can invite an expanded sense of self, a more integrated identity, and a broader belonging that can support the health of our wider, waiting world.

The Patterns of Developmental Pathways—PDP—framework will offer you a powerful proposal about how personality emerges in our lives and what we can do with these insights to enable these enduring ways we feel, think, and behave to become less restricting and more freeing. The scientific and conceptual foundations you'll explore in the first five chapters of this book will provide an in-depth discussion of the model; the therapeutic applications of this framework in the next five chapters will give you the tools to utilize this approach in practical ways to cultivate integration and growth in psychotherapy. We welcome you to the journey ahead!

PERSONALITY *and* WHOLENESS *in* THERAPY

CHAPTER 1

Three Fundamental Ideas

Welcome to a scientifically informed proposal about how to make sense of the patterns of thought, emotion, and behavior that are often simply called "personality." We'll be drawing upon thousands of narrative reflections that provide an inner view of those processes, and then we'll apply the lens of science in attempting to both make sense of them and propose a neuroscience-informed view of how personality may originate and carry forward in our lifespan development. The patterns of developmental pathways framework also helps us to understand how psychotherapy can catalyze positive growth in therapeutic change.

The study of personality is hardly new (Caspi et al., 2005; Eysenck, 1952; Mayer, 2005). As Louis Breger, psychologist and former associate professor at California Institute of Technology, suggests in his academic text, *From Instinct to Identity: The Development of Personality* (1974):

> The development of human personality is one of those grand topics—the concern of philosophers, novelists, psychologists, and theologians (not to mention parents) for centuries. All cultures and societies contain beliefs or theories about the psychological development of their people. Such beliefs or theories, which are usually not stated in any formal sense, are embodied in child-rearing practices; social institutions such as schools; beliefs about human nature, man's "instincts" and how they can be legitimately expressed or how they must be controlled; the sorts of expectations held for children; and a host of other ideas, laws, values and social practices. Such views enable parents to

raise their children, and institutions to influence them, so that they become functioning members of their societies. (p. 1)

Here in *Personality and Wholeness in Therapy*, we'll explore a view of fundamental patterns in the processing of information and energy that we believe provides an accurate and clinically useful framework for understanding personality. We are adding to this long history in the study of and reflection on personality. One objective of this model is to provide a novel translation of the Enneagram in ways that are scientifically grounded and clinically useful. **This PDP model offers a whole-person, inside perspective of personality that gets beneath behavior to the motivation that underlies the observable patterns.** Understanding the likely neural networks that develop early in life and continue to influence these patterns of personality can help make sense of the tangle of feelings, thoughts, and behaviors that clients bring to therapy. This perspective can be useful in providing a framework for clients' individual, inner-self development and growth, as well as for their relationships with others, their "relational self," thus leading to a more flexible and fulfilling way of life. Importantly, our framework also provides a unique opportunity for the therapist to "know thyself," which can in turn lead to a more effective therapeutic approach.

It's important to note, here at the beginning, that the simple word "self" can be viewed as a "center of experience" (Siegel, 2023). In this linguistic use of this common term, we want to emphasize that the center of experience— sensation, perspective, and agency (SPA)—can be experienced within our body (inner self), and in our relationships with other people and the planet (relational self). Our identity lens can adjust to zoom in on our inner self and expand out to our connections with people and nature as our relational self. "Know thyself" is an old phrase about knowing the inner self; but we can also use that same term in the expanded sense to remind us that truly "knowing who we are" invites us to explore an expanded sense of who we are beyond the individualistic view of a solo-self.

Going inside our mental lives is an opportunity to develop our mindsight skills. The PDP framework offers a comprehensive inside-out view that facilitates that journey of discovery. We are not aware of any other developmental neuroscience and attachment-informed model of personality that offers the opportunity to "see what's underneath the hood" and provides a framework for growth and change for both the therapist and client.

The PDP Model: Three Key Ideas

This is a client-friendly clinical framework to help address the kinds of recurring problems in which individuals may often ask, *"Why in the world* do I keep doing this?" A first principle is that the PDP perspective provides a **clinically useful neurobiologically informed framework of personality** that can greatly aid in unique ways toward understanding ourselves and our relationships with others. This framework also provides a way for therapists to know *themselves* on a deeper level, how their own personality comes into play when working with clients. These ways of gaining insight into personality offer a powerful and fresh perspective for psychotherapists utilizing an array of modalities in their work. Therapists can use this framework as an exciting and effective new developmental neuroscience-informed approach to therapy and therapeutic change as they become attuned to themselves and their clients.

Second, the PDP framework proposes a much-needed **lifespan model of personality** that fills a void in linking infant and child temperament to adult personality (see Roberts & DelVecchio, 2000; Rothbart & Bates, 1998; Rothbart et al., 2000). The science-based consilient basis for our hypothesis of how these personality patterns emerge from infancy can be linked to Kenneth Davis and Jaak Panksepp's work found in *The Emotional Foundations of Personality* (2018), another text in this IPNB series. The PDP framework links three primal emotion systems explored in Panksepp's lifelong work in affective neuroscience—anger, separation distress, and fear—with the infant's needs in three domains we call agency, bonding, and certainty. These three distinct subcortical motivational networks, when the drive is frustrated, each activate their respective primary affects of anger, separation distress, and fear.

Third, we believe that the **main driver of the development of personality across the lifespan involves the seeking of a sense of "wholeness."** This is a drive for a feeling that has a range of ways of being experienced and expressed, such as coherence, completion, contentment, or connection. A seeking of wholeness may be a driving impetus that organizes individuals into certain patterns of both inner experience and outwardly manifest behavior. By itself, having a sense of something being whole with that feeling of being complete, of feeling at ease and content, of being connected, would be an understandable state to be motivated to achieve, especially when considered in contrast to its opposite of being incomplete, with dis-ease and disconnection.

The PDP model posits that infant temperament and early life experiences shape the differences in the relative activation of specific subcortical motivational circuits that then create enduring patterns in what has priority in our mental life as development unfolds. Part of the activation of these motivational networks is to try, as best we can, to come to feel whole—complete, connected, content—with a sense of balance and homeostasis. Temperament can be considered an early aspect of an infant's propensities (Lengua & Gartstein, 2024; Thomas & Chess, 1997; Thomas et al., 1963), shaped primarily by neural proclivities in firing patterns (Posner & Rothbart, 2018; Rothbart & Posner, 2022). As an infant experiences life, this inner temperament forms a kind of filter that directly shapes what sensory input is attended to and how our emotional and physiological responses emerge. In a sense, temperament serves to select from a wide array of what is possible and filters those possibilities into what is most probable. In this very foundational way, temperament is a template for the filter that selectively screens how we subjectively sense life and how we objectively behave in the world.

It is these proclivities of temperament and how we learn to have strategies of adaptation to experiences—and even to our own responses to them—that form the characteristics of our personality. In a simple equation, features of temperament plus our adaptive strategies lead to our personality patterns. Recurring neural activations will create their own synaptic reinforcements, strengthening an initial, and perhaps subtle, propensity into a more robust network of interconnected neurons. **This, we propose, is how temperament forms an initial bias of the neural system, a filtering process that selects what is being attended to and given more energy and intention, and that then reinforces its own initial leanings.**

The PDP view also proposes that attachment relationships in which we grow then shape the level of integration, or how well these emerging patterns of temperament and adaptive strategies lead to what we can name as high versus low levels of functioning of these patterns. Low levels mean we are challenged to adapt well with these patterns; high levels mean we can adapt and function well. We can think of this as how suboptimal attachment may deepen and narrow the "groove" of a neural pathway that temperament initially sets in motion. When that neural groove is very deep and narrow, other more flexible ways of responding become less easily accessed and the individual's personality may become more intense and less adaptive. Psychotherapy may help a person move toward higher levels of functioning through a process of integration—the linking of differentiated parts of a system as it "widens" the groove of a PDP.

Ultimately, understanding personality seen through this model as PDPs—patterns of developmental pathways—can provide a framework for growth and change, a guide to becoming more integrated as clients learn to recognize and then relax their patterns. This integrative transformation allows them, and us, to find ways of aspiring to cognitive and emotional "higher capacities" within and across other patterns. These higher states of functioning enable us to be more fluid and flexible, less trapped in a singular neural groove, and more capable of accessing a wider range of more adaptive functions with freedom.

Wholeness, Personality, and Development

During my college education studying biochemistry, I also had the opportunity to work on a suicide-prevention phone service and was assigned various repeat callers to support their lives. I noticed that certain repeating patterns of ways of feeling and dealing with emotion, particular enduring ways of thinking and reasoning about life's challenges, and specific recurrent behavioral strategies of coping with life were distinctly present in the various individuals I had the privilege to work with on those calls. There was a sense I would feel in these callers that something was "off," something missing from leading a vibrant, whole life. That sense of wholeness, a feeling of being fundamentally connected to someone or something that felt complete and coherent, seemed to be missing. I wondered how the experience of one's personality might be related in some ways to this sense of being whole. The "psychache," a term coined by Ed Shneidman, the founder of the field of suicidology, might be the feeling that this something of the psyche, the soul, the mind was missing in an individual's existence (Shneidman, 1993, p. 258).

When I went through medical school training, I also noticed that my peers had distinct and enduring patterns of feeling, thinking, and behaving that pretty much stayed with them for the first two years of our indoctrination into the medical profession. As we went on in our training, though we had different personalities, the pain of that experience, which led to an empirically documented diminishment in empathy in young doctors and an accompanying increase in their emotional distress, was also a kind of departure from wholeness. Years later, at our 40th medical school reunion, those same patterns of what we simply call personality seemed to continue in their ways of being in the world after four decades of living.

When I finished my initial training in pediatrics and noted such distinct ways in which children, adolescents, and their parents would have these same overall patterns of feeling, thinking, and acting, I began to wonder about the developmental origins of this organizing aspect of the mind, our personality, and what role it played in our lives as we move toward or away from wholeness and health. Why did an individual act in such enduring ways? Why were there patterns of personality that seemed somewhat distinct across individuals? What were they "made of" and why did they endure? When I transferred over to psychiatry to complete my clinical education, I was able to learn that attempts to find meaningful links between later aspects of adult personality and what I had learned in pediatrics about the early emotional and behavioral traits of a child—what we could observe in their ways of interacting with others, characteristics that were often simply named *temperament*—were for the most part *not* successful. These traits seemed to be present early in life; perhaps we could call them "inborn" or "innate." Some temperament traits might have a dominant influence from genetics; others might be shaped by in utero neural development; still others might be a direct impact of random physiological variables.

We'll use this term, "temperament," to refer to early features and early propensities—like reactivity, sensitivity, rhythmicity—for the kinds of processes that can be seen in the first years of life. Whatever their origins, the notion of temperament was a useful construct to acknowledge that *not* all variables shaping a child's development were caused by the child's relationship experiences with their attachment figures, most often but not limited to the parents, or other potential experiential sources of stress. Yet children need to develop *adaptive strategies* to survive; and might these be some ways in which temperament and early experiences, including attachment, influence the pathways a child takes?

After my clinical training in adult, adolescent, and child psychiatry, I chose to pursue a National Institute of Mental Health research training fellowship in which I was able to study attachment. The empirical study of attachment, sometimes known as "attachment theory and research," would later demonstrate how temperament generally does not influence attachment patterns in a statistically robust way across each of the different attachment strategies; and in fact, a child with one set of temperament traits could have multiple forms of attachment, each with a different caregiver (see Groh et al., 2017; Sroufe et al., 2005; Van Ijzendoorn & Bakermans-Kranenburg, 2012). Personally, that made sense to me as a new father. Professionally, as a young psychiatrist just building my practice of psychotherapy with children, adolescents, adults, couples, and families, it helped distinguish between the later acquired learnings and the early inherent features of a child. From a practical point of view, this distinction between inborn temperament and experiential adaptations helped clarify how later acquired learnings built on top of early innate features of a child.

This distinction also made sense to me as a scientist. In medical school, my neuroscience professor, David Hubel, MD, was awarded the Nobel Prize, along with Torsten Wiesel, PhD, for demonstrating how experience shapes the brain. That same year, 1981, that prize in physiology or medicine was also given to Roger Sperry, PhD, for demonstrating the innate asymmetries in the human brain. What those prizes recognized were two fundamental principles: The brain is shaped by experience *and* the brain has structural and functional proclivities that are innate. Naturally, experience will interact with neural structure and influence it based on the innate functional propensities of that nervous system. Experience is sometimes labeled "nurture," while the inborn features, sometimes genetically influenced, are labeled "nature." The old debate of nature *versus* nurture dissolves away to yield the current thinking that nature needs nurture and nurture molds nature (Briley & Tucker-Drob, 2014). It is not an either/or, but rather a *both/and* process. Understanding this finding is essential for effective psychotherapy, and helpful in simply being a human navigating through the inner sea of the mind and negotiating our ways in the world across the lifespan.

Temperament and Personality in Psychotherapy

You might imagine, or even experience yourself if you are a clinician, how these scientific ideas inspire questions about how personality forms, what it is made of, and what we can do with these enduring patterns of feeling, thought, and action in our lives. Yet it may seem strange to find, if you are not in the field of mental health, that a survey of numerous professionals in this discipline reveals that few of us are offered a clear view of how temperament and attachment influence personality in such a way that we can either understand these developmental pathways or do something with them in the clinical work we do. Even yesterday I asked, yet again, a group of clinicians if they'd been offered anything in their training about how to work with personality in therapy, with the familiar outcome of not a single professional answering yes. Certainly, there are many therapists who focus on personality as "personality dynamics" or even study the Enneagram system. But a science-based neurobiologically informed developmental model of personality, and its use in psychotherapy, is rarely if ever offered in the traditional training of mental health practitioners. My own education in psychiatry focused only on personality disorder, not personality itself.

Understanding the nature of personality can be a foundation for offering more effective ways of helping people thrive. While there is a large amount of academic literature studying personality, the applications in psychotherapy are often not readily available. One possible reason for this is the often-held belief that personality is just what you have; there is nothing that can be done to change these traits. Ironically, if we think that these patterns we call personality are fixed, they may remain unchanged; yet if we imagine that they can change, at least to various degrees, they may in fact be open to modification in our lives. This relates directly to the findings of Carol Dweck (2006) that our fixed or growth mindset can determine whether we can grow and change, or not, which means that being open to change is itself the beginning of being able to change.

But what is it, exactly, that we are trying to change if we are working with personality? Work in psychotherapy around issues related to personality evokes the teachings embedded in the serenity prayer: "May I have the courage to change the things I can, the serenity to accept the things I cannot change, and the wisdom to know the difference." What in fact is changeable and what is not? And for those aspects of our personality that can change, how would we change them, and why would we even want to? We may not be able to alter a baseline set of features of temperament to a large degree, but we can transform the adaptive strategies that may emerge from them that form our personality patterns.

As a student of therapy, I became fascinated with how we develop into who we become. How might we learn to accept our innate nature while also changing those adaptive strategies toward wellness? And what does it truly mean to be well, to be "whole"? The study of personality in the empirical field of psychology (Graziano, 2003; Heine & Buchtel, 2009; Kubzansky et al., 2009) has revealed some fundamental principles that may surprise those who've learned only the popular view of the topic. One is that rather than a commonly held notion of *types* that fall into distinct categories, research in fact suggests we have personality *traits* that are characteristics that fall along a spectrum of values. A second finding is that popular approaches that postulate types, such as the Myers-Briggs Type Indicator, do not hold up with close empirical scrutiny. In contrast to popularized notions of personality, a carefully collected set of data across many cultures with large numbers of research subjects revealed universal linguistic terms that ultimately could be seen as belonging to one of five general and seemingly distinct traits. This, we've seen, is the OCEAN view of the "Big Five" personality traits (John &

Srivastava, 1999). A third finding is that we all have these traits, and that not only do they vary along a continuum of values but they can be changed with development and effort.

As far as we can tell, there is no clear developmental pathway in the Big Five or any other personality system that helps us see *how* to apply these important features of personality to the process of understanding how early traits, what we are naming temperament, move forward in our lives to become both childhood and adult personality. The importance of temperament in general for predicting adult outcome may be an intuitive sense many of us have, and is supported by an extensive research analysis by Wright and Jackson (2022):

> We tested the predictive validity of childhood personality for life outcomes up to 30 years later. Two main findings emerged. First, temperament measured between ages 0–6 was able to predict a wide-ranging number of life outcomes. Second, temperament often provided incremental predictive validity above adult based personality, suggesting that there is unique information in childhood assessments despite being assessed farther away in time. These findings establish the importance of both distal and proximal personality predictors of outcomes, supporting the need to understand who an individual is throughout the lifespan. . . . For a set of traits that were measured between infancy and age six, the ability of temperament to predict outcomes in adulthood, decades later, was noteworthy. . . . Our temperament assessments completed at an average age of 3.76 years lend support that personality can be measured early on in life and have predictive validity for important life outcomes decades later. Our wide-ranging array of outcome variables further supports the broad and far-reaching predictive abilities of childhood temperament. . . . Thus, our study indeed found that early assessments of temperament are associated with a broad array of outcomes, up to decades later. . . . Using a large-scale longitudinal study across a 30-year time frame, we identified non-redundant predictions of life outcomes for temperament and personality. Temperament explained the most variance for outcomes

such as cognitive ability and educational attainment whereas personality performed best for outcomes such as health status, substance use,
and most internalizing outcomes. Our results highlight the benefit of
a lifespan approach to understanding life outcomes, where adult-based
outcomes are informed by child-based assessments. (pp. 130–131)

Our hope is to offer some possible insights that are therapeutically useful
into how early childhood features of temperament and personality may continue through adolescent development and shape adult personality. Even in
Jerome Kagan's study of behaviorally inhibited children and their growth
into early adulthood (Kagan, 1997), the ways parents raised their children
directly impacted how a given individual would retain the essential manifestations of that inhibition, or grow beyond them. Children who had passive or
unstructured parenting and those with authoritarian parents retained their
inhibition to engaging in new experiences; those with *authoritative* parents,
caregivers who tuned in to the child's particular temperament and experience, could learn, with their parents' support, how to feel their fear and move
out into the world despite its presence internally. In this way, we can see how
supportive experiences can influence how a temperament trait is manifested
outwardly, even though, as the research found, the sensitivity of the brain—
in this case of the amygdala—remained in all the subjects. This finding has
important implications for teaching parents about temperament and how to
attune to their child's particular proclivities to optimize their development
toward flexibility and resilience.

One way to envision this is that the higher cortical structures could
"learn" the skill of inhibiting the lower subcortical regions with their parents' connection and support. One of those subcortical areas, the amygdala, may have been especially sensitive to new experiences, creating a
paralyzing sense of fear. But with attuned parenting, despite these innate
temperament traits that may be subcortically mediated, a "cortical override" that was learned would change how that amygdala reactivity would
ultimately be expressed as emotion, thought, or behavior as the child
grew into adolescence and adulthood. In other words, this could be seen
to demonstrate how personality might be a combination of subcortical

temperament combined with cortical adaptive learning to create our patterns of personality.

Since 2004, after we scientists who met at the weeklong Enneagram workshop convened and came to name ourselves the PDP group, we have worked to seek a way of understanding how that popular personality system might emerge from some empirically established mechanisms in various fields, especially those of attachment and developmental, affective, and social neuroscience. From this two-decades-long endeavor, applying these new perspectives to old views, we have come to propose three key ideas of this Patterns of Developmental Pathways framework (PDP).

Integration and the PDP as a Clinically Useful Framework (Key Idea #1)

The PDP breaks ground in the therapeutic world in two ways. First, it is more than a system of individual development and well-being. It simultaneously provides rapid insights into interpersonal relationships, what we can call *wholeness between*, and provides clients with a larger understanding of themselves, what we call *wholeness of being*. Second, the PDP provides insights and tools for working toward integration cognitively, emotionally, and somatically, a *"wholeness within."* We believe the framework will:

1. Help you become a more effective therapist by becoming aware of your own personality-based biases that can sometimes make it difficult for you to be with your clients in an open, receptive manner, so that you can become more present, attuned, and resonant with them.
2. Help provide your clients with a powerful framework for (a) understanding personality and its role in ongoing personal problems, and (b) making changes in aspects of personality that aren't supporting them in getting along well with others and better cultivating their own well-being—we call this working at their *growth-edge*.
3. Acquaint you with a body of phenomenological knowledge—insights into how things unfold in our inner lives—that is beginning to enter mainstream psychology, and that we expect many of your current and

prospective clients may already know about, regarding contemplative, psychedelic, and spiritual experiences.

4. Inspire you to pursue this *inner understanding of personality* by exploring it first within yourself, which will promote your own growth toward wholeness as well as enhance your therapeutic practice. Like us, you may find it profoundly helpful to find *your baseline pattern*, which is the pattern in your life that, up to this point, may have developed most predominantly.

The PDP as a Life-Span Model of Personality (Key Idea #2)

The PDP framework fills an important gap in our understanding of personality in that it provides plausible hypotheses about how personality develops from temperament characteristics of infancy and emerges and is expressed throughout the lifespan as adaptive strategies. We provide a framework of personality that arises from three basic, subcortical emotional-motivational systems combined with attention and somatic processes that, from birth and throughout life, help us shape adaptive strategies that become important aspects of personality. We present a simple framework that shows how three motivational systems combined with three attentional orientations describe nine personality patterns, which we call patterns of developmental pathways. We provide an inside view of personality as PDPs, using the framework of interpersonal neurobiology, drawing especially from affective neuroscience, attachment research, and the mathematics of quantum physics and systems theory, to present what we see as a powerful approach for an in-depth understanding of individuals and their relationships with others. Unlike other personality systems in modern psychology of which we are aware, the PDP approach provides powerful tools for development, growth, and change that can be readily used in psychotherapy.

We propose that a set of patterns exists in which a collection of subcortical motivational networks forming early in life sets the stage for differences in three *reactive tendencies* that an individual will have a propensity to experience. These subcortical regions—related to emotion, motivation, and attention—interact with the cortex above them in a "bottom-up" way to influence the whole of the embodied brain—the nervous system distributed throughout the body, including its head—and shape our inner subjective sense of what matters and where we focus our attention.

When we say "patterns of developmental pathways," our hypothesis is that a **pathway** (specifying this reinforced network and its accompanying processing of emotion, cognition, and behavior) involves

1. innate, constitutional, non-learned leanings, and other early-forming proclivities of the nervous system that are the biological basis of what we shall simply refer to as "temperament," which
2. recursively ingrain their own tendencies in a self-reinforcing positive feedback loop of activation, neural growth, and
3. further activation that enhances the probability of this particular network or sets of networks being activated and becoming prevalent in a person's life as a specific pathway.

Our hypothesis is that a personality's features arise from the cluster of motivation, emotion, instinct, cognition, and attention that would then make up the "pattern" of that developmental pathway. This is the basis of *personality patterns* as the patterns of developmental pathways we are abbreviating as PDPs. In various settings we shall use "PDP," "patterns," and "pathways" as linguistic ways of referring to this set of propensities that cluster into what we call our personality. The PDP framework is a contemporary, interpersonal, neurobiologically based view of personality, with proposed hypotheses that can be challenged and refined both in future research and in clinical practice.

The PDP as a Framework for Wholeness and Integration (Key Idea #3)

"Wholeness" is a term we were hesitant to use, as it is a word used in so many ways in the popular literature: People who feel fractured are far from wholeness; those disconnected from purpose do not feel whole; feeling out of touch with nature is feeling a loss of wholeness. Many approaches to psychotherapy not derived from scientific foundations may emphasize wholeness, integrity, and coherence, and we hope that this developmental approach to personality through the cross-disciplinary framework of interpersonal neurobiology will provide a complementary perspective of interest and utility in clinical work. With all the various meanings attributed to the term "wholeness," wouldn't it be better to find another linguistic symbol for an experience of being that is free, content, connected, open, joyful, and even loving? Yet as we moved ahead in our work together, we found that in the tens of thousands of narratives David had accumulated of individuals who explored the journey toward change using a personality framework, "wholeness" was the linguistic term they chose to use in attempting to describe their experience of positive growth. "I became whole; I felt at peace and complete, I was whole; I felt connected and joyful in the sense of wholeness that emerged."

By using the term "wholeness," you and I are challenged to be sure we have a shared understanding of its intended meaning. And by deciding to explore what the concept of wholeness might mean in our lives, how it relates to personality, and how it might be used in clinical practice, we also will be aided by attempting to be as specific as possible so that the utility of the term and the experience we are trying to articulate are as specific as possible.

Here is one way to proceed. We can suggest that when a human being experiences something that they name linguistically as being "whole," the term may be referring to certain features that share some or all of at least these three qualities:

1. A *state of being* that is receptive, open, and capable of holding in awareness a wide range of emotions, thoughts, and memories with clarity and stability. This makes the term akin to the experience sometimes referred to as "presence." "Coherent" or the experience of being "complete" might be apt summary terms.

2. An experience in which the sense of self expands and a feeling of being at ease and connected to "something larger" than an individual identity emerges. This makes the term akin to the states of transcendence that the emotions of awe, compassion, and gratitude are sometimes said to evoke. This could also be stated as a sense of an

expanded feeling of one's identity and belonging, an *integrative* self we can call "intraconnected." "Connected" is a summary term.

3. A flowing *experience of harmony*. This use of the term "whole" suggests that as a complex system emerges with a self-organizing process, a synergy arises in which the "whole is greater than the sum of its parts" and has the qualities of optimal self-organization: flexibility, adaptability, coherence, energy, and stability. This is the FACES flow that emerges with integration, the linkage of differentiated facets of a complex system's optimal self-organization. "Content" is a summary term.

In this book, we will refer to these three facets of wholeness or being whole with this very specific meaning: *an integrative, harmonious, and receptive state of being*. We might also remember this as an experience of feeling coherent, complete, content, and connected. This notion of moving toward wholeness is not intended to imply that we achieve some permanent state of bliss in life, but rather that we can more readily access this experience of being whole, of wholeness, with certain personal transformations that the process of psychotherapy can facilitate.

Wholeness, Attachment, Personality, and Psychotherapy

Wholeness as a theme of our human development will be explored from the perspective of how our innate features—which to a large extent influence what is often called temperament—interact with our experiential learning throughout life. We may each have a drive toward this sense of coherence, completion, connection, and contentment: a drive toward wholeness. Part of the seeking drive to achieve these may be inherent because they are aspects of integration, the linking of differentiated parts of a system. With integration, we achieve a sense of harmony, bounded on one side by chaos, the other by rigidity. In that "river of integration" rests the integrative state, one that can be characterized as fostering coherence, and a sense of being complete, connected, content. Wholeness in this way would be a natural outcome of integration. As complex systems move toward differentiating and linking their elements to optimize a process called "self-organization," this movement toward integrative wholeness can be seen as a natural "push" of a self-organizing system to optimize its emergence over time. In other words, we may have a natural drive to move toward being coherent, complete, connected, and content. This may be an innate aspect of our self-organizing property as complex systems, rather than a learned proclivity.

Another potential contributor to this seeking journey toward wholeness might be related to our memory systems. The experience of effortless existence that we begin with in the womb can become embedded into what is known as "implicit memory" (see Siegel, 2001a). Once we are born, life becomes different in fundamental ways from that intrauterine existence. At a basic level, we've now shifted from an effortless state of relative ease to a need to "work for a living" in a "do-or-die," totally new setup. We propose that the large contrast between this implicitly remembered state of coherence, contentment, connection, and completion and the new, effortful life we lead once we are out in the world is huge. This contrast with what we once had as wholeness may be experienced now as "something missing." But how could we possibly remember such an early experience of our prebirth days?

Research reveals the finding that an implicit aspect of memory becomes active in the last months of life in utero (Siegel, 2020). This effortless state of all needs being met and no separation from the world around us, what we can call being an experience "at one with the womb," even in the face of potential stressors during pregnancy, would then be encoded into neural storage. The retrieval of pure implicit memory would have the activation of a similar neural set of activations, but the sense of something familiar might be present without being identified as coming from a past experience. Pure implicit memory, when retrieved, fills our here-and-now experience without a sense of its origins in the past. This implicit recollection is quite distinct from an explicit memory for facts and autobiographical knowledge, what we usually think of as "remembering." Explicit memory becomes available later in our lives, after about 18 months of age. Implicit memory begins early and remains with us, with the features of bodily sensations, emotions, perceptions, and behaviors. Implicit memory also includes mental models, our generalizations of experience also known as "schemas," as well as priming—which gets us ready with a sense of familiarity for what might come next (see Siegel, 2020 for details). In this way, we propose that an implicit memory sense of that effortless state of existence is something we are familiar with, yet we would not necessarily identify it as coming from anything we can explicitly recall from past experiences in our lives.

Here is the broad foundational idea. We start life in a state of oneness in utero when all needs are met—what we might consider to be original wholeness—but have a journey beginning at birth that takes us away from this effortless state. This state, we are proposing, would likely be encoded into implicit memory in its facets of bodily sensation, perception, emotion, and behavior. We would then have a familiarity with that sense of wholeness without an explicit notion of where it is coming from. As we meet the challenges of "working to live" after we are born, we begin to develop adaptive strategies to get our needs to be seen, safe, and soothed met.

We propose that three motivational systems beneath the cortex become activated in response to this "do-or-die" new life we lead, no matter how wonderfully attuned our caregivers may be. In other words, life is harder out here in the world no matter how good our family environment is. Being alive is hard, and then you die. Personality is how we come to deal with that existential reality. It is, literally, a journey of a lifetime.

The motivational drive of these subcortical networks is to ensure: that we build and maintain important bonding and connection with others; that we be able to predict what will happen as we seek confidence that we will be safe; and that we know when and how to be fully embodied and empower ourselves to take agency.

Depending on how well integrated these systems become, how we can differentiate and link them, and how effectively our strategies enable our needs to be met, our ways of being in the world can be more or less harmonious. When we move away from integration, the more out of harmony we become and the more we move toward states of chaos or rigidity. In other words, the less integrated our motivational systems, the more prone we are to be in chaos or rigidity, far from the harmony of wholeness—that *integrative, harmonious, and receptive state of being* that has the qualities of coherence, completion, connection, and contentment.

Depending on how rigid the strategies that develop become, we experience a departure from wholeness throughout development. If the patterns become rigid or chaotic, that reveals a low level of integration and we may find ourselves engaging in maladaptive habits of thinking, feeling, and behaving, encountering recurring problems in relationships, and lacking fulfillment in everyday life. Eventually, we may seek to understand these habitual patterns and find ways to move back toward greater levels of integration and regain access to wholeness, even if only for intermittent moments.

Our paths toward accessing wholeness take many directions, depending upon our innate neural proclivities and our adaptations to the attachment experiences that also shape us. In our view, from surveying dozens of individuals in a range of workshops and working in more depth with those in therapy, our preliminary hypothesis—one that might be wrong, partially correct, or entirely accurate—is that the patterns that emerge seem to be intensified by the attachment history of various forms of nonsecure attachment, that is, for those individuals with a history of avoidant, ambivalent, or disorganized attachment. The essential idea in our proposal is that attachment experiences directly affect the child through the impact of those experiences on the developing brain, and how they acquire strategies to get their needs met in those relationships. The way the child develops strategies of survival is a product of their innate temperamental proclivities, which become more deeply embedded when the attachment is nonsecure.

Even with a history of secure attachment, the experience of being born and living out here beyond the womb entails a set of challenges that at times makes us feel that we do not belong, that we are not connected, that we are not safe, that we are not whole. Those with secure attachment seem to have one of the nine patterns of developmental pathways as their baseline in life. In a nutshell, nonsecure attachment seems to compromise the integrative growth of security (see Siegel, 2020). This overlay of nonsecurity on top of the universal challenge of working-for-a-living outside the womb that drives the emergence of a personality pattern may lead to a blockage in the integration of PDP patterns—making the individual more prone to chaos or rigidity because the wider range of pathways beyond their baseline are not readily available. In this perspective, each of us would have a primary PDP pattern that might serve as a *baseline* or default way of being in life, especially under stress. With adaptation to nonsecure experiences or other forms of adversity in life, a more limited set of skills is available, perhaps manifesting as a deep and narrow groove of a singular PDP. This can be envisioned as one baseline PDP strengthened relative to other differentiated ways of being, and less well-linked to other possible pathways and their alternate ways of being in the world.

In a range of prior writings (Siegel, 2010a, 2010b, 2018, 2020), I've explored the notion that optimal self-organization emerges with *integration*—the linkage of differentiated parts of a complex system. When a system is not optimally self-organizing, it moves away from that flow of FACES (flexible, adaptive, coherent, energized, and stable) toward its opposite, IMIDU (inflexible, maladaptive, incoherent, de-energized, and unstable). When individuals are not in an integrative flow in their life, they "don't feel whole" and they have "something not right" in how life is going for them. Our view is that when one of the nine PDP patterns has become fixed, when it is *excessively differentiated* from and *less well-linked* with other potential pathways and their proclivities, there is more likelihood of the nonintegrative IMIDU state to emerge. IMIDU is far from wholeness.

In our view, *integration* is the essential mechanism underlying the experience of being whole. When PDP features that make up personality are not integrative, that means there is imbalance among the many differentiated alternative pathways and they are not well linked into an integrative life. The PDP framework points therapists to specific and clear strategies to guide clients to greater well-being by accessing the experience of wholeness.

As a therapist, this PDP framework will enable you to have a more neutral and unbiased, yet "prepared" mind, as Louis Pasteur suggested in the saying "Chance favors the prepared mind." You, as a therapist, will be provided science-based insights into the blend of attachment and temperament that shapes patterns of thinking, feeling, and behaving that we call personality. The journey to "know thyself" is given new inroads with the PDP framework of personality and wholeness. When the change we seek is liberation from the suffering of chaos and rigidity by way of cultivating integration, we then can free up our capacity for more harmonious living. In personality terms, when we differentiate and link across pathways, we integrate personality. This integration enables individuals to access a "higher personality-potential" of developmental pathways, enabling a shift toward living with wholeness—toward the harmony of integration—which is what this approach is all about. Welcome.

Summing Up

1. Patterns of developmental pathways, or PDPs, emerge early in life;
2. PDPs are likely intensified by suboptimal attachment experiences;
3. PDPs can be experienced as restrictive prisons when nonintegrated;
4. PDPs can be worked with in therapy and life by integrating toward being more of a playground;
5. Understanding one's own and others' PDPs can help facilitate the growth toward a life of wholeness.

CHAPTER 2

The Foundations of the PDP Framework

What do these personality patterns look like and, more importantly, *feel* like from the inside? In Chapter 3, we'll go through them one by one and describe major characteristics as we see them from the perspective of our PDP framework. But first let's consider a few key points about how we have come to regard the narrative data from which our views are created, and the framework in which they are presented.

Our Data Sources and Conceptual Context on Personality

A current understanding of the Enneagram of personality has emerged over the past 60 or so years and continues to be refined, through mostly anthropological narrative inquiry approaches, in communities of individuals curious about themselves and the dynamics of their relationships with others, identifying ways of feeling, thinking, and behaving that somehow tend, in an enduring way over time, to get in the way of individuals being their best personal selves. The Enneagram system is also in widespread use in personal-improvement workshops, workplace settings, and the practices of a growing number of psychotherapists who find it a useful addition to their therapeutic tool kit.

Although the Enneagram system originated outside of empirical science, today a very large number of individuals around the globe have found it to be quite useful in gaining deep insight into the inner self and effective in making their lives less restrictive and more empowering, having more successful relationships or marriages, or being better parents. It is in widespread use by consultants and coaches in personal and business settings and by psychotherapists. Even though the empirical research on its clinical effectiveness is still in its early stages, there is nonetheless a growing number of research studies on the Enneagram and its effects on a wide range of important health and behavioral outcomes. We are encouraged to see so many early-stage Enneagram efficacy studies on five continents, with Google Scholar showing 1,050 entries with Enneagram in the title from 1990 through October 2023.

The state of empirical research to date is very well summarized in a recent systematic review by Hook et al. (2020) on the Enneagram of personality. They found mixed evidence of reliability and validity of the personality constructs and their measurement. They noted partial but interesting alignment with psychodynamic theory and attachment theory, and theory-consistent relationships with other personality constructs such as the Big Five. (Similarly, Bland [2010] notes interesting parallels between the personality patterns and conventional diagnostic categories by several authors.)

Hook et al. (2020) also found mixed results in their assessment of a number of early clinical studies measuring many different outcomes in workplace, mental health, and personal/spiritual-growth settings. Overall, they suggest that current evidence points toward the potential to increase workplace effectiveness and promote personal growth, and believe additional research aimed at developing the Enneagram as a therapeutic tool is warranted. A recent peer-reviewed study by David and colleagues (Daniels et al., 2018), which explored effects of an intensive immersion in Enneagram training (like that in which our group first came together) on the Loevinger assessment of adult development (Loevinger, 1976), exemplifies the kind of research on methods development and feasibility needed to confirm or refute current evidence derived from a number of small studies with various methodological limitations.

It is mainly the compelling nature of the experience of those who explore the Enneagram of personality that has led us as a group to seek a scientifically plausible account of the developmental roots of the patterns, and their function in later life. David and colleagues have accumulated tens of thousands of narrative reflections. It is this robust set of first-person reports that serves as our primary data bank. The PDP framework we propose is consilient with the Enneagram of personality perspective as it is derived from this rich source of narrative data. Harnessing the reflections of thousands of individuals on the nature of their inner mental lives has enabled us to establish what we as scientists see as a plausible developmental and neural view of what might actually be going on beneath these nine ways of feeling, thinking, and behaving in life.

As we've seen, most of the individuals offering these reflections were themselves interested in and open to seeing things through the lens of the Enneagram viewpoint. Our more recent, much smaller data subset of hundreds of individuals trying out this new PDP framework in workshops and clinical settings, without initial reference to the Enneagram, has yielded fascinating new insights and continues to support the impression that these nine patterns are a human phenomenon, not just something skewed by those who've sought out a particular form of exploration of the inner world.

For some, the traditional Enneagram exploration has been more spiritually oriented, while for others it has been more focused on psychological issues, professional growth and group dynamics in workplace settings, or peak performance seeking in the context of personal coaching. Why it has not been a subject of careful empirical validation to this point is a fascinating question. It's a very heterogeneous group of individuals who've been drawn to explore the Enneagram from numerous countries on all continents, an extremely diverse set of cultural, educational, age, and gender backgrounds, and with a variety of motives, but all oriented toward growth and change. All share the notion that these identified repeating ways of their personality, although adaptive for functioning in the world, eventually become highly automatic, habitual, and potentially "trouble causing." This awareness leads them to seek out workshops, or at least be open in work-based settings, to the growth work involving relaxing or moving beyond their detected personality patterns. That growth-edge work entails becoming less reactive and more intentionally seeking to practice the more positive, "higher" human qualities that are specific capacities of each of the personality patterns.

Our collective understanding as a PDP group of the Enneagram of personality is grounded primarily in the knowledge base called the narrative method, founded by our coauthor David Daniels and his colleague Helen

Palmer in 1988. Since 2011, the method has been carried forward as a school of inquiry and teaching known as The Narrative Enneagram (www .narrativeenneagram.org/). As workshop participants have explored and then shared narrative accounts of carefully observing the inner experience of their own minds as they face challenges and successes at being their best selves, they have come through the narrative inquiry processes of this workshop approach to identify *nine different patterns of inner experience*. These patterns are characterized by *tendencies*, which seem automatic, in the ways in which attentional focus, emotions, perceptions, thinking, and somatic sensations are shaped by the mind and, at least to us, seem to flow from and into *motivations beneath behavior*. In this regard, the patterns are a novel, unique, inside, deeply personal, whole-person perspective on how humans manage *attention and the motivational energy of emotions*. They are not, by far, the entirety of one's personality, though as we shall see they do deal with hugely important aspects of it. In this sense, exploring personality is open to only a part—perhaps small in some, perhaps large in others—of how we experience life that shapes our sense of "who we are."

In fact, it may be that "who we truly are" is someone and something *beneath* personality, not personality itself. What this means is that if we use a term like "baseline personality pattern," this may actually signify a way that emotions, thinking, and behaving—your "personality"—keep you away from a deeper essence, an essence that might be akin to what we have named wholeness. In psychological and spiritual-growth terms, as we'll discuss in greater detail in Chapters 10 and 11, this would imply that **the *integrative, harmonious, and receptive state of being* is our true "home," what we "truly are" at our essence, our core, our "original nature."** When we feel coherent, complete, connected, and content, that is coming home. This view is consilient with a range of contemplative and Indigenous teachings, and with the poetic images and philosophical notions that we are already home, already whole—we simply need to let the "junk" of life get out of the way. That junk may be the rigid expression of personality.

So why focus on personality in therapy and in life if it's not who we truly are? It is the inflexible experience and expression of personality that may block us from living with a sense of wholeness; a way of living that is, in fact, our birthright. And in this way, wholeness is inside each of us and does not need to be constructed or created; it needs to be revealed and released by relaxing or removing that "junk" of personality.

On the other hand, it may be that we need these personality filters of sensory experience to prioritize what matters most and shape what can and cannot be attended to with vigilance. It may be that personality reveals the filters we have acquired, in part due to temperament and then intensified by adaptations to experience that then shape our predominant developmental pathway, our PDP. In this sense, we may never be able to, nor would it even be desirable to, fully discard our personality, but rather relax its potential stranglehold on our lives—to make it more a playground than a prison, as we've said earlier. But what does this therapeutic stance really mean from a larger standpoint of growth toward well-being and wholeness?

As these "autopilot" patterns of inner experience are illuminated, we'll address this question. These patterns of inner experience seem to originate in the fast-thinking, autopilot *models* the mind builds and uses to navigate us efficiently through day-to-day life, and the *tendencies*, which seem to emerge automatically—outside consciousness though they may have implicit intention behind them—as they operate mostly beneath the surface of day-to-day awareness yet nevertheless powerfully structure our experience (Kahneman, 2011). Implicit processes are often not in awareness but are filled with structure and driven with intention, with motivation. And so while many may wish to believe that their conscious minds are in charge of the show, in many ways implicit processes are on the stage of both our internal experiences and external patterns of action, and we—our conscious minds—are either asleep in the foyer or, at best, aware as audience members, sometimes simply watching the performance. If experience is energy flow, as we see it from an IPNB perspective, then the shaping of that flow does not require consciousness. The show of the mind goes on even if we are not the conscious mind directing the actors on the stage.

However, these implicit models and tendencies are not immutable—we can, with effort, identify them and change them. This is the "so what" of the whole PDP approach: When we name a pattern, we can frame it with a narrative that makes sense of it; we can sense the feeling of it, identify the motivations driving it, and then shape how it may be keeping us—often with "good intentions"—away from the well-being of wholeness.

With conscious intention and effort, aspects of our inner mental life can be brought into awareness, and the patterns revealed that shape many facets of what is most salient to us and how our emotions emerge; and the inner workings beneath enduring biases in perception, attention, and behavior can all be "made sense of" and something done to integrate them. In other words, instead of being prone to rigid or chaotic reactions to life, we can access a more harmonious FACES flow and experience being more flexible, adaptive, coherent, energized, and stable. As we explore the growth-edge therapeutic work for each pathway ahead, we'll see how this integrative transformation is applied in very specific ways depending on the nature of the stuff that is keeping us, unintentionally, from being whole.

Becoming mindful of these streams of energy and attention flow is the foundational stance of working with the personality patterns. **The more we become aware of how the mind on autopilot works, the more opportunity we will have to make intentional integrative course corrections when other ways of responding to life are in the best interests of all concerned. This integration involves differentiating the distinct patterns and then linking to the higher capacities of one's own baseline pathway and of the other pathways as well.**

A Few Initial Observations and Interpretations of Conventional Enneagram Teaching

Patterns, Not Types

While in most of the Enneagram world the nine personality patterns are called "personality types," the word "type" is convenient shorthand for constructs that are more like *hues* on the color wheel. That is, they are not fixed or mutually exclusive categories, which the word "type" suggests in conventional psychological parlance. Each of the "types" is defined by a few *features of inner experience* involving attention, feelings, somatic sensations, and cognitions, which seem to motivate related patterns of behavior. This inner view of personality is in contrast to a focus on externally observable and therefore more easily measurable traits. In the beginning of growth-oriented work, one uses this "map" of hues to help discern *patterns of tendencies* in one's own inner experience by exploring questions like "Which of these patterns of inner experience most resembles my own over time, and which least?" and "In what directions do I tend to lean?"

In Narrative Enneagram teaching, unearthing answers is very much an inside job. In and of itself, this part of working with the patterns is extremely valuable in developing capacities of what is called the inner observer—the ability to observe one's inner experience objectively. The most resonant pattern(s) become focal point(s) for the work of change. While very often one pattern is dominant and more than enough to work with at the start, most people find something more like one predominant pattern with notable "streaks" of others, or blends of two or more. The PDP framework embraces this reality of *patterns, not types.* At the same time, it offers an account that is consistent with current scientific understanding of personality as more verb-like and context dependent than rigid and noun-like.

Individual Variation

We cannot overemphasize the importance of individual differences in the traditional conception of personality. While a few features of inner experience define each personality pattern, there is tremendous variation in expression of personality, between individuals and even within individuals over time. This occurs along scales of functionality, rigidity or flexibility, focus of attention, mode of regulating emotion, and so on. Also described are dynamics in which some aspects of other patterns are more likely to emerge under stress or when times are good. Given this variation, the external and observable can provide clues but often do not directly reveal the underlying pattern of inner experience. As you approach growth and change, it is the stuff of *inner* experience that becomes a key part of understanding and moving toward greater well-being. For us, this is one of the most compelling features of the traditional Narrative Enneagram approach that drew each of us to explore the insights it might provide: personality from the inside out.

An additional important pattern of individual variation within the Enneagram of personality system is typically described as "somatic

imperatives" or "instinctual variants" or "subtypes." These involve important differences in the ways the personality patterns tend to "play out" in
different *relational* arenas of life experience. In the Narrative Enneagram
school, these are the arenas of relationship with personal self, relationship
with close or intimate others, and relationship with the larger social networks in which we are inevitably bound. Other Enneagram schools define
these arenas somewhat differently. There are various accounts of how and
why these cross-cutting variations might emerge. We will return to our
thoughts on these variations later, but in just a few words we suggest they
reflect the simple fact that these different arenas of experience each become
more or less salient at different times in the specific context of each individual's developmental trajectory.

Can Patterns Change, or Does Everyone Have One Lifelong Pattern?

There are several points to be made here. First, most in the Enneagram
world believe that one of the nine patterns emerges as predominant during
childhood and becomes an enduring feature of personality throughout life
in *every individual*. This claim is highly consistent with available narrative
evidence, but from a scientific perspective must be regarded as unsettled and
in need of future research, given all the potential biases inherent in those
data such as the non-random subject pool and the bias of the interviewers to
find responses that fit into the existing Enneagram system.

As scientists, we are well aware of and respect these important aspects of
where our initial data set is emerging from. This limitation is, in fact, part of
our motivation to find a scientific framework—the PDP approach—that can
be rigorously challenged, tested, modified, discarded altogether, or affirmed,
refined, and elaborated. As we've said, and will intentionally reemphasize
here, we want you to know where the initial data come from, where we are
drawing consilient observations across data sets and ways of knowing, and
how this PDP framework is a proposal that you can try on and challenge,
and see if it works for you and your clients. **Please don't take our word for
it; take in these words and see for yourself how it sits with you and your
own experiences in life and work.**

Second, for our purposes the entirely separate claim of usefulness of working with the map of "grown-up" patterns of inner experience—which is another reason we are writing this book—does not depend on the veracity of the "*everyone* has only one *lifelong* type" claim, or for that matter on the need to "determine a singular type" before beginning serious work. The PDP pathways have fascinating implications, as you'll see, for how we feel, think, and behave in different settings and in different individuals.

Third, the available evidence suggests strongly that these personality patterns involve certain important "default" aspects of how we feel, think, and act, a repeating and often enduring pattern to how we organize our inner and interactive ways of functioning in life. Accordingly, transformational work with them in therapeutic settings should be approached with due diligence to the potential hazards of destabilizing that structure. This is an important truth about therapy in general. We have the challenging paradox of accepting people just as they are so they can "feel felt" and connected; and then we are there to help them find ways to change, if this is what will bring more well-being into their lives. That change can be subtle and slow, or it can be intense and rapid. "First, do no harm" is the physician's commitment, and it should be that for our work as psychotherapists as well. That being said, complex systems, like us human beings, may need to go through periods of disorganization in order to move to reorganization and the establishment of new levels of functioning. In this way, a "dark night of the soul" is sometimes a part of the journey to release the shackles of personality that have imprisoned us, keeping us away from living the wholeness that is already there. That is a lifelong journey and we have the privilege, and responsibility as therapists, to be sherpas on that path, carrying the luggage and supporting our clients along their exploration and transformation.

Fourth, and most important, *the goal of inner work with these personality patterns is not about eliminating them or switching them to some other "type" or pathway!*

Instead, it entails learning to recognize and "soften" or "relax" aspects of that baseline personality structure that may be habitually limiting and constricting the flow of attention and emotional energy into behavior. This integrative transformation also can involve developing access to other less-practiced ways of responding to life—the higher capacities of other pathways—and thus building a more flexible and adaptive mind that can allow other ways of perceiving and responding in life to become more accessible.

Higher Qualities and Challenges

These personality patterns can be major features of a very healthy "ego structure," the ways we learn to deal with the world, or they can be problematic. Problems can emerge when a pattern becomes both an "automatic" *and* restricted way of responding to life. In traditional Enneagram teaching, none of the personality patterns are in any way better or worse per se than any of the others. They are just different. Each can manifest in both highly virtuous and laudable "upsides," and problematic or even psychopathological "downsides," demonstrating in very concrete ways how one's best assets and biggest liabilities are often two sides of the same coin.

Might "personality disorders" be related to extreme states of PDPs? Possibly—and this would be a potentially fruitful focus of future research. Might working with the PDP approach in therapy be harnessed for a range of personality challenges, including those formerly diagnosed as borderline or narcissistic? Again, a question worthy of future study (see Alexander & Schnipke, 2020). For now, taking this model as a general "personality development across the lifespan" view would mean it would be useful for any human being at any age in psychotherapy.

Realizing this, in various ways most Enneagram experts recognize a spectrum of what are often called *levels of development* or functionality associated with each type. In most individuals, higher or lower levels of function are possible at certain times in their lives and in certain situations. In the PDP perspective, we'll just say that "healthy" or "problematic" depends on the extent to which a pattern becomes a limiting adaptive strategy for perceiving and being in the world. David would also urge that the Enneagram be used for mostly functionally effective individuals and not for those with serious mental health challenges, which should be carefully evaluated for their own impacts on an individual's life. It may be that future research could reveal that extreme low-functioning states may overlap with some forms of conventionally described personality disorders, but studies supporting that possibility have yet to be done, or at least published, as far as we can discern. This book will explore this notion of lower and higher levels of functioning, how to work with the pattern-specific challenges, and how to access and cultivate pattern-specific strengths, as we explore what in the PDP framework we call "high" and "low" levels of integration.

Nature or Nurture?

In conventional teaching there are widely differing opinions, none supported by rigorous scientific evidence, along the nature-versus-nurture spectrum of how the patterns come to be. At the nature end are those who believe they are purely genetic or inborn. At the nurture end are those like us who suspect that early life experiences—including environmental trauma, parental encouragement or indulgences, and socialization—drive their development. In accord with most contemporary developmental theory, we view it more likely that the patterns in adults arise in the interplay of innate proclivities and a large learning effect (Fox et al., 2005, 2007).

More specifically, in our PDP view, each of the nine personality patterns reflects a repertoire of essential working strategies of adaptation that we call *adaptive strategies* and that all children must learn in order to get along in human social life. In the unique circumstances of each individual life journey, specific strategies can become important features of personality by the mechanisms of salience and neuroplasticity—what has meaning and how the brain adapts to ongoing experience. In other words, as the inner networks of the brain assign a priority to outer and inner flows of energy and filter and amplify what is attended to, specific neural firing patterns are created. I made up a phrase that captures this fundamental process to help remember the sequence: "Where attention goes, neural firing flows, and neural connection grows." These experientially acquired learnings will become embedded through neuroplasticity as changes in brain structure and function.

We also recognize that certain aspects of temperament—our early tendencies of the nervous system to have propensities in how we respond to stimuli, how sensitive we are, and how open to novelty we feel—may be mostly innate, that is, not learned, aspects of our constitution. In addition to genetic and epigenetic inheritance, perhaps some early in utero conditions and very early life experiences around birth directly shape the structure and function of the brain to create these neural proclivities. As we've stated, we will use the term "temperament" to signify this notion that we have an essential nature of the nervous system, innate or inborn, that was not determined by how we adapted to events in a learning sense, even if it may be partly shaped by early experience and not just genetics. This set of temperament propensities means that we come with an inner world that will directly influence how we come to adapt, how we learn how to live in the world, how we develop a personality.

A simple equation for this viewpoint is this: temperament plus experience equals personality. We will explore this matter in Chapter 4 when we discuss our developmental model of how the patterns may come to be and persist across the lifespan.

A Personal Reflection

In the Narrative Enneagram approach to teaching about these patterns, individuals attending workshops sit on panels with others who have identified most strongly with a certain "personality type." Panel members are then interviewed, with their consent, by teachers or more advanced students about their inner experience and behavioral tendencies in dealing with the challenges and opportunities of their lives. Those chosen for panels are usually familiar with mindfulness and the concept and skill of using their inner observer to witness their own thoughts, feelings, and somatic sensations. Alternatively, a skilled interviewer might guide the process of inquiry in real time with those less familiar with this process of inner exploration. As a style of teaching, these firsthand narrative accounts provide deep insight into the felt nature of patterns in operation. As we've mentioned, these narratives, accumulated and assimilated by David and his colleagues, are the main source of our "data."

Clearly there are sources of bias built into this data-collection arrangement, and I, Dan, in my first encounter, was quite leery of the validity of the approach. What struck me, though, was how from the inside, the group that I did ultimately find myself up on the panel with shared so many internally felt views—of emotions, of what was important in our lives, of what we thought no one else saw or knew, of what we cared most about—that were actually quite distinct from the other eight panels' discussions. The scientist in me said to myself, and likely others, that I doubted the validity of what we were doing. Interestingly, so did other members of my "loyal skeptic" pattern group. It was quite hilarious, too, as an example, when we were all waiting for another panel to appear, that the panel members were found in the restroom making sure they looked acceptable before getting up "on stage." And these individuals were in a grouping that prioritized others' opinions about them first and foremost. From my first encounter with the Enneagram, I began my own (still ongoing) inquiry of the nine patterns using this narrative approach, first identifying consistent emotional patterns, then motivations and needs. I could see for myself in my clinical practice and in workshops that very often the patterns reveal themselves, and that this new clarity could be a powerful catalyst for change in problematic patterns of behavior. Simply put, awareness of what your mind is doing, often on autopilot, offers the opportunity to pause and respond differently.

From a scientific perspective, as we've also mentioned, we must acknowledge the limitations of such selectively accumulated narrative data. At the same time, I found it impossible to ignore three things. First was the potential of this approach to offer a unique *insider's* view of personality. Second was the scope of evidence of the resonance people found with the patterns. For example, thousands of people—of all ages, socioeconomic status, education levels, cultures, religions, races, ethnicities, gender identities, sexual orientations, and nationalities, and not only in The Narrative Enneagram workshops but in all manner of settings, including psychotherapy, spiritual counseling, workplaces, prisons, and vocational rehabilitation—report extremely similar experiences within each of the nine patterns. Third, I found it impossible to ignore the wealth of first-person anecdotal evidence that working with these patterns of personality can help people make deep and lasting changes, improving the qualities of their lives and relationships, and more readily accessing wholeness, as we have defined that term.

Perhaps a reason these findings never made it into the academic, empirical literature was their essential subjective nature. These are, after all, inner accounts of personally experienced processes of meaning, emotion, and attention. But with caution and skepticism to always "think again" about the model (as Adam Grant's *Think Again* [2021] would suggest), I felt it was filled with an exciting potential to explore these data and see what might emerge. What these experiences each hold in common in workshop settings is that using the personality framework, participants have developed greater capacity to mindfully witness their own "automatic" or "autopilot" thoughts, emotions, attention, and motivations, and as a result have opportunities to perceive and behave differently. As David and colleagues' study had demonstrated, too, intensive immersion in studying these nine patterns yielded positive growth in one's sense of self as assessed by validated ego-development surveys (Daniels et al., 2018). Whatever any future empirical studies might ultimately demonstrate about neural mechanisms that may be at play, it felt as if there was something meaningful and real in this data set. What these Enneagram personality patterns were really all about became a fascinating topic with potentially great scientific and psychotherapeutic value.

Core IPNB Principles: Mind, Attention, Neuroplasticity, and Integration

From its inception, our exploration to address this topic of what the underlying mechanisms are beneath these narrative findings was grounded in principles and insights of the transdisciplinary approach of interpersonal neurobiology, IPNB. The result is our PDP hypothesis, a framework that proposes both a *process* account (the dynamics of a set of functions we suggest is going on "beneath the hood" of the personality pattern) and a *developmental* account (the forces and factors that might influence how a personality pattern might come to be). We will return to the developmental account in Chapter 4. The remainder of this chapter will focus on the process aspects of the PDP model.

Several IPNB concepts and principles are central to our framework. First is the IPNB definition of *mind,* one aspect of which is an embodied and relational *process* that regulates the flow of energy and information. We propose that the personality patterns arise from the processes of three interconnected, open, and dynamic systems, what can be named **systems of mind**, as our innate temperament encounters life experience. In effect, these interconnected systems operate as "fast-thinking" processes that channel the flow of attention and emotion-driven motivational energy along different pathways toward satisfaction of certain fundamental needs that humans (and many other animals) are highly motivated to pursue throughout life. As we will see, the different pathways associated with each system provide a repertoire of adaptive strategies for addressing different circumstances.

We hypothesize that personality patterns develop when the need set associated with one of the systems and its particular adaptive strategies becomes more salient, more dominant, than others over the course of early development. These differences in salience then lead to differences in integration and robustness of the neural pathways in which the strategies are embedded. We hypothesize that each of the three systems has three potential ways that energy is directed as properties we will describe shortly. Three systems of mind, three ways to direct energy: This yields nine potential clusters of ways of feeling, thinking, and behaving that constitute the nine patterns of developmental pathways. Every person has and can potentially utilize all three of these systems and pathways all the time in navigating life and relationships with others with varying degrees of functionality.

For clarity, when we use the term "energy" we are usually referring to the literal electrochemical energy of neural firing, which transmits information "inward" from the body's many internal and external sensory systems, and also "outward" into mobilization of the body into behavior. Energy has an internal flow and it has an external flow—it is how we process information in the embodied brain and how we connect with one another as communication patterns in our interpersonal relationships. Attachment, for example, is composed of energy flow between parent and child. And this relational flow shapes the inner flow of energy within the body, shaping how the nervous system processes information. This flow of energy is often accompanied by perceptible "energetic" somatic sensations, the feeling of what is happening as it happens. Experience is energy flow.

One central IPNB principle is that human development emerges from the interface of human relationships and inborn tendencies influenced by growth of the brain. What this means for personality is that our innate temperament—proclivities not initially shaped by experience but formed by constitution and from in utero environmental conditions (including those affecting the mother and her social situation), genetics, epigenetic influences, chance, or other factors before or just after birth—will interact with our attachment experiences and other experiential events that shape the brain as it adapts and learns through its neuroplastic growth. It is this intertwining of the innate and the acquired that is how temperament and experience shape our personality and influence how we become who we are.

A second principle is this: *Where attention goes, neural firing flows, and neural connection grows.* What this means for personality is that early experience and innate temperament can lead to an early tendency for energy and information flow to be directed along particular neural pathways—activating specific networks more than others, for example—and that an initial small propensity can gain momentum and develop into a larger proclivity for activation of a particular set of neural circuits along that pathway, which further reinforces neural connectivity, and then still further enhances that neural pathway. It is these positive, reinforcing feedback loops of neural pathways that shape normal development of neural networks—collections of pathways shaped by this fundamental process of neuroplasticity. Neural activation shapes our subjective experience, and at the same time it can, with repetition, make that same activation more likely to occur in the future because of the strengthening of the neural connections that allow that neural flow to occur with more intensity.

These same processes can, under various developmental scenarios (as we shall see in Chapter 4), lead to preferential "reliance" of the mind on some pathways more than others, ultimately creating personality patterns by these straightforward mechanisms of neuroplasticity. Another layer of neural activation is how we adapt to input not only from the external environment but from our own inner activations. These adaptations can be considered "strategic" in the sense that they are our own strategies to function well given both what is happening in the outside world, such as interactions with our caregivers, and what is happening inside of us in response, such as our own features of temperament.

Strategic adaptations are activated to help us survive; and these very adaptations become themselves expressed in more intensely developed neural networks that are reinforced in their activity, their anatomy further strengthened with repetition. Direct and adaptive neural activations reinforce their own becoming and, in these ways, small subtle differences can become large, persistent distinctions. It is these persistent patterns over time and situations that we believe shape what we come to experience as personality.

In other words, we begin with a certain set of tendencies, our temperament and its neural propensities. We then have our experiences interacting with the world outside and in. And from this interface of innate and experiential, we adapt as best we can to get along. This interaction of innate and experiential, we speculate, is the process that leads a **developmental pathway** to become set in our lives as what we generically refer to as our personality. This is a combination of our temperament and our adaptive strategies.

This need not be, but can become, problematic if the flow of attention and energy becomes skewed toward one pathway over others, as it becomes nonintegrative in a state of "low integration." Why low? When one set of patterns is excessively differentiated and not linked to other options of neural firing, that compromises the capacity to access other avenues of response. This low integrative state, we are proposing, creates biases and "blind spots" in attention, and patterns of dysfunctional reactivity. Low integration makes an individual prone to chaos and rigidity. Integration leads to harmony. This is the reasoning in our proposal that working at the growth-edge in therapy will involve integrative transformation, as we'll explore in great depth ahead.

Importantly, a predominant and persistent pattern of "automatic" inner experience or the behavior it motivates may be misinterpreted as a noun-like entity, a type; and this mistaken identity—"That's just the way I am and I cannot change who I am"—can reify that pattern itself into an enhanced propensity, furthering the illusion of its essence as an entity-identity. In this way we have innate vulnerabilities of "seeing what we're looking for," which creates yet another layer of the self-reinforcing feedback loop that can dig even more deeply the "neural groove" of a particular network activation and its repeated activation over other possible patterns of motivation, emotion, and attention. On the other hand, there is a noun-like solidity to how these verb-like patterns stay with us over a lifetime. If we see through the persistence of a process into its verb-like essence, we can see how these energy flow patterns are truly processes, not "things" that trap us and constrain us.

Fortunately, personality patterns emerging from these "developmental pathways" seem to be malleable. At a clinical level, habitual or rigid tendencies of personality can be softened. At a neural level, we hypothesize that while they set a certain network activation course in motion, they also have the potential throughout life to develop, branch out, and grow, given the right circumstances. The initial goal of therapy is to identify which of the nine pathways and accompanying strategies tend to create problems in a person's life, and then help that person develop a larger, more flexible, and adaptable repertoire of strategies. This frees an individual to be amused by their pattern rather than annoyed by it—to transform their pathway into a playground over time and across contexts, rather than continue to experience it as the prison it may have become in their life.

This leads us to a third cornerstone IPNB principle—that the process of linking differentiated elements of a complex system, something simply called "integration," is at the root of well-being and wholeness. A wide array of studies support this view (see Siegel, 2020). What matters about this for now is that using the PDP framework in therapy is fundamentally about improving the state of neurobiological and relational integration—that is, linking various differentiated parts of the complex system. This is the platform, if you will, on which mind operates.

Both Noun and Verb

The words we use can themselves shape the concepts and categories we have that are being expressed by these linguistic symbols. What this means is that each of us has the vulnerability of perceiving what we believe, which creates one aspect of a self-reinforcing feedback loop that can dig even more deeply the "neural groove" of a particular network activation. Then, with repeated activation reinforced by the terms we say or hear others use, a proclivity for a certain pattern of motivation, emotion, and attention can be inadvertently reinforced. We cannot emphasize enough that this "nounification" is a vulnerability of our linguistic minds that can be limiting. And yet there is a deep value in being able to explore and express the nature of our lives and the inner nature of our mind with words. In this way, words can be both limiting and liberating.

There may be a utility at times to think in noun terms, to consider aspects of who we are as entities with an enduring quality to them. Yet our languaging matters, and it may be more useful to at least think, if not speak and write, in a more verb-like way, as in the "verbing" of a present participle—Dan is Dan-ing and you are you-ing, instead of us being "you" and "Dan," as nouns alone. On the other hand, some processes, like those of personality patterns, do have enduring features that are upheld across time and across contexts. These patterns of personality may have a feeling of an "entity"—even a self-organizing process—that a verb feeling doesn't quite capture. Not all processes are fluid and emergent without "functional structures," such as neural network connectivity, that lend them a more noun-like, entity feeling. I hope you get the point: We are both noun-like and verb-like. Let's try to be open to the fluid, process nature of even enduring patterns, while acknowledging the persistent features of patterns that can feel like process-entities in our lives, even ones that may last a lifetime of becoming what they are.

Here is the major point of this issue. It is essential to conceive of these personality patterns as **tendencies or propensities** for patterns of perception, feeling, thought, somatic sensation, and behavior to arise over the course of the lifespan. We will use both nouns and verbs to attempt to articulate the nature of these mental processes that shape our lives (see Mesulam, 1998). David Daniels would use terms like "pattern-verbs" but also hold for the importance of something he called "pattern-nouns," a kind of both/and approach rather than either/or thinking. Our overall point in emphasizing both patterns over types and verbs as well as nouns is to embrace the dynamic, fluid nature of experience, even the experience of personality. There are indeed enduring patterns that may feel like entities, and in that persistence using nouns, or "pattern-nouns," as wording may be accurate. Holding personality patterns, our PDPs, as emergent as well as persistent processes in this way is more consistent with the ways in which the nine patterns actually manifest and operate in almost endlessly complex individual variations even in the face of their common grounding.

CHAPTER 3

The PDP Framework in a Nutshell

Before diving deeply into the specific details, here is a high-level overview of our PDP framework. It describes three sets of **fundamental needs** that humans (and many other species) are strongly motivated by nature to satisfy, and three open, dynamic, interconnected **motivational systems**, which provide first-level, "fast-thinking" monitoring and modifying of those **core motivational energies**. Drawing on the foundational affective neuroscience work of Jaak Panksepp's lifelong exploration of subcortical motivational systems (see Davis & Panksepp, 2018; Panksepp, 1998; and Panksepp & Biven, 2012), we extend this view into a developmental framework of lifelong growth. We use the following labels to describe both the need sets and their accompanying systems of mind. Here are the three systems:

agency for embodied empowerment;
bonding for relational connection; and
certainty for prediction and safety.

For ease of recall, these systems of mind can be simplified as A, B, C: agency, bonding, and certainty. Each of these distinct systems carries out a motivational drive to achieve the experience of embodied empowerment, relational connection, or prediction and safety. It turns out that each of these systems, too, is associated with what Panksepp called a "primal" affect—a deep, evolutionarily based, subcortically mediated emotional state that arises from these distinct motivational neural networks. Some of these key affects are pleasant, some are unpleasant. The terms often used to distinguish these two valences are "appetitive" for the positive states an organism seeks to enhance and "aversive" for those the organism seeks to minimize.

As we will explain further below, each of these three motivational systems is tightly linked with a specific **core aversive emotion**, an uncomfortable affective state, and drives efforts to respond in an adaptive way to reduce its emergence. Each system is also associated with positive affective sensations, ones we can call **appetitive states**. The core aversive emotion is aroused when threats to well-being in the form of obstacles to satisfaction of the need set are encountered. The appetitive states emerge when those needs are sought and satisfied. When the motivation is frustrated or impeded, the correlated affective states include a range of

> anger or rage associated with agency;
> separation-distress or sadness with bonding; and
> anxiety or fear with certainty.

In addition, appetitive *states* are harnessed to fuel pursuit of opportunities to satisfy needs associated with agency, bonding, and certainty. Some appetitive states associated with each motivation being satisfied include a wide range of

> coherence, satisfaction, strength, and integrity with agency;
> connection, affection, recognition, and approval for bonding; and
> confidence, curiosity, playfulness, and trust with certainty.

Vectors

The term **vector** is helpful in describing the energetic quality of these aversive and appetitive affects and their corresponding motivations, as it conveys setting a direction for the focus of attention on salient elements of experience related to meaning, and placement of energy into behavior. A vector includes the subcortical motivation network that initiates both a drive to satisfy fundamental needs and its accompanying primal affects; it also involves the extended neural pathways connecting to a wider range of subcortical and cortical processes to satisfy that drive. In other words, a vector will have a specific pattern of energy directed in pursuit of these needs, and will motivate a sense of striving to achieve satisfaction of those needs. A vector will involve activation of certain specific patterns of emotion, thinking, and ways of behaving that we propose are the underlying mechanisms of at least some aspects of what we call personality.

One possibility is that the experience of just being in the womb, of just being in life, is far from the post-uterine life out here in the world. As we've suggested, no matter how wondrous one's parents might be, life now has the quality that if we don't get our needs met, we will die. We need to have agency for an embodied empowerment to have our bodily needs met in order to survive; we need to bond for relational connection to survive; and we need to be certain with some capacity for prediction and safety to survive. In this way, these three aversive motivational systems become activated with a threat to our survival; the appetitive states emerge when we satisfy those drives.

While the aversive emotions Panksepp emphasized are central in these subcortical networks, and also described in traditional Enneagram teaching, the proposed A, B, and C motivational systems involve a wide range of experience. For this reason, we will instead emphasize the motivation of that network and then try to keep in the front of our minds that this motivational system involves both uncomfortable aversive affects and comfortable affective states. As we'll see below, there are primal or core appetitive *affects* that emerge from four other distinct subcortical networks, and for this reason we will distinguish the terms appetitive "affect" of this distinct origin from a more general, positive, or appetitive "state" that can arise from any of the motivational networks, including those Jaak Panksepp denoted as "aversive." In other words, when the motivation of that aversive subcortical network is satisfied, the result is a rewarding, comfortable, "appetitive" state of being—of a sense of empowerment, of connection, and of ease.

In a state of wholeness there is the feeling of empowerment, of connection, and of safety. In a state of wholeness, you can see how the agency, bonding, and certainty systems are satisfied. This is our hypothesis that links the developmental journey of being here in the do-or-die lives we lead out in the world and the ways our attachment relationships and other experiences we engage in shape how we respond to this seeking for wholeness.

In Darcia Narvaez and colleagues' work on the evolving nest (Narvaez et al., 2023), we can see that we humans try to have what has been called a "continuum" to retain this holding, this sense of belonging, this human way we can be certain in life that we are a part of something whole rather than alone in the world, isolated, and with our very existence threatened. This is how the PDP view sees personality and the search to access wholeness as a journey of a lifetime.

You can think of these three motivational systems as gateways that channel attention and motivational neural energy along neural pathways toward various goal-oriented states of mind. We use this term, "state of mind," rather than "state of brain activation," as in IPNB we view the mind as both fully embodied and fully relational. In this sense, a vector creates mental states—not just head-brain states of firing—that involve the whole embodied brain as well as the relational fields in which the mind is embedded.

Together, the various pathways involve an essential repertoire of what we call **adaptive strategies**. These amount to different ways of streaming attention and emotional energy down specific pathways into behavior that is most likely to be functionally useful and socially acceptable according to the situation in the moment.

Each pattern also involves a configuration of directionality of attention and energy we call **attendency**, and a **mode** of **emotion regulation** that monitors and modifies our affective state. I made up the term "attendency" to indicate the tendency of attention and energy in general to be in a particular direction. That focus of attention and energy can be inward, outward, or divided between inward and outward. This pairing or dyadic state of attendency is consistent with a brain-based finding by Mary Helen Immordino-Yang and colleagues (2012) and fits with the sense that in this latter condition of both inward and outward, there is a kind of fluctuation between the two directionalities of attention, a shuttling between inward and outward. In our observations, this dyadic attendency is a kind of duet when working well or a duel when in conflict. We will refer to this inward and outward combination with the term "dyadic," meaning pair, and with the label "d"; inward will be designated with an "i" and outward with an "o."

Where does this tendency of attention arise from? Our hypothesis at this moment, one in need of testing further, is that one's attendency may be an innate feature we can place under the broad notion of temperament. Alternatively, it may come to be found that attendency is a learned adaptation, not an innate component of our temperament. For example, some children innately seem to be inwardly focused; some, outwardly focused; some, shifting between the two. Could this simply be a component of temperament that shapes how we subsequently adapt to life's experiences? Or is this, even if early on, something we actually learn as an early response to adapt as best we can to experience? These questions can be explored in future research studies.

It is fascinating that these characteristics of where we focus attention do not appear to correlate with the terms "introversion" and "extraversion" in the existing personality research. These latter features have more a quality of one's social relatedness. Our initial attempts to explore those features of the OCEAN Big Five traits of personality with the PDP model suggest that there is no direct correlation of attendency to extraversion or introversion. For example, there are many whose baseline PDP has an attendency of inward yet they enjoy social engagement and would likely score high on the Big Five extraversion scale.

Each of the patterns also involves a specific way in which emotional motivations tend to be processed and then expressed, or not. We label these **modes of emotion regulation** and they include *upregulating* (allowing the emotion to flow into fully embodied experience and expression), *downregulating* (containing and channeling the energy into some way more likely to be effective or socially acceptable), or *shifting* (allowing a different emotional state to emerge by releasing and redirecting the motivational energy). The term "mode" can be seen as an acronym: a regulatory capacity signifying the "*means of deploying emotion.*" Interestingly, the science of emotion regulation reveals the many ways individuals can modify attention, appraisal, or the situations in which they find themselves, in order to achieve this general range of responses—which can be highly adaptive or maladaptive depending on the situation—when emotion is activated (Gross, 2014; Izard et al., 2008; Thompson et al., 2008). As we'll see, the attendency does not predict a specific pattern's form of emotion-regulation mode. For now, we propose that while attendency may be a part of temperament's proclivity, one's emotion-regulation mode may be more a learned part of one's overall adaptive strategy. That, too, is a current hypothesis open for exploration and modification. It may also be that given a particular combination of vector with attendency, the most adaptive way of attempting to handle key arising emotion is with the mode that is then "learned" in this sense to cope with one's own temperament. The specifics of these various aspects of how these elements of the PDP arise, like the whole model itself, should be tested with empirical studies, and abandoned, refined, or elaborated with future research.

Most everything about the repertoire of adaptive strategies is shaped through development, to varying degrees of proficiency, in the interplay of genetics, temperament, and life experience in attachment and later social relationships. In this way each adaptive strategy contributes to a **developmental pathway** of learning how to cope with life given both one's temperament—including vector and attendency—and the learned adaptation to experiences that emerge, inside one's own inner world and outside in interaction with the external world.

We are proposing that these adaptive strategies are the roots of what have been described as the nine Enneagram personality types. A **pattern of developmental pathway**, a PDP, would then involve a neural groove, a set of neural networks strengthened from temperament *and* experience, a literal neural pathway that is reinforced to enable the individual to adapt well. A **PDP groove** creates an enhanced probability of a certain way of feeling, thinking, and behaving that we call personality. Put another way, our personality tendencies emerge when a particular pathway and its adaptive strategy become a predominant way of orienting attention and channeling emotional motivation. This happens as genetics, temperament, and relational experiences shape the relative salience of the different need sets. It is these need sets—for agency, bonding, and certainty—that are directly related, we propose, to the vector that is most likely to become active based on temperament. In other words, one set of needs has become most salient— more relevant and dominant—creating what we call a **core motivation**, and one of the various possible strategies has become an **adaptive strategy** for coping with life. These motivations and strategies reveal what creates a priority in an individual's life.

Such a pattern of personality can be a central element of what is sometimes called a well-developed ego structure, using the term "ego" to signify the aspect of the mind that is how we handle our external environment and our internal drives (Valiant, 1992). That executive function can be well developed *if* the differentiated elements—that is, the three vectors and the various pathways of each—are all well integrated, so that the entire repertoire of ways of focusing attention and channeling energy into behavioral responses is readily available to the individual. Integration means differentiated and linked, and integration is the core mechanism beneath well-being and adaptive functioning. This is a fundamental principle of interpersonal neurobiology we are suggesting illuminates the nature of low- or high-functioning levels of personality pathways. With well-being, we can say that development has led to a higher state of integration and a more flexible, adaptable, and highly functional pattern of personality, which allows the expression of the best qualities of one's PDP.

Conversely, problems arise when integration is impaired, essentially meaning that over time and in the unique context of the individual's developmental trajectory, one of the sets of needs (agency, bonding, or certainty) becomes more salient and reinforced than the others. This may be how the prioritizing of one has become excessively differentiated while not being linked to the capacities of the other vectors. This low integrative state leads to an excessively dominant attendency of the individual as well as a dominance of one of the vectors of that system, thus limiting available ways of seeking satisfaction and restricting how other vectors and attendencies may be accessed and developed. The net result is a tendency for skewed perceptions, and channeling of attention and motivational energy in a limited, habitual, and "force-fitted" way in situations where another vector, attendency, or mode of emotion regulation would provide a more optimal and adaptive response to conditions at hand. Here we can say the individual's particular developmental pathway has led to a lower state of integration and a more dysfunctional side of the personality pattern in that moment of life, and that this pathway is unbalanced, because the individual is challenged to access other capacities.

Naturally, there are many other neural networks and fundamental needs involved in both our life and our repeating patterns of feeling, thinking, and behaving beyond these three core needs and their motivational drives. In other words, there is much more to personality than these PDPs address, much more than the PDP framework focuses upon. Nevertheless, starting with this framework not only matches the Narrative Enneagram data we have, it serves clinically as a powerful framework to deepen an understanding of at least one component, perhaps even an important part, of what makes up the underlying motivation of a person's inner life, and then offers suggestions on what to do practically with those insights. In other words, while we readily acknowledge the inherent limitations to what the PDP examines, we also recognize its usefulness in psychotherapy and personal growth. Work with the patterns of personality toward growth and wholeness is fundamentally the work of building higher states of integration and functioning by harnessing neuroplasticity, lessening the restrictive "depth" of a particular groove of a pathway, and in this manner making higher human capacities of wisely embodied agency, bonding for connection, and embracing of uncertainty more accessible.

Three Trios of Personality Patterns

A central concept of most Enneagram teaching is that the nine personality patterns involve three clusters (known as "triads") of three personality patterns, each triad sharing at least two well-characterized features. There are many of these triads linking various combinations of the fundamental nine categories of personality in that system. This classical teaching, which seemed clear and highly consistent with our own assessment of the available narrative tradition evidence, became a key starting point for our work. It is worth reemphasizing here that we began as a PDP group with narrative data from tens of thousands of individuals harnessing the Enneagram view. We sought a developmental neuroscience perspective from empirical data derived from non-personality studies to then construct a model of personality that translates the Enneagram view. In this way, the PDP model is not a parallel view; it is intentionally built from the Narrative Enneagram findings and then takes these insights into personality into significantly distinct ways of understanding what our lives are shaped by and what, then, we can do with these new insights during psychotherapy, relational functioning, and lifespan growth of the individual.

One of the key triad groupings the Enneagram nomenclature describes is organized by a "center of intelligence" of the body and gut, the heart, or the head. The center of intelligence terminology emerged because three of the patterns were seen as tending to perceive or know the world through bodily sensations and movement, three through heartfelt feelings, and three through logic and critical thinking. When describing the three triads, we prefer to group them around motivations we are calling the vectors of agency, bonding, and certainty. We see this particular three-way division as correlating with a tendency for emotional reactivity to adversity to be flavored initially and most strongly by a dominance of anger, separation distress, or fear, emerging from the subcortical motivation networks underlying the vectors. However, these aversive emotions tend to be processed very differently in the three patterns within each triad.

Second, the three personality patterns within each triad, what we will call a **trio within a given vector**, seem to place a lot of value on a set of shared concerns that we will describe momentarily. In other words, we have three vectors—agency, bonding, and certainty—and within each vector there is a trio of patterns. That makes nine patterns in total. Our proposal is that a trio within a vector is determined by which of the three attendencies is dominant—inward, outward, or dyadic (both inward and outward).

The PDP framework provides an IPNB-based hypothesis for understanding why the traditional Enneagram system groups patterns according to what are known as the body, heart, and head centers of intelligence. Again, when the Enneagram uses the term "intelligence," it is referring to how the world is perceived and how knowledge about the world is gained. Also, we do not view these associations of physical experience as meaning the primary physical location of information processing is in these locations, such that the agency system is in the so-called "gut brain" or the bonding system is in the so-called "heart brain." As neuroscientist Antonio Damasio notes (2019), these so-called first and second brains are vitally important in contributing to the experience of emotional arousal, and it is the third, "head brain," that is in service of them, not the other way around. Undoubtedly, we do concur that there is energy flow that seems to be primary or dominant initially in the responses of each of these three vectors. Yet each of these anatomical locations of energy flow is ultimately available to each of us, no matter our baseline vector. In this way, some literal, somatically-mediated energy flow seems to be involved in both the physiological responses and the resulting felt experience of the patterns in operation. But these **anatomical locations of energy activation and flow (ALEAFs)** are likely a part of, but not the central information-processing regions for, each of the vector's systems of mind. While our gut feelings and heartfelt sensations are important for knowing how we feel and gaining insight into our intuition, a conservative neuroscientific view would suggest that these anatomical regions lack the neural computational capacities for building the kinds of memory or cognitive trains of thought that are clearly involved in the structure and functioning of the personality patterns and their "intelligences." For this reason, we will not be using the term "center of intelligence." We do acknowledge the important role the experience of ALEAFs—what we feel in our body as energy flows in our interactions and reflections—plays in shaping our perception and cognition, but that is distinct from being the anatomical location of complex mental processes beneath the patterns. An ALEAF arising in the head's cortex with the planning and expectations of cortical thinking may seem "far from the body" and even distant from emotions in its cognitive processing nature. Noting these anatomical locations can help illuminate the characteristic reactivity associated with each vector.

As the Enneagram diagram had origins in mathematical patterns, it uses a number designation for each of the types it postulates, 1 to 9, using the numerical indicators. The three anger-associated personality patterns (8, 9, and 1 in conventional Enneagram terminology of the gut-body triad, as they often begin with an ALEAF of sensate and kinesthetic flow, a gut-driven response) all share concerns around the state of empowerment and control of the body and sense of individual agency and inclusion, ensuring well-being and integrity of body and sense of self, comfort and satisfaction of needs and desires, protection from violation, attention to right versus wrong and just versus unjust. Patterns of aversive emotional reactivity involving **anger** are a common thread across all three, but expression of anger tends to be experienced in very different ways in each pattern within this triad. We came to call this the vector of agency for embodied empowerment (or simply, agency). As we'll discover, the contrast of empowerment versus helplessness has a relevant autonomic nervous system mechanism with a dominant presence in the subdiaphragmatic organs; the viscera in the gut of the digestive system. Stephen Porges's Polyvagal Theory (Porges, 2001, 2024) posits that the dorsal branch of the vagus nerve is activated in states of helplessness. This is the branch that extends below the diaphragm and involves our abdominally located "gut feelings."

The three patterns associated with separation distress and sadness (2, 3, and 4 in conventional Enneagram terminology) are grouped in the heart center, as they tend to initiate energy flow from a heartfelt intuitive and emotional source. All share concerns around a felt sense of supportive connection with others, especially important others, and what is seen in the reflection of the "mirror" they provide. Each of the personality patterns within this triad appears to be organized around some aspect of life's inevitable tensions with caretakers and subsequent important and vital people in one's life. That is, it involves union versus individuation, connection versus separation, togetherness versus aloneness, and ways in which one seeks to present images of one's personal self, which can be more or less authentic, to others to draw them in and ensure connection in their eyes. Patterns of emotional reactivity related to **separation distress or sadness** are a thread across all three, but distress and sadness tend to be experienced and expressed in very different ways in each pattern. We came to call this a vector of bonding for relational connection (or simply, bonding). We'll also see that the ventral branch of the tenth cranial nerve, the vagus nerve, may be a relevant autonomic subcortical mechanism here. The vagus nerve mediates what Polyvagal Theory calls the "social engagement system" (Porges, 2001). The ventral branch of the vagus nerve is distributed above the diaphragm, in the lungs and heart. It may be this ALEAF that leads to this heartfelt sense when it comes to the issues of connection versus disconnection of social engagement in this grouping of patterns.

The three patterns associated with fear and anticipatory anxiety (5, 6, and 7 in conventional Enneagram terminology) are grouped in the head center, because they initiate responses with logic, planning, and cognitive processing that we can simply refer to as "cortical thinking." All three in this group share concerns, mostly future-oriented, around safety, certainty, and assuredness about what will be. Each of the personality patterns appears to be organized around some aspect of life's inevitable tensions between assuredness and doubt about the future. Patterns of emotional reactivity related to **anxiety or fear** are a common thread across all three, but anxiety and fear tend to be expressed in very different ways in each pattern. We call this the vector of certainty for prediction and safety (or simply, certainty). We can also see that Porges's notion of a "neuroception" process—in which the cortical regions are continually scanning for signs of threat—may be a relevant neural mechanism for determining the ALEAF: the "head" location of initial response for this grouping of three patterns (Porges, 2001, 2011).

Fundamental Needs and Core Motivations

As we set out to see if we could develop an explanation for these observations about the Enneagram's nine personality patterns that was consilient with the field of IPNB, which includes the various domains of neuroscience, the general idea of developmental adaptations seemed most plausible to us from psychological and neuroscientific perspectives. We began by exploring some of David's earlier ideas that various aspects of infants' "original undivided state" (that is, unconditioned by life experience) of feeling worthy, loved, and safe "went into the background" as the child came to believe, beginning in the interaction of temperament and early life experience, that "the world" required a more limited way of being. In this conception, "feeling worthy, loved, and safe" was meant to capture the essence of deep, primal goals that seem to motivate the personality patterns of what we have named the agency, bonding, and certainty groups, respectively. It is that state of feeling worthy, loved, and safe, too, that would emerge with the experience of feeling whole.

After much exploration and discussion of science and practical insights, this search ultimately led us to a general hypothesis that the adult personality structures we observed were rooted in **core motivations** to pursue satisfaction of three sets of **fundamental needs**. That is, throughout life—not just during infancy—humans are highly motivated to pursue:

- Agency: Seek and pursue satisfaction of all the many needs and desires of the body and its sense of existence, and protect the integrity of the body and personal self from violation from which may emerge the affect of anger. The deep sources of these seeking-like motivations are a host of physiological (body) and psychological (mental experience of being) regulatory processes that serve to maintain homeostasis.
- Bonding: Establish and maintain *mutually supportive* relationships with other individuals. The deep sources of these emotionally fueled motivations toward connection are innate systems that effectively "hardwire" us to attune in early life with attachment figures or in later life with individuals in our social bonds of connection; feel the pain of loss or motivation to restore vital connections when they are disrupted; care for others around us in need; and bring connection by presenting an image of a personal self that will draw others in and keep them close.
- Certainty: Seek a sense of certainty, confidence, and safety in what lies ahead. The sources of these motivations ultimately arise from the mind's relentless building and modifying of predictive models, and emotional responses ranging from fear to delight when experience defies expectations.

Looking to these three core needs of infants' development is not an original idea. Consilience can be found in many lines of research that even newborn infants are highly motivated by deep biological mechanisms to feel valued/comforted, loved/connected, and secure/assured. For example, these *core needs* can be seen in the early 1980s temperament work of Buss and Plomin

(1975, 1984) and in the seven irreducible needs of children (beyond physical nurturance) identified by Brazelton and Greenspan (1983, 2000). Similarly, they are seen in the foundational understanding of secure attachment: When attachment relationships are filled with the experience of being soothed, seen, and safe, and when repairs are made in the event that these essentials of security do not happen, then an overall set of integrative connections are set up allowing optimal regulation that we call "secure attachment" (see Siegel, 2020).

We came to see how these needs are also reflected in a large body of research from the field of affective neuroscience on the evolutionary functions and biology of anger, separation distress, and fear. They are also reflected in Paul Gilbert's compassion-focused psychotherapy (Gilbert, 2010), as well, which focuses on the importance of distinguishing, detecting, and working with these three core emotions, described as the "big three": anger, sadness, and fear.

Emotion Energizes Motivation; Motivation Energizes Emotion

Our PDP framework builds directly on the theoretical framework described by Kenneth Davis and Jaak Panksepp, described in detail in *The Emotional Foundations of Personality: A Neurobiological and Evolutionary Approach*, published in the IPNB series in 2018. The text makes a compelling argument that primal emotion systems and the networks that emerge in development to regulate their expression create the foundations of personality. We suggest our PDP framework puts "clinical flesh" on the bones of their important theoretical framework, providing a developmental perspective and therapeutic ways of helping individuals grow toward a more integrative way of living. While not originally intended, their book and ours form a useful pair for neurobiological insights into personality, one on research foundations and the other on clinical concepts and applications. If you'd like to dive more deeply into the basic science of these subcortical networks, that text along with with Jaak Panksepp's other books (1998; 2012; 2018) offer excellent resources.

Why turn to areas of the brain beneath the cortex, such as the brain stem and related structures, to understand our personality and emotional lives? As Venkatraman et al. (2017) explain in their review article in *Frontiers of Neuroanatomy*:

> Emotions depend upon the integrated activity of neural networks that modulate arousal, autonomic function, motor control, and somatosensation. Brainstem nodes play critical roles in each of these networks, but prior studies of the neuroanatomic basis of emotion, particularly in the human neuropsychological literature, have mostly focused on the contributions of cortical rather than subcortical structures. Given the size and complexity of brainstem circuits, elucidating their structural and functional properties involves technical challenges. However, recent advances in neuroimaging have begun to accelerate research into the brainstem's role in emotion. . . . The brainstem is home to a group of modulatory neurotransmitter pathways, such as those arising from the raphe nuclei (serotonergic), ventral tegmental area (dopaminergic) and locus coeruleus (noradrenergic), which form a Modulatory network that coordinates interactions between the Ascending and Descending networks. Integration of signaling within these three networks occurs at all levels of the brainstem, with progressively more complex forms of integration occurring in the hypothalamus and thalamus. These intermediary structures, in turn, provide input for the most complex integrations, which occur in the frontal, insular, cingulate and other regions of the cerebral cortex. Phylogenetically older brainstem networks inform the functioning of evolutionarily newer rostral regions, which in turn regulate and modulate the older structures. Via these bidirectional interactions, the human brainstem contributes to the evaluation of sensory information and triggers fixed-action pattern responses that together constitute the finely differentiated spectrum of possible emotions.

We had initially been drawn to the work of Panksepp regarding these older brain stem networks in the first year or two of our early explorations of the associations between anger, separation distress, and fear with the nine patterns of personality described in the Enneagram approach. Our primary reference point was Jaak Panksepp's framework of emotion systems described in detail in his earlier seminal text, *Affective Neuroscience* (1998), and later summarized in *The Archaeology of Mind*, coauthored with Lucy Biven and published in Norton's IPNB series in 2012.

Over the course of his career, Panksepp characterized "at least seven 'blue ribbon'" emotion systems that encode primal survival values inherited from our mammalian evolutionary ancestors. In effect they aim to keep us in a state of satisfactory homeostasis, where needs are met and all is well. They are somewhat distinct anatomically and physiologically in terms of neurotransmitters and interconnectivity and are each rooted in distinct, deeply subcortical circuits. These are the sources of our core, primary motivations and their associated affects—what Jaak called "primal affects." Networks that then come to regulate emotional expression emerge and become "trained and tuned" by working on the job of early life. These networks involve connection upward into areas of the cortex, as also described above by Venkatraman and colleagues.

Each system creates specific states of mind that cluster into two distinct valences—one is a set of pleasant, or appetitive, sensations and drives; the other is unpleasant, or aversive. We are driven to move toward contexts that are pleasant—we have an "appetite" for them—and we move away from those that are aversive, that are unpleasant. What are these seven fundamental circuits of our primal emotions?

First, there are the three **aversive emotion** systems that we've been exploring—for simplicity we will call them anger, separation distress, and fear—which generate states of mind that signal different ways in which survival may be in jeopardy and motivate responsive behavior to different kinds of perceived threat. There is striking congruence between Panksepp's insights into the biological functions served by anger, separation distress, and fear, and the kinds of concerns, attractors of attention, and patterns of emotional tone and reactivity that characterize the agency, bonding, and certainty patterns of personality in the PDP system, respectively. More specifically:

- Anger plays a prominent role in patterns of reactivity of the trio of agency patterns. Panksepp's anger system specializes in mobilizing embodiment of assertively protective responses to potential violations of integrity of the body and its larger sense of self in the world, or obstructions to satisfaction of needs. When threat is sufficient, consciously experienced feelings spanning a range from irritation to uncontrolled rage can arise.

- Separation distress and the related affect of sadness play a prominent role in patterns of reactivity of the trio of bonding patterns. The separation distress system (Panksepp also called this PANIC/Sadness) specifically monitors the state of bonding and connection with important others. It signals a state of alarm when connection is disrupted, and it mobilizes behavior to restore vital connections with, or attract supportive attention of, others. In awareness it registers in the spectrum of feelings spanning sadness, loss, abandonment, "panicky" aloneness, or elements of the pain of shame.

- As you might by now imagine, fear, which plays a prominent role in patterns of reactivity of the trio of certainty patterns, alerts the organism to potential danger ahead in time and space and mobilizes body and being to look for sources of danger and prepare for action. Certainty is a fundamental drive because with prediction comes protection. Feelings, when they rise in awareness, can span the spectrum of mild anxiety to abject terror, and behavior from heightened awareness to full-throttle classical fear responses.

As in any field of scientific inquiry, some of the details of Panksepp's framework are controversial, particularly his thinking about the innate processes that create the distinct feeling states associated with them. For example, some proposals suggest that emotion draws primarily from learning in the cortex rather than being a part of the primary affective processes that Panksepp suggests are derived from evolutionarily shaped subcortical neural circuits (see Barrett, 2017; Barrett et al., 2007). Far less controversial are his and many others' basic and clinical research findings that the three aversive emotional states are functionally distinct from one another, provide innate threat-detection capacities in major domains of life experience, and create states of mind that motivate reactive, protective behaviors that play important roles in how humans are motivated to be and act in the world.

Panksepp also identified at least four distinct **appetitive emotion** systems, which energize pursuit of goals or objects of need or desire, and which are associated with pleasurable states of mind when feelings associated with their activation enter awareness. These pleasurable states are also fundamental to our survival.

- *SEEKING* is essentially the anticipation-reward system. It is harnessed in service of all manner of needs and desires, creates eager anticipation of the reward in their satisfaction, and motivates exploration of the world in those pursuits.
- **CARE** fuels the drive to help others when resonant emotional connection puts us in touch with their distress and need for attention.
- *PLAY/SOCIAL JOY* fuels exactly what its name implies—the drive, seemingly limitless in young children, to have fun and be creative and spontaneous. In play they learn all sorts of lessons about how to exert their agency wisely, manage interpersonal connections, and discern the difference between opportunity and threat.
- *LUST* involves the motivational energy of sexual attraction and feelings of desire for sexual activity.

These *appetitive* emotion systems also play important roles in the nine personality patterns, though in ways less specifically associated with agency, bonding, and certainty. For example, the ubiquitous and multipurpose seeking system is undoubtedly harnessed to fuel pursuit of agency, bonding, and certainty needs in all sorts of ways. In other words, in addition to the particular manner of regulating aversive reactivity described above, there is always a SEEKING-like quality associated with each pattern, a striving and directing of energy resources that likely engages the seeking system. This subcortical motivation network places primal importance in whatever direction for what is being sought. CARE is clearly deeply engaged in the bonding patterns, but nurturing is a part of each of the other vectors as well. The narrative findings also suggest that the LUST and PLAY networks activate actions that put people into situations in which the aversive reactivity of the agency, bonding, or certainty networks stands a good chance of also being aroused. In other words, Panksepp's four appetitive motivational networks are likely all involved to various and nonspecific degrees in each of the three aversive motivational networks' activations. Said differently, we do not see the four appetitive motivational networks as distinguishing the core nine personality patterns. What we do see beneath the fascinating descriptions in our narrative data is that the subcortical aversive affect—motivational networks involving anger, sadness/separation distress, or fear, which we've renamed as part of the vectors of agency, bonding, and certainty—are the underlying foundation of at least one triad grouping of the Enneagram categories.

At a different level, it is also extremely likely that at least some of the primal appetitive affects—notably seeking and care, and perhaps play—are harnessed to fuel specific ways people feel highly motivated, in a positive way, to be, to think, and to carry themselves in their interactions in life. That is, associated with each pattern is a kind of appetitive striving to be a certain kind of person, one who seeks certain kinds of goals, behaves in certain ways, and attends more to certain things than others. Some things are simply more important than others and this salience organizes one's attention, feelings, thinking, and behaviors. For example, one agency pattern is associated with a kind of implicit underlying "mission" to be a good and virtuous person who strives to make themselves and their world better. One of the bonding patterns is associated with always being the kind of person who is deeply devoted to helping others in need. And one of the certainty patterns is associated with a deep drive to seek greater knowledge and understanding. All the nine patterns have an analog of this.

Keep in mind that these repeating patterns of emotion, thought, and behavior are mostly beneath conscious intention or even awareness—that is, personality may be primarily about autopilot functions of mind. Fortunately, such enduring patterns can be made conscious and then, with intention, overridden with top-down efforts, which may be how cortical processes can intervene with subcortically initiated energy as affect and attention. I've named this "cortical override" and it may be one way of describing how we learn to overcome autopilot in the moment and then intentionally grow new neural connections to alter, at least to some extent, how such ingrained subcortical patterning can be made less intense and restrictive in our lives. Transforming our personality pathways from a prison to a playground may involve the first-level, subcortically originating assessment of the autopilot saying, "Head that way!"—and it may always say that across our lives, to some degree—but a second, learned, cortically added mechanism can then intervene and say, "Take a pause here to reflect and choose; there are many paths we can take beyond our initial impulse."

So, while aversive reactivity is very often involved in the kinds of things that bring clients to therapy, the seeking-like and "striving-to-be" qualities of the vector are also very important to work with in therapy because they are tightly entangled with self-image and identity. In net effect, this striving seems to contribute to the durability of the patterns. Whether or not that is problematic is partly a function of how well the whole system is integrated.

In sum, Jaak Panksepp's descriptions of the three aversive affective states of anger, sadness/separation distress, and fear seem to help in distinguishing the three clusters of personality patterns, while the four core subcortically mediated appetitive ones do not divide into these groupings seen in the narrative data we have. Might there be another system that could use these appetitive emotions to organize another aspect of personality? Possibly—and this is why we emphasize that both the Enneagram system and the PDP model certainly do not account for all of personality, simply one aspect that seems to be both important and useful in cultivating personal growth. Our coauthor Jack Killen is exploring issues of Enneagram subtypes that might involve a combination of various subcortical network activations. In our informal observations as a PDP group, we do see these four appetitive systems equally distributed across the nine PDPs, but are fascinated to see how each subtype within each of these pathways might be shown to correlate with these other appetitive networks' activity with future research.

We are also excited to see how future research will explore these many ways the PDP framework offers new insights that can be both immediately clinically useful and, with future research, testable. We cannot emphasize enough that the PDP model addresses just one aspect of who we are and how our personality forms, not by any means the whole of what shapes our development or our subjective experience of being alive at any given moment. We have chosen to dive deeply into the fundamental nine patterns to provide a starting place for using these ideas in a practical manner in psychotherapy. In our discussions it became clear to us that most likely these three motivational subcortical networks we came to name agency, bonding, and certainty might be useful in parsing out the distinct mechanisms underlying each of the personality pattern groupings the Enneagram was describing and that appeared in the narrative data we were drawing upon.

Temperament and Adaptive Strategies, Attendency, and Emotion Regulation

This brings us back to the fundamental Davis–Panksepp hypothesis that emotions and the networks from which they emerge—and that then develop to regulate their expression—create the foundations of personality. Although the view that they propose looks at six of the seven fundamental primal affects (they exclude lust from their survey), we see the aspects of personality described in the Enneagram perspective as involving three of those subcortical networks and then the elaborated other cortical processes that arise in adaptation to both those innate features and the experiences the individual has in life.

In our view, the networks they describe that mediate the aversive emotions of anger, sadness/separation-distress, and fear as the primal affects found across the mammalian species can be understood at their core as being the motivational systems involving what we've named agency, bonding, and certainty, respectively. At birth the rich emotional palette of these systems is little more than a set of nascent emotional *capacities*. The job of learning to use these capacities in ways that are effective and socially appropriate in a variety of contexts and situations—the essence of emotion regulation—begins immediately after birth within attachment relationships. This learning of how to adapt to life in the inner world and the outer, relational world (developing what we are naming adaptive strategies) is the main job of childhood and adolescence. Indeed, we must learn virtually everything about the meaning of affective experience, and how to wisely and safely embody emotional motivations to pursue all manner of goals, protect ourselves from harm, establish and maintain effective and mutually supportive relationships with others, and discern differences between opportunities and threats.

From an IPNB perspective, emotion is a shift in integration. Emotion involves our states of well-being that arise from how integrated our lives are as they unfold. In this way, I've proposed that "positive emotions," or what can also be named appetitive affects or states, involve enhanced integration and the ensuing experience of harmony as a FACES flow of flexibility, adaptability, coherence, energy, and stability. "Negative emotions" would be the aversive affective states that lead to the IMIDU outcome of nonintegrative states of being inflexible, maladaptive, incoherent, de-energized, and unstable. Learning to regulate emotion, then, is learning to move toward integration for that regulatory process to create well-being.

Emotion involves motion of the body; as "e-motion" it can be seen to "evoke motion" and to direct behavior, even without our awareness or conscious intention. Emotion also involves our inner feeling states, the body's sensations and affects. And emotion involves what is given priority, what is salient or has meaning, and therefore taps into our core motivations. Notice how emotion does not in any way require consciousness but may nevertheless involve the motivations that drive where energy is focused and how behaviors unfold. Emotion also involves meaning, creating and reflecting what has salience in our lives. Emotion weaves our inner lives with those of others in our close interpersonal relationships as articulated in terms such as "emotionally close" or "emotionally meaningful connections" in our lives. When we speak, then, about the centrality of emotion in personality, we can see that it is all about the body, meaning, and relationships.

As we learn to regulate emotion, we are learning to manage the embodied felt sense of meaning and connection in our lives. Regulation involves two features, as in the example of riding a bicycle. To regulate a bike, we perceive with our vision, hearing, and sense of balance. And we must learn to pedal faster or slower, press the brakes, and shift our weight to keep the bike balanced. In other foundational terms, learning to "regulate" involves learning to (1) monitor what is happening as it is happening, and (2) modulate what is happening. Emotion regulation in this way involves sensing what is going on in our emotional inner lives and then shaping that important energetic feeling of states of integration. When we regulate well, we cultivate more integration. Emotion regulation is a foundational aspect of our learning to adapt well—a cornerstone of our adaptive strategy.

We propose that the nine personality patterns of the PDP framework reflect a repertoire of necessary adaptive strategies humans must learn for just that—learning to track and transform energetic flow to emotionally feel and deal with what has meaning. The fundamental motivation, emotion, and meaning of an experience emerge from empowerment, connection, and safety, our three vectors of agency, bonding, and certainty. In its simplest formulation, our hypothesis is that the adaptive strategies arise from these three interconnected vectors, which monitor and modify inner states of what we are calling (1) *agency for embodied empowerment* and its sense of self, (2) *bonding for relational connection* in mutually supportive relationships with others, and (3) *certainty for prediction and safety* in what will be coming next.

The vectors and specific attendencies of each PDP will essentially place priority on our embodied and relational energy flow. What then arises with experience is an adaptive strategy that operates mainly in the background of consciousness and in this way puts us on autopilot as it involves fast thinking, providing first-level navigation through most day-to-day situations with efficiency and with minimal need for the resource-consuming process of awareness. It's simply more energy efficient to carry out functions automatically than to consciously reflect on them.

Conscious attention, or what is known formally as focal attention, to the state of agency, bonding, or connection is summoned when needed and can pull us out of autopilot. For patterns in a given vector, one of these becomes more salient; it is given more priority and therefore more energy and attention. Within a given vector's trio of PDPs determined by the specific attendency of inward, outward, or both as dyadic, it is a fascinating and relevant issue which patterns enable awareness of certain emotional sensations, and which actually shut that awareness off. This aspect of emotion regulation becomes an important facet distinguishing the trio of patterns within a vector from one another.

Within each vector we hypothesize that **monitoring** involves simultaneous attention to and assimilation of two very different streams of information and energy. One exteroceptive stream brings information from the five primary senses about the ever-changing stream of events and relationships in the world beyond the limits of the physical body as experience and situations unfold. The other fundamentally interoceptive stream (sometimes known as the sixth sense) contains information from the bodily organs and the head's brain about the conditions and state of arousal within the body and its sense of mental activities, such as emotions, thoughts, and memories (which I've named the "seventh sense": our awareness of this inner mental life).

Emotion-Regulation Modes

Within each PDP, we suggest **regulation** involves directing how the subsequent activation of neural energy should flow and motivate responsive behavior. Thus, when emotional motivations arise from subcortical origins, the larger cortical-subcortical systems use templates and schemas sculpted on the job of working-for-a-living to determine (1) where attention should subsequently be focused as a form of monitoring, and (2) whether the modification of that emotional state should be **upregulated**, that is, allowed to flow freely outward into behavioral expression; **downregulated**, that is, channeled into more tempered, disciplined, contained, reined-in, or guarded behavioral expression because that would be more adaptive to the situation at hand or more socially acceptable than unbridled expression; or **shifted** into a qualitatively different motivational state, such as would be the functional way to respond when initial perception of an immediate state of threat or opportunity has changed, when a state of need has passed, or when pursuit would be fruitless or pose unacceptable risk.

Notice how attendency refers to the *monitoring* function of mind while emotion regulation indicates the *modification* or *modulation* function of mind. In interpersonal neurobiology, we define one facet of the mind as "the embodied and relational, self-organizing, emergent process that regulates the flow of energy and information." As a regulatory process, then, mind has both a monitoring and modifying facet: Attendency monitors, emotion-regulation mode modifies. This reveals how the mind is itself organized by these personality patterns and how they develop across the lifespan.

A mnemonic we can propose that helps in the recall of these three research-established emotion-regulation strategies is this:

1. Upregulate ↑ means EE: experience and express a particular emotion;
2. Downregulate ↓ means CC: contain and channel a particular emotion;
3. Shift ➔ means RR: reframe and redirect a particular emotion into a different emotional state

These three fundamentally different modes of emotion regulation are distinguishing features of the three adaptive strategies associated with each vector. Do these emerge with experiences of interacting with the outside world and their filtering through one's innate predisposition of a vector and an attendency? Are emotion-regulation modes a more natural outcome of the vector and attendency independent of experience? These are unanswered but important questions of how a PDP develops with its characteristic ways of feeling, thinking, and behaving that arise from the pathway's adaptive strategies. Given that adaptive strategies are likely open to elaboration and integration across the lifespan, this implies that PDPs are (1) *innate* as well as *learned* and *reinforced* in the "work" of individual development beginning in earliest life, and (2) remain capable of *further development* and learning throughout life, including in the inner-development work of therapy. To what extent our innate proclivities can change with intention is also an open question, but our learned aspects—the intensity, depth, and width of the PDP groove that has been carved by our adapting to experience—certainly appear to be open to robust modification in being less deeply carved, and therefore our overall functioning made more flexible and free as that groove becomes less restrictive in an individual's life.

CHAPTER 4

A Developmental Perspective: Vectors, Attendencies, and Emotion-Regulation Modes

PDP as a Life-Span Model of Personality Based on Patterns of Motivation, Emotion, and Attention

How do we come to have an identity shaped by automatic processes happening beneath awareness? Two researchers offer relevant insights:

> The oddest thing about the upper reaches of a consciousness performance is the conspicuous absence of a conductor before the performance begins, although, as the performance unfolds, a conductor comes into being. For all intents and purposes, a conductor is now leading the orchestra, although the performance has created the conductor—the self—not the other way around. The conductor is cobbled together by feelings and by a narrative brain device, although this fact does not make the conductor any less real. The conductor undeniably exists in our minds, and nothing is gained by dismissing it as an illusion. (Damasio, 2010)

> All pathways are thought to start close together so that, initially, an individual has access to a large range of pathways along any one of

which he might travel. The one chosen, it is held, turns at each and every stage of the journey on an interaction between the organism as it has developed up to that moment and the environment in which it then finds itself. Thus, at conception development turns on interaction between the newly formed genome and the intrauterine environment; at birth it turns on interaction between the physiological constitution, including germinal mental structure, of the neonate and the family, or non-family, into which he is born; and at each age successively it turns on the personality structure then present and the family and, later, the wider social environments then current. . . . As development proceeds and structures progressively differentiate, the number of pathways that remain open diminishes. (Bowlby, 1973, p. 412)

In this way, our "narrative identity" may emerge as we witness our ways of being in the world—our feelings, thoughts, and behaviors—which in turn can reinforce these automatic processes that now we come to feel we are either choosing or beholden to continue.

Although the idea of developmental adaptations is a familiar concept in the Enneagram community, we also see that the PDP framework fills a theoretical and conceptual void in developmental psychology about connections between infant temperament and adult personality. At the same time, our ideas about the development of patterns expands on the Davis and Panksepp (2018) theoretical model of the emotional foundations of personality, as it provides insights into opportunities for growth and change not only as a developmental model but as a valuable framework for psychotherapy.

Under various developmental circumstances the constructed adaptive strategies can become personality patterns to greater or lesser degrees of intensity—with more or less deeply carved PDP grooves. Lower states of functioning within a given PDP would result from a deep, narrow groove; higher states of functioning within a PDP would be a wider groove. Let's continue to build our understanding of the three systems of mind, our three vectors that serve the three primal needs for agency, bonding, and certainty. Each of these three vectors sets a directionality in the assignment of meaning or salience that then shapes the flow of attention and energy into feelings, thoughts, and actions on behalf of achieving agency, connection, and safety. When under threat, activation of each vector is filled with the centrality of the reactive core protective emotions of anger, sadness and separation distress, or fear. Then, within each vector, a trio of pathways and the adaptive strategies they instantiate emerge in the course of development, shaped by whether attendency is mainly inward, outward, or dyadic as it wavers between inward and outward (yielding a trio for each of the three vectors, resulting in the nine pathways).

Here are brief sketches of the adaptive functionality provided by each system and its pathways and concomitant strategies. When the three pathways within a given vector are well differentiated and linked, they each can function as an integrated system that provides a flexible repertoire of adaptations to the circumstances at hand. Our hypothesis is that these nine pathways and general strategies for adapting to life's circumstances are the developmental root of the personality patterns.

> For ease of reference, here is a simple chart with the vector and the attendency for the nine pathways:
>
> Agency: inward; outward; dyadic—
>   A-i; A-o; A-d
> Bonding: inward; outward; dyadic—
>   B-i; B-o; B-d
> Certainty: inward; outward; dyadic—
>   C-i; C-o; C-d

The **agency vector** monitors and regulates the energetic state of empowerment of the body and its sense of self (i.e., agency) when all manner of seeking-like motivations to pursue satisfaction of needs and desires, or reactive anger at potential violations or threats to body and being, arise. Three developmental pathways provide a repertoire of **adaptive strategies**, shaped and reinforced in development, for empowering the body and its sense of self in useful and socially functional ways, depending on the circumstances at hand. Each can become a personality pattern. The ways this emotional energy is handled fall into one of three tendencies to experience and express (EE), contain and channel (CC), or reframe and redirect (RR)—each in service of adaptation to up- or down-regulate, or to shift that emotional state.

Said differently, in development you must learn when and how it is most adaptive to:

- Channel, temper, or discipline motivational energy in ways that are more socially acceptable or likely to be more effective. In the A-i PDP, attention and energy are inward-centered around learned internalized templates of standards of right versus wrong, good versus bad, or useful versus ineffective, and rules of social engagement. Here, expression of seeking-like motivational energies and anger are *downregulated*, tempered, or contained and channeled accordingly because that will be most effective or adaptive. This is the downregulation of the CC, contain-and-channel mode.
- Allow agency vector motivations to blossom into fully embodied expressions. In the A-o PDP, attention and energy are outward-centered toward objects of need, desire, or threat. Seeking-like emotional motivations and anger are allowed to flow relatively unconstrained outward into embodied expression in a generally *upregulated*, self-assertive, powerful kind of energetic stance, and "go for what I need or want," "protect me and mine," or "make it happen" behavior. Anger is experienced and expressed. Said simply, sometimes in life it is most adaptive to be big, to be powerful, and to be assertive. This is upregulation of the EE, experience-and-express mode.
- Let motivational energy dissipate and attention be redirected, as when continued pursuit would be useless or fruitless, something more compelling has come along, or the need has passed. In the A-d PDP, attention and energy are both inward- and outward-centered around conflicting information from inward and outward sources—e.g., "I" need "that" but "that" is unattainable, or "I" want this but "You" want that. Attention and energy flow are *shifted* as they are reframed and redirected into a reconciling or accommodating stance and behavior that will attempt to shift the state of mind to an unconflicted calm and peaceful motivational state. Said simply,

sometimes it is most adaptive to "let things be." Yet while this may be an immediate reaction, especially to a rising tension or conflict, this shifting away from a state of anger may yield a numbing and underlying agitation when the motivation for agency toward empowerment remains unfulfilled and the individual becomes invisible in the face of compromise and mediation. This is the shifting of the RR, reframe-and-redirect mode.

The **bonding vector** and its three pathways monitor and regulate the complicated relational dynamics involved in important interpersonal connections. These include very deeply ingrained human motivations, both appetitive and reactive (separation distress and sadness), to establish and maintain existentially vital connections with others to whom you can turn in times of need but who sometimes may need you in theirs. With this system involving interpersonal dynamics, inward attendency is essentially about you and your connection with an inner self, while outward is essentially about them and their state of connection with you. The foundations of the system are laid in the context of childhood dilemmas of union-individuation. The bonding vector monitors and regulates the lifelong challenges and tensions of together versus alone, and the images of self you project to keep others close and connected. Three developmental pathways provide a repertoire of useful and socially functional **adaptive strategies**, shaped and reinforced in development, for responding to different situations. Each can become a personality pattern. We call these the bonding-inward (B-i), bonding-outward (B-o), and bonding-dyadic (B-d) pathways.

Said differently, in development you must learn when and how it is most adaptive to:

- Allow your needs for others' attention and care to blossom into fully embodied expression. In the B-i PDP, attention and energy are centered inward around your bonding-connecting emotional motivations when they arise. The emotional energy of separation distress flows relatively freely in a fundamentally *upregulated* way toward being seen, standing out, and creating an image to bring attention to you and your needs for bonding and connection. Said simply, sometimes you need to "call out" for bonding and connection with others when you are in need or connection is disrupted. This is upregulation of the EE, experience-and-express mode.

- Make your needs for others' attention and care secondary to their needs for you to attend to them by focusing on their needs. In the B-o PDP, attention and the subsequent flow of bonding-connecting emotional energies are outward-centered toward perceptions of another's need for connection with you. This requires making their need for bonding and connection primary, and your needs secondary. That is, your motivational energy is *shifted* to caring. This is fundamentally the pathway of caring for others who you perceive to be in need. This is the shifting of the RR, reframe-and-redirect mode.

- Contain and channel expression of your innate and effectively hardwired need for a sense of bonding and connection with others so you can safely and effectively move out into the world as an autonomous agent maintaining connection with your safe havens if you need them. The B-d PDP is rooted most deeply in the pathway of early individuation from union with caregivers, and is experienced as the shuttling between an inward and an outward focus of attention and energy; the dyadic attendency. Do you stay put in the safe harbor of union with others on whom you depend, literally, to keep you out of harm's way, or move away from connection as an autonomous being pursuing your own goals and interests out in the world? The inner bonding and connection energies are kept in check by diligent outward seeking for evidence of supportive and approving connection with those others. Your self-image of success becomes key in inward-outward balance. This is downregulation of the CC, contain-and-channel mode.

The **certainty vector** monitors and modulates our sense of certainty and safety, given the reality of uncertainty and potential dangers ahead, as we pursue the work of staying alive, well, and connected with others. This system is configured by evolution with an innate negativity bias—a tendency to be wary of the unknown and lean toward allowing expression of fear and anxiety when uncertainty prevails. That means holding enough doubt about what you perceive and have come to understand about the world through inheritance and learning, and enough readiness and resources to respond to future dangers you might encounter, but not so much that you become inca-pacitated by anxiety or fear and are unable to pursue goals with confidence. Three developmental pathways provide a repertoire of useful and socially functional **adaptive strategies** for responding to different situations. Each can become a pattern of personality. We call these the certainty-inward, certainty-outward, and certainty-dyadic pathways.

Said differently, in development you must learn when and how it is most adaptive to:

- Contain vigilant uncertainty and channel that anxious energy into attempting to understand the unfamiliar, preparing for adversity, and gathering information and other resources that might be needed. In the C-i PDP, attention and the flow of motivational energy are inwardly oriented toward the states of readiness of psychological and material resources and information that might be needed if danger comes. Expres-sion of anxiety or fear, and expenditure of emotional energy in general, are relatively *downregulated*. Attention and energy are contained and channeled into gathering information and guarding personal and material resources that might be needed in the future. This is the downregulation of the CC, contain-and-channel mode.

- Let go of vigilant uncertainty because there is nothing to fear, and allow appetitive motivations to flow into pursuit of opportunity. In the C-o PDP, attention and the flow of motivational energy are outwardly oriented toward objects of need and desire out in the world, and *shifted* as they are reframed and redirected into optimistic pursuit of them. The innate pro-cess of negativity bias is shifted toward confidence, and appetitive emo-tions are allowed to flow freely outward in optimistic pursuit of goals and desires. This is the shifting of the RR, reframe-and-redirect mode.

- Maintain doubtful, vigilant uncertainty and channel between both outward objects and events and inward understanding, knowledge, and perceptions. In the C-d PDP, attention and the flow of motivational energy are oriented toward the uncertainty and doubt about both what is understood and believed (i.e., inward) and what is perceived about others and the world (i.e., outward) in the moment. Seeking of certainty and the experience and expression of anxiety and fear are relatively *upreg-ulated*. Attention and energy are focused toward doubting of the inner self and perceptions of others and the world, and imagining worst-case scenarios as a way to be prepared. This is the upregulation of the EE, experience-and-express mode.

A Developmental Perspective: 24 Foundational Steps in the PDP Framework

What follows is a set of foundational cornerstones that enable us to build the scaffold of the PDP framework. Even without each of these hypotheses ulti-mately being proved to be necessary or a part of personality development, the structure of the PDP framework is quite robust and, in its consilience, quite illuminating with clinical observation and with the thousands of Enneagram narratives we are using as first- and second-person data points in our effort to dive deeply into personality and its transformation.

The PDP framework suggests that the following sequence may be hypoth-esized to be at the heart of both the development and the maintenance of adult personality—the patterns of our emotions, thinking, and behavior. If you are not inclined to think in a "developmental model" of the human mind, this may not appeal to you and is not necessary in order for you to take in the entries that follow later on in the book. And as we've said earlier, some parts of this—such as the implicit memory of being in the womb—may seem to you "too out there" to be useful, so feel free to skim over those parts and take in the gist of this flow. But for others, this is a very compelling aspect of the developmental model that might fit with the reality of what many of us experience. If you are interested in a possible view of "how we get to be who we are," then you may find this quite interesting, and even very useful. Here is the sequence.

1. Conception. We are conceived in the union of egg and sperm.
2. The ectodermal layer. The outside surface of the growing conceptus invaginates to form the neural tube.
3. Nervous system as interface of inner/outer. The growing nervous

system, then, is really "sophisticated skin cells" whose main function, like the skin, is to be the interface of "inner and outer."

4. Implicit memory by seven months in the womb. By the last two months of in utero life, implicit memory systems form and likely "remember" (they encode and store the experience) of simply being in the womb. We postulate that this implicit bodily sense, perceptual image, emotional tone, and action state—the four foundational pillars of implicit memory—are encoded at this stage and form an implicit mental model, a summary of repeated experiences known also as a schema, for what we are naming "simply being" or experiencing "wholeness."

The womb experience becomes encoded and stored in a whole host of homeostatic, physiological, and emotion-regulatory mechanisms as a state of stability, biochemical homeostasis, thermal normality, need satisfaction, emotional equanimity, contentment, and other aspects of emotion regulation. These implicit mechanisms develop in the womb but then seek to maintain or restore the internal state when perturbed when we get out on our own, "alone in the world" and striving to survive in this new experience, this new environment that surrounds us. This homeostatic capacity to achieve an inner state of well-being is at the core of simply being or experiencing wholeness. For an adult's journey, the issue is not going back to the womb; rather it is opening to a deeper reality, one often experienced in contemplative practices by accessing open awareness, which is the developmental version of releasing or liberating our minds to experience wholeness and simply being.

5. "Temperament" is sometimes used as a term for the innate or constitutional. That is, there is at least a part of our temperament that is not acquired by experiential learning—it involves innate features of the nervous system. Some of these innate propensities, proclivities, or tendencies of the neuronal firing of the individual may be related to genetics and epigenetics; some may arise from conditions in the womb; still others may emerge as some simply random properties of the complex system of billions of neurons in the growing individual.

6. Birth is a big deal. The transition—a traumatic one, to say the least—from the in utero state of simply being is now replaced by needing to *do*, to do things to survive. We call this working-for-a-living in a "do-or-die" mode and it, too, becomes a source of encoding into implicit memory, which remains the dominant form of the way the individual learns into the second year of life, when explicit memory begins to also become available.

7. Diversity in adaptive strategies of working to live. Working-for-a-living means that the four foundations of implicit memory—bodily sensation, emotion, perception, and action sequences—will be stimulated and perturbed in quite different ways from simply being.

8. Early survival is a big deal. Whether number 4's postulation of the state of simply being is important or not, the experience of life-after-birth involves very real experiences in which survival is literally a matter of life or death: We need to breathe, eat, drink, stay warm; we need to clean out toxins by sleeping, urinating, and defecating; and we need our social connections with physical affection and caretaking from our attachment figures. In other words, we have NEEDS that must be met and that we did not need to initiate in the womb. Again, even if you don't believe in number 4's postulation, or if this proposal of simply being as a stark contrast to the extrauterine experience of working-for-a-living just does not seem relevant or even real for you, everything in this PDP view that follows still holds together as a plausible, scientifically explorable, practical framework. (We just happen to feel—literally, to implicitly sense without intellectual reasoning—that the inner state of simply being is a default state, something we and others have described in a range of psychological, poetic, musical, spiritual, and other human ways, that is so common it may simply be, well, simply being.)

9. Discomfort leads us to act—to exert our agency. Whether in contrast to simply being as postulated in number 4, the number 8 experiences—survival-based inner states and actions in the world of the body's needing to breathe, eat, cleanse, connect, and communicate—all involve an interior sensation of discomfort and the motivation to act.

That is, if I don't breathe, I die. If I don't eat, I die. If I am not connected with and protected by caregivers, I die. It's literally a do-or-die new setup in this life of ours outside the womb. These working-for-a-living conditions are not casual; and, in fact, they may be *causal* in activating emotional and motivational circuits present early on in extrauterine life.

10. Temperament and emotion are linked from the beginning. Affective neuroscience suggests that deep below the cortex, developed to some extent at birth, are subcortical networks that are involved in at least three emotional/motivational systems that involve a subjective feeling of discomfort. These include the emotion of an affective state that is coupled with a motivational drive related to survival. The PDP framework suggests that our temperament (see number 5 above) involves a particular emotion/motivation system that is especially active in each individual. When energy flows through a neuronally connected network, ions flow in and out of membranes as an "action potential" and neurotransmitters are released to activate or inhibit the downstream synaptically connected neuron. Genetics, epigenetics, or other innate factors may make a particular network more likely to fire off than another; and these constitutional factors form temperament.

11. Discomfort and the activation of the aversive emotions. The discomfort of working-for-a-living after birth will activate one, two, or all three of the distress-related, "uncomfortable," aversive emotion/motivation networks associated with what we call vectors. The proposal is that *which* network or networks become activated is shaped by the innate aspects of temperament, not by experience. This might be wrong—that is, it might be the experiential conditions that shape which of the three vectors gets mobilized more than the others. One of many possibilities is that attachment histories *do not* determine which emotion/motivation network becomes dominant in a person's life. Instead, the attachment experience *may* shape the unfolding of *how* that network becomes utilized. This point is open for further exploration, as is, of course, the whole model we are proposing!

12. Attachment is the vital factor in short- and long-term psychological

well-being. With attachment secure, the emotion/motivation network that becomes the "baseline" or default mode most readily activated, especially under stress, is more fluid in its development and can more easily access its "higher capacities" and those of other systems, such as the receptive, integrative experience of harmony, joy, and courage. This, we are proposing, is a high state of integration for a given pathway. In contrast, with attachment nonsecure, the intensity and inflexibility of the default, baseline motivational network is increased, and a person may be more fixated in the "lower integration side" of that system. The pathway is then more entrenched, and the higher capacities of all three systems and their vectors and attendencies are less available to be utilized. What results in such nonintegrative states are the chaos and rigidity of impairments to integration, experienced as a range of mental distress including a tendency toward rage, righteous anger, resentful anger, passive-aggressive anger; panic, emotional manipulation, sadness; anxiety, fear, and terror; and the fight, flight, freeze, or fainting collapse of a reactive state's activation. Note that the positive, receptive emotional states—harmony, joy, courage—for each pathway can become a part of the individual's lived experience as well, especially in the higher states of integration.

13. Early interactions between temperament and experience form our personality. Personality in childhood, adolescence, and adulthood is formed by an interaction of temperament and experience, especially within families and in attachment relationships. As indicated in both 11 and 12 above, our working hypothesis is that temperament determines the sensitivity and therefore activation of which emotion/motivation network underlying the personality vector and likely the proposed attention-orientation bias, or attendency, becomes a baseline; but experience, especially of our attachment relationships, intensifies *how* this PDP develops rather than *which* PDP becomes baseline.

14. Working with the multidimensional and inside-out personality patterns of the PDP reveals paths to integration, access to the higher, more integrative human capacities, and a process of restoring wholeness. In this way, the innate aspects of temperament can blend with

experience to form personality patterns of emotion, thought, and behavior. Psychotherapy can cultivate integration—the linkage of differentiated parts of a system—by focusing on the personality pattern of the individual and recognizing and linking the non-utilized networks of emotion and motivation. In this way, the higher cognitive and emotional capacities can be accessed to enable a more flexible, adaptive, coherent, energized, and stable—FACES—flow of the individual's life to be cultivated and an experience of wholeness to be made more readily available. Higher integration means a more fluid way the individual can draw upon the many strengths of not only the baseline pathway but the other paths as well.

15. Where attention goes, energy flows. Therapeutic growth utilizing the PDP framework builds on the adage "Where attention goes, neural firing flows, and neural connection grows" to focus energy and information flow in ways that harness the power of neuroplasticity to change enduring patterns of feeling, thinking, and behaving toward a more integrative way of living and being in the world.

16. Wholeness as an integrated way of living. "Wholeness" is a term in the PDP framework for an integrated state of living—one in which the wide range of differentiated emotions and motivations can be linked into a FACES flow of living across the lifespan. We've offered a definition of wholeness this way in Chapter 1: *an integrative, harmonious, and receptive state of being*. Wholeness also suggests a state in which belonging is a natural outcome of life, a feeling of ease, of connection, of coherence. There may be many paths to wholeness. One is when each of the three core motivations is satisfied; when one's needs are met, the experience of wholeness is made possible. Another is the accessing of an open, receptive state of awareness—a formless source of all form—that enables a state of freedom and clarity to be experienced. When the personality pattern is relaxed and one is attuned to a higher understanding of and access to agency, bonding, and certainty, experiencing a sense of wholeness is made possible. In these ways, wholeness may be what we experienced in the womb, but the life journey to "feel and be whole" is not about returning to that

physical existence; rather, it is the journey to access a plane of possibility, as we will discuss in Chapter 11, and experience a wider sense of potentiality and freedom across time and space.

17. What activates the seeking of wholeness? A proposal of the PDP framework, one that, as pointed out above, is not necessary to harness the practical implications and applications of this approach, is that the implicit recollection of simply being in the womb, and perhaps other aspects of energy flow related to an open awareness, each forms a "ground of being" that individuals know implicitly but may not have the explicit sense of how to articulate or understand. Nevertheless, there may be a sense of something missing, something possible to experience but not quite here, some disconnection that feels off, that feels wrong. It is this sense that "something is not quite right" that may be the driving force of the activation of both the appetitive and aversive emotion/motivation networks early in life, as we begin to "work for a living," and that persists in certain developmental phases throughout adolescence and adulthood. In the following final points of this developmental framework presented here, we'll name the three aversive networks and just review them briefly. Our proposal is that each network is activated in an attempt to experience—to achieve or, perhaps more accurately, to return to—wholeness. The "feeling of not being whole" is what we are proposing arises when the survival drives of working-for-a-living are activated. We believe this to be an accurate proposal—but you may not agree with it, and it may not ultimately be true. Perhaps this view is correct, partially accurate, or possibly even simply off base. Let's keep an open mind about this—but for us, while it helps deeply to understand the sequence of the development of personality in the PDP framework, it is not necessary and its disqualification does not reduce the usefulness, or even accuracy, of the PDP framework as a whole. It is this journey toward wholeness, we are proposing, whatever the specific details, that is the initiator of personality itself and the guiding principle for the integration of personality in psychotherapy and personal growth across the lifespan.

18. The drive for agency, bonding, and certainty. The three motivational networks with a drive to reduce discomfort and distress are outlined as the primal affective tone and its motivational drive:
    - Anger–resentment/agency and embodied empowerment: The drive to care for basic bodily needs;
    - Sadness–separation distress/bonding, connection, and recognition: The drive to join;
    - Fear–anticipatory anxiety/certainty and preparedness: The drive for safety.
    - A-B-C: agency, bonding, and certainty. Each vector sets the directionality of energy flow in the individual's experience. A trio of pathways is found within each vector.

19. Do we tend to focus externally, internally, or both? What we call attendency is how an initial and dominant focus of energy and information the mind tends to harness is an
    - INWARD information stream (about ME, inside the skin-encased body);
    - OUTWARD information stream (about the world out there, outside the body); or a
    - DYADIC information stream, a kind of toggling or shimmering focus, holding the tension between inward and outward.

    The processes of attention in general suggest we have the capacity to focus our energy and information processing in specific ways; in the PDP framework we are hypothesizing three directionalities of that attention that we are calling attendencies, which are primary attentional orientation biases of inward, outward, or both inward and outward. Attention is the process that directs energy and information flow, and to give a feeling for these three ways of directing the energy of a given vector, we can also state that this is "where an individual tends to put their energy"—"energy" meaning the literal electrochemical energy flow of neural firing, or the engagement with others in the sharing of energy and information flow in interpersonal communication, or the intake of external sources of energy flow in the form of our first five senses. For someone with an inward attendency, the energy flow from the head's brain and from the bodily organs—something we take in with interoception, known as the sixth sense—would be a tendency. With an outward bias, focusing on energy input from the social or physical world via the five senses would be dominant. And for an attendency that is dyadic, there would be a challenge to blend, balance, or reconcile these inward and outward directions of energy flow that can at times be at odds with each other.

20. Nine motivational patterns emerging from three vectors and their three possible attendencies. In the PDP framework, we find that individuals seem to fall into patterns emphasizing an emotional/motivational network vector and an attentional orientation bias, or attendency. When we combine three vectors with three attendencies, we get nine patterns of developmental pathways—nine PDPs. Here we then see groupings of proclivities into generally one of the vector networks and one of the attendencies. This is how patterns tend to fall into one of *nine pathways*, and this is where the correlation with the Enneagram narrative data seems to fall into place as well. Research will need to discern how reliable and how valid these observations are; in clinical practice, the PDP model seems to fit with direct subjective reports and therapeutic progress.

21. Reinforcing pathways of emotional-motivational patterns and personality. A developmental pathway can be established in the brain's networks by an initial propensity of the nervous system to become activated in certain ways. This neural *propensity* may result from a number of possible innate neuronal features, including a *sensitivity* to a minimal threshold of stimuli in order to be activated, an *intensity* of neural firing once activated, and a *regulatory capacity* to limit the duration and extent of the impact of the firing patterns of an activated network. Each of these aspects of propensity—sensitivity, intensity, regulation—may be a fundamental feature of temperament. Then once this propensity of activation—say, of the agency-anger network—is engaged, the property of neuroplasticity (that neural firing itself leads to enhanced neural connectivity) means that an initial propensity can lead to an ingrained pathway in the brain's network

connectivity. As the analogy is often stated, once a walking path is set up along a snow-covered hill, the next hikers are likely to take that same path of least resistance and further ingrain that particular path down the hill. Likewise, as neural firing might be a small propensity initially—as an innate aspect of temperament—repeated firing will increase that propensity; it will strengthen, making it more likely to be activated, which then in turn strengthens its own propensity. This is, literally, self-reinforcing. If nonsecure attachment is present, this lack of a reliable experience of being seen, safe, or soothed, and therefore not secure, will create a nonintegrative internal milieu from that nonintegrative relational milieu, and the PDP will be more deeply differentiated and other paths not as available for linkage. This is our proposal for how the temperament of a propensity can then become the pathway of patterns of neural firing that develop as personality that, with nonsecure experiences, may then become less integrative in the individual's life. This is how the nonintegrative PDP is experienced more as a prison than a playground.

22. Attachment experience and developmental levels of well-being. Subcortical networks and the resulting pathways each present their own unique challenges of finding a way to live a full and free life of wholeness. We are proposing that temperament makes one vector and one attendency bias more likely than others, and the experience of nonsecure attachment can deepen a divide from other potential ways of being and acting in the world. Differentiating these various networks as vectors with their accompanying biases in attention orientation as the attendency and linking them to one another through a day, a week, a lifetime, is what we mean by integrating our lives and moving toward wholeness. When the connections of attachment are nonsecure, the developmental pathways are more likely to become intense and their patterns more inflexible than when attachment has been secure. That, at least for now, is our educated guess. The reason for this proposal stems from the notion that working-for-a-living is hard on anyone, no matter how wonderfully attuned our attachment figures are. In this way, *we may tend to develop a PDP pattern no matter*

our attachment history. However, when avoidance, ambivalence, or disorganization is our nonsecure attachment experience, then our PDP will be intensified. What this means is that our drive toward wholeness will be increased and the development of a particular pathway will become an ingrained personality pattern that will be dug deeper into the network's connectivity, reinforcing its own existence. We would say that the "groove" of that pathway is then deeper. In this way, as we've stated, the particular pattern of emotion/motivation network vector and attendency are not determined by experience, but the intensity and inflexibility of them are.

23. Attuning to the inner journey of nine paths to wholeness. The therapeutic journey toward wholeness involves cultivating an attuned relational connection with the client that focuses attention on their inner experience to identify the inner and outer conditions that activate the motivational network vector and the attendency, and how these might relate to the experience of non-wholeness needing agency, bonding, or certainty. With agency, embodied empowerment is the motivation and anger in all its ranges, from resentment to rage, is the emotion; with bonding, relational connection and recognition is the motivation and sadness in all its ranges, from separation distress to despair, is the emotion; with certainty, prediction and safety is the motivation and fear, in all its ranges from anticipatory anxiety to terror, is the emotion. Positive emotional states for each of the vectors, including contentment, joy, and courage, fill the life of the individual more as integrative states are accessed. Each of these emerges with the activation of the subcortical emotions and motivations key to the complete range of personality patterns that are part of living a full life—and therapy can help access those underdeveloped and underaccessed networks. We each need a sense of agency, bonding, and certainty to various extents across the lifespan. By utilizing the biases of attention inwardly, outwardly, or dyadically (both inward and outward), the therapist can help guide the client toward integrating the focus of energy and information within each vector in the most flexible, adaptive, coherent, energized, and stable (FACES) ways needed for a given situation. Instead of a pathway

being fixed in the snow, therapy helps the whole hillside of life become available for exploration, inside and out.

24. Liberation from limiting and repetitive habits. Liberation from recurrent experiences of chaos and rigidity enable the question of "Why am I doing this again and again?" to be addressed and the individual to access a wider range of now integrative ways of shaping energy and information flow in their lives. While temperament may persist across the lifespan as an innate propensity, personality is changeable as we intentionally differentiate and link previously nonintegrated alternative proclivities—alternative vectors and attendencies—that shape our deep emotional and motivational experiences. In these ways, therapy utilizing the PDP framework both liberates the individual from unhelpful patterns of emotion, thought, and behavior and also frees them to access and experience a state of simply being, of resting in the coherent state of belonging to a larger whole. One way of articulating this freedom is that we can differentiate the now freed inner Me of the individual to not only become connected in relationships with others and with nature as a We, but also to feel the wholeness of the integrative state of being Me plus We as MWe, as an intraconnected self in life.

Levels of Functioning, Levels of Integration

In the following chapters, we will explore in detail our ideas about the ways in which important aspects of our overall personality can emerge from each of these patterns of developmental pathways. For now, all we need to say is that personality patterns can emerge in development because the salience of the different need sets, or of the different adaptive strategies, varies according to the individual's unique developmental experience. Important factors can include inborn proclivities; particular circumstances involving rare or repeated traumatic events at key times; authoritarian, punitive, or overly permissive parenting styles; relational interaction and communication that directly shapes inner responses and outer behavior; positive reinforcement of good qualities; or combinations of these and many other experiential factors.

In other words, innate aspects of what we are naming temperament form a filter through which energy flows within an individual in response to the ongoing experiences of life. Our vectors and attendencies form one aspect of that set of predispositions of temperament. Experiences in our world, especially our interpersonal relationships, then shape a set of energy patterns within and surrounding us that we respond to with adaptive strategies that help us survive and thrive as best we can. Illuminating these fundamental aspects of the temperament foundations of personality as adaptive strategies of working-for-a-living in the journey toward wholeness can provide liberating insights into finding freer ways of living a more integrative life.

The emergence of personality patterns appears to be a common aspect of being a human from our earliest days. These enduring patterns of how we feel, think, and behave act as a kind of filter to help us effectively respond to our ever-changing world of experience. Personality can help us, and it can also sometimes become intense and inflexible. In this way, personality itself is not necessarily or only problematic. We are proposing that personality patterns are most likely to be flexible with a secure attachment history. With security, we can envision a "wide groove," making other capacities more accessible as contributory characteristics of an integrative, healthy mind, which might be more likely to support the cognitive flexibility, emotional agility, and behavioral connectivity of resilience. This is described clearly in the narrative evidence and traditional teachings of the Enneagram, where each type is associated with a set of laudable and virtuous higher qualities, states of mind, and behaviors that contribute in major ways to individual and collective well-being and social cohesion. And, at the same time, even very developed, high functioning, healthy individuals also share habitual, autopilot behaviors that they may not be aware of or that get activated under stress. In other words, each of us seems to develop a personality pattern no matter how challenging or ideal our childhood experiences may have been.

This brings us back to the IPNB concept of integration, the process of linking differentiated elements of a system into a whole greater than the sum of its parts. We hypothesize that when development has been integrative, neural linkages between the networks within each vector are robust, and the various adaptive strategies are all well developed and balanced by one another. The result is that attention and energy can be developed to flow more freely down each pathway and access its more integrative capacities. Ideally, through conscious practice, we come to enable developmental capacities that allow us to better motivate behavior that is most adaptive to the circumstances at hand. In other words, when a fuller repertoire of responses is available, there is greater response flexibility, adaptability, and well-being, and the most beneficial and socially functional qualities of each of the patterns can emerge more freely according to the situation at hand. This is a resilient and resourceful mind. We've seen that this can be recalled with the mnemonic FACES: flexible, adaptive, coherent (resilient over time), energized, and stable (reliable rather than rigid). This FACES flow is more likely to arise within a pathway and also as we access the other vectors and other attendencies that are not our baseline. This is how we differentiate and link the vectors and attendencies in our life as we move to more highly integrative states of functioning.

Integration is seen not only within the many systems of the body, including in the nervous system, for example, but also within our relationships with other people, and with the planet. (See Siegel, 2023, for a deeper dive into this broader view of integration, belonging, and identity.) When parents sense a child's unique characteristics, for example, they are differentiating themselves from their child and then can link with compassionate, attuned communication. With such interpersonal integration at the heart of secure attachment relationships, one sees the growth of neural integration in the child that serves as the heart of resilience and well-being (see Siegel, 2020 for further details). In simple terms, relational integration cultivates neural integration, which is the basis of mental well-being and human flourishing.

When development has been less optimally integrative, salience of different needs is skewed, and some pathways are more robust while others are less so. This is the source of our proposal that nonintegrative attachment relationships—ones that lead to nonsecure attachment patterns—may make a personality pattern more deeply ingrained. Here we see a developmental overlap in the move away from wholeness. Each person's vectors are activated in response to that new life out in this do-or-die world. If attachment is secure, we still may lean on one vector or another, as a function of our temperament and its innate neural propensities. Where our attendency is directed may also be a part of our innate temperament profile and then shapes how the pathway of our personality becomes activated within that vector. If we also have nonsecure attachment, that vector and attendency's activation to handle our being far from wholeness will become intensified. The relational world is not holding us as it potentially could out here in the extrauterine world; now our personality pathway becomes intensified to deal with the challenges to our feeling whole. The result is that attention and perceptions become biased, and the flow of energy into behavior is constricted and limited to the most robust neural pathways in their now habitual, compulsive, impulsive, or "force-fitted" ways as they conform to the vector and attendency's funneling process. The result of impaired integration is a more dysfunctional personality pattern in the present moment, one we've described as a PDP with a deep, narrow groove. Over time, this personality becomes a pathway that then reinforces its own proclivities. These patterns in current interactions and persistent pathway features across time can then become the focus of growth-edge work for each PDP.

Attachment experiences do not specify personality patterns; they can intensify personality as they deepen that PDP groove with nonsecure relationships, or they enable a wider groove to be carved with security. With secure and nonsecure attachment, we still develop a proclivity of experiencing emotion, thought, and behavior that we call personality. That is our best guess, our hypothesis, at this moment. Future research can help clarify the accuracy of this proposal. In the meantime, when using the PDP framework clinically, we can take a neutral stance about causation and specific developmental mechanisms while simply exploring what the subjective experience of a client is now and how these core motivations of agency, bonding, and certainty are playing a role across their life. While each of these vectors is important for each of us, some of us may find one set of motivations more a priority in our lives than others. The reason for this favoring of one vector over another perhaps may be some combination of temperament and experiences that shapes our learned adaptations to what we've encountered in life.

CHAPTER 5

Why One Dominant Pathway?

Why "Pathways"? A Model of Personality Based on the Science of Interpersonal Neurobiology

We chose the notion of "developmental pathways" as it provides a solid way to envision how a child grows into the range of ways they respond to ongoing life experience.

As Robbie Duschinsky (2020) explores:

> From *Separation* onwards, Bowlby [1981, 1988] emphasised that clinicians and researchers should note the importance of "developmental pathways," self-reinforcing patterns in children's trajectories towards or away from mental health. Bowlby was inspired by Waddington's description of how cells can initially develop in a variety of different ways, but that once they do begin to develop, they become canalised such that a change from the established pathway requires greater and greater intervention (Waddington, 1957). Bowlby reflected that, with human development conceptualised in terms of pathways, we can expect "adverse childhood experiences [to] have effects of at least two kinds. First they make the individual more vulnerable to later adverse experiences. Secondly they make it more likely that he or she will meet with further such experiences."

By focusing on developmental pathways, we could build on the broad fields of developmental psychology and developmental neuroscience in attempting to find consilience with the fields of personality and psychotherapy. As we are seeing, the general term "pathway" offers important meanings that relate to neural networks and their growth as well as a journey of life down a particular path that involves our subjective experiences, embodied processes, and relational interactions. The term with the meaning of a verb-like journey, an unfolding, captures the importance of a dynamic, ever-changing, interactive process rather than a noun-like fixed entity or type. Yet these are enduring pathways across time with patterns in a given moment, and so a PDP has noun-like features of being a "something" even if it is a coalescence of neural pathways and their processes that shapes our interpersonal fields we co-create throughout life.

As we move into our framework's proposal of how these pathways get ingrained with deeper or gentler grooves, and how these are fundamentally related to the subcortical motivational networks that make up our vectors, we'll see how certain patterns seem to be associated with each of them in distinct ways. We are also proposing that a tendency of attention—an attendency—to be inward, outward, or dyadic (as both inward and outward), when coupled together with the vector, comprise a set of what we'll simply refer to as *early organizing features* that begin at birth and continue to dominate the inner landscape of a child through early infancy. In sum, a vector and its accompanying motivation and affects and one's attendency with its focus of attentional energy organize our early patterns of neural firing and relational interactions, which we can simply name temperament.

Next in our proposed framework is that as the individual develops across childhood and adolescence, the vector and attendency combination shapes energy flow in a way that initiates the construction of *adaptive strategies*, ways we learn to get along in the world, which in turn manifest as patterns of *expressed personality* (feelings, thoughts, somatic sensations, and behavior) that can be most readily seen in adulthood as the nine patterns of developmental pathways, the PDPs, of which one, or perhaps a few for some individuals, may become dominant in an individual's life. This issue of the prominence of only one pathway versus features of a few distinct pathways is an open question seeking empirical validation. At this moment in our narrative data, as biased as it may be, it appears that for the majority of individuals, one pathway becomes a baseline while others may be present as secondary patterns. We express this finding as "leading with" a baseline pattern and "leaning into" a secondary bridging pattern, one that may bridge to the baseline pathway by sharing a vector, attendency, or emotion-regulation mode in common. We'll be exploring these findings in greater detail here and in the chapters ahead.

It's illuminating to explore the questions of pathways and their predominance by picturing these early organizing features graphically in Figure 5.1, where you can see the initial stages within our developmental framework, which is how we can move from *one* single state of unity—being "at one

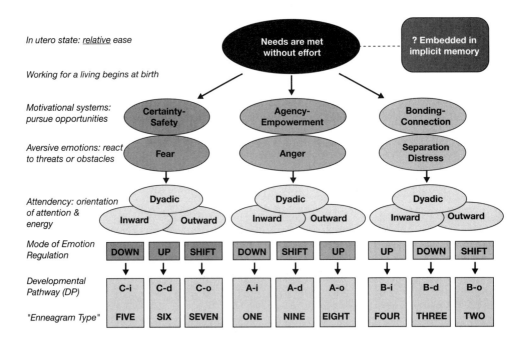

FIGURE 5.1: DEVELOPMENTAL PATHWAYS Highlights of major features of the nine patterns of developmental pathways. The vector involves the motivation toward A, B, or C: agency, bonding, or certainty. The attendency is the orientation of attention and energy and can be inward, outward, or a shimmering or assimilation of the two, not a blending—this can be named dyadic and labeled as "d."

Image used with permission from Jack Killen and the PDP Group.

with the womb," or perhaps "wholeness in utero," or even the state of simply being before doing—to *three* motivational networks underlying the vectors. Each vector aligns with a cluster of receptive, appetitive emotions and one of the reactive, core aversive affects of anger, separation distress/sadness, and fear. When a trio within each vector is created by the *three* attendencies, we get to *nine* personality patterns—patterns of developmental pathways. While a minority of individuals may readily and evenly tap into each of the nine patterns, most people seem to experience one pathway as particularly dominant in their life, shaping how they focus their attention, experience emotion, and interact with the world. We can simply say that most individuals seem to lead with a particular pattern as their baseline. The corresponding Enneagram personalities are included in Figure 5.1, as a reminder of how the PDPs of our framework were initially derived from and correlate with each of the "types" in the narrative teaching of the Enneagram personality system.

Importantly, each individual's regulatory networks are unique because each individual's life situation is unique. As Davis and Panksepp (2018) state:

> Each emotion not only has its own characteristic feelings but also guides perceptual interpretations, thoughts, and behavioral reactions, both unlearned and learned. However, the strength and sensitivity of each brain emotion system, as well as the developmental learning it has guided, vary from individual to individual. So, there is substantial variation across different people in each of these basic emotion systems, part of it inherited and part of it learned. (p. 16)

As we began to think more deeply about the origins of the patterns, we kept in mind that numerous studies in behavioral genetics have shown that both genes and environment are important both to childhood temperament and to personality in adulthood, with about 40% heritability for most traits and 60% environmental influence (Rutter, 2007; Vukasović & Bratko, 2015; see also Daniels, 1986; Plomin & Daniels, 1987). Genetic influences are evident from the findings that monozygotic (MZ) twins are consistently more similar to each other than are dizygotic (DZ) twins for each of the Big Five personality traits, among others (Bergeman, et al., 1993; Jang et al., 1996). Evidence for environment comes from the finding that MZ twins do not have exactly the same personality, as the correlations between two twins are far from 100%. The fact that MZ twins (who share 100% of their genes) can be quite different from each other indicates that the environmental influences on personality traits are generally of the "non-shared" variety, meaning that they are not experiences shared by twins and other family members, but instead are idiosyncratic, person-specific effects. Our unique experiences acquired after birth, in addition to inborn predispositions, shape our personality. These well-established findings about moderately heritable personality traits pertain to studies of adults as well as children (Baker & Daniels, 1990; Saudino, 2005; Shiner & Caspi, 2003).

For our developmental model to be consistent with what we already know in the science of personality, we realized that the adaptive strategies in the PDPs would likely be the result of both innate factors—including moderately heritable temperament—and a person's unique experiences. And this is exactly what our model proposes, although the specific ways in which the "nature" and the "nurture" play a role are still being explored and need empirical studies to confirm in the future.

It's worth noting that, in spite of the vast literature on the gene-environment underpinnings of personality and temperament, there has been only one published twin study of the Enneagram personalities that we are aware of. This study was coauthored by our colleague David (Maxon & Daniels, 2008). It was a small study (36 MZ twin pairs), with a large age range (8–60 years old), and the Enneagram was relatively new to many of the participants. They used the Essential Enneagram test (Daniels & Price, 2009) to identify each twin's personality "type." The main finding was that MZ twins were no more similar in "type" than randomly matched controls. While it is somewhat surprising that no evidence of genetic influence was found, we think this may be a limitation of using the typing approach, although the large age range and varied familiarity with the Enneagram may have also played a role.

But this finding *is* consistent with the idea that unique experiences are extremely important to personality development since there were so many discordant pairs in their Enneagram types. Twins—like all children in a family—need to individuate from each other, so they may be similar on some aspects but their need to function as individuals in the same family may lead them to seek differences. This is also consistent with what Laura has learned in 30 years of twin research, that twins need their own identity for healthy development (Segal, 2000, 2017).

Translating the Enneagram into the PDP framework could lead to more refined twin studies, which could investigate the gene-environment interplay in the various components—that is, the strength of the *vectors, core aversive emotions,* and *attendencies*—rather than relying simply on which of the nine patterns may dominate for each individual twin.

In short, our hypothesis—which has practical clinical utility and also requires research validation, especially for the causal suggestions—is something along these lines: Temperament (subcortical proclivities) interweaves with attachment and other key early life experiences (subcortical affects and needs along with cortical strategies of adaptation) to lead to personality (subcortical and cortical networks in concert with one another achieving various degrees of integration in specific contexts and across the lifespan). Might the sensitivity of the temperament's vector aspect set the likely baseline patterns, while the attendency then is shaped more by experience? If this hypothesis were to be evaluated empirically, we might find a genetic influence on which vector a set of twins found themselves sharing while their environmental need to differentiate might push for differing attendencies to be acquired early in life. The PDP framework can help guide both researchers and clinicians to explore these facets of how nature and nurture intertwine in the development of personality.

The visual image of the juggler in Figure 5.2 aptly depicts our PDP conception of an optimal state of high integration of the three motivational systems and the three developmental pathways of each, as well as the fluid and dynamic ability to cope with the challenges of life in an often uncertain and dangerous world, which such an integrative state provides. Here, the mind is relatively adept at monitoring and reconciling inner and outer information regarding states of agency, bonding, and certainty moment to

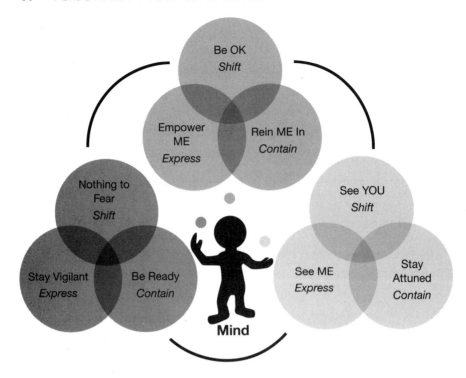

FIGURE 5.2: JUGGLING AGENCY, BONDING, CERTAINTY Each vector has a trio of attendency pathways that lead to a mental stance characterized here by a simple everyday phrase and an emotion-regulation mode abbreviated as "express" (upregulating), "contain" (downregulating), or "shift" or reframe (to activate another emotional state).

moment, and then directing the subsequent flow of attention and motivational energy along pathway(s) leading to the upregulating, downregulating, or shifting mode of emotional regulation and consequent response in somatic activation, perception, thinking, and behavior most likely to be adaptive to the situation at hand. For purposes of illustration, these states of mind are summarized in very simple, accessible, everyday phrases. That is a lot to juggle at any given moment of time, and in real time no less. It's no wonder few people are adept over the long haul at the whole repertoire of adaptations! The PDP framework, summarized in this image, offers a practical guide to becoming a better juggler by elucidating where and how attention and energy flow might be habitually skewed, and by conceptualizing alternative response strategies that will probably require practice to become better differentiated and linked in a more integrative way. Most of us may always have—and perhaps need—a baseline or primary PDP that serves as a fundamental organizer of life, but with practice we can move through life with more adaptive flexibility. Perhaps others naturally, without effort, have ready access to these many pathways in their life for reasons future research may elucidate. Finally, the juggler metaphor invites compassion for our inner self and other individuals as well on the lifelong journey of learning and practice toward the goal of living an integrative life toward wholeness.

Attendency: A Primary Attentional Orientation Bias

TABLE 5.1 Nine Patterns According to the Motivational Vectors and Attendencies

VECTOR	ATTENDENCY—How attention and energy are oriented and flow		
	Outward	*Dyadic (Inward + Outward)*	*Inward*
Agency	A-o: toward objects of need, desire, or threat	A-d: toward assimilating and resolving conflicting information from inward and outward sources	A-i: toward learned internalized templates and templates of engagement
Bonding	B-o: toward perceptions of another's needs to be seen	B-d: toward assimilating the needs to be seen while individuating and moving away from connection	B-i: toward emotional motivations to be seen
Certainty	C-o: toward objects of need and desire out in the world	C-d: toward the inherent uncertainty and doubt about BOTH what is understood and believed (i.e., inward), and what is perceived about others and the world (i.e., outward)	C-i: toward the states of readiness of psychological and material resources and information that might be needed if danger comes

The nine patterns in Table 5.1 are differentiated by the early organizing features of vectors and attendencies. These early features we can simply name temperament, with the provision that some may early on be molded, in part, by experience as well as genetics, which shape these two key aspects of our early development. One's vector and attendency will then directly influence how energy flows in the embodied brain, the extended nervous system, and will play central roles in how the individual both experiences life and also learns to live in this particular inner and relational world. These learned mechanisms of adaptation, acquired within the foundational developmental conditions of both vectors and attendencies and their interaction with lived experience, are what we call *adaptive strategies.* In other words, the early organizing features of one's vector and attendency combine with lived experience to shape how individuals learn to cope with life and how they develop adaptive strategies to survive and thrive as best they can. It is these adaptive strategies, emerging from one's baseline vector and attendency, that then underlie personality expressed as patterns of emotion, thought, and behavior.

Adaptive strategies emerge out of early life experience as "default" or baseline ways of orienting attention, regulating emotion, and responding behaviorally in order to maintain or restore homeostasis. You can think of these strategies as templates for processing information across the major domains of cognitive, emotional, and somatic information. What results for each pattern are cognitive, emotional, and somatic strategies to restore homeostasis. It may be, we are proposing, that this physiological and emotional drive for homeostasis is in some ways a resonant process to regain that state resembling an implicit memory of wholeness.

Life out of the womb for any child is a massive change toward "doing to survive." As a newborn infant who must start working for a living in a do-or-die new world, a big part of your job is to begin building those three motivational systems:

- The agency system will enable you, throughout life, to *attend to the state of your body, and use it to navigate the world* so as to keep it and its embodied sense of existence safe, connected, intact, and satisfied.
- The bonding system will enable you, throughout life, to *establish and*

maintain the vital relationships you need with other individuals, and they need with you, to get along in the world of human social life.

- The certainty system will enable you, throughout life, to deal appropriately with the inherent uncertainty of life, and help you identify and make meaning of *opportunities to pursue your needs, and potential threats to your future well-being,* informed by the sum of your inheritance and learning from past experiences.

This brings us to a summary of the three parts of our developmental hypothesis:

1. The trio of baseline personality patterns associated with each of the three motivational vectors reveals a repertoire of adaptive strategies to pursue empowerment, connection, and safety. These three patterns within a vector vary in the ways in which the motivational energy is upregulated, downregulated, or shifted to a different motivational and emotional state. Said differently, they represent the general range of effective ways of responding to, and being in, different situations when motivations to restore or maintain homeostasis arise. These patterns may become especially activated and then apparent during conditions of stress—when something meaningful is at stake. Our "stress solutions" are repeatedly encoded in broad patterns of response as adaptive strategies that help form the developmental pathways underlying our personality in life.

2. A pattern of personality arises in an individual when one developmental pathway and its adaptive strategy becomes especially dominant as a recurrent and habitual way of responding, compared to the other two in that vector or any from the other vectors. This can happen for any number of reasons. One or more pathways may be most salient to your unique developmental experience, which may include nonsecure early attachment or trauma at any time during development. Or perhaps a lot of positive feedback reinforces the good and helpful aspects of a particular way of being. Family composition and dynamics may play a role in developing a differentiated way of being. Even chance can play a role. It's likely that an accumulation of these

kinds of things as well as others over the early years of life shapes the emergence of these personality traits. Although it is the habitual and sometimes rigidly held adaptive strategy that leads to the emergence of personality patterns, ironically, we become more adaptive by recognizing and relaxing the pattern and being able to move more flexibly among a variety of adaptive strategies—enabling more freedom, growth, and integration, and ultimately greater access to wholeness.

3. A healthy, high-functioning, well-integrated system does not hold rigidly and maladaptively to a single, habitual pattern, but can move flexibly among the adaptive strategies, leaning toward the higher qualities of the "baseline" pattern and ultimately of all nine pathways. What this means is not so much "becoming another baseline pattern" but rather being able to access a wide and flexible range of the other vectors of motivation, directions of attendency, and modes of emotion regulation. This is what we mean by the phrase "the higher qualities" of other patterns—the more integrative states that enable flexibility across these motivations and attendencies, as well as emotion-regulation modes appropriate for a given situation. It is an empirical question—one that can be tested—as to whether the general view that one's baseline pattern stays with the individual across the lifespan is in fact true. Our impression is that it does, but let's keep an open mind about that question, realizing that deep subcortical networks likely underlying temperament may be less moldable than the higher cortically mediated neuroplastic networks of lifelong learning. When we ask, "Why does this keep happening?" and other questions about all sorts of problems we repeatedly encounter in life, it may be that a particular pathway has a "deeper groove" and comes to be more habitually—that is, more rigidly and less flexibly—applied to all situations as they evoke the motivational energy of that vector and the orientation of attention and energy flow of that attendency.

To emphasize this important issue, we are not stating that the therapeutic work or personally guided growth journeys integrating the PDPs lead to some "permanent state of bliss" or anything like a fixed state of being whole. And we are not saying that the "growth-edge work" we'll be exploring in the chapters ahead using the PDP framework are attempting to "rid a person" of their baseline pattern. Instead, the notion of accessing this integrative state more readily, more frequently, and with more depth seems to be what working at the growth-edge for each particular PDP enables an individual to achieve. Moving toward wholeness is, in our view, a lifelong journey toward integration. Under severe stress, our subcortical networks' particular sensitivities may be activated no matter how much personal growth or therapy we've successfully engaged in. In day-to-day experience, these journeys of personal growth may enable us to drop beneath the specific adaptive strategies of our pathway we learned early in life and access the underlying capacity to feel whole even as we are working-for-a-living in these bodies during this do-or-die lifetime on Earth. The result is experiencing longer periods of harmonious states, joyfulness, open awareness, and richer, more mutually rewarding relationships with others and with nature.

Tables 5.2, 5.3, and 5.4 provide a recapitulation of the detailed components of the PDP framework and our hypotheses about their development across the lifespan.

In a nutshell, our developmental model proposes that the *early organizing features, likely a part of temperament* (Table 5.2), involving these three sets of fundamental needs and the associated motivational *vector* and core *aversive emotion*, along with the three variations in *attendency*, begin to emerge at birth and through infancy. Throughout childhood and adolescence, these give rise to nine *adaptive strategies* (Table 5.3), including their cognitive and emotional processes, as well as somatic propensities. Eventually the *expressed personalities* (Table 5.4) emerge as the manifest traits or characteristics most visible to the self and others and include both strengths and weaknesses and, we hypothesize, become most stable from adolescence through young adulthood and onward. Strengths include the characteristics, skills, and capacities that support well-being for the individual and the collective; weaknesses can be considered sources of vulnerability and challenge. We propose that the extent to which strengths and weaknesses, these opportunities and challenges, may appear to different degrees depends on the level of integration in the individual in a given moment or at that stage in lifespan growth.

TABLE 5.2: Early Organizing Features, Likely of Temperament

Vector ***Motivational System for Core Need*** ***Core Aversive Affect—the Initial Reactive Emotion***	One of three universal psychological need sets that may become activated with a perceived lack or deficiency: • *Agency for embodied empowerment*: empowers and uses the body and sense of existence to keep both alive and well; brings a sense of congruence, comfort, harmony, respect • *Bonding for relational connection*: maintains vital connection with others; brings a sense of recognition, approval, being seen, affection, support • *Certainty for prediction and safety*: attempts to detect danger and construct patterns to create a sense of safety, preparedness, predictability, opportunity All three sets of motivational needs are essential, but one often becomes more salient, depending on genetic and other constitutional factors, early experiences, and their interaction. The aversive emotion system—anger, separation distress and sadness, or fear—that serves the core needs of agency, bonding, or certainty, respectively. Associated with a pattern of emotional tone and reactivity.
Attendency	The directionality of attention and energy that organizes the subsequent flow of attention and energy into behavior—either inward, outward, or dyadic (both inward and outward, which leads to assimilating or reconciling).

TABLE 5.3: Adaptive Strategies

Cognitive Processing ***Verbal Thoughts and Narrative Themes***	One of nine patterns of flow of information and energy into habitual, limited, and recurring patterns of thoughts and ideas, stories we tell ourselves to make sense of and cope with life, beliefs, mental preoccupations, and mental focus.
Emotional Processing ***Emotional Tone, Drive, and Reactivity*** ***Mode of Emotion Regulation***	One of nine patterns of flow of emotional energy and information into habitual, limited, and recurring patterns of emotional drive, tone, reactivity, expression, waxing and waning of feelings, emotional preoccupations, and affective focus. How the motivational system processes motivational energy as it arises: upregulating ↑(EE: experience and express), downregulating ↓ (CC: contain and channel), or shifting → to a different motivational state (RR: reframe and redirect).

TABLE 5.3: cont.

ALEAF: Anatomic Location of Energy Activation and Flow	Agency vector: gut/body Bonding vector: heart Certainty vector: head
Focus of Attention and Blind Spots	Nine patterns of the kinds of things attention is directed toward, and the kinds of things that in effect become "blind spots" for each of the nine patterns.

TABLE 5.4: Expressed Personalities

Potential Strengths	Personality traits considered to be valuable and important assets of the pathway and its adaptive strategy.
Potential Challenges	Personality traits considered to be liabilities, weaknesses, or vulnerabilities of the pathway and its adaptive strategy. Can vary over time within an individual, and on average across individuals.

It's important to understand that while we are proposing a temporal unfolding of these different components (early organizing features, adaptive strategies, and expressed personality) across the lifespan, we are not suggesting that they are discrete processes that are confined strictly to particular stages of development. Rather, the various components may very well interact with one another and emerge in a continuous way across the lifespan. When we consider the notion that the move away from wholeness is ultimately what drives the activation of a vector and attendency combination fundamental to our early organizing features, then we can understand that this move toward wholeness is a lifelong mission, one that can be shaped by inner and outer factors that mold our adaptive strategies and patterns of personality across our lifespan.

How One PDP May Come to Dominate and Shape Personality

From the core motivations—the **vectors**—activated by essential early needs, there are various scenarios that could be hypothesized to explain the emergence of one or more patterns as dominant features of personality within an individual. One impression, in need of careful systematic exploration and testing, is that the majority of the over 2,000 individuals I have informally surveyed in the PDP framework can find themselves with a "primary" baseline pathway. In various educational and workshop settings, this averages to about 85%, with a range in different groups from about 70 to 90%. In the more intensive setting of psychotherapy, over 90% of my patients have been able to readily find at least a baseline pair of patterns that emerge as a primary and secondary PDP in their lives. Some have sensed a change from their adolescent years, with transformation seeming to involve a switching of the primary and secondary roles of each baseline pattern. It feels at times that the overlay of attachment strategies when nonsecure with the timing of this transition may be part of the developmental journey for some.

Perhaps with more extensive investigation outside such group assessments, this survey number may be found to be higher, as future research may explore broad population distribution patterns. Many individuals, even in this survey setting, describe a "runner-up" group of one or two of what we are naming "secondary" pathways, ones that our initial exploration suggests may share either a vector or an attendency in common, as mentioned earlier. These secondary PDPs can be called "bridging pathways" in that they bridge across one of the fundamental defining features of the primary, baseline PDP. Perhaps the combination of life experience as it unfolds pulls one of these bridging pathways to become more useful at various times in the lifespan. But we can also ask the fundamental question, why wouldn't all nine potential pathways be equally active in a given individual? Why would there seem to be a finding of a set of primary and secondary pathways that dominate a person's lived experience as revealed in survey and psychotherapy settings?

One plausible hypothesis is that inborn temperament, whether heritable as genetic or epigenetic influences or as a result of the particular circumstances of the fetus's emergence in utero, might create a predisposition for one of the three motivational vectors to become most salient in early life— that is, agency with its drive for embodied empowerment, bonding with its drive for relational connection, or certainty with its drive for prediction and safety. For a minority of individuals, those in the average of 15% of subjects surveyed to date, perhaps these three vectors are simply equally sensitive and one does not come to predominate the unfolding developmental journey.

A second hypothesis is that the young child's feelings of anger, separation distress and sadness, or fear, the three **core aversive emotions**, play a central role. As we have described, they are each associated with one of the three core motivations stemming from the salient need sets in our do-or-die life outside the womb. In effect, it would be as though one of these systems has an initial sensitivity that makes it more likely to be activated with the challenges of our extrauterine life—no matter how wonderful our caregivers are. Even an initial slight sensitivity could then lead to a feedback loop in which the neural activation leads to strengthening of the neural connections in that neural network based on the adage we've discussed: Where attention goes, neural firing flows, and neural connection grows. An initial slight dominance of one vector over the others could then become manifest as hypersensitivity to perceived threats in that one vector's focus, so aversive reactivity would tend to be flavored more with one of the core emotions than the others. This would be the metaphoric trail in the snow that beckons others to follow that same initial pathway. This may ultimately be the outcome of the subtle initial propensity that drives the carving of one pathway to become more dominant in the majority of individuals' lives with repeated activation of that particular network. *Fear* alerts the child to their need to seek *safety*, while *separation distress* provides an alert to seek secure *connection* with their caretaker, and *anger* signals to the child to *assert the bodily self* in seeking a sense of agency, control, and harmony with the environment. These three core aversive emotions are life-supporting when they alert to real needs and vital behaviors. However, chronic stress and less-than-ideal environments can fuel habitual patterns of counterproductive or even destructive personality traits. In effect, they can drive attention and perception to see threats that are not objectively there.

A third possibility is that the feature we are calling attendency—the directionality of the flow of attention and motivational energy—may also have a key role in early development. Individuals may have an *inward* attendency, an *outward* attendency, or a *dyadic*—inward and outward—attendency.

This placement of the initial processing of energy flow may create a reinforcing loop, as we've discussed, in which those networks that are activated strengthen their synaptic connections and even the myelin sheaths that support more rapid and coordinated neural communication among those interlinked neurons and the networks in which they function. Whether attendency follows a vector or the activation of a vector follows attendency is another open question to consider—both in the research protocols that might explore this question and in the clinical formulations in which these developmental possibilities may illuminate not only the nature of how a pathway came to be but the steps that may be most useful in relaxing it and linking to other vectors and attendencies.

What this question also raises is how in clinical practice we can look at shared characteristics and how a given individual client may find resonance with the other *bridging pathways* we've named earlier. What this means is that we can have at least three bridges. One is the vector trio in which we may find similarities in all those, say, who share the agency vector (A-i, A-o, A-d). In the Enneagram system, this would sometimes be indicated as the sharing of a "center of intelligence," which overlaps with the PDP view of the trio within a vector. For those familiar with the Enneagram typing, we will use the indicator of the numerical type in parentheses, so that the Enneagram 1 data yield our inner view of the agency vector with an inward attendency, and this would be depicted this way: A-i (1). A bridging pattern for this PDP would then be one that shares the vector; for example, for A-i (1), it would be A-o (8) and A-d (9). While that may be true for someone whose vector drove developmental processes, perhaps another individual finds more resonance with those who share their attendency, bridging to all those who are inward, for example as A-i (1) would bridge to B-i (4) and C-i (5). Another possibility for bridging might be the emotion-regulation mode, such as all those that share the downregulation of the contain-and-channel mode of the A-i (1): B-d (3) and C-i (5). Even doing a mental exercise as we move along to name all the bridging triads would be a helpful way to reinforce your own learning of each of the nine pathways as we move ahead to explore these pathways in greater depth. Perhaps these may relate to the Enneagram notions of what are called "wings" and "connecting points," as future research could also explore. Please note: Emotion-regulation mode does *not* always correlate with attendency, but you may have observed that each vector trio has both each of the attendencies and each of the modes of emotion regulation.

Please don't worry if these details feel a bit overwhelming at this moment. As we go forward, step by step, and explore each of the pathways, I hope you'll sense an elegant and accessible set of insights into how these factors—vector, attendency, mode of emotion regulation—each help illuminate the adaptive strategy of that personality pattern. I hope you'll also find that once this becomes more familiar in your conceptual framework, the inner journey to understand your own baseline and bridging PDPs (and those of the individuals with whom you work) will become a helpful, and even enjoyable, way of understanding our lives.

A fourth hypothesis about developmental processes potentially relevant to the emergence of the patterns across the lifespan, and also how we work with them in psychotherapy, is that the beneficial and positive aspects, the strengths and opportunities, of the pathway and its adaptive strategy pattern are reinforced in social interactions, first and foremost with caregivers in childhood, and increasingly with others as social circles expand in early development and through adolescence. Knowing this as a therapist can greatly aid in understanding how the therapeutic relationship may be influencing the integration, or not, of a client's PDP's state of rigidity. It is also an exciting matter of clinical discovery to see how a pathway might have an emergence in childhood based on these relational experiences and perhaps have a natural persistence, or even characteristic change, during the important social transitions, and challenges, of the adolescent years and the impacts on them by modern culture such as social media and the isolation of viral pandemics. Our impression from the adult narrative data, as we've said, is that the actual baseline adult pathways do not change to other pathways in the course of development, though they do transform in their impact on clients and close others as they move from low to high levels of integrative functioning.

A fifth hypothesis concerns the development of inner narratives and stories we tell ourselves that align with each of the three vectors. Are these narratives themselves a source of persistence of the features of a pathway? Personality dynamics is a field whose investigations draw upon the narrative identity model to explore such a possibility. Might the stories we tell, to others and to ourselves, construct an unintended self-fulfilling prophecy? And is this what our narrative data are revealing—a bias of self-report that is the source of perhaps actual personality pattern differences, but ones that the narrative as much creates as expresses? One of the fascinating findings is that even those unfamiliar with the Enneagram or other personality systems who have been surveyed through the lens of the PDP framework can, in the majority of individuals, find a primary and sometimes secondary baseline pattern that resonates deeply with their lived experience—sometimes in ways that were outside their awareness.

A sixth—and perhaps most likely—possibility is that combinations of these various hypothesized developmental influences or other similar ones create early propensities for one or several pathways to become most robust and shape an important aspect of the individual's personality. This possibility helps us as clinicians to carefully and humbly express our viewpoints, for example, about not knowing with certainty how and why a person acts the way they do in persistent patterns. Now with this PDP framework in our minds—and sometimes shared directly, if that is useful for a particular person—we can simply and compassionately attune to what a client is saying and help them explore the unknown territory of the developmental origins of the way we are. We can play our PART as therapists with presence, attunement, resonance, and trust, so that together we can help facilitate integrative growth, not premature closure of exploration by offering seemingly definitive answers about how development has actually occurred. Therapy is a co-constructive, interpersonal joining and narrative process that, when taken with deep respect and humility, can be deeply liberating—opening a person to new ways of being.

All of these, and likely many other unnamed and unthought-of processes, remain open developmental possibilities. Nevertheless, however it is determined in human development, it appears that "where attention goes" directly influences the neural pathway set out by an early propensity to focus the energy of subsequent neural activation, which in turn activates genes to produce proteins to enable the momentary neural activations linking interconnected neurons to then make structural changes in the strengthening of synaptic linkages, sometimes growing new neurons, and the laying down of a myelin sheath—and thus the neural connections of the brain change based on what was happening with the mind's attention. Yes, I agree, that's a long sentence, but one attempting to state an important multilayered sequence, one related to not only how we came to be but who we can become. This is the fundamental developmental process of neuroplasticity that likely underlies each of the possibilities we've reviewed here.

In this way, in where energy is flowing and how that energy is constructed into information, the essence of the mind—with or without awareness—directly shapes not only neural firing but neural wiring. We will be using this adage frequently—"Where attention goes, neural firing flows, and neural connection grows"—as it reveals why and how an initial propensity for an emotional motivational neural network to dominate, to be a proclivity we call temperament, can then reinforce its own origins as a personality pathway emerges in our lives. Attention does not require our being aware—it can be "focal attention" with awareness or "non-focal attention" without awareness. In this manner, a motivational vector can activate attentional processes that drive the direction of energy flow by way of neural activations that do not need or perhaps even often involve the intricate process of consciousness. Nevertheless, "where attention goes, neural firing flows, and neural connection grows" still applies.

In psychotherapy, we harness the power of neuroplasticity by using awareness to activate a choice in our focal attention: We can not only choose what to attend to but also then cultivate the capacity for response flexibility (see Siegel, 2020), which allows us to select something other than an immediate reaction in our considered decision. This shift in our conscious mind's use of attention then can also change the brain's function in the moment, and structure in the long term. This is how therapy changes us: A *state* in a session, when repeated between sessions and in subsequent interactions in therapy, can then become *traits* in our lives. When we see how response flexibility emerges with the integrative growth of the prefrontal cortex, we can see a neural mechanism that may underlie the power of therapy to transform a person's life by growing processes in the brain by how we focus attention, guided initially in our interpersonal therapeutic relationship.

These patterns are themselves ingrained tendencies with marked variations in intensity and detail. Because of the nature of neuroplastic growth, it may be that a primary baseline pattern that gets established may remain across the lifespan, that we don't "switch patterns" or "leave that pattern behind" in our lifelong journey to liberate ourselves from the blockages to experiencing wholeness in our lives. In this very real sense, a baseline may remain just that—a basic way that our temperamental proclivities have interacted with our attachment experiences and other important interactions in our lives to shape our neural networks' strengths or weaknesses. The more challenging the experiences we need to adapt to early in life, the deeper the groove may be carved from experience for that particular pathway. Accessing other vectors and attendencies as integration is enhanced, as well as harnessing other emotion-regulation modes, may be envisioned as "softening" or "widening" that groove as it becomes less restrictive and therefore emotions, thinking, and behavior become more flexible. Opening those neural networks to become more integrative does not mean eliminating them; it means opening to higher states of differentiation and linkage within that pathway and opening to those higher states of other pathways—accessing other vectors and attendencies, and other emotion-regulation modes as well, to become more adaptive to all that life brings us.

We may also find that under stress and challenging situations, the wholeness we may be feeling when we are thriving may be punctuated by reactive emotions that fit with our baseline pathway's vector. This retention of some deep subcortical proclivities released from the cortical override we've learned in therapy and personal reflection may mean simply one thing: We are human. Opening to our humanity means accepting our imperfections and weaknesses. One of those vulnerabilities may be a reality that a baseline pattern of developmental pathway remains our pathway even as it becomes more integrated as a life of wholeness. These developmental lifespan issues are something you as a therapist can assist your client in learning to embrace with skill and intention as they work with you on their lifelong journey ahead.

Some Clinical Considerations in Preparation for the Details of the Patterns

As a clinician, you may get the feeling of an energetic "oomph" of a core need that has *salience*—it is meaningful and drawing energy and attention. Having a sense of both the details of these proposed patterns and a feeling for *possible* developmental mechanisms that we've been exploring can help you in the process of psychotherapy. You'll be able to understand your own internal mental life with more refinement, gain insights into the inner life of your client, and be able to "see in four dimensions" as you picture where your client has been, where they are now, and where, with your guidance and support, they may be able to develop toward in the therapeutic journey. This is a "4-D approach" to therapy. Part of these layered dimensions are your own vectors and attendencies, coming to "know thyself" and realize how unavoidably we as individuals participate in the emergent, co-constructive process of psychotherapy. Knowing our own PDPs, primary and secondary, can greatly assist our insights into the inevitable emotional and cognitive bias we—as human beings with minds and histories, with personality pathways—bring to the therapeutic process. Sometimes those biases can lead to misunderstandings, leading to a temporary rupture in our connection with clients. Recognizing such disconnections is essential to making a therapeutic repair and reconnecting to enable therapy to proceed well. Knowing our own PDP and how it interfaces with the PDP of our client can greatly assist in this important repair process central to the learning and healing of the therapeutic relationship.

The energy flow of our lives is shaped by both appetitive motivational energy—meaning how we move receptively *toward* opportunities to satisfy needs—and reactive motivational energy that is protective and defensive—meaning moving *away from* or against things perceived to be unpleasant or harmful, such as threats or obstacles to satisfaction of salient needs. A vector shapes what is salient by the motivational network from which it arises—and this salience can initiate both receptive appetitive and reactive aversive states that influence our feelings, thoughts, and behaviors. Given that this may all be beneath and before awareness, knowing about these deep subcortical systems can greatly facilitate insights into the therapeutic journey.

The core of each personality pathway *over time* is in how these motivational energies have a propensity to become channeled into patterns in the *present moment* of inner experiences of attention, feelings, thoughts, and somatic activation. As we've stated, a PDP across time can be linguistically named as a pathway; the experience of a PDP in any given moment in time can be indicated as a pattern. One pattern of developmental pathway can dominate our lives with great intensity; or a PDP can be less intense. And while we may also have more than one PDP that has a propensity to be active in our lives, as the narratives reveal in Enneagram terms as wings and connected points, for most individuals it seems one or two may be especially prominent in shaping how they feel, think, and behave across the lifespan. What may be indicated as a type in Enneagram terminology we call a primary PDP, which is the PDP that the individual "leads with." We may also have one or more secondary PDPs, which are other aspects of what has particularly strong meaning in our lives. "Secondary" means it serves less as a leading edge, not that it is less important—just less prevalent. As we've seen, we can use the term "leaning toward" to indicate this secondary, bridging pathway's role in our lives.

As you and I go through each of these exercises of empathic imagination and insight cultivation in the specific-PDP-focused chapters ahead, let your mindsight map of imaging the mind of your client, or of your inner self, come into focus. We are drawing out a map of the mind and bringing an initial viewing, an image, of each of the PDPs into focus. What this will entail is constructing an image of the *felt* quality of energy and information flowing through the individual or inside of you, because that, much more than only observable behaviors alone, is what defines each of the pathways.

Try to notice how the *feeling* of a PDP involves a directionality of energy and information flow. This energetic force of the attendency, this push of both attention and the fuel driving it forward, is both shaped by the vector's motivation and textured by its affective tone, which includes both appetitive and aversive emotional energy—what drives a person toward or away. We can also conceive of this as what creates a *receptive* state or, instead, a *reactive* state. This energetic push is also directed by an attentional focus inward, outward, or both in what we've named dyadic.

While there are seven identified motivational subcortical networks (with four being seeking, nurturing/caregiving, sex, and play as the appetitive set), as we've discussed, we have found that the aversive three of agency, bonding, and certainty are most useful in making sense of the nine Enneagram types in our extensive narrative data. These three motivational networks are a fundamental part of systems of mind we've called vectors, which organize how our inner and our relational energy flow is shaped: agency, bonding, and certainty.

The vector involves a general set of salience features in the moment, making certain aspects of experience priorities, relevant and important to lending energy to go toward or away. The specific attendency (inward, outward, or dyadic) shapes a propensity that organizes the flow of attention and information with particular characteristics over time and across situations. This appears on initial explorations, and is worthy of future study, to be distinct from the Big Five notion of introversion or extraversion, which seems to relate more to social features than an initial focusing of energy flow.

The mind adapts to these two features of what we are proposing is likely its own temperament early in life—vector and attendency—with one of its strategies being how affect is modulated as a mode of emotion regulation (upregulating, downregulating, or shifting). Emotion regulation shapes a characteristic emotional *dynamic*, that is, a default pattern of how motivational affects, including aversive reactivity and appetitive receptivity, tend to be managed in day-to-day life. "Dynamic" is a term we are using to mean the processes underlying a set of forces that interact and are in continual unfolding. As you read the details of the chapters ahead, it might be helpful to observe and note how much you personally "resonate" with each of these in your own life, especially if this is your first encounter with them. You'll find resonance, perhaps, with some aspect of the vector, attendency, or mode of emotion regulation.

As a therapist, try to imagine how understanding dominant patterns, meaning both primary and secondary PDPs in *both* you and your client, can provide important and valuable perspectives on the dynamics of the therapeutic relationship between you. It also might be helpful to try to imagine how the individual circumstances of very early life—for example, some kind of subtle or perhaps intensely challenging circumstances, some disconnecting experiences, or even positive reinforcements that were part of early life—might make the needs of one vector most salient for the developing mind and thereby initiate a reinforcing loop shaping an individual's developmental trajectory.

Notice how the PDP framework invites you to consider both innate temperament, as vector and attendency, and the way in which these filter the energy flow of experience with prioritization, giving meaning to what is determined to have salience and be worthy of the expenditure of energy. Perhaps the mode of emotion regulation stands out for you or your clients, sensing how there might be a prevalence for upregulating, downregulating, or shifting emotional states especially when of the aversive sort in a given vector—anger, sadness and separation distress, or fear. You may also notice how a history of nonsecure attachment might intensify the robustness of a particular personality pattern it leads to, making emotional reactivity to experiences involving this particular aspect of life more intense, rapid, and entrenched. The adaptive strategies we constructed during earlier development are efforts to help us survive and attempt to thrive given our life circumstances. Yet the nature of these particular strategies may be directly shaped by the inner setting of our temperament's motivational and therefore emotional propensities. These adaptive strategies can have low levels of integration, as with a history of remaining nonsecure in attachment, and sometimes they may have higher states of integration as we work toward security and wholeness.

Low states of integration can lead to a propensity toward chaos and rigidity. High states of integration enable harmony and the FACES flow of life to emerge. The term "window of tolerance" (see Siegel, 2020) was coined to embrace a span of experience that remains in a harmonious flow *within* the window; whereas moving *beyond* the boundaries of that window reveals nonintegrative states of either chaos on one side or rigidity on the other. Our suggestion is that the experience of wholeness emerges as energy enters that harmonious integrative flow. In this way, the growth-edge work in therapy is to free up the blockages to integration that have created low states of integration and have made individuals prone to chaos or rigidity in their lives. With the developmental growth toward higher states of integration, the FACES flow is then liberated, and the experience of wholeness emerges in that integrative flow. Each PDP may have its own unique ways in which emotional reactivity toward chaos and rigidity are experienced as narrow windows of tolerance for particular emotionally salient experiences and as impediments to accessing wholeness.

When energy is flowing in a specific inner and inter context, that flow can be in harmony whether it is highly activated or with low activation; likewise, we can be in various degrees of arousal, the intensity of activations, and become either chaotic or rigid. In this way, a window of tolerance describes where an individual is at a given moment within a given context of what is happening. Certain PDPs may have narrow windows for certain emotions, such as anger, separation distress and sadness, or fear, and we may then see how an adaptive strategy might be to reframe and redirect that particular emotion in specific moments involving emotional experience, or in many situations across contexts. For one person, anger is no problem, and it might be experienced and expressed readily—upregulated—yet for another person, emotion may be downregulated as it is contained and channeled to maintain functioning within the window for anger. While each of us is unique, we may actually share similar patterns in our enduring distinctions of these motivations, energy flows, and emotions.

In this way, adaptive strategies—the acquired ways we learn to deal with the outer world and our inner world of motivational responses to it—include emotion-regulation modes. In IPNB we view emotion as a shift in integration, and so the notion of windows of tolerance—in which the within-window state is integrative, but the out-of-window zones are the nonintegrative experience of chaos or rigidity—fits well with these being a window of emotional experience. How we come to regulate emotion is directly related to how we attempt to stay within the window of tolerance in any given experience.

Assessing which issues push the individual outside the boundaries of the window such that chaos and rigidity are likely to emerge is a PDP way of viewing what "reactivity" signifies in general, and specifically in the patterns that arise repeatedly in a person's life that we call personality. In this way, avoiding a topic is a strategy of survival, of trying to stay within the window—and this then becomes fundamental to what an adaptive strategy strives to accomplish in the shift mode of emotion regulation as reframe and redirect, to keep the individual in the overall integrative flow within the window of tolerance.

It is for this reason, by the way, that simply utilizing the Affective Neuroscience Personality Scales (see Davis & Panksepp, 2018) unfortunately does not offer an accurate approach to assessing or fully understanding PDPs. The ways in which a specific vector has all three of the emotion-regulation modes within it reveals how much more complex this PDP framework is than simply assessing which of six or seven motivational networks may be particularly active in a person's life. In a trio of a given vector, say, for agency, how the accompanying anger is handled—how that emotion tends to be regulated—will be a part of the adaptive strategy that might be to reframe and redirect that emotion, to shift away from it, and this would yield a formal scale finding of a low rating on the affective experience of anger in this very motivational network. We also think that our exploring the depths and details of the PDP model with you here as a clinician will be the more useful way for you to gain insights into the therapeutic applications of the PDP framework at this moment in the model's development.

Each vector and its attendency, each pattern of developmental pathway, has its own set of challenges to integration and the experience of wholeness. In this way, each pathway has its own particular growth-edge focus—the areas that are especially relevant for helping an individual move away from tendencies of chaos and rigidity and move toward states of integrative harmony and the experience of being whole. Working at the growth-edge helps individuals widen their windows of tolerance and experience more harmony, even in the face of challenging conditions.

While the findings of those Enneagram narrative data from the nearly 50,000 individuals David and his colleagues acquired over many decades have organized our initial thinking, this view of Patterns of Developmental Pathways, our proposed PDP framework, stands on its own—and has many distinct insights and implications, as well as clinical applications, ones that emerge from this new way of thinking about how temperament and attachment shape personality across the lifespan.

Terminology of PDP and the Enneagram System

Finally, a brief word about nomenclature: Different Enneagram sources use different word labels for the personality patterns as convenient shorthand. These can provide an interesting and useful high-level glimpse of how the patterns in the narrative nomenclature tend to manifest in adults. However, there is broad agreement in traditional Enneagram circles that one-word labels cannot begin to capture all the nuances of *internal* experience and *outward* behavior—the subtle yet important features these groupings delineate. Behavioral labels such as "loyal skeptic," "helper," or "performer" are more like shadows of an object, not the object itself. To circumvent the limitations of word labels, a convention of identifying the patterns by number (as we've seen, represented as 1 through 9) is widely used in Enneagram teaching. As a convenience of recollection for those who may be already familiar with the traditional nomenclature as well as for those seeking to correlate PDP views with the existing Enneagram literature, we'll use these same numerical indicators, but we will not be using the popular semantic labels.

A self-reinforcing prison can be inadvertently created by naming oneself as a this or a that type of person, by name—and at least a number pulls back, even if just a bit, from that vulnerability to pigeonholing oneself in a narrow category. In the PDP system, we will be using the vector-attendency combination, which has the intention of emphasizing the dynamic processing—the tension of energy flows of motivation and directionality of that flow—inherent to motivation and emotion patterns, rather than potentially rigidifying as a named "type of person." Also, as we focus on these dynamic processes, we will use classifications such as "emotional" or "cognitive" dynamics or processes to refer to these more affective and information-processing layers of experience, while we recognize that emotion and thought are profoundly interwoven in our daily lives.

Another emphasis we'd like to make is how some who use the Ennea-gram system of personality will use understandable shorthand phrases such as "I am a 3" or "What are you—a 5 or a 9?" These linguistic phrasings are ways we speak with one another, but have the unfortunate implicit impact of presuming our whole identity is a particular "type" of Enneagram personality. To attempt (as clumsily as initially it may feel) to avoid this rigidification of a noun-like type view rather than the more open, verb-like pattern perspective, it can be helpful to use phrases such as "I lead with an A-i (1) pattern" or "sometimes I lean toward a C-o (7) pathway." This can open our ways of communicating with others, and even with ourselves. But even if we take the shorthand route of saying "My baseline is a B-i (4) pattern" or, even shorter, "I lead with a B-i (4)," or, even more concise, "I am a B-i (4)," it may be a step toward embracing the dynamic nature of the vector and attendency processes underlying personality that are inherently fluid processes.

For each of the reflections that emerge in you as you read the chapters ahead, I suggest that you simply soak these in, SIFT them through your mind's gut, heart, and head—the sensations, images, feelings, and thoughts of the energy and information flow of the "embodied brain" we've been exploring—and just sit with this awhile. Soak, sift, and sit. If you want, take some notes, perhaps in a journal, and then we will move through the other aspects of that particular PDP and its growth-edge. You may find one PDP resonates greatly with you, someone close to you, a patient or client, or someone from your past. Knowing how we may have many layers of asso-ciations can be quite helpful in seeing how we are open, or not, to being empathically understanding of what a PDP's experience from the inside out actually might be. "Knowing thyself" is a phrase to remind us that our own awareness, knowing our own blind spots as best we can, and knowing where we are on this life's journey toward wholeness, will be important ways to bringing insight to empathy. Knowing ourselves opens us to become free to know more fully another person.

As we go through each pathway in depth in the following chapters, we will use the following descriptive framework, terminology, and related con-cepts. The notion is for you to be able to get a feeling for the details of each pathway, a sense of how someone might present in clinical work with specific types of issues, and then what strategies might be appropriate for each pathway's specific growth-edge work. Here are the broad organizing sections to get you oriented and ready to dive in.

- Expressed Personality—a capsule summary of some of the major and more externally visible characteristics of the personality pattern.
- Developmental Pathway and Adaptive Strategy—our view of the deeper developmental roots of the pattern from the perspective of the PDP framework.
- Integration and Individual Variation: Strengths and Challenges—a description of how the state of integration of the individual affects expression of the pattern in "higher" and "lower" integrative ways, including an overview of the integrative capacities that yield benefits to a person's life and those vulnerabilities that may create chaos and rigidity when not integrated well.
- Focus of Attention and Blind Spots—a description of the kinds of things or experiences that often attract attention, and the kinds of things or experiences that are often overlooked when the pattern is "running the show" as we live on autopilot, especially with low levels of integration.
- Emotional Processing—a description of major tendencies in the emotional experience and expression of the felt sense of experience and how shifts in integration—the basis of emotion—are handled. Windows of tolerance may be characteristically narrowed for certain emotions within each PDP.
- Cognitive Processing—a description of patterns of thoughts, ideas, perceptions, and concerns that tend to occupy the cognitive aspects of mind, the mental information processing, and then to potentially be expressed in words as thoughts and as external communication such as autobiographical narrative reflections.
- Summing Up—a brief overview of the key features of the pathway.
- Growth-Edge Work—the PDP-specific approaches to cultivating integration that can be the focus of psychotherapeutic work, "widening the

groove" of a PDP, relaxing the habits of mind, focusing on windows of tolerance, personal reactivity, and accessing other adaptive strategies. This section will include a focus on strategies for development, tips for growth in relationships, a clinical example, and short reflections to cultivate integration.

- Integrative Transformation—an overview of the key features of the pattern of developmental pathway and how linking differentiated aspects of the individual's life journey—accessing higher states of integrative functioning of other pathways by tapping into other vectors, attendencies, and emotion-regulation modes—can promote higher integrative levels of functioning and long-lasting change.

As we will see, all nine patterns have distinct yet equally important and valuable gifts, what we are naming *strengths*, which emerge when development is going well, or when intentional growth work has created a well-developed and well-integrated system. As a community of differentiated human beings, having a differentiated set of patterns may be evolutionarily beneficial to achieve more adaptive collective functioning. No pathway is better than another; each has challenges, each has strengths. Helping liberate the integrative capacity to achieve higher functioning at the growth-edge of clinical work is what you will learn in the pages ahead. That growth-edge will be specific to each pathway, and learning about this as a clinician will greatly enhance your capacity to provide specific strategies, skill development, and guidance for your clients.

You can use this PDP model in a range of ways. Interviews with numerous therapists harnessing the Enneagram system, and David's and my use of the PDP framework over many years, reveal how a therapist's use of one of these two personality models in psychotherapy may be expressed and experienced by **(1) helping them understand the nature of a client's life course without ever directly mentioning the personality system to them; (2) guiding their clients directly by exploring with them their likely personality patterns and then addressing the growth-edge work explicitly in the course of therapeutic sessions; and (3) gaining insight into their own personality pattern as a therapist and how their own proclivities and blind**

spots may be impacting how they are understanding clearly and helping effectively their clients in their growth journey.

In utilizing the PDP model as a psychotherapist, I have found that this robust range of usefulness applies as well, with the added benefit of being able to articulate a neuroscience-based developmental model. This sharing of the PDP framework is often readily grasped by clients for the possible origins of their pattern and the ways in which these neural networks can be harnessed now to construct new neural capacities with awareness and intention as we work at their growth-edge toward integration. Based on the science of how the brain develops, the PDP model has also enabled me to provide direct educational input in my role as a therapist into how temperament, subcortical and cortical brain structure and function, attachment, interpersonal relationships more broadly, and the embodied and relational mind itself, can each influence these repeating patterns we call personality. The PDP framework of personality also empowers the process of psychotherapy, as it is fundamentally about how our focus of attention within a trusting relationship can harness the power of neuroplasticity to help cultivate more neural integration in our lives.

As we've seen, it may be that our personality is not the true or core essence of our being—but a way we've adaptively come to filter experience by selectively prioritizing what we attend to and how we tend to respond to get our basic needs met. In everyday life, we may need such a filtering process to sort through the myriad stimuli that come at us from outside and that are generated from within us. Each vector highlights a fundamental need and our motivation to fulfill that need as a sense of agency, bonding, or certainty that serves to filter our experience, set our priorities, focus our attention, and shape what has meaning in our lives. Each attendency confers specific ways we can drive energy through our inner or external world, or dyadically as both. Our temperament of vector and attendency then shapes how we filter the perceptual system's input into meaningful ways of processing what we experience. This is how we survive as we adapt to life's unfolding. Now with therapeutic collaboration, life can move beyond autopilot tendencies of reactivity and surviving to awakened choice of receptivity and thriving. As we've said, this lifetime journey may entail shifting our personality from a limiting prison to a liberating playground.

In other words, to thrive and not merely survive, we may need to learn to live beyond these initial mechanisms of adaptation, shaped by our temperament's proclivities, and learn to more readily access a state of wholeness in our lives. Ironically, as we go deeply into the origins of how we've come to develop into who we think we are, we may find that our true identity, our core essence, is actually more fluid and flexible, more connected, coherent, and content, than we ever may have imagined could be possible. As we journey forward toward security and integration, in life and in this book, we'll have an opportunity to explore how each pathway offers both challenges and strengths in accessing the experience of wholeness. And we'll come to explore how to help those you work with, and yourself, to integrate these pathways for a freer, more fulfilling life.

David and I also found as therapists that various ways of using our emerging PDP framework of personality in the therapeutic process were illuminating and empowering. David did not see this new PDP framework as a contradiction to the Enneagram approach he had been using for decades, though we all recognized it was addressing just a portion of that narrative tradition of the Enneagram as well as the broad field of personality in general. I have also found applying the PDP framework to be consilient with the overall interpersonal neurobiology foundations of psychotherapy, focusing on domains of integration. And while the PDP framework readily acknowledges it is focusing on only a portion of how we become who we are, it serves as a useful cornerstone in a much larger exploration in which we can join with our clients as they grow across many domains of integration in therapy. Together as a PDP group, as scientists and clinicians, we hope you will find that the chapters ahead support and enhance your clinical work.

As David is a co-adventurer with us on this journey to understand wholeness, and as he was, in his loving and wondrous ways, open to lifelong learning throughout his life and into his 80s, we feel confident that he would embrace the reflections we are offering in this PDP view in response to the exquisite details of clinically rich material found in his original writings, some offered here with permission from his literary estate, and on occasion including coauthors when indicated. As we discussed, his direct wording will be placed in *italics* for ease of reference to its origins.

In the following three chapters and their three sections, you'll be invited to explore an in-depth view of the developmental background, presentation, and growth-edge work for each of the nine patterns of developmental pathways. As we've seen, there is a great amount of science that is consilient with these groupings, which form a clinically useful way for you to understand your clients and to "know thyself." Reflecting on the personal as well as the professional as you move ahead is a synthesis that I hope will serve you well in the deep dive we're about to share.

The nine PDPs, organized as a trio of sections within a given vector, can be taken in any sequence that you want, and in this way, the pathway sections of each—Vector A (Chapter 6), Vector B (Chapter 7), and Vector C (Chapter 8)—are independent of one another. What this means is that you are welcome to jump around in this set of the nine ensuing PDP-focused sections as you explore what lies ahead. As mentioned earlier, we will place David Daniels's direct statements in *italics*, and the source of his words that are in any prior publications besides his website and unpublished writings in [brackets]. The final chapters (9, 10, and 11) of the book will offer reflections and integrations that might be best explored after reading at least one of the vectors' sections in depth. Enjoy!

CHAPTER 6

The Agency Vector Personality Patterns

The agency vector includes the agency-inward (A-i), agency-outward (A-o), and agency-dyadic (A-d) pathways. From a developmental perspective, we are proposing these as the underlying mechanisms of the Enneagram personality patterns 1, 8, and 9, respectively. This motivational system provides first-level monitoring and regulation of the general state of empowerment of the body and its sense of self—the empowerment of agency—in interactions with the world. That is, it governs the "volume" of exertion of one's agency in embodying a host of seeking-like appetitive energies as well as the aversive emotion of anger, all of which serve the primal needs for well-being and integrity of the body and its sense of existence in relationship. In traditional Enneagram terms, we might say it regulates how strongly or not the "life force" is poured into the pursuit of goals, needs, and desires. When satisfied, the experiences of congruence, worth, and belonging emerge.

When the trio of pathways within this vector are well integrated, the three agency PDPs provide a general repertoire of equally important but different adaptive strategies for managing the empowerment of agency, depending on the circumstances at hand and the nature of the attendency that is the baseline focus of energy. We are proposing that an adaptive strategy is created that serves as a gateway directing whether this motivational energy is (1) upregulated and allowed to flow freely into empowerment of agency and to become fully embodied in behavior—it is EE: experienced and expressed; (2) downregulated and channeled into more contained or disciplined behavioral expression as CC: contain and channel; or (3) shifted into some other emotional and/or motivational state and RR: reframe and redirect.

Depending on circumstances, each of these general strategies can be what is the most adaptive way of empowering agency; if it is not functioning well, it can instead create significant challenges to well-being. Sometimes it is most adaptive or even vital to allow energy to flow freely into empowered agency, the essence of the A-o pathway. Sometimes, motivational energy is better tempered or disciplined in some way to be maximally effective or socially acceptable, the essence of the A-i pathway. And sometimes it is most adaptive or necessary to shift the motivational state in a different direction—to "let things go"—for example, when pursuit would be fruitless or in some way too risky, or a more compelling need comes along. That is the essence of the A-d pathway. Upregulate, downregulate, or shift. Obviously, these emotion-regulation modes can be either functional and adaptive, or dysfunctional and damaging, depending on the circumstances. Ideal functioning differentiates them and links them in a functional whole. Low integration would mean not having the fluidity and flexibility to draw on different emotion-regulation modes and then be prone to chaos and rigidity as the flow left the window of tolerance in that situation or interaction.

Keep in mind that we are talking here about learned and subsequently reinforced schemas of the fast-thinking "autopilot" functions of mind, rather than top-down, consciously formulated, intentional plans of action. Thus, each of us, at various times, can and often does move through these different modes, adjusting here and there, with little or no conscious intention. The better integrated the PDP system, the more freely that kind of movement can occur. The less well integrated, the less freedom one has to respond most adaptively. **That is all to say that pattern-related problems that bring clients to therapy are more likely to occur when the trio of differentiated pathways within a vector system are not linked, and when the higher functions of other vectors and their trios are less accessible.** When we are limited to just one kind of tool, say, a hammer, we treat everything like a nail. This can happen because in the unique developmental trajectory of each individual, the salience of the different adaptive strategies can vary such that some work better, on average or at sentinel times, than others—and therefore become deeply ingrained. We've named this a "PDP with a deep groove." Therapy makes that neural groove less restrictive, less ingrained, to become what we can simply name "a wider groove," which enables access to a wider range of options.

TABLE 6.1 Developmental Pathways for the Agency Vector

Pathway	Attendency	Regulation of anger and motivation vector
A-i	Inward	Downregulate
A-o	Outward	Upregulate
A-d	Dyadic (inward + outward)	Shift

Anger plays a particularly prominent role in this system when the individual is challenged or threatened and it is the primary aversive reactive energy that the agency vector system manages. Whether or not it is overtly expressed in word or behavior, or even registers in awareness, anger or irritation is an often-palpable undercurrent across all three patterns in this vector. What Panksepp describes as RAGE/Anger is the primal affective system that motivates us to "ramp up" assertive or aggressive power to protect ourselves from violation or to push past barriers to goals (Davis & Panksepp, 2018; Panksepp, 1998). As we shall see in the clinically oriented descriptions of the three personality patterns below, the regulation and processing of anger is distinctly different within each pathway. This is an important point for clinicians to note: Even though anger may be the common baseline initial emotion, especially when a person becomes reactive, some may feel that anger fully, some may channel that anger to minimize it, and some may say they don't experience anger readily at all. Nevertheless, we believe that the correlation of this subcortical motivational network of agency and its accompanying reactive affect of anger, in all its range of intensity, with the trio of these PDPs is robust and likely to be an accurate subcortical source of the motivational drive for these three pathways of this vector.

Please also keep in mind that the initial descriptions that follow lean in the direction of what is typically seen when the individual's agency system is *not* optimally integrated and well developed, and the pattern in that moment is exerting a dominant, largely nonconscious, and often inflexible role in managing the flow of motivational energy and attention. These are likely the less integrative states that you may see in your clinical practice and that motivate people to seek therapeutic help. It is important to keep in mind, however, that each pathway over time has strengths as well as challenges. Each also has a corresponding growth-edge focus of psychotherapy to help cultivate integration in the individual's life. The descriptions ahead are also focused on understanding the dynamics beneath these challenging and commonly shared problems that often bring a client to therapy. The ways you will be able to help a given client will be shaped by which of the nine PDPs may be their go-to, or baseline, primary and secondary pathways.

In Enneagram terms, this set of three personality patterns is considered part of the "body/gut" center of intelligence. We agree that patterns 1, 8, and 9 may experience energy flow as sensate and kinesthetic origins, as gut feelings, but we prefer not to use the notion of a "center of intelligence." Instead, we turn to a motivational system and its accompanying core affects with an ALEAF, the anatomical location of initial energy flow from which that may arise—especially when reactivity occurs. Here in this vector, the motivation network is that of agency for embodied empowerment. The fundamental drive of this system is for the basic needs of survival—for ensuring that the body's needs will be met. In this way there is a "visceral" or bodily sense that often has a feeling arising in the gut, below the diaphragm—of something being of life-and-death importance. In our PDP view, the head's brain is processing these essential needs for survival, and even the notion of agency may involve the motor system within the frontal lobe of the brain's cortex. This cortical processing gives an elaborated meaning or "value" to the core subcortical bodily needs mediated by the brain stem—to regulate digestion, respiration, and the functioning of the cardiovascular system.

While each of the vectors is about survival in this "do-or-die" new life outside the womb, the felt sense of energy flow often seems to originate from an anatomical bodily location—gut, heart, head—an ALEAF that becomes more activated, or at least becomes more salient, more noticed, when the particular subcortical motivational network's propensity is engaged.

From the perspective of Stephen Porges's Polyvagal Theory (2001, 2011, 2024), as we've mentioned earlier, the dorsal branch of the vagus nerve extends down into the subdiaphragmatic organs—including but not limited to the stomach and intestines, mediating our "gut feelings." Of relevance in that theory is the finding that a sense of helplessness and despair is associated with activation of that dorsal vagal branch. In extreme conditions, the "dorsal dive" can be activated and the lowering in heart rate and blood pressure can lead the individual to collapse in a faint. This is the "faint" of the four Fs of reactivity that also include fight, flee, and freeze; these latter three each being energy-consuming states of activation instead of the collapse state of help-lessness with dorsal activation. Naturally, each of us can have these reactive states activated. It may be a part of this trio in the agency vector's emotional processing to more readily activate these reactive states around the emotion of anger than the other vectors' trios. How that PDP's mode of emotion regulation is then activated to handle this deep reactive state will make the experience of that affect of anger quite distinct across the pathways of this agency vector. (Reminder: David's words will be in italics in the entries ahead.)

Case Example

Ross entered counseling expressing anger about what he experiences as his partner, Xia's "off the wall accusations." Ross leads with the Gut/Body Center of Intelligence [PDP view—agency vector and "leads" means a primary PDP that has an anatomical location of energy activation and flow (ALEAF) in the gut/body], *just sensing things and responding sometimes quickly, sometimes slowly (since his gut reaction may take time to build), but often without much forethought or analysis. This gets his partner, Xia, who leads with the Head Center* [PDP view—a baseline certainty vector], *really upset. She tenses up, pulls away, and starts asking Ross challenging questions. From Xia's perspective she is just trying to figure out Ross's reaction, "What does that mean? How did you come up with that?"* [PDP view in plain font: She is driven toward and prioritizes certainty] *Xia loves his grounded energy and ability to truly be present to her, yet she often reacts this way when he doesn't seem clear to her or when she just doesn't understand him. In turn, Ross feels demeaned and accused, leading to angry gut reactivity* [The subcortical motivation network of agency has the primal core affect of anger]*—sometimes he sinks into a sulking withdrawal and at other times* *in sudden eruption rather than pausing and thoughtfully inquiring of himself what this gut hunch, reaction, of his is about.* [Though David doesn't indicate the specific Enneagram type, we can suggest here that this mode seems more like shift than downregulate or upregulate, and so this would lean us to consider the A-d PDP of reframing and redirecting the emotion of anger] *This leads to a circle of escalating conflict resulting in them both withdrawing.*

In our work together, he came to better understand the strengths and challenges of his body-based intelligence [his gut feelings and drive for embodied empowerment via the agency vector], *and learned to pause before responding, do more analysis first (a Head Center attribute)* [Note how he is differentiating and linking to another vector, this one of certainty], and realize and appreciate Xia's leading with the head-based intelligence [the ALEAF of the head initiated by her baseline primary vector of certainty]. *As he became aware of his own leading with body-based, gut intelligence, appreciated Xia's leading with her analytical, head-based intelligence, and worked with his challenges, it greatly reduced these repeated and disruptive episodes in their lives. While she never entered the counseling process, she did extensive reading about the Enneagram and the three centers of intelligence. As a result of her study and Ross's changes, Xia greatly reduced her accusatory questioning and has been more forthcoming to apologize when needed for her over-questioning, at least according to Ross. It's remarkable the changes that take place from understanding the function of the three centers of intelligence and how this functionality manifests in our thoughts, feelings, and actions and they impact our transactions with one another.*

[Source: Daniels & Dion, 2018, pp. 74–75]

Understanding the inner structural dynamics of personality by focusing on which anatomical locations of energy flow and of information processing, which "center of intelligence" in Enneagram terms (or ALEAF and motivational vector in the PDP framework), is being utilized can help open an individual to using other sources of energy flow and motivation, the other ALEAFs and vectors. In our PDP view, these personality patterns are not organized by these physical locations of activation. Instead, they originate from the subcortical motivation network that is particularly active and therefore preferentially cultivated in that pathway. The agency vector is a motivational drive for embodied empowerment to satisfy the individual's basic bodily needs. We have a visceral, gut reaction when our basic bodily needs are not satisfied. When we see this case study through the lens of the motivation of agency for empowerment—the drive to have autonomy, to be able to exert agency to make a difference, to have the capacity to right a wrong—we can understand how one partner may be experiencing the conflict of those needs with the other partner's drive for safety and predictability of the certainty vector.

These vectors set up a state of mind, both within an individual and in the relationship interactions that unfold. Recall that in the interpersonal neurobiological view, our mind is both fully embodied and relational, not just an output of the brain in the head. In this way, the "systems of mind" that are part of a vector may be derived from the subcortical motivational networks in the head's brain, but they directly involve energy flow through the body and through the relational connections that all make up our experience of "mind." Understanding vectors and these systems of mind in couples therapy can be greatly empowering, as the individuals gain insight into the neural processes driving their emotional subjective experience and their interpersonal interactions. Here agency meets certainty, and working out these differences can greatly enable a relationship to become more flexible, compassionate, and kind.

A-i: Agency-inward (A-i Pathway; Enneagram 1)

Expressed Personality

In the agency-inward (A-i) pattern we see a personality that is highly motivated to be and stand for good, right, and better, and one that avoids being bad, wrong, or lazy. It is as though life orients around highly held ethical and moral standards of right and wrong, competence, correctness, improvement, discipline, and idealism. An inner critical voice is always close at hand, judging how things, others, and especially an inner self are falling short of expectations. This personality pattern seems to operate as if there is a deeply embedded belief along the lines of "My worthiness and lovability depend on being and standing for good and right in this imperfect world." It is as though there is an ultimate fear of being so bad as to be totally unworthy of regard or love. As a result, there is a pressure to be good and right. Being bad or wrong is judged harshly and a source of shame or reason for punishment. This means it's important to restrain impulse and expression of anger.

Brief Description	The 1 believes you must be good and right to be worthy. Consequently, 1s are conscientious, responsible, improvement-oriented, and self-controlled, but also can be critical, resentful, and self-judging.
Key Interventions	Help 1s notice and reduce the dominance of the critical mind, appreciate error as difference, and accept and integrate desire and instinct as the path to wholeness.

[Source: The Narrative Enneagram, 2020, pp. 48–49]

Developmental Pathway and Adaptive Strategy

This personality pattern is rooted in how the agency vector and the attendency inward drives the motivational energy to become tempered into effective and socially acceptable ways of being. Attention and the subsequent flow of energy are inwardly oriented around internalized maps—schemas and templates of learned standards of right versus wrong and "rules of engagement." Embodied expression of the host of motivations to nurture and protect the integrity of the body and its sense of self, notably including anger, is generally *downregulated* by being contained and channeled into a more disciplined, tempered, or constrained stance.

Integration and Individual Variation: Strengths and Challenges

As with all the personality patterns, there is a wide spectrum of variation in the rigidity or flexibility with which this PDP is held and drives behavior.

When the A-i pattern is dominant and the higher functions of the other vectors, attendencies, and modes are well integrated, the flow of attention and energy into behavioral expression is well tempered and wisely harnessed. Differences can be seen as differences rather than imperfections or wrongs. The personality is well but compassionately disciplined, embodying the highest standards of ethical and moral integrity with grace both in personal conduct and leadership, inspiring in orientation to improvement, highly dependable, self-reliant, clear in an inner map of intention, and highly motivated to do the best possible at whatever the individual sets out to do.

On the other hand, when integration is impaired, the expressed personality takes on a more strident and forceful feel, as if worthiness and love are contingent on always being good, correcting error, never being wrong or making mistakes, and complying with the dictates of an ever-present, often harsh inner critic demanding better in everything, first and foremost of one's individual, inner self. When less than perfect happens, there can be what feels like an imperative to correct and make the inner self, other individuals, or situations better. Here the individual can be overly judgmental, demanding, controlling, nitpicking, patronizing, critical of others and even more so of the personal inward self, and can seem constantly annoyed or resentful at life and others in a righteously perfectionistic way. In sharp contrast to the A-o pattern, where anger is freely expressed, anger that does come out tends to be more contained in the form of simmering resentment or annoyed judgment.

Behavioral Profile	**Strengths:** *Persistent effort, correct action, honesty, responsibility, concern for improvement, accomplishment, idealism, high standards, self-reliance, dedication.*
	Difficulties: *Critical of self and others, never satisfied with performance, compulsive need to improve, preoccupied with "should" and "what must be done," difficulty in accepting imperfection, will not cooperate if standards are too high.*

[Source: David Daniels, "Enneagram Type 1 Description: The Perfectionist."
https://drdaviddaniels.com/type-1]

Focus of Attention and Blind Spots

Attention is almost magnetically drawn to what is wrong, bad, or in need of improvement or correction, whether major or minor, according to the individual's own highly held internal standards. Mostly these standards conform to general social or externally imposed norms, but not always. For example, defiance of "wrong" social norms can be "right" according to the individual's own inner template of good and right. That inner template can be specific to each individual, differing across a group of those in the A-i PDP for example, and not always simply conforming to accepted norms of behavior.

If errors and what needs correction or improvement occupy the filter of attention and screen of awareness, other aspects of experience become blind spots or are harder to take in. It can be very difficult to see the value or good in others' behaviors or points of view or ways of doing things, or to be comfortable with ambiguity or the middle ground. And it can be easy to underappreciate what is good, done well, or going well. Very importantly, a tendency to keep a tight lid on expression of anger can make one oblivious to how annoyance or irritation at the many things in life that don't go as they "should" can leak out in body language and affective tone *at* others.

Emotional Processing

More than any other feature, a strong superego or conscience reigns supreme, and is the focal point for much of the work toward change. This may unfold in several interesting ways. First, there is very often a pattern of keeping a well-tempered lid on expression of impulse and desire, as if to avoid "bad" overindulgence, or to not make a spectacle of oneself. The typical result is a somewhat buttoned-up, serious, no-nonsense, play-only-after-work demeanor.

Second, exaggerated feelings of failure, guilt, or shame come quickly to the fore when things don't work out perfectly or live up to ideals. Avoiding these contributes significantly to the motivational energy to be better, work hard, and fix wrongs. They also contribute to an exaggerated sense of personal responsibility when things don't go well, even when fault lies elsewhere.

While everyone's anger is triggered by violations of standards of right and good or irresponsibility, in this case the threshold for such triggering out of receptivity and into reactivity is low because the standards are especially high. However, things can get complicated, because in general, allowing spontaneous expression of anger is "bad" behavior. So, expression of anger tends mostly to be contained—often beneath the radar of awareness—and channeled by rules and standards into a tight-lipped, controlling, and critical demeanor often flavored with simmering frustration or resentment palpable to others, but with occasional outbursts of righteous anger. This can set up obvious difficulties in personal and professional relationships where, from the A-i client's perspective, correction of others is a way of helping them be their very best, but from the others' perspective it is perceived as critical, judgmental control.

Cognitive Processing

A harshly critical inner voice manifests in thought and narrative themes revolving around annoyance or judgment of situations or others *but even more, of one's inner self*, and a tendency to take responsibility when things don't go well. Also, black-or-white thinking tends to frame things in polarities of good or bad, right or wrong. What was good or well done is often given little notice or even discounted because that is expected. Simmering anger can reveal itself in bulldog holds on resentments, refusals to forgive, talk of annoyances, or righteous indignation. Righteous causes are embraced with righteous energy.

A fascinating dynamic around play, which comes only after work as if pleasure must be earned, is often seen. For example, many in whom this pattern is dominant describe being able to let go of their typical reins of inhibition and indulge fully in pleasurable or impulsive behavior—sometimes to a degree that seems antithetical to the normal character—by intentionally stepping out of their usual environment. It's as if the superego stays home when you go away on vacation. In traditional teaching this is called "trap door behavior."

Summing Up

All of the above is often summed up with the label "perfectionist," "moralist," or "reformer" in conventional Enneagram terminology. When the A-i pattern is running the show, when it is not integrated with other vectors, attendencies, and modes of emotion regulation, behavioral patterns that lead to problems sometimes needing to be addressed in therapy are neatly summed up by Beatrice Chestnut (2013, pp. 412–413) as follows:

1. "Measuring everything against an ideal standard and driving for perfection in yourself, others, and/or the external environment through the operation of an 'inner critic.'"
2. "Conscientiously following the rules as part of an overall effort to avoid making mistakes."
3. "Repressing and over-controlling feelings, needs and impulses."

Note how all reflect an inward orientation of attention to rules and standards, and how the second and third reflect the tendency to lean toward restraint in the central dilemma of *agency versus restraint*, which we see as an outcome of the contain-and-channel downregulation of emotion as an adaptive strategy for the A-i PDP.

Growth-Edge Work

For Type 1 the inner critic or judging mind dominates life, dividing almost everything into right and wrong. In a world that severely punished impulse and bad behavior, pattern one must follow the dictates of the inner judge. To be up to this task, the critical mind, the voice of judgment, hypertrophies all out of proportion. So for Type 1, healing primarily involves becoming less dominated by the dictates of the critical mind and, in time, becoming again more undivided, whole. This means coming to appreciate that which was judged as wrong as actually differences among us. There are many ways, many paths. In fact, amongst pattern one there are as many "one right ways" as there are pattern ones since we all are

*different. What is right and wrong really depends on where you "sit in the world"
and ones learn that right and wrong are very relative to the culture.*

[Source: The Narrative Enneagram, 2020, p. 49]

Strategies for Development

- *Release the critical mind's domination y working with the negative superego
  (become discerning about the "shoulds").*
- *Replace "should" with "what do I want?"*
- *Appreciate errors, mistakes, and imperfection as differences.*
- *Make little "mistakes" deliberately, such as not making the bed.*
- *Observe the constant monitoring for comparison purposes (good/bad, perfect/
  imperfect).*
- *Welcome anger and guilt as signals for "unacceptable" behavior, which is
  often. "forbidden" or pleasurable.*
- *Explore all your feelings.*
- *Practice acceptance and forgiveness, rather than improvement.*
- *Integrate instinct and desire.*
- *Reconnect the mind and body through meditation, breathing.*
- *Pay attention to basic physical needs (I'm tired, hungry, etc.).*
- *Stop hourly to sense the body and physically relax any tightness.*
- *Make a list of pleasurable activities when the critical mind lets go; schedule at
  least one a day.*
- *Practice playing before working on occasion.*
- *Discriminate between the perfectionism of the mind and perfection in the moment.*
- *Spend equal time noticing what is "right."*
- *Use humor.*
- *Be as compassionate as possible [toward yourself.*

[Source: The Narrative Enneagram, 2020, p. 49]

Tips for Growth in Relationships
Relational Triggers

*Unfairness. Irresponsibility. Things being done the wrong way. The flagrant ignor-
ing or disobeying of sound rules. Being unjustly criticized. Being lied to, manipulated, tricked or unjustly blamed.*

Relational Reflections

As a Type 1, we need to notice and then give ourselves permission to reduce the power we give away to critical judgment. Instead, we need to learn to rely on thoughtful discernment. We can and will be safe without that critical voice so harshly running the show. Observe the tendency to self- and other-punish—judge, scold, or berate—when errors are made. This automatic dynamic can be hard on relationships, in particular, the relationship to ourselves can suffer under such scrutiny and incrimination and impact our availability to love and receive. Learn new ways of engaging with perceived error and interacting with more conducive-to-well-being solutions for improvement and correction.

Also, as Type 1s, we need to accept and integrate our personal desires and pleasures into our lives, alongside our conscientiousness, dutifulness, high standards and commitment to responsibilities. This not only enhances our own lives, but the lives of all those who love us and interact with us. Becoming more tolerant is a virtue worth exploring and allowing, as it can ease much unnecessary tension held in the soma (body).

We will also want to learn to discern if what we judge to be errors or wrongdoings are actually, or more simply, differences, ones that come from our fundamentally different aptitudes and talents. Allow ourselves to see these differences appreciatively and with gratitude, instead of with condemnation or frustration. Remind ourselves that the goal is to be whole, not perfect.

[Source: Daniels & Dion, 2018, pp. 105–106]

In relationships, the challenge for this pattern is to tap into the capacity to soften how experience is received with curiosity, openness, acceptance, and love (COAL). This COAL state is the essence of being mindful and likely mediated by the capacity to tap into an open, receptive state of awareness. In essence, the PDP framework suggests that the drive to control can be replaced with the equanimity and serenity that comes from resting in open awareness. The COAL acronym can also be used in a slightly different manner (connection, open awareness, and love) as well as its alternative usage (curious, open, accepting, and loving) and is helpful to summarizing the core of the integration of consciousness. In many ways, this aligns with David Daniels and Terry Saracino's five-A approach to working with the Enneagram that includes awareness, acceptance, appreciation, action, and adherence (see pages 15–16 of The Narrative Enneagram's *The Enneagram for Therapists, Counselors, and Coaches* [2020]).

Growing toward wholeness with the PDP of A-i involves differentiation and linkage. First, the deep differentiation of the ways one developed adaptive strategies to find an inner sense of peace amid a world quite distinct from the ideal template we generate inside our minds can be acknowledged. Then the individual can link these to other differentiated attendencies, vectors, and emotion-regulation modes to gain the freedom of integrative transformation. Letting that inner map and drive for an ideal world soften, we come to rest in the clarity of seeing life as it is, and embracing with gratitude, compassion, and awe a wider and freer sense of an expanded self at peace in the world.

The mind is both embodied and relational—and as a PDP is a pattern in which the self-organizing functions of the mind may have followed a certain pathway, we can see how the ways we connect with others within close interpersonal relationships will be a fundamental part of our lives. In this way, the A-i PDP, though with an inward attendency, directly shapes relational ways in which the mental life of the individual is woven into the relational fabric of that person's world. Mind is fully embodied and fully relational. Personality is one way the mind is expressing its way of shaping its emergence in the world.

Clinical Vignette

A 45-year-old woman, Sue Ellen, was ending her 15-year marriage when she came to me for therapy at the urging of her office mate at work. Resigned to leaving her husband, she told me that his "way of being with her" had changed from his following her directives as he had since their months of first living together to his becoming more assertive and "unhelpful" around the house. She wasn't sure why he had changed, she said, but this new "roommate" wasn't what she had "signed up for." When we explored her feelings with this shift in his behavior, she described a resentment toward his finding a way to irritate her with his inattentiveness to the details of their lives—the cleanliness of the kitchen, the commitments to what they had decided to do on the weekends, his insistence on not consulting with her when things were done by workers around the house.

When I conducted an Adult Attachment Interview (AAI) with Sue Ellen and could sense that she had a dismissive adult state of mind with respect to attachment—with the classic findings of her not being able to recall much of her childhood and yet insisting that her childhood experiences "did not impact" her development or life in general—it also fit with the impression that her primary mode of relating to others was in a logical, analytic, transactional manner. When we explored aspects of her PDP with simply a set of initial exploratory questions about what emotions dominated her life, especially when she became stressed, her dominant vector was that of agency, expressed as irritation and anger and an intense focus on how things "should be," consistent with an inward attendency in this vector. She had a well-developed inner template for how things ought to be in the world and tried to contain and channel her anger when things didn't go as expected.

Though they had chosen to not have children, this patient said that she and her husband never quite came to a shared understanding of why that was their choice. On some level she felt that something "was missing" from her life; she had always thought she would be a mother but never really wanted to have her own children. In that session, while discussing this topic, she became irritated with herself, saying how she really couldn't "keep up with my own expectations." I wanted to laugh along with her but kept quiet, as she was dead serious.

This combination of a dismissing attachment strategy and her A-i PDP led to a feeling in the room of an inward focus, a lack of connection with me as her therapist, and possibly with her husband by way of her historical descriptions. In my own mind, it felt as if the key work was to sense into how she might come to feel connected with me in therapy, to lighten up the intensity of her dismissing attachment strategy, and then see if the groove of her A-i PDP might be made a bit less deep. From a conceptual approach, this would mean enabling her to come to feel the importance of relational connection via the bonding vector, and perhaps even embrace the uncertainty and risks of being vulnerable that would evoke the certainty vector and the experience of fear. This is how we'd try to tap into the motivational energy of the other vectors.

I decided to directly name both the attachment strategy and the PDP as ways her life course may have been shaped up to this moment. Naturally, with the dismissive AAI findings, the strategy of survival in that state of mind with respect to attachment is to minimize the need for others and to deny the importance of ongoing relationships. Having a high set of internal standards in her PDP of A-i would synergize with that attachment mindset, and likely would have deepened the groove of that pathway for her. I offered questions as to whether she'd like to know more about these and other developmental issues, and if so, how much scientific detail to provide. I was attempting to join with her logical, language-based left hemisphere, which might have served as a haven from the likely avoidant attachment of her youth, and the unfulfilled longings that as a child she would have felt emotionally more within her growing right hemisphere, as it receives direct input from the signals of the body. While you might think this was reinforcing her already dominant left cortical mode—and you'd be correct—I thought of it more as aligning both with her strengths and with an aspect of her that might be quite resistant to change in either the attachment strategy domain or in the widening of the groove of her PDP. An inner template of the "should" of life and the rights-and-wrongs likely have a left-hemisphere dominance as well. The right hemisphere is more comfortable with ambiguity than the left's drive for predictability and certainty. Once we could align with each other in this way, connecting directly to her potential resistance at first, we could then proceed and explore other networks in her nervous system that may have lain dormant for decades.

Going into new ways of relating immediately activates the certainty vector's fear of the unknown and unfamiliar; and it activates the bonding vector's longing for relational connection and potential separation distress. Attachment-wise, working toward closeness and coming to feel the reality that relationships do, in fact, actually matter also goes against the understandable strategies someone with a likely avoidant attachment of disconnection had to learn, as best they could, when they were young and dependent on those who were not dependable to meet their emotional needs for closeness. Notice how in this case, the PDP framework suggests that her temperament's early organizing features of a vector of agency and an inward attendency would be intensified—not created—by her likely history of avoidant attachment relationships. Her longings to be connected, unfulfilled in that emotionally disconnected family world, could have made her bonding vector more sensitive or even her certainty vector more engaged. But here we are seeing through the PDP lens how the drive of the agency vector, likely present as a sensitivity of her temperament, helps us to envision how her inward attendency of temperament gets expressed. The emotional mode of contain and channel then drives the further adaptation to downregulate anger into the template of inner "should-maps" of life and she is able to be the adaptable daughter to fit into the cold emotional world of her parents' home.

As Sue Ellen's therapy unfolded, a number of relational moments ultimately arose focusing on the connection she and I were sharing. As she began to pursue other romantic opportunities after her divorce, she could now name her PDP proclivities as "shoulding on myself" and began to have a sense of humor about how this had been useful to her in her youth but then had become a prison for her in her adult life. As we continue our work to this day, this perspective is helping the strengths of her PDP—to be comprehensive, conscientious, and detail-oriented in her work and personal life—to blossom. She is also embracing the uncertainty of life with more ease and the need for closeness in bonding with more equanimity. True connection through becoming present, to have a serenity in simply being with a partner, is the new way of relating that is emerging in her life now. In these ways, a more integrative PDP for Sue Ellen is her powerful A-i pathway becoming more a playground than a prison in her life.

Short Reflections for Integration
What the mind sees as wrong or needing to be corrected
Simply stop to notice how your mind repeatedly goes to error and what you judge as needing correcting and practice discerning what really needs correcting.

Inner critical voice

Simply stop to notice the judgmental edge and bodily energy in your inner critical voice and how often it is present and practice softening and releasing from it.

Judging others and being judged

Simply notice how often you are in reactivity in your body and how this points to judging yourself and feeling judged. Then inquire of yourself about just releasing from judgments that are just associated with old no longer valid beliefs.

[Source: David Daniels, "Growth for Type 1: The Perfectionist." https://drdaviddaniels.com/growth-for-type-1]

Integrative Transformation

The agency-inward pathway is an invitation to accept the reality that many of life's challenges do not need our control and are not our fault. The "serenity" of this acceptance is more than a cognitive shift in perspective; the integrative growth enables the agency motivational network to be empowered with the movement from a doing mode of existence to a being mode of living.

Accessing the other vectors and attendencies is the work of integration— to differentiate and link to the higher, more developed, more actualized capacities of the bonding vector and to broaden attendency to include outward and dyadic. Ironically and marvelously, the conscientious map-making mind and visceral drive of the A-i PDP can be released from low integrative states of a hyperfocus on right-versus-wrong judgment to the powerful energy of careful and thorough attention to creating gifts of doing and of being in the world in which we live.

The journey back to wholeness invites an acknowledgment that our needs are not always able to be met by having a preset map of how "things should be"—and in this integrative growth, opening to a broader sense of simply being rather than "should being" is at the heart of this change. The vulnerability that arises with such a relaxing of inward control can be challenging. This shift to "letting life happen" opens the individual to the strengths of bonding with others and letting go of the need for absolute certainty while embracing the reality that predictability does not need to be attained to feel whole. Wholeness entails an open state of awareness, not something that needs to be controlled, predicted, or constructed. In this way, moving attention outward and opening to the experience of awe and beauty in the world that does not need to be controlled but simply appreciated is a liberating shift in this transformative growth.

A-o: Agency-outward (A-o Pathway; Enneagram 8)

Expressed Personality

This is a big personality, often occupying more space than the physical body. With attention oriented most prominently by the stream of information about external objects of need or desire, and threats or obstacles to well-being, the directionality or "oomph" of this pathway is aimed distinctly outward toward direct energetic engagement with the world and others.

Here, we see a powerfully energized personality full of appetitive gusto in pursuing all manner of needs and desires. At the same time, we see directness and ease in projecting strength and directing others to ensure justice, fairness, and a sense that situations are under control, and comfort expressing anger when it is needed to push against people or situations threatening to a personal self or close others. To others the fully expressed persona can seem impulsive, overly impactful, excessive, or worse when in low states of integration.

Beneath—often far beneath—the strong, powerful, and outwardly directed persona is a vulnerable and surprisingly tender heart. Yet inner feelings of vulnerability and dependency tend to be denied, particularly when the system is less well developed. There is a deeply embedded belief along the lines of "I must be strong and powerful to ensure protection and regard for myself and others I care about in this rough-and-tumble world."

Brief Description	*The 8 believes you must be strong and powerful to assure protection and regard in a tough world. Consequently, Protectors seek justice and are direct, strong and action-oriented, but also can be overly impactful, excessive and sometimes impulsive.*
Key Interventions	*Help 8s notice intensity and reduce impulsiveness, appreciate differences and vulnerability, and realize and moderate impact on others.*

[Source: The Narrative Enneagram, 2020, pp. 42–44]

Developmental Pathway and Adaptive Strategy

In the PDP framework this personality pattern is rooted in the developmental pathway and adaptive strategy of allowing embodied expression of both appetitive motivations to empower agency to pursue satisfaction of all manner of somatic needs and desires, and the empowering motivation of anger in defense of the body and its sense of existence in the world. Attention and the subsequent flow of motivational energy are outwardly oriented by objects of need, desire, or threat. Emotional motivations are allowed to flow freely outward, into embodied expression in an upregulated "take charge of the situation and go for it" stance of agency.

Integration and Individual Variation: Strengths and Challenges

When this personality pattern is well integrated, the flow of attention and energy into behavioral expression is well tempered and wisely channeled through access to the balancing proclivities of the other pathways—the other vectors and attendencies. Notably, awareness and acceptance of one's own vulnerability (going inward) and the impact of one's big energy on others (accessing the motivational drive for bonding) brings powerful capacities for empathy and caring. The personality is equally generous of its big spirit and courageous in confronting threats to a personal self and others; a natural leader willing and able to take charge and exert power wisely in the service of truth, justice, honesty, fairness, and protecting the vulnerable. Anger is expressed freely when it needs to be but is regulated productively, effectively, and sensitively. Such a high-functioning A-o pattern of personality could arise with a history of secure attachment, where these positive qualities of this pathway would be valued and reinforced.

On the other hand, when integration is impaired and not well developed and the A-o pathway is a baseline and quite dominant in regulating empowerment, we see a "my way or the highway" personality that tends to be impulsive; self-serving and prone to excess in pursuit of needs and desires; overly assertive and controlling; anger-driven, in the extreme, to the point of being intimidating or abusive; unaware of the impact of their energy and anger on others; and in denial of weakness or vulnerability of a personal inner self. It's easy to imagine how a history of nonsecure attachment in circumstances that led the child to feel vulnerable, or where coherent discipline was not exercised, could make this pathway particularly adaptive and magnify its development.

Behavioral Profile	**Strengths:** *Strong and powerful, exciting, intense, determined, courageous, persistent, protective of others, just, friendly, truthful, fair, clear and straightforward, firm.*
	Difficulties: *Too much, too soon, too loud, too long, too many—all lead to exhaustion, self-abuse, rejection, and other self-defeating behaviors; denial of fear, weakness, vulnerability, and limits; desire for control may result in a counterattack, loss, defeat of own goals, or trouble with authority, mixing up justice with revenge, sometimes with resulting self-vengeance, missing the virtues of tenderness, dependency, passivity, and sensitivity.*

[Source: David Daniels, "Enneagram Type 8 Description: The Protector."
https://drdaviddaniels.com/type-8]

Focus of Attention and Blind Spots

Attention (and therefore energy) is attracted quickly toward objects of desire and need and the pursuit of pleasure. It is also drawn to evidence of threats to integrity of body or self, injustices, unfairness, untruth, betrayals, provocation, and to vulnerable others or underdogs who need protection. The state and competence of power and control of situations in which individuals with this pattern find themselves also get special attention. This is less about a stereotypical notion that they must always be the controller, and more about a deep "need" to feel the situation is under control.

While these things mostly occupy the radar of attention and fill the screen of awareness, other aspects of experience tend to get less attention and become blind spots or are harder to take in. Notable can be a lack of awareness of the overwhelming impact of their big energy on others. Relationship difficulties related to this often bring clients to therapy. In this state, there may be a tremendous amount of caring yet with little revealed as empathic understanding or insight into the importance of being vulnerable in life. Equally important, as they forge ahead ensuring justice, fairness, and competence in the world, they have a strong tendency to overlook or disregard physical or psychological pain, as well as their own real limitations and vulnerabilities. Instead, vulnerability tends to be projected onto others.

Emotional Processing

Several features of this pattern merit emphasis. First and foremost, while anger issues are often prominent in what brings clients to therapy and get a lot of attention from others, this pattern is about much more than just big expression of anger. It is about expressing appetitive emotions and passions with gusto. There is a driving lust for life with big expression all around, and an almost constitutional push against *external* obstacles and boundaries.

Second, anger tends to be freely experienced and expressed, and anger-fueled engagement with others comes relatively easily. Many in whom this pattern is dominant agree with the notion that "anger has gotten a bad rap," and report that confrontation feels clarifying because you know who stands where about what and you know what you're dealing with. Conversely, failure of others to engage energetically can raise anxiety about trustworthiness and potential hidden agendas. You may imagine how problems with anger management in relationships of all sorts often bring clients to therapy at the request of their partner.

Third, the free expression of anger is part of a larger pattern of projecting power and control to conceal a sensitive core of vulnerability, as mentioned earlier. Denial of feelings of weakness or vulnerability is characteristic (though not unique to this pattern). Health crises also may bring these clients to therapy. In general, the root cause can be traced to the combination of blindness to their own limitations and vulnerabilities, and the tendency to "burn the candle at both ends." The attuned therapist will be alert to cues of the denial of vulnerability behind this "big energy" and excessiveness.

At the same time, the sensitive and tender core often shows itself in the way these clients step boldly forward—and sometimes overextend themselves in the process—to protect or care for others who are vulnerable, in pain, and needing help. It is very much as if vulnerability of a personal self, which tends to be denied, resonates in the reflection of others' vulnerability and then motivates caring and protective behavior.

Cognitive Processing

Thoughts and ideas tend to be expressed very freely and directly, with passion and little censorship, often "colorfully," and with the same "what you see is what you get" subtext. Themes of thought and narrative tend to revolve around untruth, unfairness, injustice, betrayal, incompetence, and the state of power and control in their environment, and what needs to be done to fix the situation. There is often preoccupation with righting injustices or, in the extreme, retribution or vengeance. Perceptions of threat or danger are prone to mental amplification, and action taken in response tends to be out of proportion. There is a tendency to magnify the threat of injustices, betrayals, deceit, enemies, or incompetence, or see more than in actuality exists.

Summing Up

All of the above is often summed up with the label "protector," "challenger," "active controller," or "boss" in conventional Enneagram terminology. When the A-o pattern is dominant, behavioral patterns that lead to problems are neatly summed up by Beatrice Chestnut (2013, pp. 123–126) as follows:

1. "Rebelling against outside authority and denying (internal and external) limitations."
2. "Focusing on and acting from power and strength as overcompensation for denied powerlessness and weakness."
3. "Avoiding and denying vulnerable feelings and dependence on others."

Growth-Edge Work

Growth for the A-o PDP invites an accessing of inner reflection and an acceptance of the needs for relying on others and for becoming curious and accepting of others' inner mental lives. The challenge is to enable such transformations to work with the tension that comes with relaxing the belief that empowerment only comes with assertion, rather than that true power comes with vulnerability and acceptance.

Strategies for Development

- *Moving from a cognitive habit of my truth and retribution to a cognitive awareness that the world naturally will sense and arrive at the truth and find balance organically.*
- *Moving from emotional intensity imposed on others/outward to more of an internal emotional feeling of innocence and unprejudiced feelings or unbiased power.*
- *Developing wholeness requires integration of personality and essence. This is the work of living well and of well-being. The higher state work of reclaiming essence and the personal work of developing a high functioning personality, not*

only augment each other, they require each other. The work of integration of being is both/and not either/or.

[Source: David Daniels, "Integrating the Higher Qualities of our Essence into our Lives." https://drdaviddaniels.com/integrating-essence-true-nature-lives/]

Notice and moderate your intensity, excess, and impact

- *Allow a gap between impulse and action so there is time to consider consequences (count to 10 and breathe).*
- *Observe the all-or-nothing style of paying attention.*
- *Consider the virtue in the mundane, the moderate and the mild.*
- *Practice delaying gratification and stimulation.*
- *Investigate the difference between weakness and vulnerability.*
- *Practice doing things someone else's way (start small, at first).*
- *Realize that true power comes from the appropriate application of force.*
- *Learn that flexibility and adaptability are empowering.*
- *Value the truth in opposites and differences.*
- *Build kindness toward oneself and others, opening the heart.*
- *Notice what happens just before anger arises.*
- *Use anger to focus and clarify, not blame.*
- *Identify feelings other than anger.*
- *Record insights as they occur.*

[Source: The Narrative Enneagram, 2020, p. 43]

Tips for Growth in Relationships
Relational Triggers

Deceit. Manipulation. People who won't stand up for themselves. Indirectness or beating around the bush. Liars. People that we perceive as fake. People that don't have our backs. Weakness. Boundaries or rules that are too constraining. People abusing their power and that need to be put in their place. Injustice and unfairness.

Underneath, your ultimate concern or fear is being totally vulnerable and powerless. Therefore that which stresses you and makes you most personally reactive is: perceived injustices you can't correct; deceitful or manipulative people;

people who won't stand up for themselves; weakness in yourself; inaction; bound-aries or rules that are unjust or constraining; and/or attempts to control you. These reactions block your being vulnerable, impacted, and trustingly connected to others, and ultimately, your sensing reality as it comes to you freshly in each moment.

[Source: The Narrative Enneagram, 2020, pp. 42–44]

Relational Reflections

As a Type 8, we need to become aware of our intensity, exuberance, big-ger-than-life convictions, and ability to easily intimidate others. We can give our-selves permission to reduce our impulsivity, knowing it will not dull our enjoyment of and lust for life. Our task is to learn to appreciate vulnerability, tenderness, and receptivity as strengths rather than as weaknesses.

As 8s, allow ourselves to realize and moderate our impact on others, our ability to dismiss others, overpower others, and instead, to stay present to others' reactions and responses to us, in real time. Can we adjust as we become more tuned in, reciprocal, and attentive? Can we "take others in" and listen to their perspectives? Can we allow receptivity? Keep in mind, receptivity does not mean we have lost ourselves or have gone soft on something important to us.

Challenge ourselves to come freshly to each situation, as our innate inno-cence knows how to do, and allow that innocence to be cultivated within us; if we inspire it to do so, it will return to us. In the process, we can allow ourselves to appreciate others' sense of truth, justice, and fairness. We can allow others to experience their need for power, as well as to express their own authentic power, in our presence.

[Source: Daniels, 2004, p. 9]

The mind is both embodied and relational—and as a PDP is a pattern in which the self-organizing functions of the mind have followed a certain path-way, we can see how the ways we connect with others within close interper-sonal relationships will be a fundamental part of our lives. In this way, the A-o PDP, with the empowerment motivational drive of agency and the out-ward attendency, brings an intense externally focused energy of life directly into relational ways as the mental processes of the individual become woven into the relational fabric of that person's interpersonal world. Mind is fully embodied and fully relational and working with these two aspects of mind is important in growth-edge clinical work.

Clinical Vignette

Megan and Stan came for couples therapy with the presenting issue that she wanted him to accept that their daughter was marrying an unemployed sculptor. Stan told me at the start of the session that "I just don't believe in this psychobabble you therapists speak" and that he agreed to come to this one session only because Megan insisted he join her to "help her deal with their new son-in-law." Megan, in contrast, said she needed help and wasn't "getting anywhere with this stubborn man," who had let their daughter know that if she went ahead with her plans, he wasn't going to see her anymore and would write her out of their will. "Whatever of the little we have we can give to her brother—or donate it to the art museum down the street."

When I asked the couple how the two of them were getting along, it was clear they had different takes on the question. Stan said, "We get along fine. There's nothing needing fixing here, doc." Megan looked sheepishly away and then quietly said, "The main thing is Barb's marriage, that's really it." Sometimes in traditional couples therapy a strategy that is useful is to offer individual sessions during the initial evaluation phase, but when I offered this to them, Stan quickly told me this was likely the only session we'd have. Megan looked distraught at that limitation, but said she was open to meeting alone if this was helpful. I knew this first meeting would be key to any chance to help them out.

In reviewing their relationship with their daughter, Barb, it became readily apparent that Stan never approved of any of the three prior long-term romantic relationships she had, and now, at 33, she was ready to "tie the knot with the worst of them," Stan insisted. Megan offered that she had never seen Barb look so happy and fulfilled, and that her fiancé, Rick, also seemed happy and a great match for their daughter. When Megan pointed out to Stan that no matter the profession or employment of Barb's boyfriends, none of them seemed to satisfy him, Stan said that "Rick just wants her for her money" and that Barb's full-time employment as a teacher in the local school was "the stability he really is after."

It turned out that Stan had offered Rick a position in the grocery store he managed in a neighboring town. Rick declined the offer, saying he wanted to "waste his time doing his sculpting," Stan said. The intensity of Stan's bodily energy at these various dismissive comments gave me a sense of the inner drive of his potential pattern in this moment. But how could I pursue an exploration of this with someone so uninterested in diving more deeply into what might be going on? I chose to give a big-picture view of where we might go, realizing that this might be the single chance we had. In asking Stan about what it was in Rick that made him so sure he didn't want to offer his support, Stan's response was illuminating: "How in the world would you think that any reasonable father would want his daughter to marry someone who can't earn a penny?" Megan quickly stepped in and reminded Stan and told me that Rick had applied for an arts fellowship for his sculpting and was waiting to hear back soon. I asked Stan if he remembered that, and he said he did but didn't care. Stan was tough.

When I offered a long-distance view of couples "finding a way" once they have found each other, Megan reminded Stan that he, too, had been unemployed when they first met. "But I believed in you, and you came through." There was silence, and I could sense that something in Stan felt very uncomfortable. "You had been frustrated with the different things you had tried to do—the bowling alley, the laundering service, the deliveries— but once you found which way to go, you made it all work. Rick may be just the same."

Because of the press of time, I did something I don't usually do—offer, in this first session, a big-picture sense of how we all come into life with a temperament we don't choose and an attachment setting we adapt to as best we can. Whatever that combination provides us, we can go down different pathways, I told them; how we learn about these can help us shape how our brain continues down that particular direction or not. It's up to you, I said, how you'd like to proceed. They both seemed intrigued, so I continued.

I gently started the story from the beginning, as you and I have seen in our own journey—highlighting how there was a time, for each of us, that all was fine and we didn't need to do a thing, just simply be. We remember that deeply, I said to each of them, slowly and looking at Megan and then at Stan, and we know that just being at ease is something we are familiar with, something we once had that somehow—once we are born—seems a distant past. I knew that was a tricky way to start, but something about how he had responded to Megan's reminding him of his own vulnerability when they first met and then "finding his way," gave me the feeling this would be a potentially accessible way to connect—with his implicit memory of something being right, at ease, whole.

And then, depending on what deep brain circuits are particularly sensitive to this new do-or-die setup out here in the world, I told them, we may be especially tuned in to issues related to being empowered with agency. Or we may be tuned in to being connected with bonding. Or we may be especially tuned in to safety with a certainty circuit. For some of us, then, we may find our lives filled with energy around experiencing—or avoiding—certain emotions. For agency it's anger; for bonding it's sadness or being distressed with separation; for certainty it's fear. And then I asked if they could sense any one of these three as important. Now asking that is tricky, in that if the shift mode of reframing and redirecting the core emotion is the adaptive strategy, then they might easily pass over that division. But Megan said that she could relate to sadness, feeling that relationships were really important in her life—and that was why she brought Stan in today. Stan stared at me for a while and then said, "Anger. Anger is what I feel right now, and it's what Megan says I have too much of. I don't think I have too much of it or anything; I just think there's a lot to be angry about."

That began what has now become a year of couples therapy focusing on their PDPs and the nonsecure attachment experiences they both had. Megan's Adult Attachment Interview (AAI) revealed a preoccupied state of mind with respect to attachment, marked by her overly inclusive responses to the queries and a sense that her parents were each in their own ways intermittently available and at times intrusive. The result for her was what seemed to be a nonsecure ambivalent attachment as a child. Stan had the classic findings of someone with a dismissive state of mind with respect to attachment, with his lack of recall of details of his childhood and a likely set of avoidant strategies acquired during his childhood of dealing with what, according to his minimal recall and Megan's reflections on her in-laws, was a likely pair of emotionally distant parents.

In working as a therapist utilizing this PDP framework, it is always important to "know thy own inner self" and be open to whatever SIFTing brings up in you—the sensations, images, feelings, and thoughts—related to what arises. In working with Stan, I was led by the PDP survey process to a sense that he leads with the agency vector above the other two, and that his attendency is prominent for an outward focus. Megan's falls more in the bonding vector, with a dyadic attendency. This couple's combination of his A-o and her B-d PDPs leads to a challenging blend of his tendency to not embrace vulnerability or needing others, including Megan; and her prioritizing being accepted with the productions she creates—including their own daughter. When offered the PDP developmental perspective of our journeys from being to doing, the three of us could discuss how the vector baseline would set the priority for the key issue that would make approaching their daughter's marriage different for each one of them. And recognizing Stan's PDP making empowerment a priority and insight and empathy less strongly developed given his outward attendency and the ensuing A-o pattern, we could provide a non-blaming, non-pathologizing frame on what the growth-edge for them was, not just as a couple but as a family.

Stan's A-o PDP also helped us see that when their future son-in-law, Rick, had turned down his offer for employment, it had created an intense negative reaction in Stan. Yet by reframing Rick's decision as actually taking care of his own needs, and not made out of passivity or lack of empowerment, Stan could begin to see where his own pathway was getting in the way of simply seeing Rick as an autonomous individual finding his own way in life. He could also see, in his own words, that "Barb is actually showing her own strength in going against what I've told her I'd accept. That took a lot of strength, and I actually feel somehow better about the whole situation now."

Beneath our adaptive strategies and their intensities based on our own nonsecure attachment histories, we can see that each of us is simply doing the best we can. With careful steps, these pathways can become more flexible, serving as a platform in life from which to engage in the new moments we cannot control but can learn to embrace. This allows us to be fully present in life, more likely to be filled with acceptance and love.

Short Reflections on Integration

For Type 8 your central issue in healing involves reclaiming the innocence of coming freshly without prejudice or power motives to each situation, to appreciating differences and realizing that we all have our truths. To do this it is necessary to work with your own overriding boundless instinctual energy—how this energy defies boundaries, how it is excessive, and how it impacts upon others. You need to learn that power and control have limits and that real power follows the law of "requisite variety" which says the person with the most choices has indeed the greatest power, not from your extreme all-or-nothing approach to life. You need to learn proportionality, i.e., how much power is optional, and moderation, i.e., how much energy is appropriate in any given situation. It is essential in gaining proportionality and moderation that you learn to delay the tendency to go from urge to action and to consider effects and outcomes of actions, especially those accompanied by anger. And you need to lessen denial and allow in weakness and vulnerability—softness, sensitivity, and surrender.

[Source: The Narrative Enneagram, 2020, p. 42]

Observing impulsivity or impulse to action
Simply stop and notice your urge to act and where this urge resides in your body. Pause and give yourself the gift of time and receptivity. Then take action befitting the situation.

Impact on others
Simply stop, breathe back down, and witness your impact on others, knowing your tendency to be overly impactful. Then moderate your exuberant energy as best you can to fit the situation.

Distinguishing vulnerability from weakness
Simply stop and remind yourself that allowing in the vulnerability, the tender softness that accompanies genuine receptive force is a great strength to complement your exuberant active energy.

[Source: David Daniels, "Growth for Type 8: The Protector."
https://drdaviddaniels.com/growth-for-type-8]

Integrative Transformation

You may get a sense that when someone travels down the A-o pathway and is without self-reflection and access to states of higher integrative functioning, the energy of this drive for empowerment can be intense. The emotions arising when the vector of agency is frustrated under times of challenge and especially threat can lead to an intense upregulation of anger as it is experienced and expressed—how it is felt internally and communicated externally.

A growth-edge approach for those with a baseline of the A-o pathway is to invite a focus on two key ways that accessing an inward attendency may have been most challenging: feeling and accepting one's own vulnerability and need for others, and opening then to the inner life of feelings and their importance for both insight and empathy.

In this integration, not only is there a movement to include such inward attendency, but higher levels of capacity to engage empowerment by involving the more integrative states of the other vectors, those of bonding and certainty. In the PDP framework, the agency vector can be both understood and described as naturally having, for the young child, that embodied sense of do-or-die urgency. When the focus of attendency is outward, this bodily oomph of the A-o pattern creates an intensity of directing how life unfolds that, when on automatic pilot, can become overwhelming for others even in the face of helpful intentions. The work of opening to an acceptance of this drive for embodied empowerment, the vector, combined with looking inward at the vulnerability and relational needs of the individual that before were hidden from conscious knowing, can be challenging. Inviting the client to learn to SIFT their inner world, opening to sensations, images, and feelings before thoughts, can be an essential aspect of the integrative transformation facilitated both within and outside of the therapy session. Releasing this natural drive while supporting the tender vulnerability can be challenging and deeply rewarding.

A-d: Agency-dyadic (A-d Pathway; Enneagram 9)

Expressed Personality

Now let's consider the A-d pattern. Here we see a generally pleasant, agreeable, emotionally steady, unassuming, receptive, and adaptable character who seems highly motivated to "keep an even keel," "go with the flow," avoid conflict, and not "rock the boat." Sometimes, however, half-hearted engagement, passive resistance, or rare and surprising outbursts of anger point to a more ambivalent or unsettled inner state than the amiable and deferential expressed persona suggests.

This personality structure seems to operate as if there is a deeply embedded belief along the lines of, "The best way to get along in this world is to not make waves or cause trouble, find ways to blend in, and reconcile differences." The effect is a tendency to downplay or even discount one's own positions, needs, or desires, and just go with whatever others want or need. That may look and sound like restraint of one's inner needs, but on the inside it is more like disconnection from an inner sense of self. The inner experience can feel like there are no opinions or preferences. There is a head-in-the-sand quality here, a kind of "numbing out" of inner angst, and habitually deferring to others. In traditional teaching this pattern is the poster child for "self-forgetting."

Brief Description	The 9 believes that to be loved and valued, you must blend in and go along to get along. Consequently, Mediators seek harmony and are comfortable and steady, but they also can be self-forgetting, conflict-avoidant, and sometimes stubborn.
Key Interventions	Help Pattern 9s pay attention to their own self and needs, to determine priorities and take action on them, and welcome discomfort and change.

[Source: The Narrative Enneagram, 2020, pp. 45–47]

Developmental Pathway and Adaptive Strategy

In the PDP framework, this personality pattern is most deeply rooted in what we call the agency dyadic developmental pathway and an adaptive strategy that can be aptly characterized as "reconcile." The role of the A-d pathway is assimilating inward and outward streams of information, and navigating the way between them to find the most adaptive state of empowered agency needed to restore homeostasis and the felt qualities of contentment of body and existence in which the agency vector pathways are all firmly anchored. Here, attention and energy are dyadically in tension and centered on conflicting information from inward and outward sources—for example, "I" need "that" but "that" is unattainable, or "I" want "this" but "You" want "that." Attention and energy flow are reframed and redirected into reconciling the conflict (i.e., something between) or a relinquishing stance (i.e., letting go of the motivation) that will shift the motivational state of mind in a different direction. This is the shift mode of emotional regulation, which reframes and redirects the motivational drive of agency for empowerment.

In practical terms, here's what that means. Whether during childhood or later in life, the most frequently encountered inner-outer conflict situations involve the perception of being at odds with those you are connected to but who have a different agenda from yours. So, when the choice is between a harmonious relationship or having it "MY" way, it often feels necessary to be able to find your way to compromise, capitulation behind an amiable and "I'm OK" facade, or even full disconnection from your own motivations.

Even writing this out to you now feels overwhelming inside this body—and this is not even my baseline PDP, which is exactly the point. The well-attuned therapist will sense the agitated ruminative state often beneath the amiable and deferential surface appearance and then work to connect the client's awareness to the "self-forgetting" tone and habits described further below.

Integration and Individual Variation: Strengths and Challenges

This pattern brings extremely valuable and important qualities to the fore when the systems and pathways are well integrated and the flow of attention and energy into behavioral expression is well tempered and wisely regulated by access to the balancing of the other vectors and attendencies. In traditional Enneagram teaching, the individual is aware of and in touch with their own self-love, sense of agency, and priorities. The individual is solidly grounded in an inner self, but also adaptable, genuinely curious about and able to hold conflicting points of view with an open mind, highly motivated to find common ground, naturally empathic and supportive of others, adept at holding neutral space for mediating conflict and trusted by others to play that role, and able to assert personal self needs and express anger wisely.

When the pattern is dominant and the integration of the agency system is impaired, avoiding the turmoil of inner-outer conflict by relinquishing agency becomes the modus operandi of exerting agency. "I become empowered by disempowering myself." Contentment and harmony within and with the environment trumps one's own priorities, and over time it becomes hard to find or even identify what those priorities are. Attention and energy, oriented by inner conflict, go overly outward to others and the environment. Asserting one's personal self or expressing anger is assiduously avoided, with all its downstream consequences, including stubborn resistance or passive-aggressive behavior. The mind can be filled with angst about future conflict or with ruminative rehashing of unresolved conflict. Often there is a psychological merging with the wants and needs of others, and losing track of one's own boundaries, priorities, needs, and desires.

Behavioral Profile	**Strengths:** *Being caring, attentive to others, giving, empathetic, adaptive, accepting, supportive, participative, steady, calming, receptive, generally non-judgmental.* **Difficulties:** *Going along and later resenting and resisting, forgetting the self, doing what makes life comfortable instead of what is important, and sometimes not even knowing what is important to you, containing energy, especially the expression of anger, missing opportunities through delays when deciding, self-depreciation.*

[Source: David Daniels, "Enneagram Type 9 Description."
https://drdaviddaniels.com/type-9]

Focus of Attention and Blind Spots

When this pattern is active, attention seeks evidence of anything or anyone in the external environment that might create inner-outer conflicts or otherwise disrupt an inner state of ease. This comes with a tendency to see more significance in potential conflict than actually exists. Notably, this includes the agendas and perceived motivational states of others. The result can be a psychological merging, which my co-author, Jack, describes as "getting so swept up in the others' agenda and energy, that I perceive them to be my own. Without intentional energetic focus inward on myself and what I want or need, I can easily find myself engaged half-heartedly (or less) in what I'm doing, and angry (inside, of course) at the other for distracting me from my own agenda, if I have not lost track of it altogether." Thank you, Jack. Attention is also easily drawn to objects that provide distractions from the inner turmoil of conflict.

With attention focused outward, the pursuit of one's own needs, desires, goals, and personal boundaries can easily become blind spots. So too can all the well-known counterproductive effects of anger avoidance in relationships with others. And while a "blend-in" strategy may seem adaptive, legitimate needs for recognition and attention often get backgrounded and ignored.

Emotional Processing

Several features warrant emphasis. With an "automatic" tendency to avoid inner turmoil, asserting one's personal self and expressing anger present significant challenges. For example, expressing needs, desires, thoughts, and opinions, and pursuing motivational energies (whether appetitive or aversive), is often held back until others' agendas are clear. Then, if inner and outer are mostly congruent, it's easy to find a way to go along. But if there is conflict, it *seems* better and easier to keep "ME" and "MY" wants and needs inside and find a way to accommodate, either by reframing the situation and "letting go" of or releasing the motivational energy or, worse, finding a way to numb out and disconnect from the whole mess. The result: In a very real way, these clients seem unpracticed at expressing themselves, particularly their angry inner self, or even knowing their own feelings, needs, and desires. And when anger does sometimes break through, the client is likely to feel intense remorse.

A habit of blending in can make individuality and important contribution go unseen. It can also lead others to presume accommodation or, worse, that "no one is there." Not surprisingly, then, experiences of being overlooked can trigger significant turmoil inside and occasional outbursts of breakthrough anger.

Finally, being pushed to state opinions, make decisions, or take action can be similarly agitating. But allowing expression of that anger is a particular challenge, and often leads to passive-aggressiveness. The net result of these and similar emotional dynamics can be a seemingly flattened affect unperturbed by highs or lows.

Cognitive Processing

An inner stew of ruminative processing of unresolved discontent is reflected in a tendency to elaborate on or get lost in all the complex details of problem situations, or to become fragmented in a dissociative fog of disconnection from an inner self. Relating stories in a saga style is common. Other people and their agendas, needs, and desires tend to dominate thought and narrative, reflecting the tendency to relinquish agency. So too do others' roles in causing problems, reflected in themes of complaining about or blaming others or external situations for difficulties. What "I" need and want is very often missing in action and hard for the client to locate. Self-deprecating humor, which serves to take the spotlight off "me," is often seen.

Summing Up

In conventional Enneagram terminology, all of the above is often summed up with the label "mediator," "peacemaker," or "harmonizer." Here is Beatrice Chestnut's (2013, pp. 83–84) summary of key behavioral patterns that set up problems that bring clients to therapy:

1. "Forgetting yourself to more easily go along with the wishes and wills of others."
2. "Avoiding and diffusing conflict as a way of staying comfortable and connected."
3. "Getting stuck in inertia with regard to your own priorities."

Growth-Edge Work

Type 9s focus on the environment and experience themselves as reacting primarily to others and events outside ourselves. The fact that they have lost touch with their inner separate self in favor of adapting to the environment and merging with others becomes the central issue for healing and development. Type 9s struggle fundamentally with gaining or reclaiming a separate self that feels loved equally to all others. Thus, their main task is to become awake and alive to themselves, literally to love themselves from a personal reference point for which there is no substitute and to establish their own priorities and timelines instead of falling into comfortable secondary pursuits and getting resistant to over-influence.

[Source: The Narrative Enneagram, p. 45]

Strategies for Development

- Practice (inner) self-love that is equal to the love of others.
- Develop a "both/and" strategy for life, including oneself and others.
- Take responsibility for your own well-being and importance.
- Reclaim a separate self and voice; take a personal position on issues.
- Notice when an obsession with pros and cons of a decision has replaced your real feelings and desire.
- Establish and adhere to your own agenda and priorities.
- Focus on the immediate next step rather than the final goal.
- Notice when the other person becomes the reference point and find your own reference point within.
- Examine the tendency to say yes when you really mean no (the body's reaction tells you the difference).
- Welcome discomfort and conflict.
- Notice when you are withholding your opinion to avoid conflict.
- Recognize anger in its many forms since it's a signal of something important inside.
- Realize that resistance creates persistence.
- Check within several times a day to observe what you are feeling and wanting.
- Claim responsibility, actually "implicating not extricating" yourself when difficulties come up; examine your part in the conflict.
- Remember that in every complaint there is a hidden want, wish, need, or desire.
- Notice feelings that precede your attention shifting to substitutes (food, TV, etc.).
- Remember that your self-worth is self-defined; no one can define you.

[Source: The Narrative Enneagram, 2020, p. 46]

Tips for Growth in Relationships
Relational Triggers

Being treated as not important or invisible. Feeling controlled or pushed to do something by others. Being "forced" to face conflict, state an opinion we don't want to state, or feeling pushed into making decisions. Saying "yes" to something we really don't want to say "yes" to. Disharmony. Angry, mean, or pushy people. Confrontation and disruption.

Relational Reflections

As a Type 9, we need to pay attention to our own personhood and our own specific needs—to our own self-agency. It is important to determine our specific wants and priorities and take action with respect and self-honoring, accordingly. We need to learn to welcome the unavoidable discomforts of interacting with others, our innate need for differentiation, and the fact that showing up in our fullness allows others to rightfully show up in theirs.

We need to impact our world as our world impacts us. As we activate the power within us—that "familiar but readily suppressed" anger energy that is oftentimes numbed out and long repressed—that energy can instead be used to stand in the face of arising conflicts and the challenges that come with human relationships and life itself.

As we learn to love and respect ourselves equally to the love and respect we readily offer others, we regain our ability to feel and receive the unconditional love of our true nature, of our essential self. "I matter too."

[Source: David Daniels, "Enneagram Type 9 Description." https://drdaviddaniels.com/type-9/]

- *Encourage your Mediators to pay attention to their own selves and needs, express their thoughts and opinions, and welcome in discomfort and change.*
- *Encourage and reinforce Type 9s to do their own development, e.g., in taking and expressing a position, in making the self and their own needs important.*
- *Provide Type 9s with a supportive environment for determining priorities, taking action, and experiencing anger.*
- *Ask Type 9s what they want, need, and value.*
- *Help them keep their own focus and limits.*

[Source: David Daniels, "Enneagram Type 9 Description." https://drdaviddaniels.com/type-9/]

Clinical Vignette

Allan was a 52-year-old father of three teenagers who came to see me at the request of his wife of 25 years, who said that he "seemed to be losing his kindness" as he faced the challenges of raising their adolescents and being promoted in his job as corporate attorney and mediator to managing partner of his law firm. During Allan's first session with me, he expressed that he was not interested in therapy, having never thought taking time to reflect on his own life was something "of value" or that he really needed it. In fact, he told me with a calm, even expression, his "life was smooth sailing and never really required sailing lessons."

The feeling of sitting with Allan during that session had a sense of being with someone who knew how to read a room and do what would best support others. I got the impression that he didn't want me to feel discouraged that my work as a therapist was never something he thought he might benefit from. Yet at the same time, as we reviewed his wife's concerns, he said he'd resisted at first but was open to seeing what might be at the root of what she was worried about.

In my own inner mind, getting a feeling for both a client's PDPs and state of mind with respect to attachment is a natural way to sense a kind of four-dimensional image of a person's life—where they have been before this moment, what is happening now in our interaction and in their life, and where they might go with the connection and exploration of psychotherapy. 4-D imaging is a kind of mindsight mapping of how both innate temperament and immersion in attachment relationships early on would carve out the depth and width of the groove of his PDP. In this first session, the feeling was that he was taking care of me and his wife but that he was somehow absent in a gentle way. For you reading this account, which PDPs might this represent? Which attachment strategies might this involve as well?

You might imagine a look-alike pair of the A-d that attempts to avoid anger by mediating everyone else's wants and minimizing conflict and the B-o who is handling the experience of separation distress and sadness by reframing and redirecting those emotions with the regulation mode of shifting. Here the bridge would be the emotion-regulation mode that is shared. In Allan's case, the usual sense of a robust set of mirror neurons and attunement connection often found in those with the B-o pattern did not seem to be present; instead, there was more the feeling of a fine-tuned attention to avoiding conflict rather than establishing connection. These reflections you may be having now I certainly had inside of me then, but I didn't see any need, at that moment, to share them with him.

When we did the Adult Attachment Interview, Allan had a classic finding of a preoccupied state of mind with respect to attachment with its characteristics of many detailed memories that sometimes would distract his attention from clear, concise responses. This preoccupation revealed in the AAI, especially around issues related to his mother and her active alcoholism and depression during his childhood and early adolescent years, left Allan with a feeling of uncertainty about being able to rely on her, and then other close individuals later in his emerging romantic relationships as an adult.

With his wife, Allan found a reliable partner with whom he said he got along well, as they supported each other in their career paths (she became a psychotherapist) and enjoyed raising their young boys. When Allan finished law school and joined a corporate law firm, he chose acquisitions law instead of what was the more challenging area of corporate litigation. In his words, "You could find a way to have everyone get along and set up the legal documents at the moment of a merger so that you could avoid conflict in future transactions." Allan's ability to successfully anticipate the worst-case-scenario events and plan details of agreements accordingly won him acclaim with his clients and colleagues alike.

Allan said that while he enjoyed that work tremendously, he was not that fond of the rise in his administrative role when he was chosen to be the managing partner of the firm. This role entailed that he negotiate salaries with the junior partners, oversee hiring and firing of young associates, and report back to the senior partners of the firm—his direct colleagues. He was a natural mediator, but the feeling of being lost in this work was beginning to show when a new project made him irritable and exhausted.

At home, too, his daughter and two sons, now all teens from 13 to 17, challenged him and his wife to find some happy "middle road" to giving them structure but letting them have some kind of freedom. He was worried that, whatever his own mother had experienced, his daughter would now be at risk of developing an affinity for alcohol. Her moods would fluctuate between elated and flat, and he feared that her looking like his mother would be an outer manifestation of her inner vulnerability for a mood and substance set of challenges.

All of this was coming out by his fourth session, and he stated, "I didn't know I had so much to talk about." It felt time to share with him directly some reflections on possible insights we might come to together about his inner world through the lens of the PDP framework. I shared with him the overall view of the journey of life from simply being to the do-or-die situation of working for a living out here in the world. We discussed the three subcortical motivation networks—agency, bonding, and certainty—and the trio of attendencies, inward, outward, and dyadic. Allan didn't particularly resonate with the A, B, or C vectors, but said that his attention was certainly some combination of inward and outward. When we spoke about the primal affects generated when the key motivational drives were thwarted, he could relate to both sadness and fear, but said that anger was not something he experienced.

We then went through an overview of each of the trios of the three vectors, beginning with bonding and certainty. He could relate to the C-d the most, and we focused on his worst-case-scenario thinking as a useful "gift" of that PDP and its use in his legal work and even in his role as a parent. Yet fear was not a driving force in his life; and certainty really wasn't something that seemed to preoccupy his mind. When we then explored the trio of the agency vector, he could sense an aversion for the A-o, saying that he "would never be sure others knew what his opinion was," but that he did share a focus on being complete and thorough, characteristic of the A-i—not so much for feeling empowered, but simply wanting to avoid conflict. Then we explored the personality pathway of A-d. Allan listened attentively and when I was done with my brief overview—exploring how his wavering dyadic attendency and the adaptive strategy of avoiding expression of needs and desires ironically results in a habitual personality pattern of relinquishing rather than exerting agency—he just stared at me, quietly sitting with what we were discussing.

It's not uncommon for people to feel suddenly "seen" in a deep way when their primary baseline PDP is articulated. Perhaps Allan also had a secondary pathway, bridging across the attendency with the PDP C-d. But with the exploration of the A-i, Allan felt a resonance, he said. As we explored the general growth-edge work we could offer him, he felt a "liberation from the need to be the nice guy all the time"—which for him meant stating what he needed rather than tending to work it out so that everyone else would get along in the longtime peacemaking role he could now recognize.

As the sessions continued, we had the combined visions of not only his primary and secondary PDPs but also his preoccupied attachment model. We discussed the nature of attachment, the role of relationships in our development, and the possible ways in which the intermittent reinforcement of his connection with his mother, given her mental health challenges, made him especially driven to get along well with his wife and his now teenage kids.

Expressing his own needs to his wife was something that he said "dismayed her" at first, but, given her profession, she took this on as a sign of progress. Their own relationship needed tending to, as his combination of attachment and personality meant she could be "quite assertive without pushback" from him. When one person begins to change, the whole relationship needs adjustment. Fortunately, her own openness to growth and her support of his development meant they could each be open to working at their individual and relational growth-edges.

While people sometimes feel having a pathway named or an attachment strategy identified "puts them in a box" that they resent, my clinical experience is that if we as therapists offer this as a more verb-like set of four-dimensional patterns that have the potential to grow and change, then it is really more like simply shining a flashlight on the nature of a room such that we can now open some curtains, let the light in, and even move the walls around if not fully opening the door to explore the other aspects of the home of our mind. Allan could learn that even when his own pattern in the moment was to not have a point of view, he could in fact discover his own perspective and express his own opinions about things, even if they were at odds with others' views. Allan was ready to shape this life of his, at home and work, and was grateful for the chance to grow and change.

Short Reflections for Integration
Attention being pulled by multiple environmental claims
Simply stop to notice how your focus of attention tends habitually to go out to others and environment needs. Use this as a clue to come back and focus on your own priorities and needs.

Resistance in your body

Do your best to stop and notice where your resistance manifests in your body. Practice realizing that this digging in means there is something of importance to you or you wouldn't have resistance. Then explore what of importance underlies this resistance.

Seeking comfort and avoiding conflict

Stop and notice how disharmony and conflict upset you and where this is in your bodily felt sense. Use this to remind yourself that conflict is naturally occurring and the issue is dealing with conflict constructively. Then do your best to manifest this principle in your life.

[Source: David Daniels, "Growth for Type 9: The Mediator." https://drdaviddaniels.com/growth-for-type-9/]

Integrative Transformation

In the interpersonal neurobiology framework of life, integration—the linkage of differentiated aspects of a system—is the basis of well-being. When we travel down the A-d path, differentiation at the whole-person level is likely to be impeded in lower states of functioning, revealing how integration is low when only linkage is promoted in the adaptive strategy of this PDP. In this clinical example, we can see how differentiation is underdeveloped in this going-along-to-get-along kind of impediment to integration that brought rigidity into the inner and relational life of this individual. We can see here how reflections on this pathway reveal an emphasis on letting personal differentiation be cultivated at the growth-edge of individuals who then can incorporate both linkage and differentiation in their ways of living in the world.

The growth-edge work for PDP A-d is to support personal differentiation in order to complement the usually well-developed capacities for linkage. The ironic challenge, from a PDP perspective, is that while the drive of this system is toward wholeness, to achieve this integrative state of being invites *both* differentiation from other individuals and then linking from that differentiated state. Having this view of integration as the heart of being whole can greatly aid us in understanding such paradoxes and the powerful work of expanding the repertoire available to those traveling life down this pathway.

A challenge in the growth-edge work for those in the A-d PDP is to support ways of countering the often diplomatic adaptive strategy of getting along to regain some sense of wholeness, which has actually shut off individual agency. Integration at the pathway level involves accessing the higher functions of the baseline pattern and the strengths of the other attendencies within that vector and those of the other vectors as well. The main work at the growth edge toward integration for this pattern involves practice at the more assertive (A-o) and clear (A-i) skills of the other two agency patterns in expressing both appetitive and aversive emotion (not just anger) in the face of inner-outer conflict, plus practicing relaxing the autopilot urge to relinquish agency. This movement toward higher states of pathway integration would also invite accessing the other vectors, enabling bonding and certainty to become a part of the motivational drive that organizes internal emotional experience and outwardly directed behaviors.

Integrative growth invites a welcoming in, much like the sentiment of the poem "The Guest House" by Rumi, to let all experiences be invited guests with something to teach. Letting go of compulsive reliance on the adaptive strategy to have everyone get along and to avoid conflict, while challenging, may ultimately release a tremendous amount of energy to be applied in inner and relational aspects of life.

Sensing the "bind" of having both an inward and outward focus of energy with the vector of agency, we can feel how the resolution of this tension is to shift away from the energizing emotion of anger by reframing the state and then redirecting that energy in non-threatening ways. The PDP framework helps us see how attendency, and its concomitant emotion-regulation modes of upregulating, downregulating, or shifting can form a part of the adaptive strategies that arise. Learning to integrate at both the level of the individual and of the personality patterns—differentiating and linking vectors, attendencies, and modes of emotion regulation in a more flexible manner—is a gateway to living with wholeness. The art of this balance for those traveling the A-d pathway is a great gift when integrated, freeing the individual from needing to shift away from the assertive energy of agency.

CHAPTER 7

The Bonding Vector Personality Patterns

Bonding to Establish Connection

The bonding-for-connection vector specializes in first-level management of the flow of energy and attention associated with the range of emotional motivations to establish and maintain connection with others. These include the range of aversive emotional energies of separation distress, such as sadness, grief, and shame; and various appetitive, seeking-like emotional energies. Mirror neurons and attachment mechanisms are likely to be found to play key roles in the development and operation of this bonding vector's PDPs, beginning with the newborn infant's establishment of eye contact. The young child's constant seeking of assurance of connection, affection, recognition, and approval becomes the basis of this system's major developmental dilemma, which we can call union versus individuation. The bonding system channels the need to be soothed and connected into three general developmental pathways we call bonding-inward (B-i), bonding-outward (B-o), and bonding-dyadic (B-d)—according to the three variations in attendency. These pathways are the roots of Enneagram personality patterns 4, 2, and 3.

In effect, the trio of pathways provides *adaptive strategies* for managing fundamental and lifelong needs for a sense of *mutually* supportive connection with others on whom we can depend in times of need, and who can depend on us for the same in theirs. As such, the system deals with the painful feelings of separation and loss, abandonment, loneliness, neediness, shame, the dynamics of union versus individuation, and other relational opportunities and challenges, which often bring people to therapy. When the system is well developed and integrated, it provides a repertoire of equally important ways of managing the complicated interpersonal dynamics of bonding and relational connections in a wide range of situations.

Beneath each of these bonding pathways is the fact that the human brain, like that of other highly social mammals, is hardwired by evolution to seek and maintain attuned connection with others. Collectively, humans have evolved to need other individuals, and those others to need us, to thrive in this world. As infants this need for connection is a matter of life and death. We've named this the "do-or-die" setup once we are out of the womb. We need to be seen, soothed, and safe by way of our bonds with our caregivers from the first moments of our lives out here in the world. This creates the bonds of interpersonal connection, care, and social cooperation that characterize human social life, and the sense of connection and belonging for many extends beyond people to special places, to humane care of animals and the animal kingdom, and to an even more across-time-and-space connection to all of humanity, past, present, and future. We also come to realize, with an adjustment of our identity lens, that who we are is an interwoven aspect of all of nature.

At the same time, however, humans, like all animals, are also effectively hardwired toward individuation and satisfaction of our individual goals, needs, and desires, which can put us in situations of need for support and help. The bonding system helps us navigate these intricate relational waters.

The easiest way to understand this system is to briefly consider its developmental trajectory. The foundations of its strategies are laid in earliest attachment relationships, and what we can simply call the being-seen dynamic. At birth you emerge from a relatively carefree state of virtual union we've named "being at one with the womb," into a life in this world that is inherently, to greater or lesser degrees, volatile, uncertain, complex, and ambiguous (abbreviated VUCA). Fortunately, a significant part of our mind—which includes our separation distress system—is on the job on day one. Immediately this subcortically mediated system motivates us to *seek* the attuned reflection—that is, interactions to be *seen* by—caregivers, without whom we are helpless and doomed, and to cry out for their caring attention when we are in need. These are our first primal steps at creating human connection. Also, fortunately for us, our parents' drive to nurture us (driven by their subcortically mediated Care motivational emotion system) makes us an almost irresistible object of attention (assuming no major pathology on the attachment figures' part). In resonant attunement with us, they are virtually compelled to interpret our signals of discomfort, care for our many physical and psychological needs, and otherwise do their best to help us restore and maintain a state of emotional equilibrium both within us and between us and them. Said simply, at the start they are on the seeing side, and you are on the needing-to-be-seen side, of this core being-seen dynamic. The outcome of such interactive connection is being soothed and feeling whole and content.

You also have your first inevitable encounters, no matter how wondrous your caregivers are, with the pain of separation distress when you discover the universal truth that others will not always be right there, available and able to attend to you in times of need. Perceiving their absence, your separation distress system triggers painful feelings of separation, loss, and abandonment, which also motivates you to find ways to effectively stand out—to be seen—and therefore attempt to restore lost connection.

Very soon, tensions between this state of connection and togetherness and that of individuation and aloneness begin to take shape as you become more and more ambulatory. Still, even as you begin to venture out into the wider world, a big part of your mind is always seeking the assurance of connection with them, your caregivers, tuning in to their whereabouts, and sensitive to their reactions to you. Sensing that they see you and that they are there to soothe you and back you up is vital and gives you the courage to forge ahead and keep distressing feelings of separation at bay. Being seen helps you to be soothed. Automatically you look into the mirror of their reactions for clues about your well-being, which serve as guidance and care when something delights or distresses you. You take in and feel their delight at your antics, achievements, and acts of kindness toward others as signals that you are OK in their eyes. This is the power of connection to create a way we "feel felt," join as a "we" without losing a "me," and experience the sensation of being whole.

You also take in their expressions of alarm or disapproval at your inevitable steps toward danger or defiance as signals that you are not OK and need their help. This is sometimes called "relational regulation," in that the interaction you have with the caregiver helps you to regulate your internal state. Over time, that interactive regulation becomes a more autonomous internal form of regulating your emotional state. When you get too far afield, or sense your caregivers are not there—as inevitably happens from time to time in even the best of all attachment experiences—you experience alarm and are motivated to "call" for them to come to your aid. With all this happening, you are constructing inner mental models, not just about the meaning of external opportunities and threats, but also about expectations of others regarding socially acceptable ways for you to be in this world. You come to learn that even when things are distressing, connection leads to soothing and a return to the balance of homeostasis—of things being made right when they felt off-kilter. This is called repair of a rupture; a reconnection that teaches us the capacity to be in a state of distress and have the security that all will be repaired and homeostasis reestablished. Our caregivers cannot achieve perfection, but with their presence we can learn that repair is always possible. This sense that being able to rely on the connection with others to bring a sense of wholeness in life is called "security" in the field of attachment research.

As growth and maturation continue through childhood and adolescence and your circles of relational connections expand in complexity, three other big things happen. First, your inborn and largely unconditioned capacities to attune to others elaborate into more complex and nuanced capacities that you will need as an adolescent and adult to navigate the many webs of interpersonal connections that constitute human life. As you go about living, your mind continues to monitor those around you for signals that all is well with you in their eyes, and that they will be there if you need them. As in all other social species, this involves looking for signals you might have missed that all is well, through your caregivers' responses, as pertains to the rest of the world.

Second, as your own bonding system further develops throughout early childhood, you begin to learn that others have needs, too. What this means is that you learn that sometimes when you sense needs in others, a focus of attention can shift to being about them and their needs and not you and yours, and you feel motivated to help them. Importantly, you learn that the soothing of others' distress is innately pleasurable. You are beginning to learn the repertoire of skills needed to establish and maintain connection with others to whom you can turn in times of need, but who sometimes turn to you in order to have their needs met by you. When balanced later in our development, this give-and-take in relationships is a form of mutuality, a mutual beneficence.

Third, as sexual desires come on board in adolescence, another layer of connection-seeking motivations is added to the mix. Here the issues of sexual drive and interpersonal connection have a complex interplay that can evoke profound tension between internal needs of oneself and of other individuals and ways to attain and maintain relational bonding.

In the Enneagram system, this trio grouping is often referred to as the "heart center" types. For the PDP framework, as we've said, we are letting this notion and nomenclature of a "heart center" go and instead refer to the fundamental motivational drive for connection. Yes, the ALEAF may be in the heart for many reasons, including engagement in interpersonal connection. From a poetic view, we sense these relational connections with our heart— and future empirical work may explore and verify the potential mechanisms of the intrinsic nervous system surrounding the heart that may, in actuality, specialize in processing information about our relational lives. Supporting this notion is the view from polyvagal theory, which posits a "social engagement system" mediated by the ventral branch of the vagus nerve. The ventral branch extends to and from the above-diaphragm organs, such as the lungs and the heart. This is consistent with the idea that when we feel open and connected, when we feel trust and belonging, the ventral vagus and its above-diaphragm "heart-felt" sensations may be activated.

The Trio of Bonding Pathways

The three developmental pathways—B-i, B-o, and B-d—provide an essential repertoire of general strategies for coping in different situations with these various connection-seeking emotional energies that come up throughout life. As with both other vectors (agency and certainty), the bonding pathways involve either an inward, outward, or dyadic (inward and outward) orientation. In this case, inward is essentially about you and your feelings of need for connection with others, while outward is essentially about perceptions of others' states of connection with you. We will explore each pattern in more detail shortly, but here is a brief sketch of what that means.

In the B-i PDP, attention and energy are oriented inward toward motivations to be seen and connected with others. The pathway upregulates the feelings of this vector of connection-seeking motivational energy, enabling you to experience and express it freely. This robust inner sense of self may serve to drive you forward to help ensure you stand out to be seen; by being seen and deeply connected with others, the distress about disconnection can be soothed. You let your painful feelings of separation, loneliness, loss, or neediness, and your needs and desires for a deeply felt sense of connection with your authentic self, stand out in some way that may have the outcome of attracting the attention of others and satisfying the fundamental motivation for connection. If development has not been integrative and the strategy of this pathway becomes a less integrative level of this personality pattern, you can think of its manifestations as a grown-up elaboration of the infant's experience, from the distress side of being unsoothed and unseen, and then activating the being-seen dynamic to motivate others so that you will be seen and appreciated. The ultimate goal of this dynamic is to achieve bonding to ensure connection. Yet when the groove of this PDP is carved deeply into the individual's system, the challenges of this pattern become evident in a given moment, the pathway over time revealing ways in which this being-seen dynamic is on autopilot and operating often without awareness.

In contrast, the B-o pathway may become a baseline when the attendency is outward and the focus becomes not on your own needs for connection and being seen, but on those needs of other individuals in your life. While we don't know exactly how each PDP becomes shaped, we do have the sense that whatever the causal influences, the outcome is that with this particular configuration of outward attendency and a vector of bonding, what becomes dominant is a way that the individual must learn to follow others' needs for their attention and care, which then are considered more important than the individual's own needs. It remains an open question how, while our baseline vector may be an innate aspect of temperament, our relational experiences may interact with this propensity to more deeply ingrain a particular pathway. Perhaps experience sets in motion certain aspects of temperament more than others? How the attendency might be nudged toward an outward focus—by innate features, by experience, or by a combination of the two—is yet to be understood; and even our proposal of a vector being set by temperament is a sense we have from the narrative data that, as with all that we are proposing, should be open to exploration, challenge, and reconsideration. However it ultimately originated, the lived emotional experience we see in this pattern is to shift emotion by reframing one's inner needs to be projected outward as the needs of others and redirecting that energy for connection to the care of those who could be offering caring connection. This is clear: what we are inquiring about is how this pattern may have come to be the pathway this individual is following in their life.

With the outward attendency in the setting of the bonding vector, attention and energy are focused on others. The energetic flow is outward-directed to others and their needs and moves away from one's own needs. For that to work well, it is necessary to modify your own emotional state and motivations to be soothed and seen, to be cared for *by* others, to then being all about caring *for* them. When development has not been integrative and the pattern becomes a limited adaptive strategy unbalanced by the capacities of the other two of this vector's trio, being a caregiver without needs of one's own and projecting that image to the world can become a problematic way of being if held too rigidly. Research can explore whether this is an outcome of what is sometimes called a "parentified child," a situation in a family requiring that individual to care for the adult figures in their lives. This would be the experiential hypothesis of how a particular PDP is formed, in contrast to stating that the PDP is derived from temperament but experience shapes the depth of the groove of that pathway: Experience determines not the PDP but the nonintegrative or integrative level of development of that pathway in a person's life.

In the B-d PDP, attention and energy are oriented on conflicting motivations and goals around union and individuation. Inward are motivations driving you to do things out in the world on your own, to individuate; yet competing motivations to stay closely connected with others on whom you depend, to focus on union. Outward is a focus on seeing the eyes of those you need to keep you out of harm's way. This balance of union and individuation requires that you learn to downregulate powerful motivations to be closely connected as with the B-i, by diligently attending outward to other individuals for evidence that you have their encouragement, support, and approval. When development has not been integrative and the pattern becomes a limited adaptive strategy unbalanced by the capacities of the other pathways, identification with what brings the approval and figurative "applause" and approbation of others can become a problematic way of being too rigidly focused on others' opinions and chaotically prone to distress if that approval is not available.

TABLE 7.1 Developmental Pathways for the Bonding Vector

Pathway	Attendency	Regulation of separation distress and sadness emotions and motivation vector
B-i	Inward	Upregulate ↑
B-o	Outward	Shift →
B-d	Dyadic (inward + outward)	Downregulate ↓

In summary, the bonding vector manages when and how our ever-present emotional motivations to seek and maintain supportive connection with others are (1) upregulated and allowed to flow freely into being seen, standing out, and calling attention to self and its needs for connection and care, (2) downregulated and contained by diligent seeking of evidence of connection and support from others, or (3) shifted into a different emotional state focused on others and their needs. Each can be an effective way of coping with various life circumstances; each can also become a rigidly held pattern of personality. When integration of the systems and their developmental pathways is impaired and one becomes an excessively dominant, low-integration level of these personality patterns, this can lead to relatively inflexible, "forced" ways of pursuing the need for bonding and connection. Attachment and affect regulation theories provide powerful frameworks for understanding the development and operation of the bonding system and its three developmental pathways.

Case Example

Within the vector cluster of bonding, which aligns with the core aversive emotions of separation distress and sadness, the cognitive theme revolves around "being seen" or creating an image that will bring attention, love, and approval, first from caregivers and later from other important people. Even the slightest disapproval from someone important can be sensed, so the child learns to alter how they present themselves in hopes of maintaining or restoring the important connection. This cognitive preoccupation can become habitual and automatic if nonintegrative, as the child alters their image to please, win love, and begin to embody more of an image or persona than living more freely and fully as an authentic way of being in the world. When the patterns of this vector become rigid during adulthood, the therapeutic goal may be to soften, or widen, the groove so that the client can see the true self and understand they can be loved for simply who they are and not what they do. Here's a case example of David exploring the Enneagram heart center, which overlaps with what we are describing as a bonding vector.

Rosemary leads with the Heart Center of Intelligence [the ALEAF of heartfelt sensations]. *She wanted to experience what her partner, Peter, a Gut/Body Center* [an ALEAF of gut feelings] *type, feels; and not so much was Rosemary interested in what Peter senses and does. While she loves Peter's gutsy, forthright energy and concern for Rosemary getting what she wants, she keeps longing for him to express his heartfelt feelings. She wants to be admired and appreciated, not just attended to. Rosemary gets emotional, meaning expressive, emphatic, intense, and even tearful when Peter doesn't seem to approve of her—how she looks, what she feels, what she longs for. He loves the taste of good food, but how it's presented doesn't matter to him like it does to Rosemary. She would welcome long conversations about relationships and what matters to her, saying, "I want you tuned into my feelings, my emotions!" But Peter expresses love with an energetic presence and with physical contact—hugs and sexuality, which Rosemary adores, but, she says, "He never tells me he loves me, he never likes how I look nor does he tell me how I make him feel."*

This pattern repeated over and over again gradually resulted in a widening breach in their relationship. When they came upon the Enneagram and attended my seminar on the three centers of intelligence and relationships, they both became aware of the imbalance; where their respective focus of attention tended to go was not engendering compatibility. In regard to Rosemary, she almost immediately realized the way she experiences love was just different than Peter's.

Given her new awareness, Rosemary worked on noticing and better managing her rising emotional needs, their expression, and on her longing for recognition. She paused more to reflect on what really mattered and to appreciate the way Peter did express his care for her. She allowed in time for thoughtful reflection (a Head Center attribute) [an ALEAF of cortical thinking] *and moved more readily into action (a Gut/Body Center attribute)* [an ALEAF of the gut with which the agency patterns initiate responses].

Peter, in embracing the Enneagram understandings and the vital importance of the three centers of intelligence [three ALEAFs associated with each of the three vectors], *practiced bringing more attention to his Heart Center* [an ALEAF of heartfelt sensations], *asking himself what he is feeling, and importantly, expressing his love directly in words of care, admiration, and encouragement. As a result, their love thrived anew.*

[Source: Daniels & Dion, 2018, pp. 76–77]

You may be able to get a feeling for how focusing on the subcortical motivational network and its attendant initial location of energy flow can be useful not only for working with couples but for understanding individuals and how they connect with others in their lives more generally. Here, with the bonding vector, the motivation to connect with others is front and center. Poetic insights about the heart across history, coupled with newer, preliminary findings from scientific understandings of the body and how the neural system linked to the heart may possibly be directly related to social processing—such as some ideas referring to the ventral vagus nerve connecting to the heart and being involved in our social engagements, as we discussed earlier—let us see how the PDP perspective on this motivation would be connected with an initial "oomph" of a heart-centered energy flow.

As we'll continue to see in the next three chapters, one's attendency shapes the patterns of developmental pathways within a given vector in quite distinct ways, though each has this anatomical location of initial energy activation and flow, literally at its heart in the motivational drive for connection, that emerges with the bonding vector. It might be a worthwhile exercise to imagine—given the overall PDP hypothesis about the move away from wholeness leading to the activation of the vector's motivation—what a bonding drive would do to emotion regulation depending on the inward, outward, or dyadic attendency. As you consider the factors here, you may find that the central motivation to bond, the drive to achieve relational connection, will enable, minimize, or shift away from the primary reactive aversive states of separation distress and sadness. Let's see how this all unfolds as we dive in next to each of these pathways in the subchapters ahead.

B-i: Bonding-inward (B-i Pathway; Enneagram 4)

Expressed Personality

Cardinal features of the bonding-inward (B-i; Enneagram 4) personality pattern include an emotionally expressive, sensitive, authentic, and passionately idealistic demeanor. This often shines in qualities such as appreciation of aesthetics or the unique and singular, or an uncommon level of emotional intensity. Artistic expression often provides an outlet for emotional expression. Sensitivity to abandonment tends to be high.

While emotional highs tend to be intense, more prominent feelings of disappointment or deficiency in the shortcomings of current experience tend to dominate experience and are very often flavored with a sense of sadness, longing, or disappointment. Feelings about self tend to follow a similar trajectory toward shame or envy of others' good fortune, as though "I" have somehow missed out on something or am somehow lacking in comparison to others. The view that "the grass is always greener on the other side of the mountain" is an apt way of summarizing this tendency. What can seem like a dark or melodramatic existence to outside observers is perceived on the inside, by the individual, as authenticity, which is valued.

An interesting push-pull can impact relationships. It goes like this: First there is seeking of ideal connection, then finding it, then becoming disenchanted and pulling away when the other's inevitable human shortfalls from unrealistic ideals emerge, which brings longing for what once was, and on and on. Needless to say, the ensuing roller-coaster ride is more than many others can take, who then pull away.

This personality pattern seems to operate as if there is a deeply embedded belief along the lines of "I seek the kind of unique, special, and fulfilling object or love that is missing or gone from me now." In our PDP framework, this view can be understood as this vector and attendency's understandable realization that something *is* missing—living in the "just being" state without separation in the womb—that on some level is truly gone and a life's journey to try to (re)create as best one can. Attention and energy are strongly oriented by feelings, and with the inward attendency with this vector, we can understand the how and why of these feelings being a priority and prominent in the inner life of individuals on this pathway. Thoughts tend to be oriented toward what is missing or lacking here and now. To say this in different words, it can be as though the client *expects* disappointment or abandonment—and so is susceptible to seeing more of it than is really there. As I said to a client once when we came to realize these feelings she had been experiencing most of her aware life, with this pattern, focusing on what is missing comes naturally—the key is to not take it so personally, or seriously. She actually was quite relieved by that new perspective given the temperament she was born with and the deep groove her own attachment challenges had provided for her early on in her developmental journey.

| Brief Description | The 4 believes you must obtain the ideal relationship or situation to be loved. Consequently, Romantics are idealistic, deeply feeling, empathetic and authentic, but also dramatic, moody, and sometimes self-absorbed. |

Key Interventions	*Help the 4 overcome his or her longing for what is missing, appreciate what is positive in life now, and accept oneself as lovable, separate from his or her identification with being "special."*

[Source: The Narrative Enneagram, 2020, pp. 39–41]

Developmental Pathway and Adaptive Strategy

In the PDP framework, this pattern is rooted in what we call the bonding-inward (B-i) developmental pathway. This is the one where separation distress and the motivational vector of bonding are *upregulated* and channeled toward allowing expression of feelings of separation, loss, abandonment, loneliness, or neediness, and seeking to stand out in some way to attract the attention of others who can bring or restore a sense of being seen, and the sense of comforting connection we all need. The unique circumstances of an individual's development can make the effective, working strategy of this pathway particularly salient in maintaining a sense of vital connection with others. That is, it becomes an *adaptive strategy*.

It may appear outwardly as though disappointment or absence was experienced with early attachment relationships, but we don't have observational data yet to confirm that narrative impression. It may instead be a temperament proclivity to have this combination of the bonding vector along with the inward attendency that sets up the feeling that if it could speak with words they might be something along these lines: "I am no longer at one with the womb, but I do not know that this implicit memory is coming from something real in the past. Instead, I feel a longing for something I can't quite name; but I know, deep in my bones, something is just gone—and I may never get it back." This longing for union can have the feeling that nothing will meet the wholeness felt in the long-ago womb—or big bang—experience of union we all once had. Without this realization, the inward attendency enables the implicit feeling of "something missing" to be interpreted as something missing in the here and now, and in some ways that is true. We are now out in a do-or-die setup, far from the ease of simply being. Yet the reality that we can find some approximation to that wholeness in the bittersweet blend of longing for connection and sorrow over something we cannot quite name being lost is a hard pill to swallow.

I once had a friend whose adolescent daughter was filled with this kind of existential angst. When she came to see me as a family friend, we talked about the PDP system and went around the nine pathways. When she found herself resonating most with the B-i pattern, she felt both relieved and disappointed. "I thought I was unique in being the only one feeling like I was the only one feeling this way." She's doing great now, knowing she wasn't and isn't depressed, but instead is a human being with the existential angst of being "born alone and dying alone" and needing to find meaning and connection in her life. As someone traveling the B-i pathway, she's now informed and empowered to not take her sorrow and disappointments so personally, or so seriously. And she's a fabulous poet as well, placing her deep sensitivities out into the world for others to resonate with, including her now long-term partner in life who she realizes will inevitably disappoint her because she's not in the womb anymore.

If this pathway becomes an ingrained, nonintegrative personality pattern, you can think of it as a more grown-up elaboration of the infant's cry of separation distress and the pain of possible or ultimate abandonment. As we can see in my friend's daughter, great change can happen by taking on a deep understanding of the PDP framework and growing toward integration with those newfound insights and skills of opening to other vectors and other attendencies as well as transforming one's own baseline primary PDP from a prison into a playground—of poetry, purpose, and deeply loving relationships that allow us to experience and express the joys and sorrows of our relational lives and shared existential reality.

Integration and Individual Variation: Strengths and Challenges

As with all the patterns, there is a spectrum of higher and lower functionality. With higher degrees of integration, the personality pathway presents with an uncommon level of emotional authenticity, equanimity, and comfort in fully experiencing and staying with the entire spectrum of human feelings in one's inner self and inside of other individuals, and a powerful ability to bring emotional authenticity to life in ways that are helpful to other people and society in general as well as to one's individual life. For example, individuals with this pattern can be uncommonly good at holding supportive space for others in the dark places of need, grief, or depression, probably because they know that territory well and find it less alarming than others.

At the other end of the spectrum, when the groove of this pathway is deeply carved, the B-i adaptive strategy of experiencing and expressing feelings in a mostly unconscious way of being, with its drive to be seen by and secure in connection with others, can dominate life and make this pathway more a prison than it needs to be. Emotions, whether ecstatic or dark, can flood the experience of existence, and may also come to overwhelm others. Here, the expressed personality can become more self-absorbed, moody, melancholic, envious of the good fortune of others, melodramatic, or sometimes arrogantly elitist (to compensate for feelings of personal-deficiency).

Behavioral Profile	**Strengths:** *Sensitivity, empathy, especially with suffering, creative disposition, attunement to feelings, intensity, romantic, passionate, idealism, appreciative of the unique, extraordinary, and singular, being passionate and idealistic.* **Difficulties:** *Dissatisfaction and anger with life as it is, "nothing is good enough"; rejects help, dominated by fluctuating feelings; pain is associated with the D's: depression, devastation, disdain, drama, disappointment, deviancy; experiencing the painful side of uniqueness as a misfit who feels different from others, experiencing difficulties in sustaining a relationship or path, feeling pain associated with the self-created crisis, a sort of "addiction" to suffering; envy of those that allegedly have fulfillment.*

[Source: David Daniels, "Enneagram Type 4 Description: The Romantic."
https://drdaviddaniels.com/type-4/]

Focus of Attention and Blind Spots

First and foremost, when this pattern is dominant, clients are keenly attentive to and oriented by their very rich inner emotional landscape. In effect they seek a felt sense of relational connection with all experience. Almost equally strong is a tendency to seek what might be missing or falls short of ideals in relationships with self or others, or the events of day-to-day experience. While similar on the surface to what is seen as high expectations with the A-i pattern, here the emotional reaction to experience of things falling short of ideals is disappointment and longing, as opposed to irritation or anger. Even with ecstatic emotional experiences, it can be hard to stay with those feelings, as the tendency to find what's missing or how experiences fall short quickly imbues the emotional reactions with disappointment or longing for what is now gone.

As with all the other patterns, there is a tendency to find and dwell on what you are looking for. Recall the adage, "Where attention goes, neural firing flows, and neural connection grows." Each of the PDPs reinforces its own adaptive strategies, sometimes engaging the world in a manner that evokes the very thing one dreads. The differences across the pathways are in that "what" the individual tends to be looking for. For example, there is a strong tendency to "find," and so react to, evidence of abandonment in otherwise innocent gestures of others within this PDP of B-i.

As the mind seeks deeply felt connection with experience, and as attention is drawn to disappointment and shortcoming, there is a stronger-than-typical human tendency to overlook or even discount beauty or wonder in ordinary experience in the present, which others find and can stay with more readily. David often described this as "missing out on the great middle of life." Importantly, this can include their own goodness inside.

Emotional Processing

As should be clear by now, uncommonly expressive emotionality is characteristic, often with patterns of big and rapid swings between light and dark moods. Not only is there passionate pursuit of emotional connection with others and experience, but the threshold is also low for activation of the separation distress emotion system—the bonding vector's subcortical network—and the individual is therefore more prone to respond with upregulated force in intense reactivity to any perceived ruptures of connection or abandonment. Emotional intensity in those in a deeply carved groove of this PDP can leave others feeling overwhelmed, or unable to cope with what they perceive as an unacceptably mercurial, long-suffering, or self-absorbed individual. The more rigid the personality structure, the more "loudly" the emotional energies speak in body language, and the more prominent these aspects of the pattern can be.

While there can be intense joy in artistic, aesthetic, or natural beauty that approaches ideals, overall, the personality tends to lean toward feelings like loss, sadness, disappointment, longing, or shame. Not only does attention tend to seek evidence of disconnection, but the threshold for activation of the separation distress emotion system being low also means that individuals are prone to readily respond with the full force of panic-like or even rageful reactivity to any real, misperceived, or fully imagined ruptures in connection.

Not uncommonly, an overall emotional tone of sadness or melancholy can seem to others to be a worrisome sign of depression or suffering that requires intervention. While this is the case at times, at least as often it appears that the individual is not nearly as troubled as they can seem to be to those less familiar with this aspect of emotional life or to those without this personality pattern. Individuals traveling along this pathway are simply more comfortable staying with their darker feelings than most people in other PDPs because they have a lot more practice in that territory. As Helen Palmer (1988) notes, what can seem to outsiders like depression or dwelling in the pain of loss and sadness is often experienced on the inside more like "sweet regret" that has a bittersweet, pleasant quality.

The well-attuned therapist, who will easily pick up on the strong emotional orientation and tone of these individuals who "wear their hearts on their sleeve," will be cautious about prematurely leaping to a diagnosis of depression or suffering requiring medical intervention, and equally wary of unintentionally conspiring with a particularly fixated client's habitual "woe is me" strategy, or getting caught up in the client's attachment to emotional intensity. Careful evaluation and a thorough consideration of both psychiatric disorder as well as developmental pathway is essential for proper care and treatment planning. These clients do not really need deeper access to their uncomfortable feelings, unlike most others. They need to learn to understand those feelings, and regulate their intensity and movements outside the window of tolerance that make them become dysregulated.

Cognitive Processing

Thoughts and verbal narratives tend to be oriented around what is missing, lacking, or disappointing in what or who is here and now, compared to imagined ideals of what could be, or how things once were but no longer are, tinged with an "If only . . . {Sigh}" quality. A second theme revolves around an inclination to see oneself as deficient, or as an outsider, or as having somehow missed out, compared to everyone else. An interesting third common theme reflects an often-embedded belief that "people don't—or can't—understand me," which presumably feeds into behaviors consciously, or nonconsciously, intended to let them stand out in unique ways and be seen. A fourth theme concerns meaning and authenticity in just about everything or everyone, or disdain when they find meaning, depth, or authenticity lacking in others. A fifth theme is paying considerable attention to aesthetics.

Summing Up

When the B-i pattern is running the show in a person's life, psychotherapist Beatrice Chestnut (2013, pp. 300–302) identifies three key behavioral patterns that lead to problems:

1. "Holding onto a strong belief in your own deficiency such that you close yourself off from others (and love and goodness) in the expectation of abandonment."
2. "Distracting yourself in various ways from your own growth and expansion through your attachment to various emotions."

3. "Focusing on what's missing such that nothing measures up and nothing can be taken in."

Growth-Edge Work

Healing and development for Type 4 ironically involves turning inward from the outward search for the ultimate ideal, deep-heart connection, and complete fulfillment where nothing of substance is missing. This tendency only serves to perpetuate their dilemma. All the well-intentioned searching in the wrong place only creates more intense feelings of deficiency and longing. The primary task for Type 4 is to realize that wholeness and completeness come with acceptance and appreciation of what is here now in the present moment, from the inside out, not from the outside in. Disappointments and deficiencies are part of the fabric of life, not an indication of deficiency of being.

[Source: The Narrative Enneagram, 2020, p. 39]

Strategies for Development

- *Moving from a cognitive preoccupation that only I do not have, to a cognitive awareness that everyone has some things and doesn't have other things.*
- *Moving from intense internal feelings to emotional balance with what is and what is not.*
- *Developing wholeness requires integration of personality and essence. This is the work of living well and of well-being. The higher state work of reclaiming essence and the personal work of developing a high functioning personality, not only augment each other, they require each other. The work of integration of being is both/and not either/or.*

[Source: David Daniels, "Integrating the Higher Qualities of our Essence into our Lives." https://drdaviddaniels.com/integrating-essence-true-nature-lives/]

- *Accept that wholeness and realness exist now in the present moment.*
- *Focus on what is present and "what is," rather than what is missing.*
- *Resist domination by strong and fluctuating feelings while acknowledging their authenticity.*

- *Sustain a steady course of action even in the presence of intense feelings.*
- *Notice when real feelings are dramatized: "It's going to get awful again."*
- *Resist worshipping your intense feelings: "My suffering makes me special."*
- *Do a reality check: "Was it really that good or bad?"*
- *Use physical exercise to get into the body.*
- *Practice consistency—fulfilling commitments even if you don't feel like it.*
- *Fill in the middle by appreciating the ordinary.*
- *Separate self-esteem from being special or extraordinary.*
- *Notice (and release) your longing for what is missing and idealized.*
- *Become aware of your tendency to become self-absorbed, and how this blocks being present for yourself and others.*
- *Break your self-absorption by moving toward others.*
- *Realize that shame is just the feeling that goes with feeling deficient or lacking.*
- *Work through your initial loss and move on.*

[Source: The Narrative Enneagram, 2020, p. 40]

With an interpersonal neurobiology view of these patterns of belief and emotional response, the PDP framework enables us to see how the excessive differentiation of the individual in the face of disconnected linkage from others, beginning at birth, can make the individual vulnerable to the lower integrative states for the B-i pathway. As the attendency is inward yet the need is really for outward relational connection, there is a fundamental conflict in how one's needs for bonding can be met. By recognizing this imbalance, the inward attendency can be used as a source of strength to embrace the need to connect inwardly to the other vectors—agency and the feeling that arises from the gut, and certainty and the reasoning that emerges from the head. By identifying the source of a disquieting feeling of disconnection as being historical and existential, a part of one's temperament and not a "problem to be solved," the energy can be released to attempt to begin by letting that implicit sense of "something being missing" be placed in developmental reality, letting comparison diminish and release its inhibitory hold on joy, and learning to fully inhabit the present moment, linking to life as it unfolds each day.

A PDP view of a lower state of integration in the B-i pathway illuminates the origins of a "melancholy" and despair that are understandably felt when there is no realization of the original disconnection from simply being, of being at one with the womb. In a PDP sense, this is an implicit memory of wholeness. But without integration, this longing to restore wholeness is felt to be a hopeless urge to connect with perpetual disappointment. The more integrative, higher functioning within this PDP is the movement to a higher state of integration in which the differentiation of these actual experiences of disconnection from the emotional longing can be made, and then linkages to the natural drive to connect inwardly and interpersonally can be established with higher states of functioning. In a lower integrated state of affective processing, the experience of envy arises with comparison and deep-feeling inadequacy. The movement toward the higher integrative emotional process of equanimity is a place of feeling adequate, feeling whole, and feeling unthreatened by others' achievements and acquisitions.

The growth-edge work for the PDP B-i pathway involves harnessing the gift of inward reflection to realize the source of the feeling of longing and disconnection and recognize these—again bring back to mind—as states of emotion and memory, not as ultimate endpoints of disconnection and isolation. For the PDP B-i, when a recurring state of despair or feeling "I am not enough" and "They have it better than I ever will" keeps arising, this can feel as if it were another "voice" inside, one that is commanding a comparison with others, one that feels it needs to continually remind someone down this pathway that they will always be insufficient and alone.

This cultivation of integration inherent in the growth for those traveling the B-i pathway invites a liberation of the capacity for deep feeling and the opportunity to embrace the joy of being alive, here, in "this one wild and precious life" as Mary Oliver noted, a gift this PDP can offer within the individual and to the world. As Oliver also notes in her profound poem "When Death Comes," read to her by her friends as she lay in a coma days before she died, "When it's over . . . I don't want to end up simply having visited this world." The gift of the B-i pathway for all of us, even if this is not our primary, baseline way of being, is to realize the majesty and magic of this precious life we have been given.

Tips for Growth in Relationships
Relational Triggers

People that disappoint us. People that let us down. People that leave us and leave us feeling abandoned. Feeling unheard, unseen, and unimportant. Feeling slighted, invisible, rejected, and unwanted. Feeling misunderstood and not enough. Phoniness. Insincerity. Meaninglessness. Ugliness.

Relational Reflections

- *Encourage your Type 4 to not be overrun by feelings, and to appreciate what is positive in the present moment.*
- *Encourage your Type 4 to stabilize their attention and to "fill in the middle" by valuing the ordinary.*
- *Show them that you understand by showing empathy first before offering help.*
- *Stay steady when their feelings are intense, and reveal your own feelings and reactions.*
- *Appreciate their ultimate idealism.*
- *Let your Type 4 know that they are lovable, regardless of their identification with specialness, a flawed self, or unworthiness.*

[Source: David Daniels, "Type 4: The Romantic."
https://drdaviddaniels.com/type-4]

- *As a Type 4, we need to overcome the longing for what we perceive is "still" missing, disappointing, or lacking in ourselves and/or in our surroundings, all while knowing that that something missing also happens to be that something we've decided is really important.*
- *For us Type 4s, an attachment to disappointment and its resulting energy almost becomes an addiction, leading us to savor the melancholy we know so well and almost invite. It's a state of being that seems to ignite deep feelings of aliveness and intensity and specialness, ones that keep us from appreciating the ordinariness of the mundane, of the status quo.*

- *It's important to learn to appreciate what is positive in our lives right now, just as it is, and develop the gratitude that goes with putting attention on what's here, what's good about it, and what's real. In the process, we need to give ourselves permission to accept ourselves as lovable "as is." From here, we can receive our own love-ability with grace and kindness, humility, and a feeling of "enough-ness."*
- *It's important to allow ourselves to realize that a state of self- and other-acceptance is not dependent on "being special," ideal, superior, or one-of-a-kind. It is simply so because we are who we are, and all is as it is.*

[Source: Daniels & Dion, 2018, pp. 110–111]

Clinical Vignette

A 16-year-old adolescent male, Stephen, came for evaluation as he struggled with great despair and a sense of longing he could not name yet felt he was doomed to live, in a disconnected life of being isolated and alone. He was facing intense existential issues, not uncommon in adolescence. Yet the depth of his despair was profound. Before coming to see me, he had a complete psychiatric evaluation to assess for life-threatening aspects of his suffering, including suicidal thoughts and self-harming behaviors, which he did not have. But what he did have was an inner life that seemed to fit the B-i profile to a T; and when I mentioned this to his parents when they came with him for a second opinion and then discussed this notion with their son, a light bulb of recognition lit up. And then this adolescent's response was telling: "You mean there may be other people who also believe that there is no one like them and they will always be alone? If that's true—I want to meet them!" You can be certain of that, I told him. And so he did, starting a program in his high school for teens to share their inner journeys. You can picture this as activating not only his bonding vector with an outward attendency, but also engaging his agency and certainty vectors to widen the array of motivational networks becoming engaged in his life. This is one example of light bulbs going off and other enlightening ways the PDP framework can help us with our unique and shared lives. As longtime educator Russ Hudson once said about the Enneagram system, it isn't that it puts you in a box; it illuminates the box you are already in so you can become free.

The recognition of how this young man's PDP was shaping his painful life course offered us a chance to explore how he was developing and what factors, inside as temperament, and relational as attachment and friendships, were powerfully influencing him. It was profound to see at this "breakthrough" period of life, as Ellen Galinsky names it, how an opening of the mind to new ways of conceptualizing who we are can shape our own development (Galinsky, 2024). Stephen learned that with a baseline proclivity toward bonding, this primary vector would make relational connections central in his life. Yet with the inward attendency, he'd be filled with an intense sense of something being missing. We discussed the reality of implicit memory and the notion that we all have some sense of being fulfilled, of being at ease, at peace. This sense of wholeness, I offered to Stephen, was something I too longed for, but being of a different PDP as my baseline, it was simply different from his.

The PDP perspective enabled us to discuss the deep neural mechanisms shaping our subjective experience. With Stephen's inward focus in the bonding vector, there was a likelihood of feeling, inside, that something important was missing. This forlorn state, without having light shed upon it, could certainly progress, as it seemed to have done with Stephen, toward a helplessness and despair. With the intense social media attention of his adolescent peers, this "who is in and who is out" at school made him feel that some rule book he didn't sign up for was "constantly letting me know I don't belong." The subsequent withdrawal, socially from others and inwardly from his own sense of vitality and hope, created a negative spiral down into the state that, understandably, concerned his parents. The classic diagnoses of "depression" and "mood disorder" were, on the surface, logical conclusions. And certainly if Stephen didn't respond to therapy, we might consider other options of interventions.

We worked on his ability to sense his emotional life from a bit of a distance with a practice known as the Wheel of Awareness. And we looked deeply at his needing connection in a social world among his peers that seemed to be superficial and dissatisfying to him. As he began his group at school, the interest that other students had surprised him. He began meeting peers who were not in his prior social circles or athletic activities. "I can't believe that there is a whole world there that most kids just don't know about." That inner world, now a bit more illuminated for Stephen, is hopefully one that he will continue to learn about and expand upon as he grows.

It may sound odd, but learning about the neural mechanisms beneath his sorrow actually seemed to enable Stephen to "not take myself so seriously" even as he was attuning more now to the meaning of his emotional life. That lightness of being, we can both imagine and hope, is a direct outcome of how empowering our clients to gain more access to wholeness may happen by widening the groove of their PDPs so that a broader array of adaptive skills becomes available. For Stephen, this meant looking outward, not only in; trying out other modes of emotion regulation other than upregulation as experience and express; and tapping into the empowerment of the agency vector and the predictability and safety of the certainty vector. The freedom to access these other skills of life will hopefully be a gift for Stephen that keeps on giving.

Here is an example of another clinical vignette, this a transcription from David's exploration of romantic intimacy with different personality pairings:

David's Commentary: *Here we experience the deep longing for the ultimate ideal that can dominate a Type 4's life and that can profoundly affect the ability to love freely as well as can affect their lovemaking experiences. In the process, this longing can take Type 4 away from what is present and positive. Katherine's awareness is ahead of her ability to keep her heart open to herself; she's still learning and allowing herself to be receptive to what is positive in the moment. This is her next step toward integration and wholeness.*

Katherine: *My 4-ness shows up as I always find something missing in my life. I'm always seeking something, longing for more of what I feel is important. It is my life story.*

David: *The sadness to me in Type 4 is not in the seeking of quality itself, which is* *lovely, but that you are never enough, others are not enough, and you don't appreciate all that you are, or that others are. So tell me, what is love to you?*

Katherine: *A lot of energy goes into this seeking, getting disappointed, and never feeling enough. I once had a true love, but he left me [tears come up]. I have never found that love again.*

David [with intensity]: *This left you in a state of longing, which is core to your work of development [pausing]. Keep working on noticing this focus of attention—on what you feel is not enough, and let that be a reminder to go to what you appreciate in yourself and life instead.*

Katherine: *To me, it is just holding on to what is positive in both me and another person.*

David: *It means more than holding on, it means staying present to what is, not what isn't in either you or the other. There is even a definition of love that goes, "Love is appreciating differences."*

Katherine: *I need to feel that what he gives me is fine and there's not something better or more he should have done. It's so disappointing to the point I cannot enjoy what's there and being given, at all. I know I need to just hold on and stay present.*

David: *And paradoxically, truly loving and appreciating yourself, is what will allow you to truly love and appreciate another. What you are doing to another is what you are doing to yourself, deep within. This work goes beyond just holding on. This is the work of awareness. This is the work of self-acceptance. So how does all this show up for you when it comes to your sexual expression?*

Katherine: *I like to be truly there, present in the moment. All what you say about love for me is the same in my physical relationship with a partner. I just learned the enneagram, relationships, and intimacy need to be there, appreciating what is and express it as a desire, though it's not an actuality. I find myself struggling.*

David [with warmth and definiteness]: *Can you notice how you express this as an idealization? This is an awareness of the mechanism you are using to engage with another. That is different than simply being there present in the moment with acceptance for self and other. You have much awareness, so* *much so, you can see how you are actually trying to cope. I urge you to use this to become aware of the deep longing that takes you away from what is present and real and there for you. Let that be the key to being kinder to yourself. Learning how to come back to what is there in your love life, and when lovemaking, that's real; this is your practice. I urge you to take some time to reflect on this work you have just done and absorb its developmental potential for you. Thank you, Katherine.*

[Source: Daniels & Dion, 2018, pp. 365–367]

Short Reflections for Integration

Simply stop for a minute or so 3–4 times a day to center and reflect on one of the following:

Longing for what is missing

Simply stop to sense in your body and notice how your attention and energy recurrently go to what you feel is important yet missing. Then come back to what is present and positive as best you can.

Emotional intensity

Stop to observe the bodily intensity of your often fluctuating feelings and allow yourself to come back to a more calm stance.

Idealizing specialness

Simply stop to notice how you often focus on being unique, unusual, different and spurn the ordinary. Allow yourself to make the ordinary extraordinary.

[Source: David Daniels, "Growth for Type 4: The Romantic." https://drdaviddaniels.com/growth-for-type-4]

Integrative Transformation

A PDP perspective on integration for the B-i lets us envision how differentiating a feeling state of longing for a connection that is now missing can be made explicitly clear, named, and then placed in a frame in which it makes sense. By focusing on this vector's fundamental motivation for relational connection through bonding, we can see how potentially "trapped" an individual can become when their attendency is inward. The state integration of liberation, from this forlorn feeling of disconnection being a totality of reality to now being simply a feeling of an implicit memory, frees the individual to "not take these impressions and feelings so personally" and instead free these inner states to take their proper perspective in one's life.

Integration for the B-i pathway is a deeply existential journey with the potential to face our foundational feelings of longing and transform them into curiosity, gratitude, and amazement. Feeling fully, embracing joy, and not being swallowed up by any negative feelings of despair are the internal journey experiences of this growth-edge exploration and expansion. Instead of those on this journey being swept up by the waves of emotion and drowned in the disillusionment and despair, therapy can offer them emotional surfing lessons to enjoy the wondrous gifts of intense feelings of their wonderful immersive minds.

When we use the PDP lens of development, we can see that the primary vector of bonding makes this motivation for relational connection a priority. With the inward attendency, we can now understand how this deeply felt sense of something being missing in the connection would emerge. The adaptive strategy of needing to be able to be seen for the authentic, real person one is would then have the hope of finally gaining that real connection that feels so deeply absent. Yet the sad irony is that when not integrated, when in lower states of development, the intensity of that drive to be seen can actually drive people away, not toward, the connection the individual seeks. Clinical work, then, involves offering a perspective on the fundamental existential dilemma of having a subcortical motivational network to achieve something that, in its fullest form of union, can never really be achieved.

Instead of seeing life as a compromise, an integrated individual becomes empowered in their own way to find true meaning in the opportunities life affords to connect—with one's inner life, with other human beings, with nature, with beauty, with the divine. The fullness of those connections, when expressed in the world and experienced as these true opportunities rather than inadequacies, can enrich a life with a wide array of emotional intensity and meaning.

B-o: Bonding-outward (B-o Pathway; Enneagram 2)

Expressed Personality

Notable behavioral traits of this highly and often clearly relationship-oriented pattern are well characterized in the traditional label of "helper" or "giver." They include uncommon levels of attention to others and their needs, and proactive support and giving of themselves and their resources to help and care for others. Carried too far, this propensity for caregiving can lead to extreme inattentiveness to one's own needs, exhaustion of self, depletion of resources, and codependency.

As with all three of the bonding patterns, beneath these relatively nonspecific surface behaviors is a quest for a felt sense of being seen, recognized, and valued by others. When it becomes problematic, the personality structure seems to operate as though there is a deeply embedded belief that "I *must* care for and give fully to others in order to be loved and valued." Here, the quest for connection revolves around a generally nonconscious dynamic of *earning* love and connection by attending to others and their needs, and making *them* feel valued, recognized, and cared for.

When this pattern is fully running the show, the net effect can be a kind of "strategic giving" approach to life. Although not a *consciously* formulated strategy, it is nonetheless strategic in two ways. First, it is a "giving to get" strategy. The rewards are being seen as a selfless and caring giver and through that public presentation, then, feeling connected. Recall here that caring for others creates a sense of connection. Second, giving from this dynamic tends to be targeted to those whose affection and gratitude somehow feels particularly salient in some way. Importantly, for most clients, little if any of this underlying dynamic is evident in their own awareness;

they simply sense a compelling need in others, and respond by bringing their seemingly constitutional helpful, generous, and insightful self to the situation. Other individuals, however, sometimes sense the nonconscious strings that are attached to the giving behavior, and then feel manipulated or intruded upon when the deeper dynamic of the pattern is dominating that giving person's behavioral drives.

One possible mechanism arising from a PDP perspective on the B-o pathway that may be particularly apt is that of the mirror neuron system. This set of neurons, discovered initially in monkeys and then found also in human beings (see Iacoboni, 2009), enables us to gain a glimpse into a possible way in which we pick up the signals from someone else, often their nonverbal communications, and activate two processes inside of us. One is to imitate their behavior; the other is to simulate their internal state. In observing several individuals on an Enneagram panel of those with a Type 2 designation, it was remarkable, and uniquely found in this panel grouping, that when one member would cross their legs, the remainder of the panel would do the same. That behavioral imitation was nonconscious but quite evident, and mirrored (no pun intended) by their verbal reflections on how readily they could feel others' feelings since their earliest memories. One person even had "Empathic" on his license plate out in the parking lot. Whether this is a temperament feature—not learned but innate—that is then reinforced by family experiences, or simply a learned capacity, we don't really know. However, these features of emotional sensitivity to the states of others and a tendency to readily imitate behaviors observed in others suggests that a robust mirror neuron system may be present.

The brain enables us to first feel in our own bodies what is being picked up, as with an antenna, from the signals of the bodies of others. We then examine, nonconsciously, this internal state with something called interoception—the perception of the interior. And we then assess that internal state, in an adjacent prefrontal region, and then come to a sense of our own interior status by way of what is generated from what we sense in another as part of our empathic understanding. Could it be that the outward attendency coupled with the robust mirror neuron empathic resonance response makes it more readily available to feel another's feelings before we know our own? Some views from evolutionary theory in fact suggest just this—that we began in our human development with empathy before we gained the ability for insight. Perhaps we are seeing this important evolutionary sequence in the powerful empathic abilities of those along this B-o pathway. Integration would invite an expansion of these skills to now be focused inwardly, an evolutionary and developmental step (see Siegel, 2023 for a broad discussion of this topic).

Brief Description	The 2 believes you must give fully to others to be loved. Consequently, Givers are caring, helpful, supportive, and relationship-oriented, but also can be prideful, overly intrusive, and demanding.
Key Interventions	Help the 2 develop, integrate, and own the true separate self, and overcome the addiction to meeting the needs of others as a way to be cared for and loved.

[Source: The Narrative Enneagram, 2020, pp. 33–34]

Developmental Pathway and Adaptive Strategy

In the PDP framework, this personality pattern emerges when the need to establish and maintain mutually supportive connections with others becomes most highly salient, and the working strategy of the B-o developmental pathway becomes an adaptive strategy.

Here attendency is outward, meaning the flow of bonding-for-connection emotional energy is centered on perceptions of others and their needs to be seen and supported or cared for, and emotional motivations to connect with others are shifted toward the care of others, which brings feelings of connection. In effect, feelings of neediness—including one's own—tend to be seen externally in the response of others, and the solution is to become the active agent in establishing connection by making *others* feel seen, valued, and cared for.

Integration and Individual Variation: Strengths and Challenges

As in each of the pathways, this pattern of personality is not in and of itself problematic. Attentiveness to others and their needs, and generosity of spirit, are vital to social cohesion. In the growth-edge work, finding the strengths in this pathway and accessing the higher, more integrative capacities of the other pathways—the other vectors, the other attendencies—is the direction of therapeutic work. In this case the natural "gifts" of attentiveness to and resonance with the needs of others can be used wisely in giving and caring where giving and caring are needed. At the same time there can emerge a clear awareness of one's own needs for bonding, connection, and being seen when those arise, and these states can flow freely into attentiveness to self and seeking of care of self from others.

In contrast, when this pattern is dominant and integration is impaired, attending to and caring for others becomes a kind of compulsive strategy for establishing and maintaining a sense of bonding and connection with others. The individual becomes identified with and prideful about being indispensable to others' well-being as *the* strategy for establishing and maintaining their own connection with others. Attentiveness to or even awareness of the needs of one's inner self for connection, care, and help from others becomes impaired, and there is susceptibility to crossing the line between generous caring and unconsciously manipulative giving or codependency.

Behavioral Profile	**Strengths:** *Giving and generous, helpful, romantic, sensitive to others' feelings, appreciative, supportive, energetic and exuberant, willing.*
	Difficulties: *Overemphasis on relationships, especially challenging ones; making yourself vulnerable to rejection and loss, repression and indirect expression of your own real needs, which may lead to eruption of anger and emotion, manipulating others to get your own needs met, allowing your feelings to grow and overwhelm you (feelings such as hysteria, distress, and somatic complaints), repressing questions regarding your real self (e.g., who am I, really?), feeling controlled by others who have developed dependency issues, and longing for freedom.*

[Source: David Daniels, "Enneagram Type 2 Description: The Giver."
https://drdaviddaniels.com/type-2/]

Focus of Attention and Blind Spots

When the B-o pattern is active, attention and energy are centered on others, and their feelings and needs. Approaching life with this orientation over time, one develops a genuine sensitivity to others, and a knack for resonating with their feelings and sensing their needs and desires. So far, all well and good. However, when used as a nonconscious strategy for maintaining connection with others, there is a susceptibility to over-reading and perceiving more need for care than is real.

A key contributor to this susceptibility is that attention to one's own needs and care of oneself can become major blind spots. Although not exclusive to this pattern, inattentiveness to one's own needs is characteristic when integration of the B-o pattern is impaired. It is as if the client never learned how to attend to and care for themselves, or the importance of doing so. The net result: It can be very difficult for these clients to perceive the difference in their own and others' needs, and to project theirs onto—that is, to see them reflected in the mirror of—others.

An even deeper blind spot for this pattern can be experiencing a solid sense of an autonomous self. As one becomes increasingly wrapped up in the "giver" dynamic, the sense of an independent—as opposed to codependent— self can get lost in the "shape-shifting" to become what you perceive others need from you, and the reward and reinforcement you receive for being such a thoughtful, helpful, generous, and kind person.

Emotional Processing

As in all three of the bonding patterns, motivations to connect are relatively strong. Here, with a tendency to attribute emotional signals of need to others, there can be what feels like an urgent requirement to move toward, and be helpful and supportive, accompanied by a pridefully inflated sense that you know what others need, maybe better than they do, and that they cannot do without you. It is essentially a nonconscious way of reframing the motivation, releasing the hold of the situation, and shifting the emotional state of distress. This is reflected in so-called shape-shifting behavior—becoming who and what is perceived to be *needed* in the others' reflection. (While similar on the surface to what is seen in the B-d pattern, as we'll soon see, there shape-shifting is more as though becoming what is approved of in others' reflection.) The common focus is on how to ensure relational connection.

At the same time, for those on the B-o pathway, there is a hypersensitivity to rejection and abandonment, which can manifest in deep hurt, anger, or shame when others do not reflect appreciation, or pull away from connection. While the dynamic of strategic helpfulness is almost entirely beneath conscious awareness, others may sense the nonconscious strings attached to the giving, or the see-through shape-shifting and seductive flattery, and therefore feel manipulated or intruded upon, and respond by resisting or backing away. Here, the panic-like pain of rejection and separation felt by those with the B-o pattern can burn and turn to fury in that moment. "How could you treat me like that after all I've done for you!?" Alternatively, a true existential crisis of shame or depression can erupt if rejection or failure leads to the collapse of the image of being that special one, and there is no internalized solid self to step in and pick up the pieces.

The more rigid the personality structure, the less integrated the individual is at that time in their life, the more "loudly" the subcortical bonding circuit expresses itself with sadness and separation distress through body language, and the more prominent the emotionality beneath the patterns of behavior can be. Just beneath the generally hidden desire for recognition, appreciation, and affection they long for from those to whom they are giving the most, there may be a great deal of anxiety, shame, or lack of self-worth that goes unrecognized given their outward attendency. The irony is that someone so attuned to the needs of others tends, when not integrated, to be challenged to attune to their own inner needs. An attuned therapist will often pick up on these cognitive-emotional undercurrents in the narrative and behaviors of the client heartily describing their care and concern for others.

Cognitive Processing

Thoughts and narrative tend to be dominated by the needs, troubles, and concerns of others, and all that has been or must be done to ensure they are attended to and cared for. A boastful streak may show up in prideful narrative themes, suggesting "I know what they need," a cardinal feature of this personality pattern when it is really running the show. At least as much, however, it is as though the individual and the other are conflated, and true feelings and needs of one's inner life—such as exhaustion, depletion of personal or material resources from all the giving—are missing in action. Indeed, the client with a primary baseline B-o PDP will often be unable to recognize the needs of their inner self, much less articulate or focus attention and energy to do something directly about them.

Flattery, charm, seductiveness, and keeping the spotlight on others can become well-honed tools used in the strategy of keeping others close. Even in therapy, the client will have an inordinate focus on the well-being of the therapist. In therapy, clients often present with complaints of depression, exhaustion, frustration, or even rage when all their efforts to help have been unsuccessful, insufficiently appreciated, or rejected.

Summing Up

Beatrice Chestnut (2013, pp. 376–372) describes three major behavioral expression patterns for this personality archetype that are associated with problems clients tend to bring to therapy:

1. "Denying needs and repressing feelings as a way to connect more easily with others."
2. "Adapting, merging, helping, pleasing, and shape-shifting to engineer connections with specific individuals."
3. "Avoiding rejection and separation through maintaining an idealized (inflated) image of yourself, avoiding conflicts and boundaries, and managing your self-presentation (including lying and being inauthentic)."

Growth-Edge Work

Healing and development for Givers involves reclaiming their freedom from the tyranny of a need-governed (driven) world in which they must fulfill the needs of others to gain approval or love. This makes developing a separate self, and thus a sense of freedom, a difficult proposition. Since the needs and desires of others are endless, Givers never gain a sense of their own freedom, unless they learn to give what is needed and no more, pay attention to their own needs, and receive from others. They must learn, ultimately, that needs are met by a greater or universal will, and their self-worth does not depend upon being the agent of others' fulfillment. Then they can experience the pure joy of giving for its own sake, freely and lovingly.

[Source: The Narrative Enneagram, 2020, p. 33]

Strategies for Development

- Moving from a cognitive preoccupation that others need me and I need to give to them to a cognitive awareness that the world naturally gives and takes.
- Moving from emotional pride with others to an internal emotional humility.
- Developing wholeness requires integration of personality and essence. This is the work of living well and of well-being. The higher state work of reclaiming essence and the personal work of developing a high functioning personality, not only augment each other, they require each other. The work of integration of being is both/and not either/or.

  [Source: David Daniels, "Integrating the Higher Qualities of our Essence into our Lives." https://drdaviddaniels.com/integrating-essence-true-nature-lives/]

- Give and receive freely, without pride and expectations.
- Release from the pride of indispensability.
- Practice giving without anyone knowing.
- Reflect on what it would be like if no one needed you.
- Notice how your attention habitually goes out to others' needs and desires.
- Balance the active force that goes out to others' needs with the receptive force that allows your own needs to be met.
- Describe yourself around different "significant others" and learn to be authentic rather than changing in order to please.
- Learn appropriate giving (ask before giving).
- Notice a rise in your emotions as a signal you may be repressing your own needs.
- See your anger as a cue that you aren't getting your own needs met.
- Spend time alone to develop independent interests and autonomy.
- Practice self-love and appreciation.
- Make the "hidden score card" conscious—what you have given, and what you have unconsciously expected in return.
- Become aware that it is a great gift to others to receive from them.

- *Stay at home for a day and let friends completely care for you with no paybacks.*
- *Ask for something you need once a day.*

[Source: The Narrative Enneagram, 2020, p. 34]

Tips for Growth in Relationships
Relational Triggers

Feeling unappreciated or uncared for. Not being thanked for all that is given. Feeling uncaringly controlled. Having unmet personal needs and wants, when having given others so much. Being rejected. Treated as dispensable and unnecessary. Being blocked from giving.

Relational Reflections

- **Sensing others' needs and jumping in to fulfill those needs**
  Simply stop to sense in your body and notice how quickly you move forward with active energy to help others often without reflecting if this is really best or fulfilling for the other.
- **Indispensability**
  Simply stop to notice your pride in fulfilling others needs and how this imperative drives your giving.
- **Own needs and desires**
  Simply stop to ask yourself, "Have I been tending to my own needs and desires and receiving from others?" If not, work at allowing this precious gift to self and to others into your daily life.

[Source: The Narrative Enneagram, 2020, pp. 33–34]

How You Can Help a Pattern 2 Self-Develop and Fulfill Their Relationships

- Help your Type 2 develop, integrate, and own their true separate self and overcome the addiction of meeting the needs of others as a way to be taken care of and loved

- Encourage Type 2 to appreciate themselves separate from giving and to claim their own voice
- Avoid becoming the wonderment and being seduced by Type 2s over-giving
- Stay constant and provide steadiness, paying attention to their often real, unmet needs

As a Type 2, we need to develop an individuated self—without feeling guilty for doing so—as very little attention goes to proactively fulfilling the needs of our own personhood. We can give ourselves permission to ward off the deeply felt repulsion of being deemed "selfish" when we do begin to take care of ourselves and put ourselves and the satisfaction of our own needs first, if necessary, and with self-agency, as is appropriate.

We can work toward overcoming the addiction—the high—we get when meeting the needs of important others, when never saying "no," and when seeing ourselves as above others, as more altruistic and more caring. We can allow ourselves to see how we may overuse our own innately generous nature as a way to be loved, appreciated, and taken care of.

We can allow ourselves to explore our feelings when giving without conditions, when giving to ourselves without shame, and in learning to trust that others will love us, and come toward us, without us having to ingratiate ourselves to them first. We can hold the belief that love does and will come to us, organically, as we have brought it to others. As we come to trust in the natural flow of love, coming our way, and in divine reciprocity, our ability to both give and receive freely flourishes. It also gives others the joy of giving to us freely and organically, without provocation or expectation.

[Source: The Narrative Enneagram, 2020, pp. 33–34]

A PDP view of B-o and of the growth-edge needed is to illuminate the nature of a lack of differentiation of the inner experiences—emotions, needs, meanings—of the individual as "me" from the contrasting high sensitivity to those very same inner experiences of others. The challenge of an adaptive strategy with this combination of vector and attendency that leads to asymmetry of relationships is that the rigid and chaotic reactivity that can arise may seem "justified" in that the individual of the B-o pathway is so "helpful" to others that they cannot see why they would not be appreciated. Integrative growth invites an honoring of the skills of whatever adaptive strategies emerged from this PDP, and then seeing how to cultivate the differentiation and linkage within that pathway, in this case, working on growing more internal differentiation. As the other vectors and their high integrative capacities are also accessed, agency and certainty become more available for the individual's life skills as well.

Clinical Vignette

A 62-year-old physician named Eliot came to see me saying that his wife's new job was making him irritated for reasons he could not understand. Though his career was still in full swing as a cardiologist and their children were fully grown and now, in their 20s, finding their own way, he felt some "unsettled" feeling as the journalism work of his wife achieved a new level of prestige. As we discussed his new and unsettling feelings of distress, he decided to enter psychotherapy for the first time. My evaluation sessions at the beginning of therapy often involve the two assessments of adult attachment, utilizing the Adult Attachment Interview and the PDP survey of informal questions that could give us a sense of where Eliot was in both his baseline vector and his attendency.

The AAI revealed elements of a preoccupied state of mind with respect to attachment, which included both a great amount of detail with responses to the inquiries, and sometimes getting off topic. The closeness he felt with his mother was sometimes punctuated, he said, by her "mild alcoholism" where he would, during his adolescence, find her passed out at home when he and his two-years-younger sister would return from school. "She was a quiet drunk," he said, and did not describe any experience of being terrified of her or his father, who was busy as a general surgeon at a local hospital.

Eliot's PDP survey revealed a history of focusing on relationships for as far back as he could recall. He would take care of his sister when his mother was drunk and his father absent. His earliest romantic relationships were filled with him being attracted to "women with big problems" that he would try to solve in the course of their often-tumultuous relationships.

When he first met his wife in college, her parents were in the middle of an acrimonious divorce. They were "drawn to each other" early on in their dating, and when college was over, she began her career in journalism as he went on to medical school. Her career was put on hold, he said, as she raised their three children, and he trained in interventional cardiology and developed a thriving practice in our town. He said that he always felt their relationship was balanced in needs, but that he was "more the giver and she the receiver."

"Once the kids were out of the house, she really fell apart. I was there for her to help support her in the classical 'empty nest syndrome' and that felt good. I was fine. But when her writing was noticed by some awards group and she received national recognition, that worry disappeared and she seemed to do fine. I don't know why that bothers me, and I know it shouldn't, but if I am honest, it makes me irritated with her behavior."

We focused on what he might be feeling in this new situation, with her busy career and public recognition. He was able to identify a feeling that in all of his prior relationships before marriage, he was the one to take care of his partner. Now, he was able to see, for the first time she was in the position of "not needing" him. Instead of feeling free or proud of her, he felt somehow threatened by her independence.

As we explored the attachment adaptation that the likely ambivalent childhood attachment with his mother would have created, we illuminated a sense of inner turmoil that the inconsistency and sometimes overt absence of his mother's attention created inside him. That feeling of insecurity was not in his academic work, at which he excelled; but it was present in his close, romantic relationships.

Whether this attachment strategy drove his vector to be in the bonding motivational network, we don't know. And whether these early inner feelings of distress drove him toward an attendency of outward, we also don't know. But we could say that the preoccupied adult attachment he revealed would suggest some "leftover issues" that were giving him a sense of insecurity in relationships now as an adult. And this nonsecure state of mind would then dig the groove of his PDP even more deeply into his neural networks.

Sometimes just knowing this as a therapist and working with the ideas inside of me is enough; but in this situation with Eliot, I felt that sharing the developmental neuroscience PDP framework directly would be the most helpful for him. We could see that with the nonsecure attachment, there would be an intensification of the pathway he was on. The move away from being at one with the womb after birth in the do-or-die new situation would make one of his subcortical networks especially activated. In his case, the bonding vector would make the drive for relational connection intense. Perhaps because his internal world was so distressing, or simply because of his temperament, the outward attendency would be creating a way in which he'd adapt—his adaptive strategies would be to meet others' needs to vicariously satisfy his own longing for connection.

Now, with the kids out of the house and his wife's career flourishing, her dependency on him for both emotional and financial support was markedly shifted. She felt close to him, but didn't need him. For someone with a primary baseline PDP of B-o, this would mean not being able to feel fulfilled, activating his separation distress and sadness, and when she didn't need him, to feel irritated and rejected.

Knowing this was a beginning for our work. He could learn to become more aware of his own inner needs by doing practices like the Wheel of Awareness, which guided him to have interoception, the perception of his interior life. He could feel the heartfelt sensation of needing his wife, and he could begin the important shift to differentiating his own needs from satisfying hers. Fortunately, his wife was excited about these realizations, and together they could discuss these patterns and how hers in the C-i pathway created an "interesting" challenge that perhaps you can imagine. In fact, as a journalist in one of the couple's sessions we decided to have, she was intrigued as to how each of the various relational combinations would present its own unique kinds of challenges to reaching clarity and wholeness. We'll get to some of that in the final chapters of the book!

David has an intriguing exploration here, too, of how this PDP presents with experiences of sexual intimacy.

David's Commentary: *Here is a heartfelt example of doing the work of becoming whole, of personal integration. Richard, a young man in his 20s, expresses the path for Type 2 as discovering his own needs and desires and in the process, finds himself on the road to more organic, unconditional giving and receiving, to himself as well as to others—both of which are gifts. This level of development is inspiring.*

Richard: *I know I'm a Type 2 because I'm helping, and helping is a way to be. To be honest with you, that's it!*

David [smiling]: *That's concise. So then, what is love to you?*

Richard: *To be with somebody and to just be appreciated.*

David: *Say a little more; what does being appreciated mean to you?*

Richard: *It is the longing for connection. To be appreciated for who I am so that I don't have to explain myself or even, I won't have to keep doing more to feel accepted. I'm always helping people in terms of asking, "How are you?" or "How can I make you smile today?" I'm really there for the other and I expect that back too, I really do. But I don't want to say that every time. I want this back with my wife though.*

David [with concern]: *That is treacherous territory because she doesn't think the way you do as a Type 2. She may love you deeply but doesn't operate from the same habit of mind. While as a Type 2, you go out of your way to notice what another needs, others won't necessarily be doing that for you. You may need to tell her what you want and need.*

Richard [laughing]: *I may need a course in how to ask the right questions!*

David [lightly yet emphatically]: *She may need to take your course and you hers. But seriously, true love is being in a natural flow of giving and receiving, which is an unconditional flow. It's a process where both show up willfully and within their own volition, with their own freewill. It goes beyond any course that has us trying to ask the right questions, as useful as that can be.*

Richard [speaking seriously]: *What stops me is not knowing myself. To me, sex was always something difficult because I was giving something that I hadn't given myself, but I didn't know it at the time. So to really make sex not "a doing for someone else," but slowing down and just being present—I didn't have any grasp of that.*

David: *Yes, it means being there "for you." You have never put attention there. You beautifully describe the path; I can just sense your depth of understanding. The key theme for you is to have your heart actually opening to yourself. This means, continuing to practice. Come back to your own feelings, sensations, and desires every time you practice. So while you are waking up to this, what can be the difficulties in your sexual expression?*

Richard [said tenderly, kindly]: *I thought and was often confused, is there something wrong with me or with her? The answer is that I was missing being there for myself [pauses]. Now I'm finding me from the inside, which is different.*

David [said warmly with a few tears]: *Process is the path for all of us. You are on the path and that is a gift you are giving yourself. It is very moving. Thank you, Richard.*

[Source: Daniels & Dion, 2018, pp. 353–354]

Short Reflections for Integration

Sensing others' needs and jumping in to fulfill those needs

Simply stop to sense in your body and notice how quickly you move forward with active energy to help others often without reflecting if this is really best or fulfilling for the other.

Indispensability

Simply stop to notice your pride in fulfilling others' needs and how this imperative drives your giving.

Own needs and desires

Simply stop to ask yourself, "Have I been tending to my own needs and desires and receiving from others?" If not, work at allowing this precious gift to self and to others into your daily life.

[Source: David Daniels, "Growth for Type 2: The Giver."
https://drdaviddaniels.com/growth-for-type-2/]

Integrative Transformation

The outward attendency of the bonding vector can make an individual vulnerable to lower states of functioning in which the inner needs for connection are driving an outward effort to attain that interpersonal bond without being aware of the inner feeling of their own personal need. This adaptive strategy can then be to "figure out what others need and then meet those needs" in order to be needed and ensure lasting connection. This outward energy can then be intense when not integrated and the inner needs for personal states being seen by others missing, driving that outward energy even more powerfully with the shift mode of emotion regulation that reframes and redirects—this is for you, not for me (or my needs). This can be understood as not differentiating one's inner needs from the inner needs of others in the face of intense external behaviors to ensure connection.

The external drive to connect that underlies the B-o energy is a heart-centered sensation about relational connections; but the feelings when such bonding is not acknowledged can become reactive, with a "pride" experience of resenting someone not accepting a bid for meeting their needs, as we've seen in Eliot's experience. Naturally, the give-and-take of any relationship would make this asymmetry, filled with the propensity toward a chaotic or rigid pattern, signs of low integration.

Growth-edge work for the PDP B-o involves an openness to the give-and-take of meaningful relationships. Two or more individuals can each differentiate their inner states and then link them to others without losing that differentiation. In this way, interpersonal integration is not about blending; it is about joining as a We without losing the Me.

By differentiating the individual's own inner needs from those of others and then linking from a place of sufficiency and clarity, relationships can be established with the rich sensitivity that those with a B-o pattern offer in interpersonal communication and awareness. By ensuring this differentiation and linkage balance, the FACES flow—of being flexible, adaptive, coherent, energized, and stable—begins to fill the relational space with a sense of harmony that is not on the edge of either the chaos or the rigidity that marks moments of being unseen or underappreciated in low-integrated states. In some informal observations, the capacity for mirroring and empathy seemed especially high in those of this PDP pathway; and this then can become a strength if the nonintegrated states of merger are then transformed with the cultivation of differentiation that does not compromise healthy forms of linkage.

In this B-o pathway, the outer energy can be a primary challenge, for clinician and client alike, in helping guide attention inward. When the emotion-regulation mode is shift, this reframing and redirecting of the emotions of separation distress and sadness, and even of panic in the face of disconnection, can be quite difficult to work with. The wonderful skills of empathic resonance, however, can be used to help guide the client toward integration by differentiating this skill and focusing its motivation—bonding for connection—toward the inner life of the individual. In this way, by differentiating attendencies and then linking inner and outer, higher integrative states are invited to become engaged. With embracing the other higher states of the other vectors, agency and certainty, we can then see how integration as the focus of the growth-edge can yield a deeply transformative experience for the individual whose initial focus was on others' needs and not their own.

When an attendency of outward can be balanced with a focus inward within the individual, the feelings of one's own needs and perspectives can begin to emerge. This movement entails the shift mode of emotion regulation yielding to feeling the authentic feelings of need, of a longing to belong, that then can open relationships to a more flexible way of unfolding in the more symmetric sharing that is the basis of relational harmony.

The well-honed empathic skills usually aimed to the external world of others can now be harnessed to focus in a caring, kind, compassionate manner on the individual's own inner experience of emotions, desires, and needs. This is both a switch in attendency from outward to inward, and a change of the emotion-regulation mode of shift—RR, reframe and redirect. We can see from this profile how challenging it might be to make such changes in the adaptive strategy cultivated to deal with a deep sense of not being whole. This growth-edge work, then, can involve moments of profound vulnerability as attention and emotion regulation transform and an awareness of this drive for bonding becomes revealed. In the PDP view, this integrative transformation can help the individual to live with more harmony as they go about the human challenge of being both in relationship and in harmony with one's inner life, a we and a me, where both can flourish.

B-d: Bonding-dyadic (B-d Pathway; Enneagram 3)

Expressed Personality

As with all three of the bonding patterns, maintaining a felt sense of connection with important others tends to hold special salience. With this pattern, accomplishment and success provide the vehicle to being seen by others, and with that a feeling of their approval and support. In other words, the need for connection with others is channeled into making sure you always uphold the image of one who is successful, valued, does the most, and looks the best. Notable behavioral traits include a strong drive toward doing and achieving, and an eagerness to "get 'er done" and "move on to the next thing."

This personality structure seems to operate as if there is a deeply embedded belief that "I must accomplish and succeed to feel loved and valued." Many of the clinical problems associated with this pattern derive from the pressures to produce created by this orientation. Physical exhaustion or psychological breakdown brings many to therapy as it becomes increasingly difficult to sustain the relentless pace of the succession of goals and the competitive drive to be the best. Not infrequently this precipitates a deep existential crisis: "If I am what I do, and I cannot keep doing, then I will be nothing."

Brief Description	*The 3 believes you must accomplish and succeed to be loved. Consequently, Performers are industrious, fast-paced, and focused on goals and efficiency. They also can be inattentive to feelings, impatient, and image-driven.*
Key Interventions	*Help Threes slow down, welcome and appreciate their feelings, and notice that love is "being" as well as "doing and having."*

[Source: The Narrative Enneagram, 2020, pp. 36–38]

Developmental Pathway and Adaptive Strategy

As alluded to in Chapter 2, in the PDP framework this pattern is rooted in the pathway toward successful individuation in childhood and adolescence. Here the feature we call attendency—where energy and attention are first centered—has a dyadic both/between quality, where the focus can center on conflicting or competing motivations to be an autonomous being out in the world on the one hand, and staying connected with others in peaceful relationships on the other hand.

The B-d pattern is fundamentally about holding those tensions in ways that allow both individuation and a sense of supportive connection to unfold. Given that evolution has essentially hardwired humans to live connected rather than solitary lives, the solution is to keep the lifeline of connecting motivations contained—that is, downregulate them—by constantly seeking the approving reflection that you are doing well in others' eyes. This dynamic is evident in the behavior of toddlers in their early ventures away, out into the world on their own, with "one eye" on that goal and the other on their caregivers for reassuring evidence that they are being seen, recognized, and supported, and lifelines of connection are intact. It is useful to see this as the roots of the adult personality pattern. The unique circumstances of some individuals' development can, in a variety of ways, make this normal and necessary developmental approach so salient in early life that it becomes an adaptive strategy and a pattern of personality in which achievement of goals and success in the eyes of others become the modus operandi of life. That is, you become identified and connected with a kind of produced "false self" who is successful at achieving and doing what others admire but disconnected from an expression of your authentic self.

Integration and Individual Variation: Strengths and Challenges

When the B-d pattern is dominant and the higher capacities of the three systems and their trio of pathways are well integrated, the flow of attention and energy into behavioral expression is well tempered and wisely channeled by access to the balancing proclivities of the other pathways.

Here we see an inspiring, hard-working, enthusiastic, efficient, and highly competent natural leader. Doing and accomplishing and inspiring others are highly valued but balanced by an ability to experience just being or just living and taking more time to be in touch and be real, authentic, and personable. There is openness and attentiveness to others and availability to respond to their needs for bonding and connection. And there is a realistic sense of responsibility for making things happen.

The less well-integrated and dominant this pattern, the less a balance of both differentiation and linkage rather than excessive differentiation of this pathway, the more we see an egotistical, external goal-oriented and self-aggrandizing "human doing" focused on success and achievement but disconnected from their own authentic self, vulnerabilities, and needs for connection with others, as well as the needs of others, even close others, for attention and care. "Less well-integrated" can emerge from non-differentiated pathways as well as non-linked patterns. Excessive linkage without differentiation, for example, would be one way to understand a nonintegrated state. Whatever the combination, in whichever PDP, the therapeutic goal is to both differentiate and link, to cultivate integration and its FACES flow. In this pattern, individuals may be prone to predictable problems that can bring them to therapy. While not exclusive to this pattern, examples include physical or emotional exhaustion, relationship difficulties stemming from physical absence or habitually downregulated and unprocessed feelings, and workaholism.

Behavioral Profile	**Strengths:** *Effective and industrious leadership, seeing possibility, enthusiasm, hope in action, encouragement, problem solving and solutions, ability to provide, efficiency, practicality, competence.*
	Difficulties: *Self-deception about real needs, missing own feelings, moving to a new task and leaving items incomplete, avoiding reflection and acceptance by doing something instead, suffering and fear appears to come from "nowhere" and wants to be chased away, impatience with differences, which are seen as obstructions in the path toward the goal, wanting too much admiration and attention.*

[Source: David Daniels, "Enneagram Type 3 Description: The Performer." https://drdaviddaniels.com/type-3]

Focus of Attention and Blind Spots

It can be helpful to think of this personality pattern as the poster child for the "human doings" among us. While this pattern does not have a monopoly on that behavioral trait, it is a paramount feature. As such, when the pattern is active, *attention* tends to orient relentlessly toward goals and the most efficient and quickest path to their accomplishment. Related to this, perceptions of obstacles to achievement of success, or any hint of the prospect of failure, tend to loom unusually large on the screen of attention. This process also creates a tendency to exaggerate the significance of inevitable impediments to success.

While doing, goals, and obstacles occupy most of the screen of attention, *blind spots* are harder to see and take in. Most notably these include relationship-oriented feelings, both one's own and others', which are habitually downregulated and prioritized second to achievement of goals and projects on the ever-present to-do list. This is not at all to say these are non-emotional robots. On the contrary, they can be highly emotive, in both positive and negative directions, about matters related to their priorities, or which threaten their image of being a successful person. It is to say that needs and feelings related to other matters—for example tending to the emotional needs of others in important relationships—tend to be perceived as distractions to be dealt with as quickly and efficiently as possible, so as not to take time and energy away from the seemingly vital need to get things done and off the to-do list.

At a deeper level, in a very real sense they can become so wrapped up in becoming the limited image of the human-doing they strive to create—what in traditional teaching is called the false self of this pattern—that they do not recognize, value, or even know how to embody the rest of their whole, unique, human self with all its messiness and inefficiency—that is, their true self in traditional teaching. Consequently, they can be blind to their own physical and psychological vulnerability and, in a way, vain, as they take on the stance that it is only through their own hard work that things get done. They can also blame themselves for what does not succeed or allow them to move on, quickly, to the next task, project, activity, outing, or relationship.

Emotional Processing

In this pattern, when the separation distress of this bonding vector's subcortical motivation system is activated, there can be what feels like a pressing urgency to do even more to bring the rewards of others' attention, recognition, and admiration. The more rigid the personality structure, the more "loudly" those signals speak in body language, and the more prominent these pressures to produce can be.

Not surprisingly, given the roots of this dynamic, when this pathway becomes a dominant personality pattern, emotional energy seems from the outside generally channeled into a forward-moving, goal-oriented, go-get-'em disposition, often accompanied by an engaging or even charismatic leadership quality that inspires others. Inside, however, the experience tends to be a kind of time-oriented, urgent sense of responsibility to push onward, get this goal out of the way, and move on to the next. Other feelings—notably including needs of the self or of others—or attention to what else is going on in the environment tend to get unconsciously pushed aside as distractions. Such avoided feelings can create a variety of problems familiar to all therapists.

While distressing feelings of separation distress tend to be kept at bay, panic can erupt quickly and powerfully when the prospect of failure or major ruptures in the sense of supportive connection with important others threaten to undermine progress or the achiever self-image. So, too, can anger when obstacles get in the way of success. The result: When big negative feelings do intrude, the lack of practice at processing feelings undoubtedly contributes to the overwhelm that can ensue. And in private, or when triggered by music or a melancholic movie scene, weeping can release the pent-up tension of an inauthentic connection to self so often brought on by this compulsion for doing and achieving.

Cognitive Processing

With this pattern, thoughts and narrative tend to feature projects, tasks, goals, things to be done, or all that has been achieved.

Often, conversation is flavored with a streak of what is traditionally called vanity, which David described as "excessive pride in one's own appearance, qualities, good points, and achievements." Less evident to outsiders is the exaggerated and weighty sense of responsibility for making important things happen—as if "it's all on me"—and the inner feelings of responsibility when things don't go well. That, coupled with a competitive nature and a seemingly boundless forward-moving and doing energy, which others generally do not match, can become a kind of belief that everything depends on "ME" and "MY" effort, energy, and skills. It is as though the world will fall apart without "ME" and "MY" hard work and leadership. Importantly, it can be very difficult to let go of this way of thinking, because accomplishments bring a great deal of social reward and acknowledgment.

As each goal is ticked off the to-do list, the next project or task rapidly takes its place on the agenda. Just being in the moment—down time with nothing to be done—is difficult or even scary. And when things don't go well or failure has occurred, responsibility weighs heavily, even when environmental circumstances and other players, work teammates, or family and friends also were part of something that did not work out.

While the underlying motivational dynamic of seeking recognition is generally beneath conscious awareness, the attuned therapist will often sense the emotional charge beneath the client's narrative dominated by all the things they've done or are doing, and an often-self-aggrandizing demeanor.

Summing Up

Beatrice Chestnut (2013, pp. 341–343) describes three major behavioral expression patterns for this personality archetype that are associated with problems clients tend to bring to therapy:

1. "Working hard to support a (narrow) focus on tasks, goals, and achievement."
2. "Constructing and maintaining a specific image to impress others."
3. "Doing without stopping to avoid feeling."

Growth-Edge Work

Healing and development for Performers involves not making life into tasks. The simple prescription here is to expand the range of pace so that Threes can slow down enough to allow feelings to emerge, and to realize that love and acceptance come for being as well as doing. Performers depend on active force and mistrust receptive or passive force. Since Performers are hooked on producing and succeeding, they do what it takes to reach the goal, automatically adjusting their image to become what they perceive will bring them the rewards they desire. They sometimes take shortcuts or soften the truth, since they focus on approval and an image of success through the accomplishment of tasks.

[Source: The Narrative Enneagram, 2020, p. 36]

Strategies for Development

- *Moving from a mental preoccupation that I am the doer to cognitive awareness that the world organically moves forward with or without my efforts.*
- *Moving from emotional urgency/deceit to emotional honesty with self and others.*

[Source: David Daniels, "Integrating the Higher Qualities of our Essence into our Lives." https://drdaviddaniels.com/integrating-essence-true-nature-lives/]

- *Develop receptive force and patience.*
- *Slow your pace and increase its range (imagining a metronome going slowly).*
- *Practice doing one thing at a time with your full attention.*
- *Ask yourself what really matters.*
- *Work with image issues and the belief that love comes from what you do and how you look.*
- *Feel the difference between relating through an image and relating directly from your heart—become open to your true, authentic self.*
- *Notice the cues of shifting your presentation to get a "win."*
- *Lose once in awhile; allow for failure.*
- *Welcome feelings realizing that doubt and anxiety often arise first.*
- *Use imagination—remember a time when you were sad, happy, etc.*
- *Practice saying how you feel out loud.*
- *Notice that your anger is associated with obstruction to goals and accomplishments.*
- *Develop a communication link with your inner self: "How does my inner self say yes?" and "How does it say no?"*
- *Pay attention to physical cues of being tired, stressed, or feeling ill.*
- *Develop empathy and understanding for yourself and others.*
- *Take time to pay attention to others' feelings.*
- *Disconnect success/failure from love.*

[Source: The Narrative Enneagram, 2020, p. 37]

As this B-d pathway moves toward a more highly integrative state, individuals embrace the blend of an inner sense of longing to belong with an outer focus on doing in the world, and a harmony and trust in life, a "hope," emerge and a feeling of ease in doing replaces a nonintegrative experience of a tension-filled drive to produce and perform. Action in the world can become an inspiration for all involved, rather than life being governed by a focus on approval and adulation. Engagement to connect can be mutually productive for all without a fear of disappointing others and losing connection. Belief in one's abilities and place in the world begins to blossom.

The emotional reality of being disconnected from wholeness unless approval is gained by the reactions of others leads to a focus on appearance rather than authenticity in lower states of integration. The feeling of this bonding vector's motivation for connection when away from wholeness is an intense, do-or-die, focus on the personally proven achievements that will be activating the approbation of others. This focus on one's worth based on the opinions of other individuals rather than arising from within is what is sometimes known as "deception" and may be seen as an outcome of the CC mode of downregulating this motivational state and its emotions by containing and channeling this energy in a constrained direction—pleasing others with production and products rather than a belief in the essential goodness of simply being oneself.

The move away from wholeness after birth and the potential to achieve a sense of wholeness out in the world, working-for-a-living, help us see how the bonding vector with the combined inward and outward dyadic attendency yields this profile of priority, the significance, of *doing* in order to be connected. With the bonding motivation for connection as the subcortical driver, this tension between an inner focus of energy on the need to bond with the outer energy on "what can be done to attain and maintain connection" can be understood as the underlying dynamic processing that creates this contain-and-channel emotion-regulation mode in an effort to downregulate the separation distress and sadness. The adaptive strategy that unfolds, if in a low integrated state, can dominate as a person's sometimes intense and inflexible ways of doing to be connected; a high integrated state would harness that power of doing in the service of wholeness rather than a pressure to perform and achieve approval to attain connection. Underneath this outer behavior of low integration is an inner longing, one that, from the view of integration, invites both differentiation of the individual's innate wholeness, their innate goodness and being complete, and the distinct expectations and reactions of other people. In this way, those leading with a primary baseline B-d PDP are offered a challenge: how to learn to be, not just do. And in this integrative growth, how to become in touch with a true sense of what has meaning and purpose, not just what productions will meet others' criteria for what is good and praiseworthy.

In working with patients, this move from doing to being can take many forms. Sometimes it begins with mindfulness practice that enables the sensory experience of "just being in awareness" with sensations, thoughts, or even pure awareness itself to become a part of an individual's capacity. Then, depending on the attachment history of the individual, the work to explore how the therapeutic relationship can support this experience of "simply being felt" by the therapist may become a key facilitator of this "being seen" for who the client is, not just for what they do. Our PART becomes crucial in this transition, as we are *present* in an open, receptive awareness, *attuned* to the inner experience of our client's just-being mental life, and *resonant* with the client's inner state of emotional experience, and we then cultivate the *trust* needed to cultivate the learning, and unlearning, as they move from seeking approval to being seen.

Tips for Growth in Relationships
Relational Triggers

Obstacles that get in the way of the goal. Anything or anyone that threatens or thwarts progress and our ability to get to completion. Indecisiveness. Inefficiency. Criticism. Not being recognized or applauded when it's due. An insult to the image that's been constructed and wanting to be projected to others. Failing.

[Source: The Narrative Enneagram, 2020, pp. 36–38]

Relational Reflections

How you can help a Pattern 3 develop and fulfill their relationships:

- *Encourage your Type 3 to take time to smell the flowers.*
- *Pay attention to their feelings and ensure that they really listen to you.*
- *Support them in making relationships and feelings a priority.*
- *Let them know that you care for them regardless of their accomplishments.*
- *Show and tell them what is really important to you.*

[Source: David Daniels, "Enneagram Type 3
Description." https://drdaviddaniels.com/type-3/]

Clinical Vignette

A 37-year-old actor was working hard to feel a sense of accomplishment and "fullness" despite doing well in her career and achieving professional awards for her work in film. Outwardly, Andrea said that her "fans would never know how I am both happy with their applause but also feel like a fake." This impostor syndrome is shared by many—in my own class in medical school, 50% felt that they had been chosen "by accident" and that someone soon might discover the error and ask them to leave the university. We found that her Adult Attachment Interview revealed a confusing childhood setup, with a father with bipolar disorder and frequent sojourns in the hospital and a mother who felt overwhelmed by her three young children, each a year and a half apart. Andrea was the youngest, and she found that entertaining her siblings and trying to get her depressed father to laugh would "lighten the mood in that morose household."

In middle and high school, she found herself drawn to the drama opportunities, having an unusual set of skills of being able to imitate accents well and memorize lines of a script. She loved the attention and pursued her college studies in acting, finding work quickly during those years, and then becoming an employed thespian for the remainder of her 20s and now into her 30s.

Andrea's romantic life was tumultuous, with frequent unsatisfying relationships with beautiful women whom she would find at work and then feel were never satisfied with her in their intimate lives together. Her last relationship ended with intense hostility on social media a year before she came for therapy to explore how she might create "a better path for myself" as she got older.

When we did the informal survey of her PDPs, we found that while she leaned toward the C-d pattern, with worst-case-scenario thinking and a great deal of fear, she resonated most with the characteristics of the B-d profile of needing to perform in order to be loved. That was most evident in her professional life and her distress when the actor's union strike lasted for many months and led to her not being actively engaged at work. Not being able to perform made her feel "more than depressed, just deflated and empty, with no meaning" in her life. But even more, in her romantic relationship history, she was always "trying to prove she was lovable." Was this a part of what seemed to be a preoccupied state of mind with respect to attachment? Or might this nonsecure attachment strategy have intensified her baseline temperament of a bonding vector and a dyadic, inward-outward attendency?

Another bridging PDP that seemed to serve as a secondary pattern was the A-d, where she found herself struggling to stand up for herself in intimate relationships, desperate to avoid conflicts. And at work, she also would feel terrified of creating ill-will with her director, perhaps with a positive outcome in her continued work but with a limitation on how she could request better roles and more sustainable contracts from her talent agents.

As our work in therapy progressed, part of the growth-edge focus on each of these baseline dyadic forms of PDPs, her primary B-d and her two secondary bridging ones of A-d and C-d, involved an empowering moment in one session when she could see that the blend of how she had tried to deal with her confusion at home and the lack of attuned connection combined to give her a deep sense of uncertainty about who she "truly was." Yet the attention she received with her entertaining capacity, both personally and at school and then professionally, gave her a sense of being appreciated at least on some level—"which was better than being invisible." This lack of authentically connected relationships at home and her doing what Marlon Brando named "lying for a living" left her with a set of public achievements but personal despair.

As our own connection therapeutically unfolded, Andrea began to feel that she could "simply be" in a session without having to entertain me. I invited her to try out the Wheel of Awareness to cultivate a direct way of learning to be and not just do. And as the work still unfolds, we, Andrea and I, can begin to get a glimpse of how she feels more agency as she taps into a way to see from many sides in the integrative strengths of the A-d pathway, as well as to challenge authority, and not just accept what is given to her as a work-based set of conditions, in the integrative strengths of the C-d pathway.

And with her primary baseline of B-d, the growth-edge work continues to focus on her taking in a sense of her own worth in her essence rather than having to prove her value in her production. Perhaps ironically, her forced work stoppage with the actors' strike gave her a required break from the treadmill of success that sadly had left her paralyzed—the more she could produce valued products, the less free she felt to try out a new way of living. Now she feels ready to try working out a balance between the being she has learned to appreciate and the inevitable needs we all have to "do" in order to pay the rent and earn enough to eat. This is what the PDP model we were discussing taught her about our common human life journeys from being to doing.

Short Reflections for Integration

Image

Simply stop to sense in your body and notice how looking good and behaving in ways that gain approval and recognition can run your life. Then do your best to allow in your own true feelings.

Focus on tasks

Simply stop to notice how you focus attention and energy on doing and performance and do your best to expand your pace by slowing it.

Feelings

Simply stop to ask yourself, "Have I been paying any attention to my feelings?" And when not, pause further to encourage your feelings to manifest themselves.

[Source: David Daniels, "Growth for Type 3: The Performer." https://drdaviddaniels.com/growth-for-type-3]

Integrative Transformation

Each pathway has its challenges and its strengths. With the go-do energy of the B-d PDP, integration can yield a powerful force for good in the world. When this acceptance of just being as a way of living arises, the sense of wholeness can begin to be felt without the nagging sense of "I need to do more." For many, even those without this baseline of a PDP, the ways social media stimulates our feelings of being inadequate or missing out can push us down a low integrative pathway of this B-d configuration. The irony, of course, is that while the digital platforms may seem to get us connected, the kind of bonding this vector's motivation is striving for is far more authentic and deep than what those settings provide. Identifying this challenge, which may be especially familiar and forceful to those with this PDP, may be helpful in modern culture to help us all support our collective growth toward wholeness.

We can see how the dyadic attendency sets up a tension of this oscillating inward and outward attention that, when focused here on the motivation for bonding, creates this intensity of a focus on relational connection on the outside while well aware of the need for this connection on the inside. The resultant adaptive strategy to downregulate the intense separation distress and sadness by reframing and redirecting this energetic push is to focus on production, the creation of something by doing, a creation offered to seek the attention and approval of others. Unlike the motivation of the A-i PDP with an internal template of right and wrong that can lead to an intense focus on accurate and complete productions, here the motivation is to connect rather than to empower.

In the growth-edge work, this transition from doing to create a product for approval can be in service of a deeper essence, a truer sense of being whole within the inner world, and connected in service of the greater good. In this way, the higher, more integrated functioning of this pathway is filled with a richness in the "can-do" attitude of joining for collaboration and creativity rather than its prior intense focus on being accepted. Part of that journey is to embrace this sense that to live with wholeness is to be, and that doing emerges from this essential integrated place of being. As this integrative journey unfolds, too, the access to other vectors—of agency for embodied empowerment and certainty for safety and prediction—becomes more readily achieved. While the dyadic state here is already with both inward and outward attendencies, learning to focus on one or the other at certain times can be experienced within various practices, such as the inward focus on the Wheel of Awareness, which has no outward doing; and the pleasure of improvisational doing that engages others in connection without a need for approval. In this way, joining, in both the inner world of being and the outer world of relational connections, achieves a fuller, more integrative flow as this growth-edge work unfolds.

CHAPTER 8

The Certainty Vector Personality Patterns

One of the major tasks of childhood and adolescence is learning to juggle confidence and doubt about safety ahead. To get along in this world you need some, but not too much, of each—conviction and concern—as you go about the vitally important business of attending to the well-being of an inner self and relationships with others. This juggling act is the terrain of the certainty vector. It provides first-level management of innate motivational energies, which drive you to seek certainty about what will happen next in order to attain safety, and the emotional energies of anxiety and fear, which serve to warn you of potential danger to your well-being. This vector is involved in helping you discern the difference between threat and opportunity.

As described in the overall PDP framework, humans are highly motivated throughout life to seek a sense of certainty, to have a feeling of confidence, and to ensure safety in what lies ahead. The roots of this motivational vector lie in the human brain's phenomenal capacities, passed on from eons of evolution of mammalian nervous systems, to learn from experience and project that forward into expectations about the future.

Relentlessly, even before birth, the brain is building and updating predictive models of what is likely to happen next, based on all that has come before. This experience after birth is encoded in implicit and explicit memory of lived experience. Our prospective minds, shaped by this ability to anticipate what will happen next, can also learn to plan for the future based on what was learned in the past from experience. In addition, we may have inherited propensities and proclivities of the nervous system as revealed in startling new findings in the field of epigenetics, which reveals how even the experiences of our ancestors—parents and grandparents—can shape the non-DNA regulatory molecules that sit atop the genes in their sperm and eggs in ways that we literally inherit and that shape how our nervous systems develop. For example, experiencing a shock that was associated with a certain smell for our ancestors can be transmitted to us as an inherited fear of that same scent (Skvortsova et al., 2018).

As life rolls by, the brain is also constantly comparing what is being perceived in current experience with the expectations of its predictive models. When current experience matches expectations of safety, you feel a degree of confidence in continuing onward toward your goals. When experience matches expectations of danger ahead, your anxiety/fear system is activated and motivates you to take protective action appropriate to the degree of threat it detects. Between those two positions is a domain of ambiguity, which can create a mind state of anxious uncertainty.

The certainty system navigates us through this terrain of "Safe or unsafe?" as we inevitably confront the realities of potential threats ahead in this life on this planet. We've seen how these three pathways are designated as certainty-inward (C-i), certainty-outward (C-o), and certainty-dyadic (C-d). Each of these PDPs involves the key features of certainty, assurance, and predictability.

Before we describe these pathways in detail, it is helpful to consider the developmental trajectory of learning to cope with the inherent uncertainty and potential dangers of life. At birth and your emergence from the relatively carefree, effortless state of life at one with the womb, the certainty system includes undeveloped capacities and untrained potential that must be developed into life skills in on-the-job learning as we are out here learning to "work for a living." As we've discussed, this isn't just work; it is, literally, a do-or-die setup in which the things we need to be certain of are all about things that will keep us alive.

Propelled into the experience of life by birth and the gamut of motivations that move you out into the external world, you begin the lifelong experience of encountering novel situations, new things, and people you have never interacted with before. Some of those situations, things, and people will be harmless amusements, some will present opportunities that you can pursue with the confidence of safety, and some will pose threats to your well-being. So here you are, born into the lifelong dilemmas managed by the certainty system: "Will I be safe or unsafe? How confident should I be? Can I trust in myself?"

The work of developing the undeveloped capacities of the certainty system begins at birth (if not sooner) and continues throughout your entire life. Two things about this work are especially important. First, virtually everything about what is safe or unsafe in this world you must learn from experience and from the important people in your life in "on-the-job" training. For example, I recently visited an animal rescue shelter in Alaska and was struck by how the orphaned young bear, elk, and moose would never be able to survive if returned to the wild because the window of opportunity to be taught survival skills of food and shelter by their mothers closed early in life with the unfortunate deaths of their maternal attachment figures, their first teachers.

As mammals, we too, for years, take in countless lessons about what is and what isn't safe, first and foremost from the lessons of our caregivers and then from others who help us avoid threats and encourage us toward opportunity, but more and more from the bumps and bruises of mishaps that inevitably happen, even in the best of all circumstances, as we are more and more on our own in the world. This experience comes together with all the genetic and epigenetic factors we've inherited, shaping the structure and functioning of our nervous systems. From these underlying inner and outer influences, our mind builds models that aim to predict whether the situation we are in right now represents threat or opportunity. We link facets of experience associated with threats to our anxiety/fear system and learn to adapt as best we can.

Second, research suggests the brain is built with an innate negativity bias—that is, "a propensity to attend to, learn from, and use negative information more than positive information" (Vaish et al., 2008). In other words, from an evolutionary perspective it is better if our predictive models err a bit on the side of unsafe when we encounter the unknown, which in effect means favoring anxiety when things don't quite add up. This is the root of the universally disquieting state of mind when humans encounter uncertainty, and of the underlying tone of the three certainty patterns if the system comes to dominate our ways of going about the job of "working to live."

We propose that as you grow and go about life pursuing your own well-being and navigating interpersonal relationships with others, your ever-emerging, fast-thinking certainty system is automatically, mostly beneath awareness, assimilating two streams of information: (1) an outward stream about perceptions of the situation and people in the environment in the current moment, and (2) an inward stream of information from predictive models derived from prior learning and encoded in implicit memory and their associations about conditions being safe or unsafe.

The three developmental pathways of the certainty vector provide a repertoire of general adaptive strategies, which are useful and socially functional for responding to different situations when the fear system does not launch the full-fledged reactivity of the fight, flight, freeze, or faint reactions, which by "design" take over everything else in that reactive state. In contrast, when we are receptive we can work with challenge in an open, flexible manner; when we become reactive, we may err toward negativity and a tendency toward chaos and rigidity in our survival-first intensity. Each of the pathways may have its own strategies that make receptivity and reactivity have a distinctive profile, as we'll see.

In the C-i PDP, attention and the subsequent flow of motivational energy are inwardly oriented toward internal prediction models and the stream of information about the state of available resources and preparedness for danger ahead. Fear and anxiety are relatively *downregulated* into an on-guard stance of focused alertness. The energy and motivation of the vector of certainty is contained and then channeled toward gathering information, and nurturing and conserving the psychological and material resources that might be needed in event of emergency.

In the C-o PDP, attention and the subsequent flow of motivational energy are outwardly oriented toward what is going well, opportunity beckons, and you are good to pursue what you need or desire. Attention and the flow of certainty-seeking motivational energy are outwardly centered on objects of need and desire "out there" in the world and channeled into confident and optimistic pursuit of satisfaction. The innate state of cautious uncertainty is *shifted* toward confidence, and appetitive emotions are allowed to flow freely outward in optimistic pursuit of goals and desires.

In the C-d PDP, attention and the subsequent flow of motivational energy are centered on ambiguity or uncertainty coming from both the outward stream of information about others and the world in the moment, and the inward stream of information from the templates and schemas of what has been learned and taken in. Said differently, this pathway holds the reality of uncertainty about safety of life ahead on this planet. Both the vector of certainty-seeking and the flow of anxiety into behavioral expression are *upregulated*. Attention and energy are channeled into anxiously energized efforts to predict what will be, and doubting or challenging beliefs and perceptions.

TABLE 8.1 Developmental Pathways for the Fear/Safety Certainty Vector

Pathway	Attendency	Regulation of fear and anxiety motivation vector
C-i	Inward	Downregulate ↓
C-o	Outward	Shift →
C-d	Dyadic (inward + outward)	Upregulate ↑

As with the three agency and three bonding pathways, each of these pathways of responding to the existential dilemmas about safety and confidence can be the most adaptive and socially functional way of responding to what life brings, depending on the circumstances in which you find yourself. When development has been integrative, the mind is able to draw on each pathway *freely* to make the best possible safe-or-unsafe determination and set the body in motion accordingly. And each pathway can become a personality pattern when it is, overall, particularly salient to the individual's unique developmental circumstances. Problems are more likely to emerge when integration is impaired, that is, when a working strategy becomes *the* singular, primary adaptive strategy for getting along in the world.

As with all nine patterns, there is a kernel of truth in the working model that is aimed at survival and becomes an adaptive strategy shaped by the vector and the attendency. In the reality of life on this planet, a sense of certainty that you will indeed have the resources you need to cope with whatever might come along can be elusive. So is certainty, a certainty that others will be there to help in times of need, a certainty that life will unfold the way it needs to. We sometimes create a longing for the same image of certainty as what the multimodal artist Kameelah Janan Rasheed, on the Brooklyn Public Library foyer, states is the "flimsy fantasy of certainty" in this quotation: "Having abandoned the flimsy fantasy of certainty, I decided to wander." If wandering is the freedom to simply explore life unfettered by concerns about even attempting to create certainty in an uncertain world, then in many ways each of the trio of this certainty vector wrestles in distinct ways with how to achieve some semblance of freedom in life.

Why would an Enneagram notion of the "head center" correspond to our proposal of the certainty motivational system and its core affects of fear and anticipatory anxiety? With certainty we optimize safety and the sense of security to ensure survival. Being able to predict enables us to feel safe, to feel protected. How do we predict to have a sense of certainty? The cortex as the higher part of the brain in the head has been called an "anticipation machine" as well as a "pattern detector." The cortex anticipates as it learns from ongoing experiences, detects patterns in experience over time, and then predicts what will happen next based on what happened before. The PDP of the head's brain—the *parallel distributed processor* of the cortex—enables prediction and then the drive for protection to be achieved. This is what we mean by the motivation for certainty, the drive for safety in the world. The subcortical network for certainty draws on the cortex's capacity to predict. From a polyvagal view, this likely involves what Stephen Porges has named "neuroception," the neural perception of the cortex's capacity to monitor for danger (Porges, 2001, 2011).

With the attendency inward, the C-i (Enneagram 5) pattern finds the gathering of knowledge, the protection of space, the creation of internal models of knowledge, and the efficiency of spending time a pattern of living that enables a feeling of certainty through inner self-sufficiency to arise. With an outward attendency of the C-o (7) pathway, the cortex's planning of activities shapes how this proclivity focuses energy and attention outward to multiple options, exciting plans, and positive future possibilities, enabling feelings of certainty in knowing that "at least one of those options will work." And with the dyadic inward and outward attendency of the C-d (6) pattern, awareness of all that could go wrong in the outside world is now coupled with internal doubt and questioning. This adaptive strategy provides a feeling of preparedness in the outward focus; yet the awareness of the inner feeling of fear and anxiety in anticipation of things going wrong emerges and then organizes the preoccupations of those traveling down this pathway.

Each of these PDP patterns is based on the propensity of the certainty system to be engaged and the core affects of fear and of anxiety to arise and to then set the "motion" of the mind in specific patterns over time and context. That is what "personality" means, and this "mental momentum" involves emotion, thought, meaning, value, and the regulation of behavior.

Here's a clinical description from David of focusing on the center of the head. As we've stated, David's words come from before we clarified our PDP vocabulary where we see this as an ALEAF (anatomical location of energy activation and flow) taking place in the head's cortex and involving cortical thinking. In this way, the ALEAF for each of the trio may initially involve cortically mediated cognitive perceiving and processing that is dominant in the certainty vector.

Bea, leading with the Head Center of Intelligence [cortical thinking as an ALEAF], *came into counseling saying, "Juan just never stops to think. He just seems to go with whatever he is feeling." (Beatrice wasn't making any distinction between feelings and gut impulses.) She wanted more careful analysis, wanted to prepare for both the best and worst that could happen, and wanted acknowledgment for her efforts to understand things. "It drives me crazy my having to cover all the bases, figure things out, and do all the meticulous planning." Beatrice had no awareness that she was owned by the Head Center of Intelligence, which was compounded by her worrying about the well-being of their two young children. Juan, who came into counseling with Bea, leads with the Heart Center of Intelligence* [an ALEAF of heartfelt sensations].

It frustrated him that "so much of our time together just goes into figuring things out, it feels unending." And he expressed this with much emotional intensity. While they clearly cared about each other, this conflict of intelligences

had created a gulf in their relationship, pretty much ending the "honeymoon."
Here it was the guy wanting more expression of feelings, longer and deeper
conversations, and the gal is wanting more intellectual analysis. In grasping the
Enneagram's emphasis on three centers of intelligence, they could see how they
each lead with predominantly different centers. This was a huge wakeup call
for both of them.

Bea learned to pause when her mental pace picked up along with the anxiety
and tension she regularly felt in her thorax and neck; this was common, she said,
whenever she succumbed to her frenzied thinking pace. She calmed herself with
slow and conscious breathing and put attention on asking herself what she was
feeling in her heart and sensing in her body. She came to the awareness that she
was overanalyzing things, believing this was the path to security. And Juan prac-
ticed calming his feelings by noticing them rising in his gut and heart areas. He
came to appreciate Bea's Head Center point of view, as an expression of care for
him and the children, and she for his Heart Center's feeling-based point of view,
as Juan's way of caring for his family.

In a matter of a few weeks, the honeymoon was rekindled as they both came
to putting more attention on the physical relationship, the Gut/Body Center [an
ALEAF of gut and bodily sensations] being their least attended-to center. They
had begun to successfully rediscover the critical closeness they needed to grow
stronger together and stay committed.

While all three centers are essential to relationships, it's the Heart Center
that tells us most about our bonds. It's our connection to others in the end that is
most central to our experience of relationships. Understanding the neurobiology of
bonding further validates the vital importance of our connections, of the love we
receive and then cultivate in our lives. Our neurobiology is testimony to how we
are wired for relationships. We all need to grasp the simple fundamentals of this
wiring to truly appreciate how relationships are at the core of our development and
our entire experience of belonging to one another, and to the whole of humanity.

[Source: Daniels & Dion, 2018, pp. 78–79]

Now let's shift focus to what each of the associated personality patterns
looks like, with its strengths and challenges, using the same descriptive
framework we have used with the other two vectors. (How about that for

being primed to reassure your and my longing for certainty by being able to predict what will happen next in this chapter . . . Go, writing-and-ready cortex!) See you in the pages ahead.

C-i: Certainty-inward (C-i Pathway; Enneagram 5)

Expressed Personality

With this pattern, the expressed personality tends to be quiet, analytical, and require more time alone than most, preferring to adopt an observing stance as opposed to engaging at first with the world. There is a thirst for knowledge and intellectual understanding. Inside, there tends to be a sense of limited personal reserves of time and energy, and a sensitivity to the calls from other individuals for resources, time, and attention. Some people may typically perceive a "heady," cerebral kind of demeanor, and guardedness around emotional engagement. Beneath the surface appearance is a very active mental life, full of thoughts and feelings. Many in whom this pattern is active report being better able to access their feelings when alone.

The C-i pattern seems to operate as if there is a deeply embedded belief along the lines of "I cannot depend on others or the world to be there when I need their help, support, and care, so it is necessary to strive for inner self-sufficiency. And it is this sufficiency that will make my world more certain." It is as though the vector of certainty—the motivations that fuel the lifelong need for a sense of predictability and safety—is contained and then channeled into *creating, nurturing, and protecting a solid inner sense of preparedness and self-sufficiency.* Among other things, this means nurturing and guarding knowledge and material resources that might be needed to emotionally deal with whatever may come along in life.

Even your nearest and dearest may sometimes be unable to help or will leave, let you down, or drain you dry. Even your best-laid plans may fall short. Even your accumulation of knowledge and careful preparation may still not prevent accidents from occurring. So, you must learn in development how to be prepared to care for yourself, but not overdo it; to somehow find the peace in wandering freely in life, prepared, yes, but not fantasizing about a degree of control and certainty that is simply not attainable. Troubles with this pattern emerge when striving to make that flimsy fantasy of certainty a lived reality becomes a habitual and limited way of being in the world.

Brief Description	The 5 believes you must protect yourself from a world that demands too much and gives too little to assure life. Consequently, Observers seek self-sufficiency and are non-demanding, analytic, thoughtful, and unobtrusive, but also can be withholding, detached, and overly private.
Key Interventions	Help 5s appreciate the difference between detachment and non-attachment, realize that withdrawal invites intrusion, associate into experience and feelings, and move forward into life.

[Source: The Narrative Enneagram, 2020, pp. 24–25]

Developmental Pathway and Adaptive Strategy

In the certainty-inward pathway, the flow of attention and the motivational energy of certainty-seeking center inwardly on the stream of information about the state of understanding and preparedness for danger ahead. Fear and anxiety are relatively downregulated—contained and channeled—into an on-guard stance of alertness focusing on objects of potential uncertainty, and subject to conceptual analysis. More generally, the vector of certainty-seeking energy is channeled toward gathering information, and nurturing and conserving the psychological and material resources that might be needed in the event of emergency. In many ways it is like a precursor to a more full-fledged "freeze" response—pausing to deal with the threat at hand before fighting or fleeing.

Integration and Individual Variation: Strengths and Challenges

When the three vectors and three attendencies are well integrated, we see a thoughtful, curious, intellectually oriented and engaging individual who is in touch with their own feelings, generous of spirit, well able to serve as a wise and emotionally available confidant, appreciative of simplicity, and calm in crisis.

This contrasts with what is seen when integration is impaired. Here, tendencies toward what is sometimes called "avarice" or "hoarding" (of personal and material resources) are magnified. What emerges is a character profile prone to cautious withholding of personal and material resources, and a withdrawing and warily private, "hunkered-down," and emotionally detached demeanor.

Behavioral Profile	*Strengths:* Being scholarly and knowledgeable, thoughtful, dispassionate and calm in crisis, respectful, keeper of confidences, appreciative of simplicity, dependable, and ascetic. *Difficulties:* Isolation from own feelings and experiences, especially in the here and now, detachment from life and possible withdrawal into minimization, pain of loneliness with a longing for connection, feelings of inadequacy, various failures to act, missed opportunities, avarice for time and space, confusing detachment with non-attachment, seeing requests as demands.

[Source: David Daniels, "Enneagram Type 5 Description: The Observer." https://drdaviddaniels.com/type-5]

Focus of Attention and Blind Spots

It can be helpful to think of this pattern as the mind's department of emergency preparedness. It specializes in monitoring and nurturing the seemingly limited stockpile of resources of knowledge, emotion, and energy that might be needed to maintain a felt sense of confidence and readiness when danger comes along, which of course it will at various times in this world and in this human life. So, in the quest for a felt sense of safety and certainty, attention centers on the state of understanding of the situation, and on people or events likely to draw on the seemingly finite stockpile of emotional, energetic, and material reserves.

Thus, when signals of potential danger activate anxiety and fear, attention and certainty-seeking energy orient quickly inward toward available resources of information and energy for the situation at hand. Given that those resources tend to be viewed as limited or insufficient in quantity and quality, there tends to be magnification of the perception of their limitations and the toll that the object motivating anxiety is likely to take on the individual, and energy is channeled into whatever needs to be done to nurture and protect those resources from depletion.

When those sorts of concerns occupy attention quickly and automatically, it can be easy to miss signs and signals of sufficiency or even abundance, the potential likelihood and value of connection with others, and how you might be nonconsciously depriving yourself of those freely available resources. These become *blind spots* when this pattern is running the show.

Emotional Processing

As with all three of the certainty pathways, it seems the threshold for activation of the anxiety/fear system is relatively low. In this case all the narrative data suggest that the vector of certainty-seeking, which can include fear and anxiety when triggered, tends to be *downregulated* for this pathway. This means expression is tempered or contained, and then channeled into an emotionally guarded and reserved, often "hunkered-down" but highly observant, studious, and conserving general demeanor, focused on figuring out and understanding, and nurturing the seemingly limited resources needed to deal with the situation.

Emotionally, several interrelated things seem to be happening. First, there seems to be a deep belief of *scarcity of personal reserves*, as if the bank has a limited balance on which to draw, so those resources must be guarded and allocated carefully. Second is a feature sometimes called *isolation of affect*—a tendency to live life at a distance from the felt bodily experience of the mind's ever-unfolding emotional "soundtrack." Related is an often-evident tendency for mentation and intellectualization to be dominant ways of processing experience and engaging with others. This can have the sense of not only a lot of "head" activity but also, specifically, a reliance on the left hemisphere's dominant mode for logical, language-based, list-making, linear thinking. So, if your modus operandi is to carefully conserve emotional resources, approach engagement with others cautiously, and keep a distance from emotional experience, the territory of interpersonal emotional engagement can become unpracticed and unfamiliar from such a left, cortically dominant mode of processing energy—the highly developed left-dominant ALEAF of this pattern—and thus relationships may seem even more mysterious and taxing than they seem for others operating from different primary patterns.

Interestingly, some, but by no means all, individuals who identify strongly with this pattern recall childhoods with either emotionally distant or excessively intrusive caregivers. It makes intuitive sense such attachment experiences could foster emergence of tendencies to pull protectively inward, and build "walls" around emotional engagement. On the other hand, it may be that this feature of temperament—to have an inward attendency and a dominance of the certainty vector—may itself tend to make the autobiographical narrative reflections prioritize certainty and describe features of attachment that were unreliable in their distance or in their overwhelming nature. Either feature might place that narrative in the dismissing adult and avoidant child attachment or preoccupied adult and ambivalent child attachment groupings, respectively. Whether experience, temperament, or some combination of the two is the primary causal factor in the origins of this pathway, these retrospective narrative accounts provide an evocative metaphorical way of understanding what is seen and experienced in the emotional processing of the adult expression of the pattern.

As we've discussed earlier, it's an open question as to how the initial innate temperament proclivities intertwine with experience, especially that of our attachment relationships. My own impression (leaning in on my own bridging secondary C-i pathway capacities as a resource here) is that, of the four broad attachment groupings—secure/autonomous, avoidant/dismissing, ambivalent/preoccupied, and disorganized/unresolved—they actually may be equally distributed across the nine PDP groups; and this would be a numerical consistency in that *four* attachment strategies do not correlate with *nine* personality patterns. As we've also said earlier, one of our leading hypotheses is that an individual's attachment nonsecurity likely intensifies the features of their particular dominant primary baseline pattern. The question to consider, then, is whether the data from narrative reflections may be an outcome of the pattern itself and not due to the actual attachment experiences that occurred and how the individual has made sense of them.

As always, these patterns of emotional processing and expression, and the effects they have on attention, thinking, behavior, and relationships, generally operate beneath consciousness. Raising awareness is the first step toward building a more flexible and adaptable way of being. The next steps in the process of integration aim to liberate the positive aspects of the drive to be prepared and enable an embracing of the uncertainty inherent in bodily sensation, emotional experience, and interpersonal relationships.

Cognitive Processing

Typically, this personality pattern tends to seem very heady and emotionally reserved. That is, observation, logic, analysis, and reference to data, facts, and intellectual information about the world and others tend to become preferred ways of experiencing the world and engaging with others. Indeed, sharing in intellectual exchange can be a dominant and rewarding mode of connecting and relating with others. That said, the externally perceived emotional reservedness conceals a lively *inner world* of imagination, investigation, thoughts, analysis, understanding, and so on, which is emotionally alive and vibrant. Moreover, intellectual exchange can be filled with feeling and passion, even if others perceive a tendency to "think their feelings." So, the phrase "at a distance from emotional life" and the quote from James Joyce's (2008) *Dubliners*, "Mr. Duffy lived a short distance from his body," may be more about emotional expressiveness and communication in the interpersonal domain than about inner subjective experience.

Summing Up

All these patterns of emotional processing and expression, and the effects they have on attention, thinking, behavior, and relationships, are generally beneath awareness. Raising awareness is the first step toward building a more flexible and adaptable way of being. While the tendency to engage through intellectualization is often evident, the well-attuned therapist will also sense undercurrents of isolation of affect in their clients' stories and behaviors and will do well to explore whether this pattern is beneath certain typical problems that arise during therapy.

Beatrice Chestnut (2013, pp. 254–255) describes three major behavioral expression patterns for this personality archetype that are associated with problems clients tend to bring to therapy:

1. "Hoarding and withholding inner resources out of a perception of scarcity and fear of depletion."
2. "Detaching from emotions and emotional life."
3. "Distancing oneself from others through excessive boundaries, the need for control, and a fear of external demands."

Growth-Edge Work

As a Type 5, we need to learn to more fully participate in life's messy experiential possibilities. We need to engage with others and with our own need to express more of ourselves to those we love and who love us. Allow an inner knowing, which is not necessarily from our schoolbook's academic learnings, but that which comes from the experiences of life itself. Accept that participation in life—participation with others—actually leads to being energized, revitalized, and nurtured, rather than being drained and depleted. Allowing and exploring feelings reverses deeply held Type-5 fears that can cause their own brand of isolation and suffering.

[Source: Daniels & Dion, 2018, p. 110]

Strategies for Development

- Moving from a cognitive habit of stinginess or inner control to mental awareness that all can be included and dealt with as it unfolds.
- Moving from emotional greed of one's own time and space to opening to what is brought externally by the world that is really needed.

[Source: David Daniels, "Integrating the Higher Qualities of our Essence into our Lives." https://drdaviddaniels.com/integrating-essence-true-nature-lives/]

Recognize there are ample resources, consequently practicing abundance, and
- *Recognize and release the avarice for time, space, energy, and knowledge.*
- *Make the counter-instinctive move forward into life and feelings.*
- *Notice the impact of withdrawal and withholding on others, and how it invites intrusion.*
- *Stay present and engaged with others.*
- *Share or give more of yourself, while taking in more support from others.*
- *Practice compassion, care, connection, and communication.*
- *Learn to nurture and support others.*
- *Practice self-disclosure.*
- *Behave as if there were abundance.*
- *Notice how you detach from feelings and shift to the intellect.*
- *Recognize that cutting off from feelings leads to intensifying them.*
- *Welcome all feelings, both positive and negative.*
- *Use imagination—remember a time when you were sad, happy, etc.*
- *Practice saying feelings out loud.*
- *Realize that the flow of a universal energy is there to meet life's real needs.*
- *Do body work.*
- *Allow time for observation; then time for action.*

- *Stay as present as possible in each moment.*
- *Identify the cues that you are withdrawing into your mind.*

[Source: The Narrative Enneagram, 2020, p. 25]

A key to working with those with a baseline C-i pathway is to use their strengths of needing to know the nature of experience and offer the PDP framework early enough in the work that you can avoid their feeling that this psychotherapy process is a "waste of time and energy." With the inward attendency, developing insight into these processes is often ready to happen—but with the CC downregulation mode of contain and channel, the emotional reality of the fear underlying the drive for certainty may be less readily felt. Working carefully at this balance of introducing concepts while also offering direct experiential learning is one strategy that works well, a combination of noesis and gnosis.

Tips for Growth in Relationships
Relational Triggers

Being considered not smart or factually incorrect. People not interested in the information that we have to share. Demands placed on us from others, especially emotional ones or those that infringe on our private time. An overloading of emotional input. Too much stimulation. Intrusions that might tire us. Needing time alone and not being disrupted. Not being able to restore our energy as needed.

Relational Reflections

- *Encourage Type 5s to welcome their feelings in the here and now, to express. concerns, confront conflict, and release control of time and energy.*
- *Provide moderate feedback about your own feelings and concerns.*
- *Respect their need for privacy, understanding their privacy is not rejection.*
- *Make distinctions between requests and demands.*
- *Recognize intellectualization and modify as is appropriate for the situation, bringing feelings and sensitivity to others back online.*

[Source: David Daniels, "Enneagram Type 5
Description." https://drdaviddaniels.com/type-5/]

As a Type 5, we need to learn to appreciate the abundant and sustaining flow of life force energy, which is available to each of us, as it resides and is made available from within. We need to realize that withdrawal—from others, from life, from our desires—actually invites emotional loss as well as the potential for intrusion. It may also injure relationships over time, as in, when we are needed and wanted, we refuse to engage.

It's important to move into an experience of our feelings, a present-moment experience even better. Allow ourselves the time and disruption to engage with our feelings, accept them, and process them. Our feelings connect us to our humanity, to our spirit. Allow ourselves to learn to take time for feelings, spend time learning to cultivate access to them, and cherish them as we learn to articulate them to others, which is a very important developmental step.

[Source: Daniels & Dion, 2018, p. 110]

Clinical Vignette

Janette was 42 when she first came to therapy. Her "chief complaint" was that she wondered if the choice she had made to marry a divorced man with three adolescent boys was perhaps a mistake in her life. Janette had a thriving radiology practice, working as a specialist in the area of brain studies, that had both a clinical focus and a research division. She had made the decision to attend medical school to "learn everything I could about how this body works." And when it had come time to pick a specialty, radiology attracted her because she could "be the master" of her calendar and her space, without the less controllable conditions of other medical specialties she also enjoyed.

When we discussed her situation at home, she said that she and her first husband, a medical school classmate whom she adored but ultimately found "too emotionally demanding" as a person as he grew in his psychiatry training, had decided to divorce "amicably without children or much fuss." Over a decade passed as she pursued her advanced training and set up her busy but controllable clinical and academic radiology practice. "I know this sounds weird," she said, "but I love sitting in a dark room by myself and just figuring things out."

When she met her now husband at a friend's birthday party, she wasn't looking for a new relationship, being happy as a single woman in control of her life, she said. They dated for two years, and once she found their "life together more attractive than their life apart," their love for each other overcame her concerns about his three young children not being open to having her move into their home. Five years after they married, her husband's ex-wife left town abruptly, and Janette was thrust into having a full house, no longer half the time but now full-time. She felt "invaded" and found herself spending more time at work than she really needed to do; soon, her husband complained about this imbalance and asked her to find a way to be with him and the now adolescent kids. That's when she sought out my consultation.

An Adult Attachment Interview revealed the features of a secure attachment, with ready access to both positive and negative memories of her family-of-origin life history and an acknowledgment of how these experiences shaped who she was. The informal PDP survey revealed a resonance with the baseline of a certainty-inward pattern, with some leanings toward a secondary pathway of A-i as a bridge. She could also resonate with her bridging within the certainty vector, sharing some planning and go-to energy of the C-o and of the worst-case-scenario thinking of the C-d (as in, "Does this mean I'll need to get divorced again?" and "Will I have to give up my whole practice to be a stay-at-home stepmother to these teens?"). But her primary way of leading with the C-i pathway was evident to both me and to Janette for all the reasons you may see.

Letting her know about the subcortical networks involved in motivation, I felt her cue in to the neurodevelopment aspects of temperament that may underlie our proclivities we call "personality." Given her secure adult state of mind with respect to attachment, it seemed that Janette was experiencing simply the intensity of temperament transforming into personality without a deep groove being carved from nonsecure relational experiences. In this sense, her pattern was simply a manifestation, it seemed to me and to her, of a tendency of her brain to innately favor some ways of being over others. In this case, the choice of her profession was a perfect fit with her PDP. Initially, her first husband's giving her lots of "emotional space" before he became a psychiatrist (sorry, Janette!), which dissolved away once he needed more direct emotional communication, was also something that seemed to work well. But even though she had felt that space to "do her own thing" in this second marriage, the unexpected full-time presence of her new stepchildren threw this balance of connection and private time off to the point that her lack of awareness of this issue was leading to her automatic withdrawal.

When we explored the core issue of this PDP, it became clear to her logical mind that she could work with her feelings more than she had been doing to let the view of her space, knowledge, and time be a "placeholder" for the deep need for wholeness in the image of certainty. In her own words, "It's really more like a shadow we see on a radiograph. The lines are not the organs, they are not the networks of the brain; they are just a reflection we see with X-rays or with magnetic resonance and water molecule spins." In this way, we could see that space, time, and knowledge were symbols of something else: a drive for certainty in an uncertain world. When we see that life in this post-uterine world is inevitably filled with unpredictable and even unsafe elements, we can understand how one of these motivational networks can gain predominance.

Learning the Wheel of Awareness was an important component of therapeutic interventions. It helped her to understand that this three-pillar practice—teaching her to strengthen the focus of attention, opening of awareness, and kindness of intention—would likely be integrating her brain's various networks. It also helped to distinguish the emotions of her rim from the experience of simply being aware in the hub. To then become immersed in awareness gave her the capacity to feel a sense of being whole without being attached to the previous symbols of certainty—her time, space, and knowledge.

As we continue to work on her transformational changes, becoming aware of her body's signals and embracing the fullness of these layers of inner experiences will hopefully help guide Janette toward a fuller, freer way of living. She is spending more time at home, finding a new way to relate to her stepchildren and finding a new enjoyment in simply being with them. We will continue to explore how she can maintain her love of knowledge and expertise while relaxing its previous surrogate of clinging to it as a way to attempt to always be prepared and ensure that "flimsy fantasy of certainty," and instead, letting herself wander in life and simply be grateful for the family and professional life of connection she now has.

Short Reflections for Integration

Reflexively retracting

Simply stop and do your best to just come back and open your heart knowing that you will be nurtured, not drained of energy.

Detaching to observe

Simply stop to notice the contraction in your body when withdrawing away from intrusions. Use this as a signal to relax your contraction and move forward into life.

Limiting needs and desires

Simply stop to remind yourself that this protective habit of over-restricting needs and desires actually can lead to deprivation and deficiency, not sustenance and nourishment. Then accordingly allow your wants and desires to be expressed.

[Source: David Daniels, "Growth for Type 5: The Observer."
https://drdaviddaniels.com/growth-for-type-5/]

Integrative Transformation

As those traveling the C-i pathway move toward enhancing linkage in the face of intense differentiation, the sense of harmony that begins to arise comes with a trusting that certainty is not something that needs to be constructed, but rather a state of embracing uncertainty and allowing life and love to emerge. A full participation in experience innately involves taking risks and being open to this journey of life, moving beyond the constriction of fear and into the adventure of possibility. Integration moves from the differentiation of a predictive cortical processing to a state of deep acceptance and ease with uncertainty fully felt in the heart and whole body.

Within the vector, it can be helpful to shift the focus of energy from only inward to also outward and to gain that energy of the engagement with outer threats directly. When the focus of attendency can shift fully outward, the higher integrative capacity of the C-o pattern to envision future activities in planning and interaction can be an energizing outcome of such integrative growth. From the C-i baseline, we can see that this perspective helps with how we can soften that drive to always be in control and to be prepared, relaxing into a broader view. Wholeness arises as we come to realize that we are not needed to control all outcomes, but can instead let the world arise as it will and we can fully participate without being hampered by fear.

In these ways, accessing the other vectors and attendencies is part of the transformational journey to link to other motivational drives and ways of focusing energy in life. Focusing beyond the interior, embracing the other attendencies, is also part of the therapeutic change to widen the skills of life needed to live with more freedom and fulfillment. The comparatively tight focus of attention of the left hemisphere and its more neurally distant functions far from the more raw bodily input into the right hemisphere with its broader attention may explain what is my own informal observation that those traveling the C-i pathway have entered a more left-sided way of living.

As emotion can be seen as a shift in integration that arises from the body and first enters the subcortical and then the right cortical regions, we can surmise that an effort to achieve certainty may be more a left-dominant adaptive strategy. Interestingly, this is consilient—resonant with findings from other, independent pursuits—with the finding that left-hemisphere dominance is also associated with a "digital way" of deciphering energy flow into categorical divisions, such as up or down, right or left, correct or wrong. One can sense the effort to find certainty in these judgments, with a feeling that something is the right way and other approaches are the wrong ways. Relaxing away from such constructions may itself be filled with anxiety and fear, the very emotions that are attempting to be contained and channeled to downregulate the emotions arising in this pattern of C-i. Growing past those understandable concerns, the freedom to reach across the hemispheric divide and see more broadly, letting an open awareness arise, is the natural evolution toward a higher, more integrative state of living.

Letting life be experienced with a mindset of sufficiency and abundance can allow the sense of "self" to expand beyond its being defined as merely the individual. As described in Chapter 1, "SPA" is an acronym that can be used to state what self, as a center of experience, may include: sensation, perspective, and agency—what we act on behalf of. The growth-edge work to move beyond the contraction of the C-i pathway's low integrative state is to embrace abundance as well as uncertainty in a growing trust in the capacities of the universe to allow positive states to arise in their natural way without having to be controlled or predicted.

While the predictive drive of the cortex may be fueled by the emotion of fear arising from a subcortical motivation for certainty, for the inward attendency this may result in excessive cortical thinking to assure a semblance of control, prediction, and safety. Relaxing this emphasis on a head-based ALEAF (an initial flow that perhaps becomes left-hemisphere dominant) and opening to a more receptive way of living may be one key to the emotional growth for those in the C-i PDP. The shift from having energy invested in controlling life to a more receptive engagement with letting life happen—not passively but openly—is part of the shift to a higher state of integration in which linkage to life's innate potentials weaves with the differentiation of inner skills and passions. This can feel like a shift to an "ease of well-being."

Cognition as the transformation of energy into symbolic value, energy in a formation that we call "information," is itself a means to attempt to construct certainty from a virtually infinite array of energy patterns in life. At the basic level, our mental apparatus makes categories, dividing the world into groupings. We then construct from these divisions the cognitive concepts that underlie how we believe the world to be and how we come to even perceive what reality itself is made of. When we take these categories and concepts and share them with others, this often takes the form of language. A word is a symbol of what we see in the world, how we construct a coherent view, or at least a cohesive sense, of what reality is. Now we can imagine how, from this PDP framework, a certainty-inward vector-attendency combination draws heavily on cognition to attempt, as best as can be approximated, some sense of certainty in life. As this motivation for certainty is a drive for safety, the growth-edge work is to come to experience energy flow in a non-symbolized way—how we can highlight sensation, image, and feeling before the often-dominant mental experience of thought. Utilizing the acronym SIFT, each of these first three more-direct experiences of energy flow can be given attention and priority as life unfolds.

The deep challenge for those traveling the C-i pathway is that the very mechanism—prediction—that is felt as a life-or-death necessity, is exactly where the growth-edge work needs to be focused. Letting go of control and construction and letting in an openness to connection and collaboration enables the individual to become a part of a process larger than simply the individual alone. This integrative journey may involve moving beyond what might be a dominant left-hemisphere mode of dividing into chunks and narrowly focusing attention on predictable details and instead opening to a more receptive, wider view that may be more dominant in the right hemisphere. These ways of knowing are "orthogonal," meaning they are not just an elaboration, but a new way of seeing and being in the world. Letting go of control and prediction means not controlling and not being able to predict. We shift from what may be a reactive way of "doing" in the world to a new and receptive way of simply being.

The lifetime journey down the C-i pathway invites a deep reflective focus on *sensing* and not just thinking, opening to the processes of the whole of the body, including the right side of its brain, so that the understandable focus on the acquisition of knowledge and skills, the guarding of space and time, and the drive to achieve certainty to contain and channel the wish for safety are each relaxed and a wider, receptive awareness is cultivated.

C-o: Certainty-outward (C-o Pathway; Enneagram 7)

Expressed Personality

Notable behavioral traits include a generally optimistic, energetic, highly resourceful, self-assured, confident, and typically upbeat, fun-loving demeanor. As with the other certainty patterns, these behaviors are rooted in the vector of certainty-seeking, and the adaptive strategies that emerge in development for coping with the inevitable *uncertainties* of life. Unlike the other two patterns in this vector, this is the pathway of optimism and confidence about certainty and safety. Fear and anxiety are shifted as they are reframed and redirected into planning and projects.

With this pattern, the personality structure seems to operate as though there is a deeply embedded belief along the lines of "I must stay upbeat and keep positive options in sight and open in this world that limits, frustrates, and causes people pain that can be avoided." When the pattern is active, it is as though the quest for that felt sense of safety and certainty revolves around an attentional "fixation" on or "addiction" to the bright side of life. Fear and anxiety tend to be downregulated, and on the surface *seem* unrelated to the personality. But when fear is sufficiently activated, there can be what feels like an urgent need to fix the situation and head for the exit ramp out of harm's way.

Brief Description	*The 7 believes you must keep life up and open to assure a good life. Consequently, Epicures seek possibilities and pleasure, and are optimistic, upbeat, and adventurous, but also avoid pain and can be uncommitted and self-serving.*
Key Interventions	*Help 7s recognize the excesses of future planning and experience, make lasting commitments and accept all of life: pain, fear, boredom, and limits as well as pleasure, joy, excitement, and options.*

[Source: The Narrative Enneagram, 2020, pp. 30–32]

Developmental Pathway and Adaptive Strategy

As we described previously, in the PDP framework the C-o pattern is rooted in what you can think of as the pathway to opportunity, when all seems well, and you are good to go for what you need or desire. So with this pattern, attention and the flow of certainty-seeking motivational energy are outwardly centered on those objects of need and desire "out there" in the world, and motivational energies are redirected outward into pursuit of satisfaction. Equally important, the innate, baseline mind state of wary uncertainty is shifted into one of confidence and optimism. "I've got this!" is the reframe and redirection. It seems self-evident that it is a normal essential state for humans to be able to embody the confident and optimistic pursuit of goals and desires when the situation calls for it. Problems arise when it becomes a rigid and habitual approach to life in coping with uncertainty or fear.

Integration and Individual Variation: Strengths and Challenges

When the three systems and their three pathways are well integrated, we see an imaginative, inventive, inspiring, optimistic, and resourceful character full of life, attuned to sharing all of that with others to help them and the world in general come to a better place. At the same time there is discipline, focus, and emotional groundedness.

This contrasts with what is seen when integration is impaired and this pattern is excessively differentiated, dominating the individual's life, and the negative tendencies associated with it become prominent. Here we see a character prone to hedonistic self-centeredness, "monkey-mindedness," difficulty maintaining commitments, and all the familiar problems associated with pain- and conflict-avoidance.

Behavioral Profile	**Strengths:** *Loving of life, optimistic and thinking positively, playful, enjoyable, inventive and imaginative, energetic, helpful, spontaneous, open to and seeing possibilities.*
	Difficulties: *Short-term gain may lead to long-term pain ("no pain, no gain"), various losses resulting from trying to keep life up and escape the "traps" of limits, overload from trying to keep excitement going (gluttony), trying to do more may lead to loss of purpose, then anxiety and depression, distraction and diversion from deeper purposes and commitments, repeating the same mistakes, equalizing authority creates conflict.*

[Source: David Daniels, "Enneagram Type 7 Description: The Epicure." https://drdaviddaniels.com/type-7]

Focus of Attention and Blind Spots

With this personality pattern, which specializes in seeking out the "bright side of life," attention goes quickly and naturally toward what David called "positive, pleasurable possibilities." This long list includes all manner of needs and desires, routes to freedom from limitation and pain, and options for novelty, fun, interesting ideas, projects, paths to positive outcomes. This is accompanied by a tendency for attention to jump quickly and often from who or what is here and now to the next bright, shiny object "out there." Very importantly, attention seeks routes to avoid the possibility of encounters with pain or limitation.

Of course, when those sorts of things tend to call your attention easily, quickly, and automatically, other things become harder to perceive and even more challenging to take in. *Blind spots* thus include feelings of an inner self or of others on the darker side—the inevitable pains and difficulties of life in this world—and legitimate limits on pursuit of the pleasures of the bright side of life.

Emotional Processes

Several prominent themes are seen when this personality pattern is dominant. One is an affectively upbeat and distinctly appetitive emotional mindset. Beatrice Chestnut (2013) describes it as "an often-insatiable hunger for stimulating experiences of all kinds." In traditional teaching, the pattern is often said to exemplify the "deadly sin of gluttony." This is very often evident in the generally optimistic, energetic, confident, outgoing, and fun-loving demeanor, which many find attractive and inspiring. It is also evident in a tendency of attention to move often and suddenly from one "bright, shiny object" to the next.

Other features involve aversive emotions. First, as with the other two certainty patterns, the threshold for activation of the anxiety/fear system is relatively low. In this case, however, the coping strategy is to shift, and utilizes "top-down" emotion-regulation techniques, mostly nonconsciously, to avoid encounters with fear or other painful emotional states by reframing and redirecting an unpleasant mental state into one that is more optimistic and confident. Examples include distraction of attention ("whistling past the graveyard"), rationalization, and cognitive reframing of difficult situations or literally removing oneself from them. Said simply, there is an uncommon ability to see and find the bright side. While many use such techniques at various times, here they can become overused, automatic, habitual, or compulsive.

Second, and not surprisingly, things in the blind spot of attention—potential sources of pain and limitation, frustration, boredom, and so on—are particularly potent triggers of fearful reactivity. It is as though there is an ultimate fear of being forever trapped in pain or limitation, so the hazard gets magnified, and energy is quickly and automatically channeled into urgent behaviors to avoid or escape painful encounters with them. So, for example, there is a strong tendency to avoid conflict, and a susceptibility to all the familiar problems in relationships associated with that.

These clients are so adept at staying on the bright side that they and most external observers are typically unaware of the currents of anxiety and fear-avoidance beneath the surface. And they are so unpracticed at processing painful emotional states that they can become emotionally overwhelmed when one of these emotions breaks through the defensive barriers keeping them at bay. Incapacitating anxiety or depression sometimes brings clients to therapy. The well-attuned therapist will often sense a forced quality in the optimistic and self-confident demeanor. One key goal of working with this pattern is to bring these unpleasant energetic currents to a receptive awareness of the client, so the client can learn the value they offer in fully appreciating the richness of life.

Cognitive Processing

Like the other certainty patterns, this PDP also seems "heady" to others, having the anatomical location of energy activation and flow (ALEAF) in the head and experienced as cortical processing, the neural origin of the mind's future-orientation. In this case, there is a distinctly upbeat, very future-oriented, and often idealistic or even utopian quality in much of the client's narrative. The mind tends to be full of positive possibilities, options, and flexible plans about how things could be better, how problems can be fixed, what would be really interesting or novel. The "prospective mind" is filled with an attention to the future, a neural correlate of which is the prefrontal cortex's capacity to mediate "mental time travel" in which we can not only reflect on the past but project ourselves into the future with plans and imagination.

Just as attention tends to move quickly from one shiny object to the next, so does thinking. Others often experience *monkey-mindedness* in what on the inside seems like making important and helpful connections toward a bright and optimistic future. Always having positive options in mind and keeping them open as long as possible—or at least until more attractive options come along—are key features of the patterns of thinking. As a result, plans can seem to others more like placeholders for future decisions, in that they are subject to change, often and on the spur of the moment.

Living on the bright side of life also seems to include very quick leaps to confidence and certainty—"I've got this." Just as there can be a kind of façade of optimism covering over feelings of anxiety and fear, a perceived sense of mastery of new skills or fields of inquiry comes quickly, often too quickly, ahead of real expertise.

Summing Up

Beatrice Chestnut (2013 pp. 171–173) describes three major behavioral expression patterns for this personality archetype that are associated with problems clients tend to bring to therapy:

1. "Focusing on pleasure to avoid pain."
2. "Confusing indulgence and freedom from limits, with love."
3. "Living for or in the future as a way of avoiding being present now."

Growth-Edge Work

The growth-edge work for the C-o PDP focuses on the overly differentiated and well-honed prospective mind, which is filled with an outwardly-focused attention that engages in the future to shift out of anxiety and fear in the present. This new cultivation of an inward focus links to inner emotions and bodily sensations that are not predictable and that cannot be planned out in advance. Ironically, the only thing that is truly certain in life is uncertainty itself. Embracing a wider set of emotions than those that have been reframed and redirected links differentiated states in new and emergent ways. Accessing this inward attention and the emergence of energy flow it empowers invites a linkage with this newly acquired attendency, freeing up the individual to feel the freedom and trust of being in the present.

Strategies for Development

- *Moving from a cognitive preoccupation of a pleasant future to a cognitive awareness that the here and now work is just as good.*
- *Moving from emotional gluttony for external excitement to an inner knowing that I can bring in what is actually needed, both pleasure and pain.*

[Source: David Daniels, "Integrating the Higher Qualities of our Essence into our Lives." https://drdaviddaniels.com/integrating-essence-true-nature-lives/]

- *Become aware of over-scheduling, multiple projects, future plans, and other mental evasions as clues that you may be avoiding something negative.*
- *Notice your hunger for stimulation and gratification as a reminder to return to the present.*
- *Observe impulses rather than go into them.*
- *Work on one thing at a time and finish what you start.*
- *Notice that you are missing the depth of experience and pleasure when you stay on the surface.*
- *Explore realistic self-evaluation versus self-criticism, and notice how when your ideas of self-worth are challenged, the desire to promote yourself to feel superior again arises.*
- *Ground in the present.*
- *Acknowledge the desires and well-being of others in equal proportion to your own.*

- *Realize the difficulties and pain produced for yourself and others through rationalization and escapism.*
- *Notice the subtle superiority in position of "up-ness."*
- *Welcome negative feedback and criticism.*
- *Realize that the full spectrum of life and deeper purpose includes the "darker side" of life—its pains, loss, suffering, and limitations.*
- *Work with your feelings, and notice the difference (and sensations in your body) between a real feeling and the idea of a feeling.*
- *Learn to stay with feelings of fear and being trapped when you let go of options.*
- *Notice your tendency to find the silver lining in the clouds; practice the opposite of finding the clouds in the silver lining.*

[Source: The Narrative Enneagram, 2020, p. 31]

Tips for Growth in Relationships
Relational Triggers

Constraints or limits that prevent us from getting, or from doing, what we want. People that get stuck, are unhappy, depressed, or other-blaming. Debbie-downer attitudes and those who lay trips on us. Feeling trapped. Feeling restricted. Feeling beholden to others when we want to take off and be free. Getting bored. Things that are too tedious or a total hassle. Being told what to do. Being told, "You can't . . ."

[Source: The Narrative Enneagram, 2020, pp. 30–32]

Relational Reflections

As a Type 7, we need to recognize our propensity to engage in an excess of continual future planning and options-generation, which keeps us from experiencing the present moment and from dealing adequately with what's in front of us. Our desire for, and recognition of, new and stimulating experiences is a wonderful talent and attribute, but it can leave little room for the more mundane aspects of running a life and navigating obligations.

Learn to make lasting commitments, all the while, trusting in ourselves that these commitments and responsibilities will not confine us or enslave us. As a

Type 7, we can learn how to ground our body in the present moment and release the grip of stimulation-hunting, future-tripping, and day-dreaming.

Give ourselves permission to accept all of what life has to offer, because it's rich and meaningful to do so. That would include allowing any pain, fear, boredom, and limitations to be felt, without fearing that we will be trapped there forever. Experiencing the pleasures, joys, and vast array of options in life is a given for us.

We need not worry that we will ever lose these aptitudes and capacities as we allow ourselves to take on the all of life, the all of relationships, the all of our feelings, and the all of ourselves.

- *Encourage the Type 7 to make deep commitments, accept pain as well as pleasure in life, and appreciate the value and worth of all others.*
- *Provide a supportive framework for a Type 7 to move into painful situations.*
- *Make your own needs, wants, and feelings important.*
- *Apply the KISS principle (Keep It Simple, Sweetie).*

[Source: The Narrative Enneagram, 2020, pp. 30–32]

Clinical Vignette

A 73-year-old woman came for an evaluation to address her "fear of retirement" and concerns she might become depressed as she prepared to leave the company she had founded. Meg was an energetic, intense, and engaging person who seemed terrified of the new phase in her life—both what was about to happen at work and how that would impact her marriage of 45 years. Her husband had retired several years earlier and seemed to be enjoying his time reading, gardening, and simply being at home. But for Meg, this way of life "seemed like dying" rather than the "relaxed living" her husband said was so fulfilling after a life of intense travel in his work in the aerospace industry.

Meg's company was a creative consulting group that helped large corporations and governmental institutions to address how they'd become stuck and to find innovative solutions for moving forward. She was educated in business and early on found consulting a rewarding way to "look at a project, make some comments, and then move on." Her colleagues who'd found positions within a company seemed happy; but the idea of being committed to one organization and having to keep track of all the details of a given department's tasks seemed both overwhelming and dissatisfying for her.

When her consulting work led to an opportunity to form her own company, she was careful to keep her role as overseeing what her team of consultants was doing, never to have to stick with one client or another. For the last 30 years, this was her work life. But as business became more virtual and the online world of artificial intelligence not an area she felt interested in or capable of mastering, she knew it was "time to sell" and found a younger associate eager to take over her position.

"It all seemed such good timing, for me to decide to leave now and find a competent successor. I'm ready to leave, don't get me wrong. I know why I am going, and I know when that's going to happen—next month. It's just that I have no idea where I'm now going or what I'm going to do once I'm done."

Clearly, Meg is not alone in feeling the distress of changing roles, of leaving a life of work, of feeling like she may not have meaning and purpose in her profession. Yet the quality of her fear seemed more than the distress of change; it felt as if something fundamental to Meg's life energy was about to be diminished. We sometimes get "lost in familiar places" at work. Using our jobs to attempt to meet our early and ongoing attachment needs is often helpful in seeing through such challenges. Meg's AAI revealed a dismissing profile, with her lack of recall of many of the features of her childhood relational experiences. That finding suggested that she may have had avoidant attachment at home, with a lack of focus on her interior life. She would have been safe and her bodily needs cared for, but her being seen and soothed likely less a part of her attachment experiences.

The informal PDP survey—simply asking questions about how she handled emotions, where her focus tended to be, and areas related to her vectors of agency, bonding, and certainty—brought up a distant connection with her emotional life, an outward focus, and a priority on planning. She described how if she "didn't know what was happening next" she felt like she was "going to explode." Her life at work was fulfilling, she said, in that she could always have a new project she could get excited about overseeing, send her consultants in to "do the detailed work" she couldn't stand, and then move on to the next task or go out looking for more clients. At home, she was the organizer of their busy lives; busy because she was always setting up social dates and trips, and her husband, when he was around, was happy to participate.

But now all that was going to change. He seemed to want to simply stay at home, being five years her senior and having some knee and hip issues that made a sedentary life more appealing for him. But Meg couldn't imagine becoming housebound. She said, "I'd rather die." The term "retirement" drove her out of her mind, she said.

In this clinical evaluation, I thought it would be helpful after our third session to directly discuss the PDP model with her. We discussed the fundamental notion of wholeness, the vector of certainty, and the attendency outward. At that moment, it seemed she most resonated with the C-o pathway as her primary pattern. What we could do, I suggested to her as a plan (which she greatly appreciated), was to look at the drive to organize her life around avoiding uncertainty by planning, thinking of new ideas, and following her enthusiasm into its outward expression in projects. I offered her the notion of "preferment" instead of "retirement," and that she could now do the things she preferred. She seemed relieved that she didn't have to just hang out at home.

On the other hand, I suggested to her, she could learn to develop other skills to feel a wider array of abilities to handle her emotions—to broaden beyond the shift mode of reframing and redirecting her emotions. We talked about how the "fear" she had described of stopping work was a great example of letting an inner emotional state begin to enter her awareness, a new experience for her that had been quite distressing. This was a natural link to discussing her attendency, and the untapped capacity for her to look inward instead of looking outward, because of her lifelong predominance of being an externally focused individual. Could her attachment experiences have shaped these early organizing features of her life? Perhaps. And perhaps they were more inborn features of temperament, with the PDP groove made deeper by her nonsecure attachment history.

I told her about the capacity to see one's PDP when it is not integrated as a box we are trapped in, one we may not even be aware of. And that the work we might do could transform that walled container into a platform that could be where it now would serve more as a playground for her than the prison it may have been for much of her life. She liked that plan and is actively working on this now in therapy.

Short Reflections for Integration

Planning for possibilities

Simply stop and notice your recurrent planning for positive possibilities associated with your energy going up and out. Use this awareness to bring yourself back to the full spectrum of what is present in the moment including both joy and pain.

(Inner) Self-referencing

Stop to notice your thoughts often go to what pleases and fulfills you. Complement this tendency by putting equal amounts of attention and energy on others as to yourself, as best you can.

Reacting to pain or distress

Notice the felt sense in your body when painful and distressing situations arise and your tendency to either reframe these into positives or elude them. Breathe back down and with discernment do your best to face these.

[Source: David Daniels, "Growth for Type 7." https://drdaviddaniels.com/growth-for-type-7/]

Integrative Transformation

Integrating across time, linking the anticipation of the future with the events of the past and the experience of living in the present, becomes a central focus for the growth-edge work of those traveling the certainty-outward pathway. Living for the future as an adaptive strategy to handle the non-accessed, nonconscious pain of being out here, working-for-a-living, enables an avoidance of the fear of life's inevitable uncertainties. Do-or-die is shifted into do-to-live. Yet this strategy's own trap is to lock an individual into a perpetual focus on the future that keeps them far from being present now or learning from the painful lessons of the past. The energy of this forward-thinking, seeking stance can be compelling, for the individual and those around them;

yet without integration, this can become a rigid stance making exhaustion a vulnerability.

The mind is created, in part, by the human brain—an organ in the body that serves as an "anticipation machine" as it gets ready for what's next by projecting what might happen in the immediate future. Building upon this readying capacity, we also have the prospective mind, which envisions a future based on what might be possible and then can plan on these ideas being implemented at some coming time. When this information process-ing biased toward anticipating and planning for the future is fueled by the certainty vector's motivation for predictability in a complex world, the out-ward attendency will drive energy flow toward representations of informa-tion and of the future—facts, understandings, planning, possibilities, and opportunities not to be missed. To drop into the present moment and sim-ply be with what *is* means developing, or at least accessing, another mental capacity for being mindfully present now, inwardly focused in this moment, as free as possible from the seeking, planning, anticipation, and conceptu-alizations of knowledge and instead open to the uncertainty of now. This is the growth-edge journey for this pathway.

We've discussed earlier that in interpersonal neurobiology, we see "emotion" as a shift in integration. Here a higher level of integration comes with linking the capacity to simply "be" and to be with emotions rather than focusing incessantly on "doing" in action and planning and shift-ing away from the emotional life emerging, even if beneath the surface of awareness. This embracing of interoceptive awareness, of simply being aware of the body's sensations and then the emotions that emerge from the body's input, drops us into the present moment, freeing us from what can at times be a prison of planning and conceptualizing. The trust in this state, as with each of the pathways we are exploring, is to embrace a sense of wholeness that naturally emerges, without effort or intention, from this receptive awareness.

When I first participated in a week-long Enneagram gathering, a pow-erful moment emerged when someone from the Type 7 panel who I was having lunch with said that some of the issues arising from the larger group discussion were "unsettling" for him. We went for a long walk, and during the ensuing conversation we each noticed how difficult it was for him to focus inward, to sense his body's state, to be aware of the emotions that might be there after the panel. He told me that this was the "usual way" he was and that inner reflection was simply not in his skill set. Until the PDP framework emerged, it wasn't readily apparent to me why this difficulty would be so prevalent in this pattern. With the vector and attendency processes now being made clear, and with these being possible temperament features, we can see how this drive toward certainty to ensure predictability would serve as a deep life-and-death motivation; yet without the capacity to focus inwardly on the emotions that this drive activates, the ensuing anxiety and fear are themselves sources of uncertainty that now, in a low integration level, would need to be warded off. Hence, we can see at least one possible developmental process that shapes which emotion-regulation mode emerges with this vector and attendency combination—to shift by reframing and redirecting the primal affects associated with this subcortical motivational network.

This emerging PDP perspective also helps us see the common ground across different patterns, to illuminate the bridging features of some otherwise seemingly separate PDPs. We bridge to those pathways that share the same vector, attendency, or mode of emotion regulation. For example, my own secondary bridging C-o pattern may get me to engage in more activities than I can actually accommodate effectively, and so knowing this propensity of the certainty vector when in its outward attendency can greatly aid in my learning to say no to opportunities that arise.

With an outward attendency in the certainty vector, we can sense how, now far from the predictable and safe world of the womb, the anxiety and fear of the unknown would disable the individual if their realities were truly known. Out in the world we can plan for what happens next and gain some sense of certainty based on this prospective mind: imagining and organizing for future happenings far from the present moment. This engaging planning process means that uncomfortable emotions or thoughts, experiences of not being able to organize or enact plans, and the feeling of uncertainty that then arises are too much for a nonintegrative PDP of C-o to metabolize. The growth-edge from the understandable shifting emotion-regulation mode toward a more receptive state of mind entails differentiating these internal states of anxiety and fear and then linking to the larger sense that life can unfold without always being organized by the individual.

Shifting away from the pain and uncertainty of our do-or-die life out here in the world, an outward focus in the vector of certainty leads us to reframe the anxiety and fear and redirect that energy into imagining what we can do, seeking and planning out our opportunities for positive experiences in the future. All the while our inner subcortical life is busy motivating us for certainty, our cortex plans our lives away from living in the emergent, vibrant, alive, yet ultimately uncertain present.

Integrative growth within this pathway moves from this excessive focus on the future to living fully in the present and accessing whatever emotions and reflections, comfortable or uncomfortable, may arise now, or that may emerge from the past. The energy of adventure does not have to disappear, but can be channeled and expressed—the two other emotion-regulation modes—into engagement and exploration that do not need to have control as their guiding principles. With integration across vectors and attendencies, growth enables the higher levels of integration of the other pathways to be accessed. With this adventurous spirit, trying out new ways of living into a fullness of being can itself become an adventure in which uncertainty is embraced as an opportunity and not something that is a compromise to be dreaded or feared.

C-d: Certainty-dyadic (C-d Pathway; Enneagram 6)

Expressed Personality

Expression of this personality pattern is characterized primarily by an inner sense of doubt or uncertainty, heightened vigilance for potential dangers ahead, and a tendency toward catastrophizing—imagining all the possible ways in which things might go wrong down the road. As with all the fear-related certainty vector patterns, it seems from the narrative data that the need for a felt sense of safety holds special salience.

If the bridging C-i pattern is the mind's department of *preparedness* and the bridging C-o is *planning*, the C-d is a focus on *surveillance*, specializing in the search for sources of danger in the inherently uncertain future ahead. The personality structure operates as though in accord with a deeply embedded belief along the lines of "I must gain certainty and security in this hazardous world that I just can't trust." Some in the C-d pattern reveal high degrees of anxiety and fear and a shutting down of their risk-taking behavior; others in this C-d pattern have, either at times or more generally, a "counterphobic" mental stance that seems to shut off this behavioral paralysis and instead "go for it" and after some hesitancy, push through to achieve a sense of certainty. In some ways, this counterphobic manifestation of the C-d pattern in the moment may appear more like the "let's go do this" stance of the A-o pattern—but it is more like pushing through doubt to achieve a feeling of safety rather than denying vulnerability.

From early in life, these clients seem to have learned that the way to get along satisfactorily in this life is to remain constantly vigilant and on guard for all the unexpected problems, hazards, mishaps, incongruities, and untrustworthiness sure to lie ahead. In comparison with all the other eight personality patterns, uncertainty and doubt occupy the mind—about others, the world in general, confidence in the state of one's perceptions and knowledge, and even doubts about doubts themselves. (Welcome to my world!) Of course, there is an element of truth in this formulation. Everyone needs a degree of healthy wariness to survive in the real world, but trouble can happen if it becomes a habitual, limited, or compulsive way of living, which sets up problems with anxiety and trust that bring many clients to therapy.

Brief Description	The 6 believes you must gain certainty and security in a hazardous world that you just can't trust. Consequently, Loyal Skeptics are themselves trustworthy, inquisitive, good friends, and questioning, but also can be overly doubtful, accusatory, and fearful.
Key Interventions	Help 6s notice the preoccupation with hazard and the accompanying over-imagination and projection, pay attention to what is already alright, become their own authority, and develop greater trust in themselves and others.

[Source: The Narrative Enneagram, 2020, pp. 27–29]

Developmental Pathway and Adaptive Strategy

In the PDP framework, this pattern is rooted in what we call the certainty-dyadic developmental pathway and its working strategy. In effect, this is a kind of nodal pattern of the system that holds its central dilemma or tension in awareness—the need to cope with the reality of an inherently uncertain and sometimes hazardous world—as these individuals pursue satisfaction of their various needs and desires. Attention and the flow of motivational certainty-seeking energy are centered squarely on that *inherent uncertainty* concerning both the outward stream of information about others and the world as it is unfolding in the moment, and the inward stream of information from the templates and schemas of all that has been learned and taken in. Both the vector of seeking certainty and its accompanying anxiety or fearfulness flow into behavioral expression and tend to be relatively upregulated, and the subsequent flow of attention and energy is experienced and expressed toward more phobic, quietly anxious doubting and questioning in some individuals on this pathway; while in others, the pathway is more counterphobic, with a move against the fear with skeptical challenging of what is believed or perceived. These phobic and counterphobic states can also exist within the same individual across differing contexts and experiences.

Integration and Individual Variation: Strengths and Challenges

As with the other patterns, when the three vectors and their trio of pathways are well integrated, the flow of attention and energy into behavioral expression is well tempered and wisely focused by access to the balancing higher integrative states of the other pathways, meaning accessing the other vectors, attendencies, and emotion-regulation modes. Here, with integration, the individual has a flexible and adaptable repertoire of strategies for coping with the innate and healthy angst of uncertainty built into the mind by evolution, and for responding in an effective and open manner to anxiety and fear when they are triggered. Sensitivity to possible troubles ahead is well balanced by an ability to channel that energy toward grounded and cool-headed preparation, and the optimistic confidence and courage that can come from having anticipated the worst. And the full array of emotion-regulation skills is now available—not just upregulation of fear—which in this integrative state allows confidence in one's inner life and in other individuals to emerge, and opportunity, rather than uncertainty, to be seen clearly.

When integration is impaired, doubtful ambivalence, constant questioning or challenging of ideas and assessments of one's inner self and others, second-guessing, catastrophizing, and testing of the trustworthiness of others are prominent. Anxiety and fear, when they arise, are upregulated and tend to flow into sometimes more phobic flight strategies (i.e., more obviously anxious, vigilant, compliant) and at other times more counterphobic fight patterns (i.e., more confrontational, assertive, aggressive, and risk-taking).

Behavioral Profile	**Strengths:** *Being thoughtful, warm, protective, devoted to others, trusting as faith develops, intuitive, sensitive, loyal, fair, witty, and full of ideas.* **Difficulties:** *Ambivalence over "everything," leading to inaction, avoidance, procrastination, and incompletions, difficulties with authority, both in cases of obedience and rebellion (e.g., trouble with the law), seeing fearful possibilities everywhere which displeasures life, magnifying external power, dangers, and harm in a hyper vigilance which limits possibilities, over-imagination, especially regarding anger and motives of others, leading to situations in which misreading and mistrusting occurs, seeing the hidden and ignoring the obvious, creating opposition in order to take action.*

[Source: David Daniels, "Enneagram Type 6 Description: The Loyal-Skeptic." https://drdaviddaniels.com/type-6]

Focus of Attention and Blind Spots

Each of the nine pathways demonstrates a version of the truth that there is a tendency to perceive what one is "looking for." With this pathway there is a strong tendency to see threat ahead. Anchored as it is in an amplified sense of uncertainty and doubt, attention is charged with finding and focusing on any and all hints of doubt or uncertainty, which of course are many in this world, inside and out. While human minds seem constitutionally wired by evolution to see a few more threats than exist in actual reality in our negativity bias, the tendency here is to see many and everywhere in the constructed reality of a busy, questioning mind.

If that is what mostly occupies the screen of attention, other aspects of experience get less attention and become *blind spots* or are harder to take in. In this case the tendency to focus on uncertainty, doubt, and potential danger comes with a tendency to miss or dismiss compelling evidence of safety, certainty, confidence, and opportunity that are evident to others. And the fact that things sometimes do go badly or wrong as predicted—because that happens in this world—provides all the proof needed to validate and reinforce the habitual vigilant stance of looking for trouble.

Emotional Processing

Anxiety and fear, which are generally upregulated in this pattern, play a prominent role in its emotional dynamics. The less well integrated the system, the more fear and anxiety seem to flow and be expressed in thought and behavior and get projected outward onto others and the environment. As we've described, this manifests in a sense of anxious doubt, insecurity, and ambivalence about one's perceptions, one's knowledge and understanding, one's positions on issues, or the trustworthiness of others. Anxiety and the host of problems that come with it are common as a presenting issue for many seeking therapy. Enneagram-familiar therapists often report that the first half or so of each session amounts to providing the client safe space to discharge accumulated anxieties about the uncertainties and dangers that consume their attention.

Very interestingly, many who come to identify strongly with this personality pattern do not initially perceive themselves to be unusually anxious or fearful, even when others observe and experience the relatively upregulated expression of anxiety. For those with the C-d pattern's internal vantage point, they are simply giving what seems like obviously due diligence to the vital task of spotting the possibility of danger ahead, even when they seem excessively anxious doomsayers from others' external vantage point. Scanning for danger, alerting when a threat is perceived, and motivating the individual to seek safety can be part of the inner reality common along this pathway. On the other hand, those with the C-d pattern may be frustrated or confused by others' failure to appreciate the value of their well-developed habits of troubleshooting. Over time, those leading with this pathway may even grow weary of their own "what-if" questions, devil's advocacy, second-guessing of themselves or others, or analysis paralysis. They can begin to doubt their own doubts.

A spectrum of relationship difficulties, well captured in the seemingly contradictory labels "loyal skeptic" and "contrarian" often used in the Enneagram world for those traveling along this pathway, reveals other important emotional dynamics. Relationships, like most everything else, tend to be approached cautiously, with vigilance or aversion and a long period of testing, as if the other person is on probation. It can take a very long time for a sense of confidence and trust in others to develop. Even in long-standing relationships, whether personal or professional, faith can be shaken more easily than is the case for most others. David himself identified most strongly with this personality pattern, as do I. When teaching about it, he often recounted how even after decades of a highly successful marriage he could find himself worried that his beloved Judy was ready to call it quits and walk out on him. He knew full well this made no logical sense even when he was in the thick of it, but the feelings came easily and quickly at even minor, routine bumps along the way. When David and I met and shared such similar reactions, it was like finding a fellow club member, something I never imagined could be possible.

Very interestingly, once trust is established after being often and thoroughly tested, it can be held too dearly, too compliantly, too loyally, so that significant violations of trustworthiness are not clearly perceived and taken in. The result can be patterns of difficulty related to relinquishing too much authority to others!

Relationship difficulties with authority figures are frequent sources of difficulty for this personality pattern. If you are predisposed to doubt and constantly "test" and question the trustworthiness of others, it can be especially difficult to place trust in authorities, where inherent in the social contract is a view that those in positions of authority ought to be given respect and trust. While this may be troublesome for those authority figures, it has great utility in empowering the capacity to challenge a system that seems flawed, as so many of the interwoven systems are in our modern cultures. In other words, as with each of the patterns, there is both a personal and a social benefit to the inherent characteristics of a pathway—in this case, the pursuit of truth and integrity through incessant questioning of the status quo.

Cognitive Processing

As we've seen, thoughts and verbal narratives often include catastrophizing, ambivalence or doubt about the trustworthiness of others, and loops of second-guessing the soundness of one's own judgments or decisions, which can undermine confidence in the personal, individual self as much as or more than trust in others. Another common characteristic experienced by some, in some situations, is a habitual counterphobic tendency to take contrarian positions on others' opinions or assessments. Another almost opposite pattern involves the tendency already mentioned to remain overly loyal for too long to others or groups. It is as though the interest of preserving the sense of security and safety of existing relationships, even after their expiration date, outweighs the risk of moving on.

The well-attuned therapist will usually recognize the underlying anxious emotional tone, even behind the contrarian stance, and sense that these folks live very much "in their heads," a head-based ALEAF we also see in the other two certainty patterns.

Summing Up

Psychotherapist Beatrice Chestnut (2013, pp. 216–218) summarizes what she describes as the three key behavioral patterns for each of the nine personalities that are the kinds of recurring problems that often bring clients to therapy and are primary targets for deeper therapeutic work. For this pattern they are:

1. "Trying to find a sense of control and security in a dangerous world by watching, doubting, testing, and questioning."
2. "Projecting fear, anxiety, and power out onto others, especially authorities."
3. "Acting out fear in different ways instead of owning it, being with it, and consciously managing it."

Growth-Edge Work

As a Type 6, we need to become aware of our preoccupation with what could go wrong, what's unsafe and untrustworthy, and the accompanying magnification of mishaps, potential danger or fault, all the way to perceived betrayals. We are sensitive to discrepancies, inconsistencies, and double-binds. This sensitivity provides us with a tremendous sixth sense to sort through immense detail, incoherence in others or situations, and out-and-out lies that were intended to manipulate or confuse. It's critical that we learn to thoughtfully discern what really is hazardous and what we can let rest in good faith.

[Source: Daniels & Dion, 2018, p. 112]

Faith is a big stretch for the Loyal Skeptic because faith comes before proof. This means staying with situations requiring courage, feeling the fear, and resisting the impulse to move away from fear (the phobic's habit), or challenge fear (the counter-phobic's habit).

[Source: David Daniels, Healing Your Habit of Mind (1998)]

Strategies for Development
Fear
Simply stop and notice where fear in your body is and inquire of yourself to discern if there really is anything to avoid or challenge, knowing that mostly this is the result of magnifying what seems fearful. Then act accordingly.

Imagination
Simply stop to remind yourself that your "blind spot" is magnifying in your imagination what you experience as hazardous and unpredictable. Then act accordingly, moving into rather than away or against what seems fearful but truly isn't.

Doubt/contrary thinking
Stop and notice how doubtfulness, questioning, and contrary thoughts keep coming up in your mind. Do your best to release from these and move forward into action.

[Source: David Daniels, "Growth for Type 6: The Loyal Skeptic." https://drdaviddaniels.com/growth-for-type-6/]

- *Working at distinguishing true impressions from projections.*
- *Welcoming in fear and moving ahead.*
- *Reclaim your faith in self, others, and the universe.*
- *Realize proof is no substitute for trust or faith.*
- *Communicate with the part of you that is afraid—what is it trying to tell you?*
- *Imagine yourself as bigger than whatever you fear.*
- *Be aware of magnification, and work at distinguishing true impressions from projections.*
- *Relinquish the quest for certainty and control as a substitute for faith.*
- *Get a reality check—how do others view your fears and concerns.*
- *Take an action before you are fully prepared.*
- *Balance the negative spin you tend to put on situations with positives.*
- *Examine the opposite.*
- *Become your own authority and watch for cues of giving your power to others.*
- *Own your aggression (which helps Sixes get out of the victim stance).*
- *Engage in pleasurable activities.*
- *Develop the belly center through meditation and self-observation practices.*
- *Do physical exercise to move your energy out of the head.*
- *Sense your body when mental activity of doubt, anxiety, or worry arises.*
- *Doubt the doubt, and remember that faith is not foolish.*
- *Take time to focus on, name, and savor your successes—make a list!*

[Source: The Narrative Enneagram, 2020, p. 28]

Tips for Growth in Relationships
Relational Triggers

Being cornered. Being controlled or feeling overpowered. Interactions with others that feel too unreliable or that feel unsafe. Discrepancies in other's speech or behavior and inconsistencies. Being accused of something unfairly and/or wrongfully. Others' lack of responsiveness. Giving others warnings and advice that they do not take seriously. Lack of respect and/or a lack of integrity as seen in others.

[Source: The Narrative Enneagram Therapist Training]

Relational Reflections

If you are the other individual in relationship with Type 6, you can feel misread and mistrusted. The Type 6 questions your behavior, your intentions. You feel put off by the implicit and explicit accusations, the blame and even paranoia, as you, the other, don't experience yourself as "bad," untrustworthy, or harmful. Compounding this can be the 6's own guardedness and "chatter." You don't know what is really going on with them.

The Type 6's questioning mind seems like constant "butting." It feels confronting, limiting. You hear "you can't do this?" "What about that?" "Can't you see how manipulative they are?" You sense Type 6 keeps causing trouble. It seems there is never enough proof for the six, never enough reassurance. You want to get going and the six drags their heels. It gets very frustrating.

[Source: Daniels, 1998, Type 6]

If we're a counter-fear Type 6, also called, "counter-phobic 6," we'll tend to address our fears and apprehensions head-on, rather than feel paralyzed by them. We are more dispositionally wired to go toward, assert with contrary or tyrannical, oppositional thinking—confront and deal. Challenging can feel much better than waiting, stewing, and whirring.

As a Type 6, we believe we must seek certainty, trustworthiness, and security in what we believe to be a hazardous and unpredictable, often dangerous world. We must avoid becoming utterly helpless and dependent on others or anything that we cannot control, especially in this kind of world. We must be vigilant, don't-miss-a-thing observant, and cognizant to all that surrounds us, in order to protect ourselves and our loved ones.

[Source: Daniels & Dion, 2018, p. 279]

Clinical Vignette

A 24-year-old graduate student came to see me for treatment of her "obsessive-compulsive disorder" diagnosis she had been given in the campus mental health center. Tania had a long history of worries about things that could hurt her family members: fears of her parents dying in an airplane accident, images of her brother getting seriously hurt as a football player in high school. She had always assumed, she said, that this was "just the way things were" in her mind, a necessary state of being aware of what could go wrong. But after college and now into the second year of her doctoral program at a local university, she felt overwhelmed by her fears of failing her qualifying exams to move on to the next phase of her work in biochemistry research.

When the clinician on campus told her that she had OCD and recommended medications for her obsessions about failing, she decided to get a second opinion and called me. "I'm not saying he was incompetent; I'm just saying I don't trust that he is accurate." The records she obtained showed a checklist recitation of what was needed to rule out other conditions, such as mood or thought disorders, substance abuse, or other anxiety disorders. She didn't have panic or social phobia. But positive on this form were the classic findings of obsessive-compulsive disorder—replete with obsessions about failures despite excellent achievements in both graduate school and her prior academic setting, and with compulsions to enact behaviors to attempt to guarantee both success and avoidance of negative outcomes. These compulsions included saying in her mind "All is OK" and tapping 10 times on each hand before handing in a paper or taking an exam, and before her brother would start a football game at school or her parents would head to the airport for a trip.

Tania and I discussed the notion that an ancient "checker system" exists in which we've inherited a neurological way to keep us safe by a Scan–Alert–Motivate (SAM) process of scanning for danger, alerting us to threats, and mobilizing us to take action to prevent harm. Sometimes, I told her, that SAM process gets so exuberant it can lead to what one young patient of mine named "overactive checker deployment." For some people, the checker system can get overactive because of exposure to the bacterium streptococcus. She was intrigued that the protein on the surface of that bacterium seems to match the protein of the networks in the brain related to the checker and motor movements, leading to the PANDAS syndrome: psychiatric and neurological disorders associated with strep. Obsessive-compulsive issues are one outcome of PANDAS. But Tania hadn't had a strep infection for 15 years.

Then we talked about the notion of personality emerging from temperament and intensified by nonsecure attachment experiences. She was intrigued, and so we dove into the PDP survey first, finding her, as you can imagine, resonating most with the worst-case-scenario thinking of the C-d pathway. While this was her primary baseline PDP, she also felt a secondary resonance with the C-i and A-d bridging PDPs—the intense focus and love of her studies at school (even with her fears of failure and feelings of being an impostor) as well as her acting as a mediator at home with her family and in her social life now as an emerging adult.

At this point in her second opinion–seeking with me, she and I discussed the tendency of those in the C-d pattern to discount the opinions of authorities. And since she came to me as yet another authority, I felt it was important to lay out the information so that she and I could, together, co-construct what seemed like a reasonable view of what was going on and what she could choose to do about it.

Tania asked if there might be some overlap between the OCD—overactive checker deployment—and the C-d PDP. We discussed the neuroplasticity concept of "Where attention goes, neural firing flows, and neural connection grows" to illuminate the possible linkage. The subcortical networks of the certainty vector were all about attempting to predict in order to attempt to protect, to ensure some sense of safety in an inherently unsafe and uncertain world. While the "checker" system likely involved this subcortical network, it also was vertically distributed, including aspects of the reward circuitry and the prefrontal cortex's manner of determining meaning and evaluating whether an error had been made and how to both correct it and avoid mistakes. Checking for potential danger is one way of interpreting what the classic obsessive-compulsive disorder is, a kind of "doubt hiccup" that leads to an overactivity of this system.

Treatment for the OCD aspect of her life could involve the cognitive behavioral techniques aligned with mindfulness practices, an approach that I had written about in the book Mindsight in the same year I published the PDP framework in the traits chapter of The Mindful Therapist, and that was based on interventions leading to a relaxing of this excessively activated checker network in the brain. And regarding her question, she again queried, what might be the relationship between a pattern of developmental pathway and the OCD, whether it is thought of as a disorder or an overactive deployment? I told her that one of the benefits of the PDP hypothetical framework is that we could ask that question in an empirical study—were those in this pattern more likely to exhibit elements of OCD? And could an approach to integrative transformation that we are proposing for the C-d pathway be useful if in fact OCD symptomatology is simply a more extreme, nonintegrated manifestation of this PDP?

Tania started asking a lot of questions about the other pathways, and if there might be the possibility that each was associated with a "disorder" at its extreme, nonintegrated state. I told her I thought that was a fascinating idea, and that some authors had postulated it for the Enneagram personality system and personality disorders, but no formal research had proved the validity. For her, I said, what mattered was how she might find this useful at this moment in her life.

Tania dove into some of the interpersonal neurobiology foundations, taking up *The Developing Mind* and *Aware*, and was fascinated about how a low level of integration of her PDP would illuminate the origins of the chaos of her intrusive thoughts and emotions and the rigidity of her compulsive behaviors and repetitive thoughts and also make sense in terms of being outside her window of tolerance. She even mapped out moments when these obsessions and compulsions, revealing this chaos and rigidity, were triggered by life circumstances: her upcoming academic challenges, moments of risk with her parents' travels, intense times with her brother's athletic competitions. With the Wheel of Awareness as a meditative practice she then learned, the hub of that wheel—as we'll explore in our final chapter soon—became an experiential dive into maximal uncertainty. As she became more familiar with what at first was a frightening and anxious sense of "being unmoored" in the pure, receptive awareness of the hub, she came to feel a "letting it all go" sense of freedom, a way she could embrace some kind of trust in the "love of the world" that she felt in that loving-awareness place of the hub.

With time, she could also come to sense the impulses toward compulsive behaviors and obsessive cognitions to be "just points on the rim of my wheel" that she didn't need to take so personally, or so seriously. As these reflective practices became a part of her life, the propensity to need some sense of certainty in a world woven from uncertainty let her come to find a peace of mind she hadn't recalled experiencing for a long, long time. Her symptoms of "OCD" became both less intense and less frequent. When I told her my 94-year-old mother's definition of mindfulness, she appreciated the shift: "What used to annoy me now amuses me." This, we reflected on together, was how an imprisoning PDP can move from a prison to a playground. She could enjoy the values of a certainty vector's giving her a propensity to challenge existing scientific dogma, to love knowledge, and to have the enthusiasm of making plans in her life—to set a direction, but not need to be certain of the outcome.

Short Reflections for Integration

- *Moving from a cognitive habit of cowardice/doubt to cognitive awareness that the world can be accepted as is without doubt*
- *Moving from emotional fear to emotional courage with guiding oneself and with external real danger*

  [Source: David Daniels, "Integrating the Higher Qualities of our Essence into our Lives." https://drdaviddaniels.com/integrating-essence-true-nature-lives/]

- *Encourage Loyal Skeptics to notice positives, develop trust in others and the future, appreciate their own strengths, and take positive action*
- *Provide them with positive alternative meanings*
- *Be consistent and trustworthy*
- *Disclose your own personal feelings and thoughts*

  [Source: David Daniels, "Growth for Type 6: The Loyal Skeptic." https://drdaviddaniels.com/growth-for-type-6/]

Integrative Transformation

Excessive differentiation of the certainty vector can yield an intense and persistent activation of a "checker" system scanning, alerting, and motivating the individual to assess and address potential dangers and ultimately to imprison an individual in avoiding or ignoring fear. When excessive concern about danger fills our meaning-making minds, our actions, and our interactions with others, an excessive pessimism—"seeing the difficulties with every opportunity"—can imprison our freedom to be and act freely in the world. Linking a sense of trust in the universe, a "faith" that life will unfold well, to the useful checker system that manages the real risks in a more integrated way balances reasonable concern with the intellectual realization that life inevitably has risks.

One possible source of the lower integrative states is an excessive differentiation of not only the checker system, driven by the certainty vector's subcortical motivational network, but also the left side of the divided brain. The left hemisphere specializes in a narrower focus of attention than the broader focus of attention of the right side of the brain. This tight focus enables details to be the focus of attention, and then allows those details to be assembled into clusters of categories and concepts that we can label and list in language-based words. Yet the left-hemispheric cortex is also more distant from the input of the lower areas of the nervous system—the subcortical areas and the body proper. As bodily energy flow and emotion arises from these regions and first seems to enter the right hemisphere, we can state that living a left-hemisphere-dominant life is potentially less emotionally enriched. The integrative work of bilateral processing would entail taking in the nonverbal, intuitive, holistic, systems-sensing right-hemisphere information processing to allow a fuller spectrum of life to emerge.

Bilateral integration enables the individual to draw on the more non-rational, nonverbal information processing of the broad-focusing, intuitive, more body-connected right hemisphere. Rather than discarding the highly differentiated and developed left-hemisphere processes, this integrative growth-edge work entails expanding the information-processing repertoire to include what may initially feel like a world of uncertainty, but is really more a nonrationality that is quite distinct from being irrational. In this way, expanding the sense of a center of experience—a self with its sensation, perspective, and agency—may be part of the emerging growth for integrating from the baseline of one's PDP, especially the C-d pathway.

The predictive mind is also dominant in the certainty vector attempts to detect patterns in an effort to anticipate what might happen next. The subcortical vector of certainty drives energy into the predictive, pattern-detecting cortex. With a dyadic attendency both inward, to the fear and sense that knowing what might be unpredictable might just be a threat, and outward, to all that could, in reality or in imagination, go wrong and become a threat to existence, there is an upregulation of the emotion of fear and the concomitant strategies that those of us in the C-d PDP experience. Recognizing this certainty drive for safety, the individual can work at their growth-edge to transform mistrust in life into a faith, a trust in life working out and a movement from the paralysis of fear or even its counterphobic alternative—excessive risk-taking—to a more integrative way of life. As Mark Twain is reported to have quipped: "I have been through some terrible things in my life, some of which actually happened." Growing at the edge for this PDP allows us to distinguish the imagined events and irrational fears from the reasonable concerns.

A PDP view of the phobic and counterphobic C-d pathway allows us to see how the experience of subcortically originating fear in the face of uncertainty and potential life threats, of perceived danger, can be met by a strategy to either flee from the event or image, or to fight it as a way of "conquering the fear." You may wonder how this would be a low integrative state. Shutting down fear can be a useful adaptation if the evaluative mechanisms assessing the actual danger are engaged and a discerning decision is made. With counterphobia, however, the shutting off of the fear is often activated without a comprehensive and open assessment being carried out about the true nature of the risks and benefits facing the decision to go forward or retreat. By seeing the upregulation of the emotion-regulation mode of EE, experience and express, we can see that the experience of fear gets expressed robustly but in two distinct reactive ways—to flee from or to fight against and move toward the fear-initiating event or inner thought.

The growth-edge work explores how the head-based initial energy flow with cortical thinking and its potential to "overthink" even simple decisions can open to the heart-felt and gut-sensed nonrational information processing that arises with a motivation for bonding and for agency—integrating the other vectors into the individual's repertoire of higher integrative states. Within the vector, the work of sensing what an "overactive" checker system does to attempt to create a "flimsy fantasy" of certainty, as the artist Rasheed names it, is an understandable yet futile and imprisoning cognitive move to ensure safety in a basically uncertain world. Learning to relate to this survival-based motivational system and widen the attendency toward a dominance of an inner focus without obsessing about the outer dangers, gathering knowledge and relishing it in time and space (as in the C-i PDP's high integrative states) and the excitement of planning and participating in life's opportunities (as in the C-o PDP's high integrative states) enable other possibilities to be received and explored with an openness and freedom from terror or from the blindness of the counterphobic position.

Even in my own personal exploration of this system, I was filled with doubt about the popular Enneagram view, about David's framing of that system, and then about how we, as five scientists, were attempting to fit an empirical view from developmental neuroscience into the publicly embraced and widely used system. Ironically, doubt would be revealed as a key experience of those in this pattern; but this has been both amusing and at times befuddling, even annoying. "Doubting my own doubts," I would often say, before knowing about this potential to illuminate the nature of doubting as part of this particular temperament's journey into personality. Adaptive strategies that arise from the subcortical motivational networks likely emerge within our cortical strivings. In the case of the certainty vector, this push is for safety by attempting to establish a feeling of certainty that comes with predictability. Beyond the contemporary personality view of the Enneagram, this PDP perspective enables us to see how both neural propensities and life experience can help form what we are innately leaning toward.

In the PDP perspective, as we've seen throughout our journey here, the move from the wholeness of the experience of being in the womb, embedded in implicit memory systems, into the working-for-a-living of the do-or-die setup within this life out here on Earth is a prime and classic driver of the certainty vector's energy—toward planning and enthusiasm with an outward attendency; toward protecting space, knowledge, and time with an inward attendency; and toward tracking threats with the dyadic inward-outward attendency. The growth-edge, integrative work for this tension of the inner feeling of fear and outer focus on actual or imagined dangers can create an intense sense of survival-based preoccupations far from that feeling of being whole.

As an experience-and-express emotion-regulation mode of upregulation, the inner feeling of this PDP C-d can at times be quite overwhelming. In many ways, the strategies of counter-fearful versus fear-experiencing each become captivated by this certainty-drive for safety. In counter-fearful strategies, the approach is to move away from this otherwise paralyzing state. This is accomplished by pushing through the fear of danger; and can at times become just as dangerous as being consumed by fear and avoiding experiences, which also blind us to opportunities. Either approach, fearful or counter-fear-based stances, become chaotic or rigid propensities revealing low levels of integration. Embracing a deeper reality of wholeness beneath these adaptive strategies enables those in this pathway to relax the vigilance and open to a deep sense of fulfillment along their life journey.

By embracing with acceptance the reality of risk and the necessity for reasonable concern and caution, courage emerges, enabling life to be lived with enthusiasm and efficacy even in the face of fear. Rather than avoiding the emotion of fear, the experience-and-express regulation mode can allow fear to be faced—"to feel and deal"—and life to become more freely alive.

The growth-edge work of reaching the higher integrative states within this pathway builds on the strengths of questioning the nature of what is true, attention to detail, and the high energy capacity of this PDP's innate proclivities. As other vectors are also made more accessible, an emphasis on agency and bonding naturally fills an individual's life with more empowerment and connection. As I write this to you, I can feel my own need for certainty relaxing, hoping that these narrative journeys down each of these pathways have been helpful to you in your work and life in however and wherever this PDP approach may be of benefit to you and those in your journey of a lifetime.

CHAPTER 9

Therapeutic Principles for Integrating PDPs in and Into Clinical Practice

It's an Inside Job

We've been investigating a way to understand the summations of thousands of narratives from people across the globe, exploring their lives from a perspective grounded in the knowledge and practices of The Narrative Enneagram school of teaching. These details are derived from the reflections of inner experience of people of all ages, socioeconomic status, education levels, cultures, religions, races, ethnicities, sexual identity, and country of origin, who all report similar experiences within each of the nine patterns they identify with. I view all this, of course, with the important caveats we've mentioned, that this collected set of insights comes from people who were at least open to mindfulness and to change and were each seeking out the Enneagram view. In this way, the data may be skewed toward "fitting in" to one grouping or another. But even with my skeptic's perspective, listening closely to formal panels or sitting down for dinner or taking long walks with workshop participants, this had the sense of not being about narrative distortion; it seemed more about finding clarity amid the prior confusion.

Also, discussing this PDP model with people in other conferences and gatherings not related to the Enneagram, like a two-week rafting journey down the Colorado River, has yielded similar reflective sharing. Even more, the stories that emerge fit the vector framework powerfully well, with individuals dividing up, in about 90% of those asked, in the agency vector and a primacy of anger being either present or actively avoided; bonding and a focus on separation distress/sadness in oneself or others; or certainty with its accompanying predilection toward anxiety/fear being primary or actively avoided. When asked about the attendency an individual might be leading with, the initial reactions are a bit less clear, but ultimately, as in the river-rafting setting, it becomes readily apparent who is in which attendency, even independent of which vector they are in. When I have led workshops exploring the PDP framework with those unfamiliar with the Enneagram, participants have not only usually found their pathways but they've come up with their own questioning approach, once they know the framework, that helps to delineate which pathway or pathways their interview partner is traveling down in their lives.

For clinical purposes, we can use the notion of integrating PDP both *in and into* clinical practice with the intention of highlighting how our integrative transformation approach is not about blending but about honoring differentiation across the vectors and attendencies and then linking them. That's how we integrate PDPs *in* the therapeutic journey. We'll also be exploring the many ways you can use these ideas to integrate the PDP framework *into* your practice.

How the Patterns Are Used, Useful, and Misused

With the framework we now have, inspired by this accumulation of narratives, the bulk of them from the Enneagram world over many decades and a new, smaller set through the PDP framework in the last 15 years, we then can look at this high-level tour of the personality "types" from the Enneagram world viewed from a PDP perspective on patterns and ask: What does the PDP perspective offer that is clinically useful over and above a traditional Enneagram viewpoint? You may have come up with your own response to this question from the prior chapters diving into the integrative transformation of each PDP. This framework allows us to ask fundamental questions that can directly aid the therapeutic process and the understanding of client and therapist. How can therapeutic change be facilitated by insights into the potential developmental and neural underpinnings of temperament, motivation, emotion, memory, and personality? How does the PDP model help us see the connection among innate proclivities, known as temperament, and experiences in relationships, known as attachment, that have also shaped neural structure and function? And how do these two influences on neural development, the innate and the experiential, shape the emergence of personality, in childhood, adolescence, and into adulthood?

We can also ask, How do such patterns of emotion, thinking, and behaving—what is formally known as personality—change over the lifetime, on their own, or with therapeutic support? And how might low levels of functioning of a given PDP make one psychiatric disorder more likely than others at the extreme of low levels of integration? Could interventions, then, for conditions like obsessive-compulsive disorder or various personality disorders, be amenable to an integrative approach designed with neural integration in mind?

When I trained as a young psychotherapist, and as I've become an educator in the field of mental health, it became readily apparent that there were, and are, no developmental neuroscience–based models of personality nor guidelines for how to use those in a systematic way in psychotherapy. Personality disorders are named, and specific modalities of therapy, such as dialectical behavior therapy (DBT) or mentalization-based treatment (MBT), for example for those diagnosed with borderline personality, have been empirically shown to be effective approaches to alleviating suffering (Choi-Kain, et al., 2017). But how does personality as a fundamental developmental process work in all of us, not just in those with the extremes of psychiatric dysfunction? How can a therapeutic relationship be informed by the therapist's own PDP and insight into that of the client—and how might this PDP-informed therapy lead to lasting changes in a client's brain? How can an understanding of the developing mind and the study of neuroplasticity help guide our efforts to help people in therapy? And how can our understanding of that organizing process that shapes emotions, thinking, and behaving that we call "personality" come to be understood and worked with in therapy? As we've suggested, it is our intention for the PDP framework, in its broadest applications, to be a useful guide for the process of change in therapy.

Noting patterns can help you as a clinician and the person with whom you are working to gain deeper insights into the subtle or sometimes not-so-nuanced ways a vector and attendency can be in a low state of integration—and then lead you to practical ways to provide support and facilitate integrative transformation. As we've stated, and it's worth reemphasizing here, the proposal is *not* to "get rid" of the personality pattern, but to free it up to access its own integrative strengths as well as to access the strengths of other pathways—meaning accessing the other vectors and attendencies and tap into the other modes of emotion regulation. I've found this approach to be profoundly useful in my clinical practice (as well as my personal life).

One of the ways a system of identifying patterns can be misused, however, is in its application as a "diagnosis" or viewing personality as a "fixed type" that pathologizes or fixates a person and their unique journey in life. No one needs the rigidity of such an unhelpful categorization. Yet knowing patterns also can be freeing if they are seen as the verb-like, emergent, organizing—literally "self-organizing"—processes that they are. Patterns regulate our states of mind. While they may be verb-like unfoldings, they do have, as we've seen in our explorations of temperament and adaptive strategies, persistent ways of shaping our emotional life, our thinking, and our behavior. In interpersonal neurobiology, we have the nine domains of integration that serve to help organize our evaluation, intervention, and assessment components of therapy. These domains include the areas of consciousness, bilateral, vertical, memory, narrative, and identity, among the many ways we can have integrative flow in our lives. In an IPNB-informed approach to therapy, we assess for the experience of chaos and rigidity as signs that the individual is away from the harmonious FACES flow of integration: flexible, adaptive, coherent, energized, and stable. One of these domains we explore is "state integration," which entails recognizing our distinct states and their ways of being prone, in themselves or across their functioning, to creating chaos and rigidity in our lives. When we work to integrate states at the within and between levels, deep change emerges toward that FACES flow of being harmonious that comes with integration.

In some fascinating discussions, Joan Ryan, Heather Coros, and Suzanne Dion (personal communication, November 2023) explored with me their independent, unpublished, informal research findings and clinical impressions in being trained in both the Enneagram system and the therapeutic modality of internal family systems (IFS). Some suggested that the "parts" of an individual usually reflect a common "type." Others considered each "part" to have full access to each of the Enneagram patterns. Joan Ryan said that her initial findings suggested that both protective parts—managers and firefighters in the IFS nomenclature—as well as the vulnerable "exiled" parts, seemed to present themselves through the lens of a primary or "core" Enneagram type. In other words, from this data set at least, there seemed to be a filtering through a dominant core type even as different experiences might lead to certain aspects of a person being wounded and then isolated. These warded-off states are then protected by other aspects of the individual who in turn seems to be filtering energy flow through the attention, cognition, and emotion biases of that particular core type. Future research can help clarify how our multilayered minds with a range of states harness the various aspects of vectors, attendencies, and modes of emotion regulation in service of their various functions for the individual's life.

From a PDP perspective, we could imagine a scenario that could go in a number of directions. One is the notion of state integration being challenged, yielding differentiated states of mind that either were not linked—exiled—or were excessively differentiated, as other states were constructed as an adaptive way to protect those exiled parts within that pathway. We might also imagine a deeply "state-dependent" set of neural processes that, as with dissociation, might yield quite distinct skills and memory access within a given dissociative state—the clinically important condition known as dissociative identity disorder. This condition may arise as terrifying experiences lead to "fear without solution" in the situation of disorganized attachment. How the ensuing attempts to survive such biological paradoxes as being terrified by the very attachment figure who is supposed to be there to protect you from terror is the key challenge leading to how states come to exist and then persist. Future research could ask, from a PDP framework, if dissociative states might be accessing different vectors and different attendencies, as well as their corresponding modes of emotion regulation, in a desperate attempt to make sense of the non-sensical situation of disorganized attachment.

Future research can explore this notion and determine whether other disconnected aspects of a person may reflect other pathways; and we can examine the alternative view, that a given set of early organizing features—our temperament—may actually be a baseline filter through which all other "parts" or "dissociated states" may arise. Another question to be asked is how life in general may induce continued separation of "parts" of an individual, and how the journey to wholeness may influence that subjectively felt sense of differentiation in the face of emerging new capacities for linkage. In whatever ways states may find themselves not differentiated and linked, this nonintegrative condition would fit also with our fundamental proposal that the lifelong journey toward wholeness, what seems to be consilient with Richard Schwartz's notion (Schwartz, 2021) of the capital "S" Self, involves distinct primal needs and our strategies we develop to meet them from early in our lives.

Another aspect of how the PDP framework can be used well is understanding the notion from the serenity prayer: Grant me the strength to change the things I can, the serenity to accept the things I cannot change, and the wisdom to know the difference. Our PDPs are open to integration; yet our baseline pathway, especially under stress, may stay with us for a lifetime even with the joy of a robust journey of healing and integration. As we've said, the aim is to have the courage to change our state of integrative access to the higher capacities of our own baseline pathway and in fact link to the other vectors and attendencies and modes; to have the serenity—and the humor and humility—to realize we live in a body with its innate temperament that may change to only a minor degree; and that we can have the wisdom to realize integrative transformation is not about getting rid of something but about differentiating and linking something with more fullness and freedom. This is how we widen a deep and narrow PDP groove. This is how we free our PDP from being a prison to becoming a playground.

Our proposal that the mechanisms of the verb-like processes of regulation underlying how personality emerges from the self-organizing mind also gives us insight into the processes of change, highlighting the role of integration in optimizing the self-organization of complex systems. These systems—inner, as the embodied brain, and relational, as the relational fields with other humans and *intra*connected within all of nature—let us envision, as social activist and mindfulness teacher Rhonda Magee has suggested, that "healing our selves from the inside helps us to heal the world."

Within the multidisciplinary framework of interpersonal neurobiology, we've seen how we can consiliently define the self as a *center of experience* with the three facets of SPA: subjective sensation, perspective or point of view, and agency—our source of action. Subjectivity, perspective, and agency are shaped by patterns in the swirls of energy we can name "state of mind." As mind is both embodied and relational, our personality is the self-organizing process that shapes energy flow both within our bodies and in the relationships in which we exist. Our *self* is not just these somatic containers, these skin-encased bodies we inhabit, but the whole of the inner and the inter. We have many centers of self-experience, within us and between our bodies and the larger relational worlds in which we live.

The journey to wholeness is at the heart of what personality and its various pathways are all about, which means that this is a journey of a lifetime. When a clinician understands this shared view, "shared" in that we are all on such a journey, as well as a perspective that can now be experienced and expressed as a framework for our clients to consider in their lives, too, then the journey of psychotherapy itself becomes a sharing adventure. As a therapist, I have found this stance profoundly empowering and liberating—that I am joining my clients, my patients, as a fellow traveler in this amazing gift of being alive here, together on this planet.

"Look-Alikes" on the Outside

By now you may have noticed that the characteristics of expressed personality of the various patterns may sometimes look alike. This is important because it is typically behavioral issues that first bring clients to therapy, yet the work will be different depending on the inner experience—the motivations, meanings, and emotions—of the individual coming for therapy. Herein lies a major value of the PDP framework—the potential for helping clients and their therapists get closer to inner motivations beneath behaviors in working toward therapeutic change.

Consider, for example, the agency-dyadic and bonding-outward patterns (9 and 2 in conventional Enneagram nomenclature). Two individuals each traveling down one of these distinct pathways will tend to become so tangled in others' needs, wants, and desires that they lose track of their own. From the outside, this behavioral tendency would make each of these two patterns, the A-d and the B-o, "look alike." As a therapist, just sensing this common habitual way of behaving by itself, from the external perspective, wouldn't allow you to understand the *inner* mechanisms beneath that personal-self-denying tendency. Yet if we look with a PDP lens, we can see that the motivational energy, the vectors, beneath the similar behavioral patterns is very different. The B-o pathway can easily lead to a kind of loss of a personal self because those with this pattern are acting out an adaptive strategy to be seen and loved by actively exerting their inner self in caring, while the A-d pathway ends up in its behavioral version by acting out an adaptive strategy of relinquishing agency and slipping passively into merged relationships in a deferential and go-along-to-get-along way of resolving conflicting motivations. Yes, you may have noticed: Both the A-d and the B-o pathways share the shift emotion-regulation mode of reframe and redirect. But neither is a look-alike for the C-o, which also shares this mode. The PDP framework, with its foundations in vectors, attendencies, and modes, enables us to deeply understand the inner mechanisms of mind beneath externally visible repeating behaviors.

Cultivating integration *in* individuals with either the A-d or the B-o PDP is quite distinct. Working on the low integrative states of the B-o personality pattern involves learning to recognize and relax that habitual compulsion to shift the emotional state by meeting other people's needs, especially if one's own needs are not met; while therapeutic focus with the lower integration levels of the A-d pattern involves learning to recognize and relax the compulsion to relax! Obviously, that's very different work— even though the two share similar behavior and a similar emotion-regulation mode of shift. This sort of insight is one of the major values of therapeutic work as you integrate the PDP framework *into* your clinical practice. The therapist can work with the client to unearth the baseline vector(s) and forms of attendency while exploring the emotion-regulation modes, and then note the patterns of priority and meaning, feelings, thoughts, and somatic sensations beneath habits of externally visible behavior. Getting a feeling for the associated anatomical locations of energy activation and flow (ALEAFs), will also help you to understand clients' inner experience as well as the potential activation of your own reactions to them as their therapist. With these insights into the pathway's trajectory over a lifespan and the patterns of that PDP that show up in a given moment and circumstance, you as a therapist will then be more equipped to better tailor therapeutic interventions and envision the growth-edge work for that individual in their own development toward wholeness.

We can extend these general ideas to many other behavioral "look-alikes." For example, several of the personality pathways have a behavioral tendency to procrastinate, but with careful inquiry and introspection, different emotionally charged motivational vectors are revealed. When people who most identify with the certainty-inward (5) pattern procrastinate, it is often because of a craving for more information; with the agency-inward (1) pattern, putting things off is often because their inner critic demands finding the correct way and avoiding making a mistake; and with the agency-dyadic (9) pattern, it is often because choosing means risking confrontation and disturbing a sense of inner calm. They are each procrastinating—that's what we can observe outwardly—yet with different habitual mental models or states of mind that are associated with different motivational vectors and attendencies, as well as their associated modes of emotion regulation affecting how energy and attention are channeled into behavior. In other words, while procrastination may be the common behavior, the inner motivational drive beneath that habitual way of acting may be quite distinct and the therapeutic focus distinct for each individual. This reveals how knowing the inner mechanisms of the mind at work in the PDP approach can deepen how your clinical work enables you to both understand the mental lives of clients and help them gain insight and integrative development.

Mindsight is a term for our ability to have empathic understanding, insight into our inner lives, and integration to enable kindness and compassion to flourish. The PDP framework offers a powerful mindsight tool to empower ourselves as clinicians and ourselves as people on this planet to cultivate insight, empathy, and compassion in our lives. Mindsight helps us see the inner mental life of one another beneath the external manifestations of behavior.

Because different personality patterns can look alike from the outside, determining PDPs of others based on externally visible behavior alone is unreliable. We need to apply a mindsight lens to know our clients well. This is one of the valuable and at the same time challenging aspects of the PDP approach—it is an inside job requiring an inner search for motivation and emotional experience. While that may be hard at first, developing the mindsight skills of sensing this sea inside has great positive contributions to make in a person's life. We need to learn to *see inside the sea inside*, I often say to my clients. This may be one of the challenges, and limitations, of some typing instruments that may focus too readily on outer dimensions of the externally visible, and therefore more readily objectify, and sometimes quantify, aspects of personality.

Four-Dimensional Therapy

Using this framework to help others does not require making a precise personality "diagnosis" before beginning work. Instead, the therapist in effect works with the pattern(s) that show up with the client at that moment in their lives. As we've seen, the Patterns of Developmental Pathways supports a four-dimensional framework of personality that helps us see not only in the present but across time. And for this reason, doing "4-D Psychotherapy" (Siegel, forthcoming) enables you as a therapist to envision not only the PDP's manifestation as a pattern in this moment—diving deeply into subjective experience, interpersonal interactions that shape a relational field in the present, and neural processes unfolding within the whole embodied brain—but also the ways such patterns have persisted over time to reveal the pathway aspect of that PDP and where development might be able to go with help.

Together, therapist and client use the patterns as a kind of map of inner experience to identify what resonates most. The map supports a collaboration between clinician and client in working together to make sense of long-term patterns of inner experience that, as we've seen in the prior in-depth PDP chapters, have *tendencies* to emerge repeatedly across time and contexts that reveal a pathway that may be most dominant in the person's life. The purpose of unearthing these tendencies is to facilitate liberation from limitation. Clinical formulation helps clients construct a coherent narrative about their individual experience in a way that can free them up to make new possibilities available and new choices clear and attainable. The PDP narrative, either inside of you as a therapist or in the co-constructed sharing with the client as well, helps to make sense of *these patterns that tend to emerge.*

It may seem like a subtle distinction we've made in the PDP framework, but we invite a more challenging conceptualization of these tendencies as having a verb-like fluidity of life that embraces the potential for change, rather than the understandably "more certain" sense of personality types or the self and its parts as nouns with an entity-like fixed nature. Yes, persistent patterns can have a feeling of noun-like entities; yet as we'll see in the chapter ahead, even viewing this as a fixed nature of the mind's features can lend an unnecessary and sometimes unhelpful rigidity and resistance to change. As we've seen, the enduring quality of these patterns can give them the look and feel of something solid, a noun-like entity. Respecting and inspecting this persistent set of patterns of feeling, thinking, and behaving can embrace both noun- and verb-like qualities of the PDPs without rigidifying them. Client and therapist together can use these dynamic formulations to explore the nature of the client's very individual inner experience, and from this determine how to work with what they find. It is this "work" at what David would call the "growth-edge" that we've outlined in our prior chapters.

From the beginning of our conversation, we've noted how important it is to both understand and remember that these nine patterns are not regarded as pure categorical personality types—as noun-like, restricted entities. In the world of personality, including with the use of the Enneagram, we have observed that this point either is not known or is forgotten; personality type is frequently misunderstood as a *categorical* difference—I am right-handed *or* I am left-handed. This unintentional "nounificaiton" may be in large part because self-development enthusiasts often present what we are calling personality *patterns* here as personality *types* within a typology of categorically distinct entities.

In contrast to this communication vulnerability, in which we often nounify processes as things, while most people come to identify most strongly with one of the patterns, individuals' internal experience is very often "flavored" by other patterns. Jack, for example, says, "I resonate most strongly with the A-d or 9 pattern, but I also see a lot of C-i (5) and A-i (1) on inner reflection and in my behavior." We might view this as Jack's baseline primary A-d PDP with a secondary set of C-i and A-i PDPs.

In many ways, these different pathways are filled with the various approaches we may uniquely harness to deal with the challenges not only of family life early on in our development but also of our peer-to-peer relationships in our adolescence and then of the larger world in which we live throughout our adult lives. We take on the challenges of motivational drives and emotions, the seeming paradoxes of seeking connection while also needing to be individualized and develop an authentic self (our bonding vector); being confident and safe while having the courage to embrace uncertainty and rest in our awareness with not knowing (our certainty vector); and activating our agency to bring balance to the world so we have a sense of empowerment and of being able to live with the many ways inevitable conflict arises (our agency vector). Yet we do live in a body, one with an embodied nervous system molded by evolutionary history and shaped, in part, by experience. What this means is that we do have primal subcortical motivational networks. And what this also means is that those networks may be particularly sensitive and responsive to experience and may be different for me than they are for you. These differences then reinforce over time their own initial propensities and turn that subtle predilection into a more robust, and enduring, pathway. As we've also seen, the nature of genetic, epigenetic, and experiential factors on neural development would naturally push for one set of neural connections to become more dominant than others for many of us, creating a tendency of leanings and activation, not a categorical difference.

Whether or not our hypotheses concerning temperamental proclivities related to vector and attendency are accurate and complete, we can see how certain of the nine pathways may become most salient for us. Some of us may relate to each of the nine; some to three; some to mostly one. This is not about categorical division into only one grouping, but *predilections* that present as patterns in the present moment and as pathways that shape our lifelong journeys. Carefully conducted research in the future will help us to delineate what some might say is each person's having one singular baseline pattern rather than there potentially being primary and secondary patterns each of us may have. Let's keep an open mind about that issue, especially as we try to be receptive to whatever our clients are experiencing.

These pathways to becoming whole integrate the polarities of life's paradoxes—we are fluid in our continual emergence while at the same time we are shaped by enduring proclivities that reinforce our own patterned ways of experiencing life. In this way, the underlying mechanisms of vectors, orientation of energy and attention as attendency, and the adaptive strategies that emerge as we learn emotion-regulation modes and assemble cognitive narratives that we develop to make sense of our lives, each continue to shape our sense of "who we are" yet to various extents can also evolve across the lifespan. In 4-D therapy, we work with our clients to sense where they've been, where they are now, and where, often with our assistance at the growth-edge of their therapeutic development, we can support them in the movement toward wholeness in their lifelong journey.

Utilizing the PDP Framework

A "map" of the PDP vector, attendency, and mode helps us to recognize and conceptualize our own deeply ingrained, generally nonconscious biases in perception, and the patterns in the ways we tend to respond to others and to life events more broadly. This, in turn, helps us use those insights to engage in the inner and relational work of change and transformation.

In terms of understanding others, many relationship problems may stem from a failure to appreciate the fact that others have very different ways of attending, perceiving, feeling, thinking, and then behaving. A PDP map is an extremely powerful tool for working with relationships in that it helps individuals in a relationship to conceptualize, accept, and appreciate such differences in both cognitive and emotionally resonant ways. When my wife and I learned our different PDPs, it greatly helped us understand the nature of our conflicts and misunderstandings. Instead of being frequently caught in a rut, we could see the patterns underneath these relational patterns and could find each other beyond the initial reactivity that such disconnection can initiate. This understanding creates rich opportunities for building less reactive and more compassionate, empathetic, authentic, communicative, and collaborative relationships.

As clinicians we are quite familiar with the fundamental idea that deep and lasting change in challenging patterns of behavior naturally requires more than simply an aspirational goal of more constructive behavior. Such change, from a PDP perspective, requires relaxation of more deep-seated emotional drivers of attention and behavior. It requires that we open awareness to the energy flow within our heads, hearts, and viscera of the entire body—each aspects of the whole of the "embodied brain"—and to our relational connections with people and with nature. With these insights, we can help others build new neural pathways both of top-down processing and even of bottom-up motivation and emotion. By learning about the core emotion-motivation networks underlying our vectors, the attentional bias of our attendencies, and the emotion-regulation modes that tend to be dominating our clients' lives, we gain new insights that can lead to powerful opportunities for change.

By catalyzing integrative growth, unique for each PDP, there seems to be widening in the groove of one's baseline pattern, opening to other vectors and attendencies, letting other emotion-regulation modes become accessible. It may be that we never lose that baseline PDP groove but simply make other vectors, attendencies, and modes more available to make our lives more free and more whole.

Utilizing the PDP map of the personality patterns in psychotherapy also incorporates any of a variety of clinical strategies aimed at developing greater capacities for (1) focusing attention and shaping intention; (2) attending with increasing clarity to soften both the driving and reactive emotions; (3) reframing automatic counterproductive appraisals and reactions; and (4) making this understanding of developmental pathways a natural way of cultivating more integration across the lifespan. The PDP perspective empowers us as individuals to understand and transform the deep drivers and organizers of our inner life and our relational ways of behaving in the world.

CHAPTER 10

Wholeness and Integration in Psychotherapy

In the first sections of this chapter, we'll explore the relationship of the PDP framework to broader, more conceptual and theoretical issues related to spirituality, wholeness, and consciousness. This exploration may not be of interest to some, nor is it necessary to find utility in applying the PDP framework in therapy. Others may find this part of the chapter both relevant and meaningful for using the ideas we've been exploring directly in their clinical practices and lives. If you are interested in taking a deep and wild dive, welcome! If not, thanks for being on this journey all the way to this point, and feel free to skip ahead to "Therapist, Know Thyself" on page 321.

Emotion, Integration, and Wholeness

From an interpersonal neurobiology viewpoint, *experience* is energy flow. *Emotion* is a shift in the state of integration of that flow. *Attention* is that process that directs the flow of energy. When energy is in a form that symbolizes something, it is *information*, or energy-in-formation. And in this way, attention to what matters, to what is deemed salient or relevant for one's life, is how energy flow is shaped based on the evaluation of meaning. Because meaning shifts integration, it is fundamentally an emotional experience—how we find what matters and makes sense of life to cultivate a sense of *coherence*. "Coherence" is a term that implies a resilience across experiences. It is also an acronym, this acronym penchant of mine says, that includes connection, openness, harmony, emergence, resonance, energy (as in vitality), noesis (as in knowing), compassion, and engagement. We thrive with these elements of coherence in our lives. Coherence, we can propose, emerges with integration.

IPNB also proposes that the mind has four facets that include subjectivity, consciousness, information processing, and self-organization. A natural drive of a complex system is to "maximize complexity," and this drive can be translated as creating harmony. As we've seen, the FACES flow of being flexible, adaptive, coherent, energized, and stable is the natural outcome of optimal self-organization—and it has coherence at its center. This FACES flow is achieved through the process of integration—the linkage of differentiated aspects of a system. A shift in integration, then, is how emotion arises and emerges in tandem with the movement toward self-organization. Emotional well-being arises with integrative transformation, the way we allow integration to become a part of our lives.

Wholeness, Spirituality, and Science

One feature of the Enneagram system, as we've described from the beginning of our journey, is that it includes a focus on psychospiritual growth. In some individuals, using this term, referring to the psychological on the one hand and spiritual on the other, makes a lot of sense; for others, especially some mental health professionals, bringing these two ideas together brings up a sense of discomfort and doubt. Let me offer you some reflections that may help with these concerns. I once taught in a conference called "Spirituality, Education, and Science" and was given the opportunity to ask some workshop participants what their understanding of the term "spiritual" really was. Dozens of individuals revealed a similar view—that for them, "spiritual" or "spirituality" signified a life with *meaning beyond merely survival and connection beyond the boundaries of the body*. In this use of the term "spiritual," we concur with this view of a life of *meaning and connection* being made more robust by doing the PDP work of facilitating the integrative journey toward wholeness.

From the PDP view, "psychospiritual growth" means the mind (the psyche) is exploring living with meaning and connection (spiritual) as it develops across the lifespan (growth). And so, for us—defining these terms very specifically in this way—we are comfortable with translating "psychospiritual growth" as the development of integrative capacities to move toward wholeness. Wholeness, recall, we are describing as including a state of being with empowerment, connection, and ease. Yes, this would address the fundamental need sets of each of the three vectors. And this, as we shall see in this chapter, is exactly how we see the PDP approach supporting psychospiritual growth.

A PDP perspective, as we've discussed from the beginning of our journey here, includes the notion of the implicit memory of being at one with the womb embedding a sense of simply being in the world. Theoretically, there may also be the more abstract notion that we all come from the big bang in which the quantum vacuum, a sea of potential, is a "formless source of all form" that serves as a generator of diversity in which potentiality could arise and then transform into actuality (see *Mind* [Siegel, 2017] and *IntraConnected* [Siegel, 2023] in the IPNB series for a deeper dive into these ideas).

Simply put, quantum physics posits that energy is the movement from possibility to actuality. The mathematical space of all possibilities is called the quantum vacuum, which is also referred to by physicists as the sea of potential and the formless source of all form, as noted above. This space is empty of form but full of potentiality. We can propose that the experience of wholeness is felt in the implicit memory of simply being, being in the womb; and this state of wholeness we can propose may also be the quantum vacuum state of pure potential.

Wholeness can also be experienced in the world of actualization arising from that sea of potential—what we name a "plane of possibility," as we'll soon discuss—as these possibilities transform into actualities in their flow to differentiate and link, to become integrative as change unfolds, not stuck in rigidity or chaos, but emerging as an ever-changing harmony, equilibrium, disequilibrium, and change.

These actualities are the many ways we are differentiated from one another and within our own lives. How we come to link those actualities, in Newtonian dimensions of time and space, and across their various manifestations in our lives, is what we mean by "linking differentiated" aspects of a system. Isaac Newton, in the late 1600s and early 1700s, identified the properties of large objects that had a noun-like-entity characteristic of things separated in time and space. In the early 1900s, technology advanced to allow us to perceive processes smaller than an atom—such as electrons and photons—and be able to determine that the properties of these verb-like events were not the same as the macrostate Newtonian characteristics. For example, there was no variable of time; and in this microstate quantum realm, there were influences across Newtonian dimensions of space that did not impede their relationality, a process known as nonlocality or entanglement. The Nobel Prize in physics in 2022 was awarded for the detailed validation of this microstate-realm reality. The quantum physics notion of energy being the movement from possibility in a sea of potential arising into various states of actuality will be elaborated in this chapter in greater detail to offer a view of the psychospiritual-growth aspect of the PDP framework that may—or may not—match with the Enneagram aspects of this area of human development and spirituality. These ideas can be explored in further depth than this chapter will allow in other publications (see Siegel, 2017, 2018, 2020, 2023).

In the PDP model, each of us has an inchoate sense of this wholeness, and the journey of growth is our movement back in whatever various pathways we may find ourselves engaged in. "Movement back" may imply regaining a sense of homeostasis that we experienced in utero and that we are naming "being one with the womb"; and this return may also be, in a fundamental "experience-is-energy-flow" meaning, the return to possibility from our various life journeys as a range of states of actuality. The personal reactivity of our particular PDPs is specific to whichever of our subcortical networks of agency, bonding, or certainty may be our innate propensity, and then is shaped further by our attendency of inward, outward, or dyadically as both. This is how the Newtonian actuality of living in a macrostate body, a noun-like entity with survival needs, meets the quantum realm's reality of potentiality.

You'll notice that David's Enneagram terminology, the views we reviewed in the earlier chapters, uses concepts such as innate goodness and trust in the universe to take care of what needs to be done. These are often referred to as "holy ideas" or "virtues." When David used the terms "holy idea" and "virtues," from an interpersonal neurobiology perspective we might say he was referring to states of higher integration that enable a more flexible, adaptive, coherent, energized, and stable state to emerge. This FACES flow becomes more accessed as each of the pathways becomes differentiated and linked, within itself, and with tapping into the higher integrative capacities of each of the pathways.

Our PDP view of these important Enneagram notions is that a plane of possibility—the quantum vacuum—serves, literally, as that g.o.d., or generator of diversity. This plane of possibility is the sea of potential that physics has proposed is the "formless source of all form." As forms emerge from this potentiality, the complex systems that arise have the principles of self-organization as an innate emergent property—without an author or organizer, without a conductor. This innate push toward optimizing self-organization happens with differentiation on the one hand being matched with linkage on the other. We are using the term "integration" as a linguistic symbol for that process of linking differentiated parts by which optimal self-organization enables harmony and wholeness to arise. We experience coherence—including each of those elements of the acronym described earlier—when we have ready access to, and live from, this plane of possibility. As we've seen, our various PDP journeys through life include states of lower integration when we are far from accessing that plane; and we have states of higher integration when we can more readily access that plane and enable what actualizes from it to naturally be differentiating and linking. The plane of possibility is the portal through which integration effortlessly arises.

Integration emerges as a natural synergy in which the interaction of parts gives rise to something larger than their individual facets—"the whole is greater than the sum of its parts." When we "trust the universe" we come to realize we can learn to let integration arise, sometimes getting the blockages of differentiation and linkage out of the way, enabling rather than creating integration. This view means that "psychospiritual growth" from a PDP perspective entails a shift from making something happen to tapping into an innate aspect of reality, of letting that plane be the resource—a source to tap into again and again—that is liberating rather than limiting, energizing rather than depleting.

Notice, too, how our inevitable move away from wholeness after we leave the womb—no matter how wonderfully attuned our caregivers are and secure our attachment is—means that we all have the capacity to develop a pattern of developmental pathway or pathways that dominates the push from possibility to actuality in our lives. Our psychological growth, our growth-edge, how our emotions arise and become regulated or not, our thoughts and what has meaning in our lives, our behavioral patterns and relational strategies in life—each of these can be shaped by our PDPs. And each of these can enable or restrict our capacity to live from the plane of possibility.

From the spiritual-growth viewpoint, the disconnection after birth from a state of "just being," as we are being "at one with the womb" may be conceived as a loss of empowerment, connection, and safety that evokes a feeling of being away from that "something greater" than an individual view of "self." This loss may be an impetus for a "spiritual journey" in which some may seek deep inner contemplative practice while others may look to find the "sacred" or the "divine"—to discover "God." Still others may come for psychotherapy, feeling deeply that something is "wrong" or "missing" in their lives. In this way, psychospiritual growth is in a sense a redundant term: Psychological growth is spiritual growth in that leading a life of meaning and connection, which is how we are defining what "spiritual" means, is promoting mental health—the health of the mind.

From the PDP viewpoint, we take a neutral stance about theistic beliefs, yet we consider the underlying structure of many religions (bringing back to connection—*re-ligare*) as sharing this drive for something more, which we suggest might be understood as the fundamental psychospiritual drive toward wholeness. This drive initiates a spiritual quest to return to home, to return to that wholeness that we all experienced to one degree or another in the womb; that we all left after the big bang. In the PDP perspective, this view of being lost or separated from home, as reflected in Ram Dass and Mirabai Bush's book about death and dying, *Walking Each Other Home* (2018), places a new embracing framework on fundamental questions of existence. This is what we mean by using the term "psychospiritual growth"—working with the PDP framework cultivates a life of meaning and connection.

Consciousness and Wholeness

For those new to some of my vocabulary and prior writings, here I'll offer a concise summary of terminology and concepts that we can use to envision the connection between clinical work and personality, wholeness, and cultivating consciousness in the PDP framework.

On the following page is a diagram of these notions, which we will be referring to for a deeper dive into synthesizing how to integrate personality and wholeness in, and into, clinical practice. (For in-depth discussions of a proposed view of mind as an emergent property of energy flow, please see Siegel, 2017, 2018, 2020, 2023.) If this energy focus is "too much" for you or something you are simply not interested in, I've presented all the prior chapters without these ideas so the PDP framework would be understandable and useful without going to a view of mind emerging from this energy perspective of the movement from possibility to actuality. If on the other hand you are up for trying this out, or reviewing these interpersonal neurobiology views of consciousness and applying them to the PDP framework of personality, welcome, and onward we go!

In interpersonal neurobiology, we draw upon a wide range of ways of knowing, including the various disciplines of science, to understand reality. One aspect of reality is the mind. By proposing that mind is an "emergent property of energy" it is natural to look not only at the energy transformation of the human nervous system, including its head's brain, but also to the experts in energy itself, physicists. This is how we turn to the physics view of energy as "the movement from possibility to actuality." This leads to Figure 10.1, which we call a "3-P" perspective, as it entails a plane of possibility, plateaus of enhanced probability (greater than near zero), and peaks (of actualization). The mind emerges along this probability distribution curve, meaning where the energy probability position is at a given moment. Energy flow is the movement along this distribution set of values. In Figure 10.1, we can imagine the example of me thinking of, say, one of the one million words you and I hypothetically in total might share. Your chance of knowing that word is one out of a million, or "near zero," seen at the bottom of the graph. When I say "ocean" and you know that with 100% certainty, the "energy flow" is revealed as the movement from point A at the bottom to point A-1 at the top.

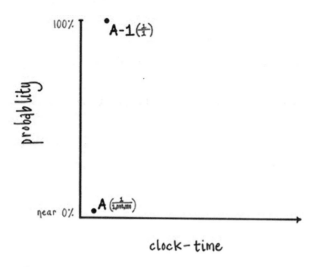

FIGURE 10.1: Energy flow is the movement from possibility (Position A) to actuality (Position A-1).

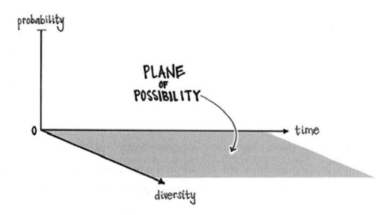

FIGURE 10.2: The plane of possibility represents all diverse possibilities.

If we add a third axis of diversity, we have a now-three-dimensional diagram, we can see how the vertical y-axis is the probability position, from near zero to 100%; the horizontal x-axis is the change, or "clock-time" or simply "time" axis; and a z-axis going in and out of the plane of the page is the diversity axis, the various elements that might be happening all at the same moment. If this is new for you, it can take a while to process this perspective, and doing an immersion in a reflective exercise can help.

A reflective practice known as the Wheel of Awareness has yielded survey findings suggesting that the knowing of consciousness—the experience of being aware—may emerge when energy is in the plane-of-possibility position (see drdansiegel.com for experiencing the wheel as a meditative practice). This position is in the quantum realm of our reality, and in this way has the features of being filled with connection, timelessness, and massively connected verb-like processes rather than noun-like entities separated across time and space. Linkage of the full range of diverse possibilities is maximal in the plane. In the macrostate, large-object world, physics has revealed what Newton explored: There are noun-like entities, such as planets, bodies, and apples, that are separated in real macrostate dimensions we've named time and space. In contrast, the microstate realm is timeless, and there are no entities, only massively connected verb-like processes. This is how the hub of the wheel—the knowing of awareness—would correspond to the plane, which may have features more of the microstate realm, "empty but full," as it is devoid of form but filled with potentiality. In contrast, the things we are typically aware of, on the rim in the practice and in our day-to-day lives in these Newtonian, macrostate bodies we live in, would correspond more closely to plateaus and peaks—our awareness itself originating in the plane. In our diagram, plateaus are a visualization of how we learn to filter all possibilities into a subset based on prior learning. These are states of higher probability but not full actualization. Plateaus serve as filters that determine which actualities may arise. We can name these "top-down" filters; they select which energy flow patterns are allowed to emerge into a peak of actualization. In contrast, we can have "bottom-up" experience, in which we sense, as directly as we can, energy flow in its fullest, unfiltered emergence as peaks arising directly from the plane without the selective filtering of a plateau.

3-P Diagram

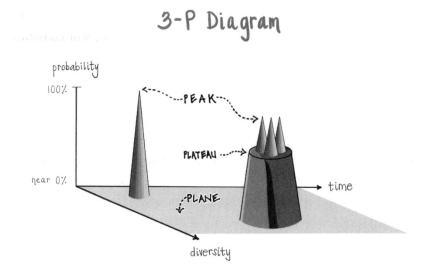

FIGURE 10.3: 3-P diagram with peaks of actualization, plateaus of increased probability filtration of activations, and a plane of possibility as the "formless source of all form."

3-P Diagram Meets the Wheel of Awareness

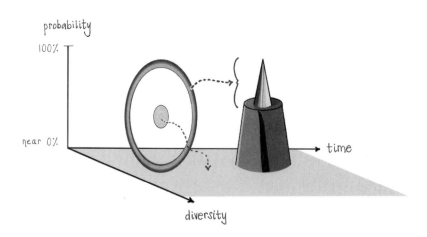

FIGURE 10.4: The Wheel of Awareness meets the 3-P diagram—the rim of the wheel represents plateaus and peaks; the hub of the wheel represents the plane of possibility.

A PDP view would be that the experiences we have, especially within our families as sibling relationships and attachment patterns, will construct top-down filters, our plateaus, that shape how we experience life. We also have our innate, unlearned, proclivities (our temperament characteristics), neural networks that become activated in the experience of being alone in the world and working-for-a-living in this do-or-die new life we lead out here, born into a body in the Newtonian macrostate world. These two factors, innate temperament and experiential learning, intertwine in the creation of a set of plateaus that form our ways of experiencing emotion, thought, and action—the underlying "structure," in energy filtering terms, of what we have been calling "personality." The contrast of the implicit memory of being at one with the womb and the now ongoing experience of this new do-or-die state of existence creates a tension in our lives—for the rest of our lifetime journeys—and stimulates the subcortical drives for agency, bonding, and certainty in our attempt to move back to a wholeness that we implicitly know, we feel deep inside, is truly possible. In various ways, depending on our vector and attendency proclivities, throughout our lives we'll be on this journey of seeking the realization of something, of a peace, a contentment, a fulfillment, what we are naming a "wholeness," that we once had and now, on the surface of everyday existence, has the appearance, at least, of being gone.

With practice at the growth-edges we have been exploring in various ways specific to the PDP proclivities of an individual, the journey to wholeness will involve cultivating access to the plane of possibility we are proposing underlies the experience of being whole. Thousands of individuals have practiced the Wheel of Awareness and have offered reflections on what the experience of the hub itself feels like: love, home, empty-but-full, complete, timeless, God, joy, peace. Often this experience is initially accessed with the aspect of the practice in which the spoke of attention is turned inward to the hub itself as in Figure 10.5.

WHEEL OF AWARENESS

FIGURE 10.5: Exploring the hub of the wheel directly by bending the spoke.

For the growth-edge work for each of the various PDP pathways, the wheel may be useful to facilitate the journey to wholeness in the face of the day-to-day challenges of living in a macrostate body by enabling the cultivation of access to the open awareness of the microstate realm. As a whole, the Wheel of Awareness practice is designed to facilitate a differentiation of the many aspects of energy flow that form the reality of our experience. Some are elements of the rim that have the macrostate qualities of the classical, Newtonian physics realm: noun-like entities of separation across the Newtonian dimensions of time and space that we, living in bodies, are quite familiar with and that organize our life journeys. Other aspects of the wheel practice enable us to access more directly the hub with its microstate quantum-realm properties that lack an "arrow of time" and are in this way timeless and filled with the experience of massive connectivity of verb-like emergent processes that, taken in their entirety, have the quality of—beyond even *inter*connectedness—something that from the sensation, perspective, and even agency of the whole we can name *intra*connected.

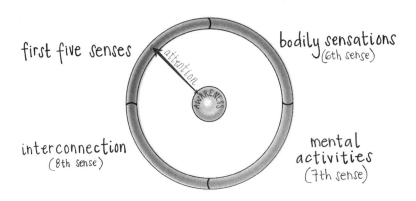

FIGURE 10.6: The components of the Wheel of Awareness.

The capacity to transition between our macrostate and microstate realms of energy flow is a skill that perhaps children have but, we can propose, are vulnerable to losing in their later childhood and through adolescence. In this way, in looking at the growth-edge PDP work, we are perhaps speaking about regaining a lost, or at least hidden, capacity we once had. And because of this, while we can speak of "learning a new skill" or "acquiring" or "cultivating" a capacity, it may be more accurate to envision this as a release of a fundamental ability that was never truly lost. Each of us is born from wholeness—whether in the context of the womb or the big bang of our universe—and as emergent properties of energy flow, we never lose the ability to transition between that flow in the macrostate realm of matter and the microstate realm of "pure energy" flow. It's all energy.

All of life is the flow of energy. When that flow gets "stuck" in only the macrostate realm it can become a prison for us, one we can unlearn as we regain the fundamental skills of living also in the microstate realm of wholeness. Being in nature, opening to the awe of simply being alive in this wondrous gift of life, expands the small sense of self to widen into what we are proposing is accessing this intraconnected reality of our shared lives. Gratitude and compassion in addition to awe, form the trio of what are classically known as "self-transcendent" emotions, which we can instead name "self-expanding" emotions, that allow us to open our sense of identity and belonging.

We have an identity lens, one that can look close-up from the sensation, perspective, and agency—the SPA—of self-experience or can be widened to include our deep weaving with all of our human family and all of nature (see Siegel, 2023). This is the Me in the body and the We of our relational lives. We do not need to choose one over the other; "MWe" is a term that integrates both the differentiated me and we to help us name the intraconnected wholeness of our essence.

Living with wholeness does not mean escaping to the hub of the wheel in an attempt to live only *in* the plane of possibility. This IPNB view of the journey is to integrate our lives, embracing the macrostate reality of our bodily existence *and* the microstate reality of our relational fullness which we can sense within that state of open awareness. In this way, consciousness arises as we flow from plane to plateaus and peaks, accessing them all, being open to the time-limited life of the body and the timeless reality of our intraconnected wholeness.

Living in a Body Out in the World

Patterns of developmental pathways are initiated, we are proposing, with the fundamental reality of being born into a body. Out of the womb, that body's evolutionary history becomes relevant as we deal with the disparity of wholeness in contrast with the do-or-die working-for-a-living necessity of being out here in a body. Our attachment experiences will directly interact with these deep evolutionary survival networks that motivate us to adapt to our newfound life in a body out in the world. The PDP framework, then, offers an inside view of how neurological, inborn systems will be engaged that, we are proposing, are unique to each of us as a part of our innate, unlearned, temperament. "Attachment," in contrast, is a term we use for how our relational experiences, also involving our basic needs for survival, will be influencing how we adapt to our interactions with others, especially attachment figures, such as our parents. The PDP perspective helps us name, explore, and work with these two aspects of what shapes our journeys toward wholeness across our lifespan.

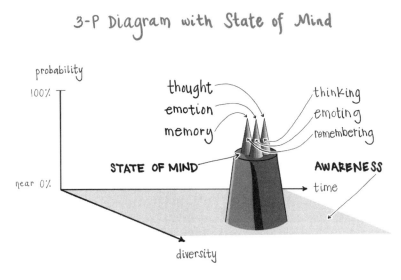

FIGURE 10.7: The mind and the 3-P diagram.

This engagement of our subcortical motivational networks may give rise to a particular developmental pathway and its specific pattern of shaping energy and information flow—the essence of our mental lives. A given pathway will involve specific plateaus that *filter* energy flow into a specific subset of peaks that are a visual way of representing our emotions, memories, and thoughts, as seen in Figure 10.7. A plateau makes information processing more efficient in that it selects which representational patterns are most salient for our handling of what is happening in the moment. A state of mind, a mood, and an intention are examples of what a plateau entails in our mental lives. These plateaus can be useful and in some ways are necessary for our survival in these Newtonian bodies we live in; and plateaus can also limit us from accessing a broader array of energy flow patterns available from the plane of possibility, and in this manner constrain our lives.

The fluidity of shifts in plateaus—in states of mind, mood, intention, knowledge, skills—is the key to plateaus not being prisons, but being platforms from which effective information processing can emerge freely from the plane of possibility. I like to offer the example that if we don't use the plateau-based skill of driving a car or riding a bicycle at a traffic intersection, if we don't step on the Newtonian macrostate brakes and stop our vehicle, we *will* become one with everything in the ensuing accident. Plateaus are not bad by themselves; plateaus are often essential for our survival. Yet the work toward wholeness may necessitate letting those plateaus relax, and it may entail accessing a way of living where actualities arise *directly* from the plane of possibility without being filtered by plateaus, as seen in Figure 10.8. We've seen how this can be viewed as a "bottom-up" flow in contrast to the "top-down" filtering by plateaus we've constructed from innate temperament or by prior learning. This we also can simply call "presence" or living with "open awareness." For this reason, reflective practices, such as the Wheel of Awareness, that enable the individual to tap into an open, receptive state of consciousness, are fundamental to working within the PDP framework of growth, no matter which pathway an individual has been living through.

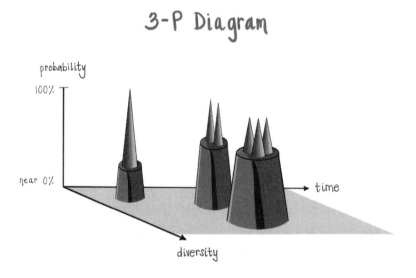

FIGURE 10.8: Some peaks arise after being filtered by plateaus; other peaks arise directly from the plane of possibility without being filtered.

In our PDP discussions we often say that we work to make personality more like a playground than a prison. With this plane-of-possibility perspective, we can illuminate the mechanisms beneath that suggestion as learning to more readily loosen our plateaus and access the plane, letting peaks arise in integrative ways directly.

In this 3-P perspective of the mind, we can also picture how a robust PDP might be envisioned. In Figure 10.9, we see how a low-lying plateau begins a filtering process that only allows a subset of all actualizations to emerge. Then, on top of the foundational plateaus, we see other plateaus constructed that continue to constrain which possibilities are allowed to arise. This selective funneling of the deeper filtering process might be how a vector could be envisioned as a deeper, more low-lying, foundational plateau. Then, depending on the attendency, another filtering plateau would be constructed on top of that vector plateau. Accessing other attendencies within a given vector would then

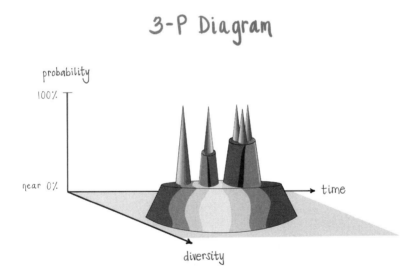

FIGURE 10.9: Layers of plateaus as filters that may be the fundamental mechanism underlying patterns of developmental pathways and their organizing ways of shaping how we feel, think, and act. A foundational plateau may be the vector, higher plateaus atop that lower one may be attendencies—and these may shape the emotion-regulation mode and other adaptive strategies that emerge as filters of experience.

widen which actualities were possible, making the individual more adaptive. Accessing other vectors would widen that set of what is possible even further. Living more directly from the plane itself, as seen in Figure 10.8, might be possible with higher states of integration. And then, in this possible scenario, under stress or with certain life circumstances, the plateau filter is reestablished to handle the Newtonian, macrostate realities of living a bodily life.

The Centrality of Wholeness

In the meditation experience of many contemplative traditions, an oceanic experience of wholeness is often described. William James, the grandfather of modern psychology, explored this in his classic text *The Varieties of Religious Experience* (James, 1902). The term "numinous" is sometimes evoked to describe the often-ineffable quality of this feeling, a state beyond cognitive understanding, an expansive sense of being embedded in the whole of the universe, a fundamental part of an essence larger than one's individual life. The timeless nature of this nonrational state is often described as having a dissolution of the distinction between a separate self and distinct other and to have a sense of familiarity, wonder, and awe. Arising from this wonder can be a feeling of understanding, "truth," appreciation, gratitude, reverence, and love toward life.

We are not making any statements as scientists about the theistic nature of these numinous feelings of wholeness, and we are not going to disentangle the many spiritual traditions that each have their own ways of making sense of this feeling of being at one with the universe, whether it is with a theistic godlike figure, or with the sense of something larger in the world in our true and deep nature as individuals, as our wholeness in the deeply woven fabric of the universe. Even from a physics point of view, as we've seen, the universe began as a big bang in which matter ultimately formed from the vast potentiality some call the quantum vacuum—that "formless source of all form." However religion or physics might interpret the origin and meaning of this timeless state that is an aspect of our lives, we can say that within its expressions is something likely related to the sense of wholeness we are attempting to articulate with words here and with this exploration of personality through the PDP framework. These are fascinating questions, some of which I take up in other texts (Siegel, 2017, 2018, 2023).

For the purposes of our exploration of the PDP framework, we are suggesting this set of possibilities: We have implicit memories of being at one with the womb, and this may give us the implicit sensation of wholeness and simply being. And we have the post-birth laying down of memory, implicit in the first 18 months of life exclusively, but then followed by the acquisition of the capacity, which lasts throughout the lifespan, to lay down explicit memory. In these ways, we may also have implicit memory for the experiences with our caregivers that involved the core experiences of being safe, seen, and soothed—integrative experiences that, if offered in a reliable and recurring way, may have also given us a relational sense of wholeness.

Explicit memory takes the form of factual memory, dominant in the left cortex and processed via the left hippocampus; and autobiographical memory, dominant in the right hemisphere and processed via the right hippocampus. Autobiographical memory has the sense of a self in some point in time. Both forms of explicit memory, when retrieved, give the "ecphoric sensation" that what is being retrieved from memory is something that was experienced in the past. In contrast, pure implicit memory may have a feeling of familiarity, a kind of recognition or "bringing back to mind" of something, but without the ecphoric sensation that would tag it as something coming from an experience of the past. (Please see Siegel, 2020, for an in-depth examination of these forms of memory and their role in human development.) What this finding implies is that the explicit memories that contribute to the literal facts and recollections of our life narratives may develop after an initial implicit encoding of core experiences of wholeness in our lives. Nevertheless, we may be driven to "get back" that sense of being at ease, of being whole, of simply being, that may be embedded in an implicit familiarity that may be missing in various degrees as we are out and about in the world.

Our proposal is that the implicit sense of wholeness is then quite distinct from the implicit and then explicit sense of working-for-a-living in the do-or-die doing life we are now in—a state of living that may feel disconnected, uncertain, and dangerous, and requiring that we ensure survival by our actions. When under threat, the brain assesses this danger and then activates the deep neural networks mediating fight-flight-freeze-or-faint states of reactivity. Some of us may be more sensitive, by inborn temperament or early experiences, to one of the key subcortical motivational networks we've suggested involve agency for embodied empowerment, bonding for relational connection, and certainty for prediction and safety. These vectors are primed to become active when something in life that we deem salient—important— triggers one of these fundamental needs. We've seen that it may be, too, that our core attachment needs to be soothed, seen, and safe correspond to these vectors of agency, bonding, and certainty. Each of us, depending on our PDP, may be especially sensitive to some of these issues more than others. When activated, we feel far from whole; when we strive to have these core needs met, we are driven to get (back) to wholeness.

As therapy progresses and existing PDP strategies are revealed and their states of integration illuminated, there can be a release of protected states of survival, thereby allowing the person to finally access and become immersed in a more direct means of meeting their needs with more flexibility and efficacy. No matter our state of integration, we still have basic needs for empowerment, connection, and safety—the issue is how we find our way to asserting our agency, bonding, and certainty vectors. As we relax those drives, higher states of integration are achieved, meaning that we can harness our higher capacities within a vector and then access both other vectors and other attendencies.

We may also have a sense of wholeness that arises in pure awareness, as we've discussed above regarding the Wheel of Awareness practice, and the possible correspondence of the hub of the metaphoric wheel to a plane of possibility. Even without the aspect of the PDP proposal about an implicit memory of experiences of wholeness from our intrauterine life, we have the notion that pure, receptive, open awareness accesses wholeness as that "integrative, harmonious, receptive state of being" that may exist before, during, and beyond any experiences we have in our bodily existence. We may intentionally cultivate an access to wholeness with nurturing the experiences of awe, gratitude, and compassion and the practice of various contemplative techniques, including the Wheel of Awareness. This is the common exploration of contemplative and Indigenous teachings for thousands of years, wisdom that reminds us that who we are is broader than the individual body we inhabit—fundamentally connected with other people and the planet, intraconnected within all of nature. While modern culture may tell us that we are a "solo-self," an identity as an individual located only in the body, our true identity is much more whole than that limited message we are often given. We do not need to lose our individuality as we differentiate and then become linked in a larger relational whole. Who we are is a MWe.

This view invites us to consider the various pathways as being plateaus we have constructed that filter the activations emerging from our common ground, the formless source of all form, the infinite possibilities of the plane, into selected aspects based on our vector and attendency. In this view, psychotherapy helps us access the wholeness that originates in the plane by relaxing the grip of necessary plateaus we've built as adaptive strategies to deal with the Newtonian macrostate world of bodies and their inherent needs for survival. This is, as we've also seen, the way therapy can be viewed as enabling access to wholeness by releasing the blockades of these life-defending reactions of the PDP. Personality, then, is not our "true essence" or "home base" but rather our baseline "best adaptive strategy" that, if rigidly enforced, keeps us away from experiencing the wholeness that is both our common ground in each moment and the shared origin across our deeply connected lives and existence.

Therapist, Know Thyself

Each of us as a therapist is also an individual person—and knowing our own PDPs is very helpful in therapeutic work, and in life! Knowing this system well, knowing it so well that it comes naturally to you in your professional capacity to sense the patterns of these developmental pathways, will support the important clinical stance you take with the diverse array of clients in your practice. It may also serve you well in your personal relationships, as I know it has in mine. This stance may involve your simply understanding, inside yourself, what a client may have been experiencing for most of their life, and it may also include discussing these patterns, the PDP framework, directly in therapeutic conversations. In the work I tend to do myself as a therapist, I see my multidimensional role to include being a growth-nurturing attachment figure, a supportive therapeutic presence, and an interpersonal neurobiologically informed educator. Each dimension of these aspects of the PART we play has presence, attunement, resonance, and the cultivation, we hope, of trust that enables the growth of integration and connection in the individual's inner and relational lives. These are the growth-edge features for applying IPNB as we integrate personality and wholeness *in and into* psychotherapy.

As we become more aware of these patterns of developmental pathways, we can then tap into other vectors, attendencies, and modes of emotion regulation, especially as we see their importance in our skills of adaptation to this ever-changing, ever-challenging world. Recognizing patterns can empower us to see trends and more fully understand underlying mechanisms of the clusters in these ways we tend to feel, think, and behave in any given circumstance—our personality in that moment. Robust patterns can be viewed as high plateaus constructed as learned adaptive strategies that serve to filter what we feel, how we perceive, and how we act in that moment. The deeper the groove of the PDP, the higher and more constrained the plateau.

When we become aware of a pattern, we can then reflect on it and do something with it. In the 3-P diagram, we would depict low states of integration of a pattern as a rigid, imprisoning plateau, and the work of integration transforms that constricting filter into a more flexible plateau, one that permits freer access to the plane and in this way facilitates a more flexible life accessing wholeness. Integration arises freely from the plane. This is a way to envision, with this proposed mechanism of the nature of mind, what we've said from the beginning of our journey: Integration enables us to transform our personality from a prison to a playground.

As we've seen, a PDP reveals how we've grown in a certain way, with a certain set of features we are naming a "pattern" in the moment and a "pathway" over the course of our lives. In therapy, we join with our clients in an evolving co-construction of a dynamic making-sense narrative of their lives. Integrating the PDP framework into therapy powerfully enables that journey of discovery and change to become one of integration and liberation, a move toward wholeness and freedom. At times, using the PDP framework to envision how those in close relationships—at work, in friendship, and at home—*might* be living out a possible pathway can help in cultivating empathy and compassion in interpersonal relationships. As therapists, "knowing thyself" invites us to reflect on how our life journey toward wholeness may be experienced through a PDP baseline way of living in the world, especially in our relationships. How our clients' PDPs evoke particular reactions from us, directly in our interactions or indirectly in the leftover issues we may have from significant others with similar patterns, will be important in not "becoming lost in familiar places." Noticing and naming patterns of each developmental pathway is a starting place of recognition; but then continuing further to change those ingrained, low integrative states toward more fluidity and dynamism of a vector and its attendency can be powerfully transformative, for our clients in clinical work, for the therapeutic relationship, and for our personal life journey. We can envision this as freeing up the energy flow that is the experience of our life to gain the freedom of enabling a wider array of actualities to emerge from that g.o.d., the plane of possibility, the formless source of all form that is the generator of diversity. The plane in this way is our resource—the source we can access again and again.

One of the benefits of this 3-P diagram is that it enables us to see how we might get stuck in life as we repeat the same ways of responding and feeling and thinking in our lives. When we access the freedom of the plane, our "energy position" is in the place of maximal uncertainty. With the familiar patterns of a PDP, we are at least in a place of higher certainty—we know how we can act to have embodied empowerment to satisfy our agency motivational network, to have relational connections to satisfy our motivation for bonding, and to have prediction and safety to satisfy our needs for certainty. Once we've followed what our nervous system has deemed salient, what is meaningful and has taken a priority in our lives, the adage "Where attention goes, neural firing flows, and neural connection grows" helps us see how that initial tendency can then become a lifelong propensity.

Integrating our personality, then, involves both differentiating and linking within our plateaus, to make them more flexible in their own patterns in the moment. And integrating our personality also would involve accessing vectors and attendencies other than those of our baseline, primary PDP. In both senses of integration, we are broadening out from the lower integrative states that make us prone to chaos and rigidity in our lives due to the restricting in what actualities might arise. With a fixed plateau, we are limited in what we can experience from the plane of possibility. With integration, we have a wider access to that wholeness from the plane, the freedom to experience whatever spontaneously emerges. The plane, as we've seen, is the portal through which integration naturally arises. Too high and rigid a plateau, accessing that integration is constrained. Too high and rigid a plateau, the further we are from wholeness. This is what a deep and narrow PDP groove entails.

What this may suggest to you as it does to me and to clients I work with is that embracing uncertainty is part of the journey toward wholeness. With this integrative transformation, we come to realize the reality that synonyms for "uncertainty" are "freedom" and "possibility."

My suggestion to you is to continue the exploration of finding your own comfort with the PDP framework, for yourself and your clients, and be flexible in how you utilize these concepts and clinical applications. As you move forward in your work ahead, please see how you feel about each specific pathway and what experiences you may have had, in your own body and in relationships with those close to you, in your childhood and in your current life now, that may have shaped any understandable bias in working with those of similar pathways. Most of us seem to have one primary, baseline PDP and a few other secondary PDPs as well. The work with the PDP framework is to be curious about where you or others tend to "lead" from, and "lean" toward, what resonates with one's inner experience, and also to see how you can work with an individual with any PDP. In addition to the PART we play as therapists being present, attuned, resonant, and trustworthy, we also have that mindful way of being that includes the components of another acronym, COAL: We are curious, open, accepting, and loving. The COAL state of mind is what the P of presence really entails.

In the prior chapters we've explored both the positive aspects of a pathway and the extreme of what it means to be an "unactualized" type, one where the core features of this grouping are not in awareness. This is how "living on automatic pilot" may be experienced by an individual who leads with a particular PDP while it is in its "low integration" state. We've seen how, in IPNB terms, this state of low integration means we may be prone to the chaos and rigidity outside our windows of tolerance. While each of us has challenging aspects to our personality, what could also be named weaknesses, difficulties, or vulnerabilities, these challenges seem to correspond to a given pattern in ways that are profoundly clinically useful in terms of identifying and then knowing where they come from and how to then work with them effectively for a given individual. As therapists, understanding the deep mechanisms of a pathway can help us offer supportive guidance to widen windows of tolerance by creating higher states of integration.

We have focused on the growth-edge for each PDP to help people find their way (back) to wholeness when they may be quite far from experiencing that state of harmony in being with open awareness in their day-to-day lives at this point along their path in life. This journey ultimately invites a process of integration, one we have highlighted in its specific applications in the chapters we've explored for each PDP. Integration of the lifetime journey of personality invites at least two somewhat distinct dimensions. One is that *within* a given PDP are potential "lower" and "higher" levels of functioning, each reflecting low or high levels of integration within that pathway. The second dimension is the accessing of the higher functioning of each of the other vectors and the other attendencies, enabling an individual a wider set of internal linkages to access the strengths inherent in other pathways—not becoming that other pathway but achieving its positive attributes—and then becoming freer in this more flexible adaptation as life unfolds.

A growth-edge for a particular pathway is an invitation for focusing attention in a particular way to bring that PDP from lower to higher states of integration. Using the notion, and even the term, of "growth-edge" invites an individual to cultivate a particular kind of inner and relational focus of energy and attention to move at the edge of their current state to higher states of integration. As we've seen, this growth and transformation is likely not about abandoning or trying to get rid of a PDP altogether; the growth-edge, in our integrative use of this term from a PDP perspective, is within the two dimensions of (1) achieving higher states of integration *within* a pathway, and (2) accessing the more highly integrative functions of other pathways as well, and in this way as an *among*-pathways dimension of integration. What this really means from a PDP perspective is being able to make other vectors and other attendencies accessible as needed to approach life with more adaptive options. Within and among dimensions of integration is the clinical work we can envision inside ourselves and focus on for each pattern of developmental pathway that helps create a flourishing and resilient life that accesses wholeness more readily: an integrative, harmonious, receptive state of being.

In our work as clinicians, knowing the inner and inter nature of mind enables us as "mind therapists" to work with energy flow patterns that are both internal, within us and our clients, and interconnected, between our inner lives and the inner lives of our clients. Taken as a whole, the inner and inter, combined, form the foundations for an *intra*connected way in which the mind is both Me and We—yielding our identity as an integrated MWe. MWe can be a way that we as psychotherapists sense into how the inner and relational fields of our lives are moving toward an integrative flow. "Inner integration" can be named as the focus on the inner life of the individual; "inter integration" would be the name we can use for the relational work of a given PDP. And then the wholeness that arises with such inner and inter integration combined we can name "intra integration." The fundamental movement of this integrative transformation is toward the *within*-pathway growth of more integrative capacities and the *among*-pathways growth of accessing the more integrative capacities of the other vectors and attendencies, which together enable the wholeness of intra-integration to be accessed.

For you, too, knowing the PDP or PDPs that are your baselines— the primary pattern you tend to *lead with*—and your potential, perhaps bridging, secondary pathways—what you tend to *lean toward* in various circumstances—can help you see your own growth-edges in the lifelong journey of integration. And a knowledge of which individuals—parent, spouse, child—may have a PDP that has been especially challenging for you, which therefore might make working with a client with a similar pattern especially difficult, can be quite useful to cultivate.

At times we may be thinking about something like which *pathway* a person might be on; at other times, it may be more appropriate to consider which *pattern* the individual is immersed in, in that moment, in that situation. We have been using both terms as simply shorthand for the longer term, "patterns of developmental pathways" or simply its abbreviation as PDP. And while our initial impression as a PDP group is that one PDP serves as a kind of baseline pathway or primary pattern in most circumstances, it may be that certain others serve as secondary baseline PDPs that may, or may not, have common ground with a vector or attendency or emotion-regulation mode bridging to that primary grouping. In other words, we need to have an open mind about how future studies of the general population may ultimately reveal the distribution of those with a singular baseline PDP or perhaps those for whom several vector and attendency combinations are a baseline instead. Likewise, it is an open question as to whether and to what degree we can completely release a baseline pathway and become "a blank slate" in our lives.

Conceptually, we can imagine accessing the plane of possibility and living more directly and more often from that sense of wholeness. However, even with such an achievement of dropping beneath learned plateaus that likely form our adaptive strategies that organize our PDPs, we may still have a vulnerability to activate, under stress and distress, when we are tired or hungry, when we are disappointed and frustrated, a familiar set of emotions, thoughts, and behaviors that reflect our baseline PDP. While these ways in which we focus our energy, regulate our emotions, and automatically prioritize different aspects of agency, bonding, and certainty may change in our lifespan growth, it is possible that our baseline primary PDP may remain a higher probability throughout our lives. How much change is truly possible is a testable question. It is for this reason we've emphasized that we may be able to move our PDP from a prison to a playground, even as that PDP may remain our baseline primary pattern of experiencing the world across the lifespan. We widen, not eliminate, our PDP groove. As my now-94-year-old mother has said about a similar way of becoming mindful, even as we may remain with our PDP, we can become amused rather than annoyed by our own automatic ways of being in life. That mindfulness, that COAL state, is what living with a personality as a playground enables us to experience.

As we get ready to bring our journey together to a close here in this exploration, you may sense that an open state of compassion, insight, and connection may be your true home, and that personality is actually covering up this core way of living, this perhaps plane-of-possibility-based, deep, grounding way of experiencing life. It is for this reason that we have chosen to use not "home base" but "baseline" as the term to indicate a default mode, in life and especially under stressful conditions, perhaps even in higher states of integration that may have been achieved, that activates plateaus of reactivity and top-down filtration that we are proposing is the structure of personality itself. Who we "truly are"—our "true home" or "home base"—may actually be more living directly from the plane of possibility. From this perspective, our personality plateaus are simply a temporary though enduring effort to deal with life's challenges, not from a place of receptive being, but from a set of perhaps necessary developmental adaptive strategies. These plateaus of our PDPs are how we attempt to keep ourselves empowered, connected, and safe in these bodies we inhabit for this time here on Earth. Agency, bonding, and certainty are vectors we may always need to various extents while living in a Newtonian, macrostate body here in the world.

It may be that living with open awareness and accessing this way of being receptive and wide awake may be a state of wholeness we come to access more readily with growth. Might this "integrative, harmonious, and receptive state of being" we've named wholeness be beneath and before "personality" as we've been exploring it? Let's rest with that question and SIFT how it arises in sensation, image, feeling, and thought. For me, this question enables us to consider that our personality is not "who we are" but instead "how we are adapting" and that our PDPs are our best efforts to adapt but not our "true selves." Just as the body is not the beginning and end of our identity, our personality may be just one aspect of who we truly are.

The three "self-expanding" emotions, sometimes known as the "self-transcendent emotions," of awe, compassion, and gratitude are likely the emergent integrative states that are involved in an expansion of our constrained sense of who we are. This widening of an identity lens through which we sense our sensation, perspective, and agency—our SPA of self—enables us to access that state of wholeness beyond the PDP's particular way of emoting, thinking, and acting in our lives. From this developmental perspective, we've survived by drawing on the vector and attendency that we may have had a predilection for as we began to "work for a living" and strive to survive as best we can.

We are proposing that to thrive, we need to develop beneath these survival strategies of adaptation, accessing both a wider range of flexible responses to life and the receptive, open awareness that imbues our lives with wholeness.

Opening to a broader sense of who we are, beyond the solo-self of the individual body as the defining feature of our identity, is the invitation to reclaim wholeness. This widening of our identity lens enables us to weave the experience of an inner me with an inter we as the intraconnected, integrative identity of MWe. This is the journey for each of us as we work with our patterns of developmental pathways, the movement toward accessing a state of wholeness that we once knew and from where we all have come, one that is available for us to immerse our integrative selves in more readily as we live our lives more fully, more freely, and in a more connected way of being in the world.

AFTERWORD: ONWARD TOGETHER

Exploring More

As we come to a close of our journey here in this final chapter, I'd like to invite you to take a moment and breathe into all that we've covered along the way. You now have experienced a deep dive into one way to understand certain aspects of personality and to harness these insights in psychotherapy. If this has been intriguing to you, there may be a feeling inside you of wanting to know more and wondering, "How can I continue to learn about this approach?" The brief reflections in this chapter will address some of these questions, and also focus on how you might place in context the information you will likely receive in your explorations ahead. What we've found as a PDP group is that some interested in the Enneagram hold the psychological and spiritual dimensions of the narrative teachings to different degrees of relevance; some find certain areas of little interest, or distracting to the other dimensions. What we'd like to offer here is a way to find a common ground—a consilience—that may help you as you move ahead in your life-long learning in this area.

All along our journey, we've emphasized that the Patterns of Developmental Pathways is a framework you can consider in both your work as a psychotherapist and in your life as a human being here on Earth. As we've said from the beginning, we welcome you to an exploration of what might be underneath the popular Enneagram of personality system, and that these proposals, as compelling and consilient with science as they may be, will need empirical validation to prove their accuracy. You can explore their coherence for yourself, and naturally can discard any and all aspects of this framework that don't work well for you; or you may just find that the intricate details of the PDP perspective are useful and true in your own life and work.

As you apply these ideas to yourself first, you have the opportunity to observe through the PDP lens how a priority might be given to one of the three vectors of agency, bonding, and certainty—in your own life, or in the lives of those with whom you work. Yes, we all have each; but it seems from the narrative data we have that one of these motivational systems, these vectors, for most of us seems to take priority in our lives. Perhaps one is primary while others are secondary, or perhaps all three of these may have equal value in your life no matter what the trends of those narratives seem to be showing for the majority of us. Your truth *is what it is* no matter what the reported experiences of others seem to be. You may also apply the same inquiry into how your baseline focus of energy—the attendency of inward, outward, or dyadic as both inward and outward—tends to go in various types of experience. Perhaps you've changed over your development, and inquiring both about now and about when you were younger—perhaps in late childhood or during adolescence—will reveal distinct changes. Inquire and explore with curiosity what your pathway or pathways may be revealing in your life. These may just be features of temperament, those early proclivities we have that shape our inner filtering of energy and directly shape our lived experience.

It may be that this combination of vector and attendency form a mental mechanism that we can conceptualize and visualize as an enduring "plateau," as we've explored in Chapter 10, one that serves to filter possibilities into certain actualities as they arise from the plane of possibility. This view of the *probability transformation of energy as the basis of mind* helps us see how the psychological and spiritual aspects of our lifelong journey toward wholeness are actually simply two facets of one process. "Psychological" may be seen as the patterns of energy and information flow that we name emotion, thinking, and behavior. "Spiritual" may be what gives us meaning beyond survival, and connection beyond our skin-encased bodies. Physics has empirically demonstrated what contemplative and Indigenous teachings have taught for thousands of years, that we have at least two "realms" of one reality—one a relative and one a universal aspect of experience; in physics terms, one a macrostate Newtonian world of spatial and temporal separation, the other a microstate quantum realm of verb-like massively connected processes without separation across those Newtonian features of time and space.

As we access the resource of the plane of possibility, that formless source of all form, in quantum physics terms, we tap into both a psychological source of resilience and a spiritual source of meaning and connection. Wholeness is an integrative, harmonious, receptive state of being, one that we might conceptualize as emerging from within the plane, if that view resonates with you; or it might be more familiarly conceptualized as a state of simply being at ease, that effortless state we all had in the womb. These two views are coherent with each other; you may prefer one over the other in your own understanding—or you may simply hold both as two lenses on the same wholeness.

From a memory perspective, as we saw at the beginning of our journey and reviewed in the preceding chapter, we have an implicit memory of being "at one with the womb" that is in stark contrast to the do-or-die conditions we each experience once we are born and out here in these bodies. As we've explored, our PDP group is proposing that this contrast leads to the selective activation of one of the three subcortical motivational networks of agency, bonding, and certainty. You can conceive of this as simply trying to attain homeostasis of our embodied reality, the physiological and relational needs we have to survive and thrive. You can also conceive of this in parallel as the move back to this state of the plane of possibility, that generator of diversity, the formless source of all form, that is the mental source of being aware. Mind, in this view, is an emergent property of energy flow. And energy, from a quantum physics perspective, is "the movement from possibility to actuality." That movement begins in the plane of possibility, the quantum vacuum or sea of potential.

Embedded in the implicit memory storage of each of us is an engram—a neural pattern encoded from a prior experience—of a state of effortless being. As our brains are pattern detectors and anticipation machines, even as this is implicit memory that lacks being tagged as coming from a past experience, we will have a sense of familiarity that allows what is happening now to be compared to what happened before. Our proposal is that this contrast between the effortless simply being and the do-or-die working-for-a-living conditions activates one of our motivational networks deep in the subcortical regions. Which of these is most sensitive, most likely to become active, is proposed to be a function of temperament. We can envision this on our mental diagram of the plane, plateaus, and peaks—our 3-P diagram—as energy flow that will now be filtered by this core motivational drive for empowered embodiment, relational connection, or prediction and safety. This is how our vector becomes a filtering plateau.

How our attendency drives this energy of life inward, outward, or dyadically as both will shape the kinds of adaptive strategies we will construct to handle life's challenges. That combination of vector with attendency will create very distinct experiences of being alive, especially in response to challenges. With suboptimal attachment experiences, for example, the groove of that vector and attendency combination, that PDP, will be dug more deeply into our neural circuitry. To handle life, we will construct adaptive strategies that generate particular priorities in our thinking, specific modes of regulating emotion, and ways in which we behave in the world. This blending of temperament and adaptation to life's experience is the fundamental basis of the development of *personality* we are proposing as patterns of developmental pathways.

We have built our PDP framework on the thousands of Narrative Enneagram participants' directly felt experiences to build a bridge between traditional views of this popular personality system and empirical science. You can continue to build these connections in your own journey by reading more on the Enneagram in the various resources we've cited, which are in our references list, and you might choose to dive into Narrative Enneagram workshops to try out what that perspective on personality feels like for you. As is true in all matters, be discerning about online resources you choose to explore. Surging contemporary interest over the past decade in the Enneagram's personality typology has resulted in a proliferation of online resources of highly variable quality. Be particularly wary of sources that offer superficial views of the patterns focused primarily on behaviors or surface characteristics rather than inner experience, that make sweeping stereotypical generalizations about traits or behaviors, or that promote assessment instruments lacking any kind of validation. In our own direct experience, we have the natural bias of knowing the Narrative Enneagram organization, as David was a cofounder with Helen Palmer, and so we invite you to consider exploring their offerings.

Given that the PDP framework is new, there may be only a few traditional Enneagram programs that incorporate this consilient approach to personal development, organizational consulting, or the process of psychotherapy. Hopefully, with the journey of this book out in the world now, there will be a growing number of interpersonal neurobiology–informed opportunities to explore the Patterns of Developmental Pathways in more depth. We hope that your growing forward will allow you to build more bridges as you learn more in your own life. We are each on a lifelong journey of discovery and growth, and I hope you may find new ways of applying and understanding this framework in psychotherapeutic practice and in everyday living.

In whatever ways you choose to proceed, "knowing thyself" is a lifelong invitation to learn more about your own inner experience and patterns of interacting with the world. We suggest you give yourself plenty of time and mental space to incorporate this PDP framework into your personal life and understanding, if you choose, as you proceed in seeing how it might apply to your work as a therapist. Chapters 6, 7, and 8 offered insights into the intricate layers of a given pattern that you can explore with your clients, and then a view of how these patterns present over time as a pathway the individual has been traveling down from early on in their life journey. Applying the PDP framework invites a continual inner examination for your own personal growth and an understanding of how your particular pathway will interact with your client's own PDP. As we've seen, you can use these insights to deepen psychotherapy even without directly discussing the PDP framework with clients. And you may also find individuals and situations in which offering input about the patterns you are perceiving may be an important part of the therapeutic conversation. I have found such moments of direct discussion about the lifelong journey we are all on to be quite illuminating and to facilitate a deeper connection between the client and me as the therapist.

Potential Bridges and Challenges Between Concepts and Language

Many readers from "mainstream" mental health, science, or business backgrounds who do choose to pursue additional study or training about the Enneagram, as many have before them, including some of our PDP team, are likely to quickly encounter concepts or language that do not sit easily, or perhaps at all, with contemporary psychology or neuroscience. Mostly these concern conjectures about how the patterns have come to be or operate. Just a few examples are concepts like "holy ideas," "lost essential qualities," and "true and false self." If you are among those who find such concepts difficult to feel at ease with, this section is for you.

There are several important things to keep in mind when such difficulties arise. First, it's important to acknowledge that such difficulties may stem from the distinctly nonscientific origins of the Enneagram of personality, and its recent development largely outside of the scientifically grounded mainstream of psychotherapy research and practice. That history is extremely interesting, and readers who wish to explore it more fully can do so from a number of resources (Callahan, 1992; Chestnut, 2013; Christlieb, 2016; Ichazo, 1998; Naranjo, 1990, 1994; Palmer, 1988; Riso & Hudson, 1999; Wertenbaker, 2017; Wiltse & Palmer, 2009). For our purposes here, what is important to understand is that the deepest historical roots of the Enneagram of personality lie in the synthesis of similar teachings, over millennia, of various philosophical and wisdom traditions, and from various contemplative, religious, or spiritual settings. Common threads of this history include accounts of attributes of character and states of being that are "higher" (i.e., virtues, divine qualities, holy ideas) and "lower" (i.e., vices, deadly sins, falls from grace). This view includes identifying and working with these challenges as patterns of obstruction to "direct knowledge," personal awareness, and spiritual growth.

In the mid-20th century, Oscar Ichazo, a Bolivian-born South American philosopher and some might say mystic, brought such teachings together in what he viewed as a comprehensive understanding of the human psyche. In this context he placed various attributes of higher and lower character and the human condition in general on a so-called Enneagram figure. The word "Enneagram" comes from the Greek and refers to a map (*gram*) with nine (*ennea*) points. The Enneagram figure has its own history in ancient esoteric and mystical thought and mathematics (see Wertenbaker, 2017). It consists of a circle on which nine roughly equally spaced points are connected by a network of lines. In traditional teaching it is seen as revealing important patterns of movement of energy and pathways to transformation (e.g., from vice to virtue). Ichazo was the first to explicitly add the concept of personality patterns associated with the character archetypes to this figure.

The Enneagram of personality as we know it today emerged in the early 1970s from a group of students of Ichazo, notably including Chilean-born psychiatrist Claudio Naranjo, who saw consilience with a large body of psychological and psychodynamic theory and psychopathology, which was his own professional training (see Naranjo, 1990, 1994). I had the opportunity to meet with Naranjo and share a very intellectually fascinating conversation at an international Enneagram conference, where we explored his views of the Enneagram with the concepts of interpersonal neurobiology. Naranjo's version of the Enneagram of personality has been further developed in the ensuing years in many different settings, but largely outside the mainstream of contemporary psychology, psychiatry, and neurobiology. Not surprisingly, the psychospiritual frame remains strong in many settings, though much less so when the approach of the Enneagram of personality is brought into the workplace.

Second, the original motivation for the PDP project was to see if we could find ways to bridge the cultural gap between this psychospiritual frame and contemporary science. We believe the PDP framework provides a way of interpreting those more spiritual accounts in ways that are fully consonant with contemporary psychology and neuroscience. What that means at a practical level is that it is not necessary to hold as literally true certain concepts that might be challenging to consider—ones that some might distinctly note as "spiritual" rather than psychological—about the development and functioning of the nine patterns in individuals. As we explored in the last chapter, there may be a way to deeply understand some aspects of that dimension of the Enneagram teaching through the lens of the plane-of-possibility view of consciousness—but even this may be "too much" for some in the mental health field to feel comfortable considering. I've had some mental health and neuroscience professionals ask that I not refer to physics in discussing mental processes. Their response when I ask them why not is telling: because, the statements generally go, "energy is not scientific." Careful application of the scientific field of physics' principles and empirical findings about energy to our lives—whether it is about how energy flows in electronic gadgets or how it just might be the underlying mechanisms of mental life, from our emotions and bodily sensations to thought and awareness—seems to me a reasonable application of consilience as we seek a common ground across distinct ways of knowing (see Siegel, 2017, 2020, and 2023 for a more complete discussion of this issue).

Why not apply the same consilient exploration to understanding personality? Building a bridge between the seemingly separate domains of the spiritual and the psychological may in fact reveal that, in their essence, there is no real separation that needs to be bridged. If spirituality is deeply about meaning and connection, our most cutting-edge psychological studies of a thriving life reveal these "spiritual fundamentals" are actually essential to wholeness and living a life of resilience and well-being. Might this be a way of imagining what "spiritual health" would entail? Individuals who work with and use the Enneagram hold these spiritual terms and concepts with something along a spectrum from rejection and skepticism to curiosity and open-mindedness. And many who work with the Enneagram in business settings do not reference them at all.

Even within our PDP team there are disagreements about the nature of the "truth" and place of such teachings. The PDP framework allows us to make peace with these differences. We all agree wholeheartedly that the psychospiritual frame of many concepts, which David embraced fully in his teaching and writing, offers language that can evoke a powerful *felt* understanding of the deepest energetic currents driving the patterns in individuals. All that's required of the skeptic is to hold these views in a more metaphorical, or "it is as if," kind of way. That's how some of us in the PDP group consider some of David's writing and teaching. Jack relates that he had several personal conversations with David about this over the years. David would chide him in his playful way about being a scientist but say clearly that what mattered was doing the work.

All this is to say that we see these kinds of differences between our PDP account and more traditional Enneagram accounts as analogous to the differences in the ways a poet and a botanist would describe a rose garden. They are about the very same thing viewed through different lenses of knowing about and understanding the truth. Each has its value and place, and together they provide a richer understanding.

A Legacy of Consilience

We as a PDP group hope that the Patterns of Developmental Pathways offers another step in a "march toward consilience." Gurdjieff, Ichazo, and others saw and taught about what we would describe as consilience across that history of older wisdom-tradition teachings. Ichazo was the first to describe them in terms of personalities (rather than character vices or virtues), which he placed on an Enneagram figure. Naranjo, in turn, saw consilience in Ichazo's teachings and recast the personalities from his vantage point. We see our framework as another step in the history of this search for consilience in understanding personality. It is a way of looking at the very same phenomena from different ways of knowing and understanding life. So, we embrace those traditional narrative teachings as extremely useful in many settings, but we see a way of interpreting them that we hope opens minds that can build on our hypotheses in the future. Whether you are a practicing clinician, an academic researcher, or an organizational leader, or are simply applying this in your own personal life, we hope this framework will offer a consilient perspective that invites challenge and exploration and continues a long history of human endeavors to understand who we are and why we do what we do.

Inherent in the books and workshops is the Enneagram figure. Here we offer David's particular descriptions of each of the Enneagram types and their key features:

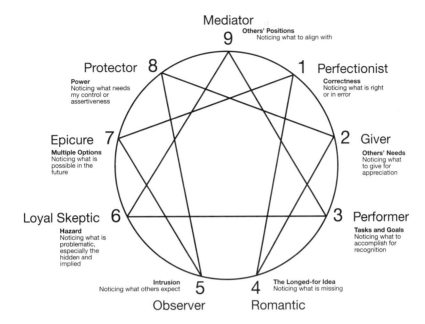

This is the classic "nine-sided figure" as the visual symbol and map of the Enneagram. We can also see here in David's version of that figure an emphasis on what the individual's particular type—what we are calling their pattern of developmental pathway, or simply PDP—has a propensity to pay attention to. What this means in neurocognitive terms is that value is placed on a certain form of information and then attention is directed toward that information as energy is focused there. Such prioritization selectively places meaning on that which is drawing our attention. You are now familiar with more of the details of these core aspects of the PDP framework:

a. the vectors and their underlying subcortical motivational networks;

b. their accompanying reactive affects that often shape our initial emotional response;

c. how each PDP within that vector has a trio of possible attendencies, an orientation bias of attention as inward, outward, or dyadic; and

d. how these each have a specific emotion-regulation mode as upregulating, downregulating, or shifting: experience and express, contain and channel, reframe and redirect.

We drew our PDP framework from the narratives David had collected of Enneagram workshop participants. Being familiar with this frequently referenced figure may be helpful for you, especially when you work with clients who themselves may know about this popular system of personality. Placing the figure here is also an opportunity to see if you can stretch your own memory system, challenge your conceptual mind, and look at this image and determine which of each of the three variables—vector, attendency, mode—apply to a particular PDP, to a specifically indicated "type" on the Enneagram figure, and then exercise your mind by naming which vector, attendency, and mode correlate with each of the nine Enneagram points on the figure. It's a fun exercise, one that will build the muscle of your mindsight skills to envision the PDPs and the underlying mechanisms of each.

We can also reemphasize what was mentioned in the introduction here in our reflections. The PDP framework offers a view of a part of personality, not the entirety of what constitutes "who we are" or our overall enduring patterns of thought, emotion, and behavior. In terms of exploring a possible developmental neuroscience view of what mechanisms may be at play in the Enneagram system, we have been focusing primarily on the core nine types, not the subtypes, and we do not attempt to explain the lines linking "connecting points" where one type goes to in stress or growth; nor do we address the wings. In this way, for example, I lead with a C-d pathway (6 Enneagram type) and would also have meaningful connections with wings of 5 and 7—which I do—and the connecting points on those lines of 3 and 9, which I also do.

From a PDP perspective, we've seen that we can speak of "bridging pathways," ones that share one of at least three features: vector, attendency, and mode of emotion regulation. In your own experience, personally and professionally, it might be of interest to see what patterns "flavor," as Jack says, the inner feelings and outer behaviors besides your baseline, primary pattern. For me, the 5 and 7 are bridges to my vector of certainty; the 3 and 9 are bridges to my attendency of dyadic. Exploring your own primary and secondary PDPs is a helpful journey of discovery, one that can greatly aid your work with other individuals and groups in exploring their own.

A Loss of Essence and Departure From Wholeness

Let me offer you two of David's descriptions of a child's loss of some essential aspect of life as a way to gain a perspective into and feeling for how David viewed the psychospiritual growth for a type in the Enneagram view. The notion of losing touch with an "essential quality" in specific ways for each type helped David make sense of how each of the Enneagram types is adapting to a specific kind of "loss." Growth-edge work in clinical practice from that viewpoint was trying to regain what was lost.

From a PDP perspective, we would see this as how the departure from wholeness is experienced differently based on the ways in which the features of temperament combined with experience to shape personality. The PDP model, as we've seen, suggests that early organizing features, including vector and attendency, will influence the adaptive strategies that are learned, which may include emotion-regulation modes and the patterns of overall thought, reactive emotions, and behaviors. In this way, David's descriptions may be about how the consequent pattern of developmental pathway shapes the inner life of the young child and forms the basis for at least some aspects of personality. Here are two illustrative examples.

Pattern 1: David's Description of Loss of Wholeness in a Young Child

For Pattern 1, the original whole state, experienced as a young child, is that undivided state of utter wholeness or oneness where everything is complete as it is in each moment. There is no division into time or space, into good or bad, into right or wrong. The universe functions perfectly, balancing out change as things move from cosmos to chaos and back to cosmos over and over. This oneness is damaged by a world that severely judges and punishes "bad" behavior and impulse. At least the emerging Pattern 1 child, perhaps especially sensitive to damage of this aspect of essence, experiences this judgment as harsh and severe. So in the interest of survival, natural evolving nonjudgmental perfection goes into the background and the developing personality substitutes the perfectionism of good versus bad, right versus wrong. The young pattern 1 child then gains worthiness and love through being good, correcting mistakes, striving to be perfect. A compensation emerges of a powerful inner critic or judging mind with exacting standards that meet vigorous criteria. You replace the undivided state of holy perfection (could say wholeness or dynamic perfection) and protect it from future damage with its mimic, the divided world of perfectionism of right and wrong, of good and bad.

[Source: Daniels, 1998, Type 1]

Pattern 6: Description of Loss of Wholeness in a Young Child

For Pattern 6 the original state of faith in self, others, and the universe is damaged by a world that is experienced as threatening, dangerous, and unpredictable. You just can't count on it. You can no longer tap into the original secure trust. Consequently, there is a fall into fear and doubt. Since you can't trust the environment, it is smart and logical to fear it, doubt it. As a replacement for faith, for the permanent security of essence, you naturally pick security and certainty. You stay out of harm's way as best you can. It only makes sense. You defy security, you face dangers and create your own certainty, or you seemingly contradictorily do the opposite. Here the logic is better to face the danger than feel fear. The only thing worse than facing dangers is trying to flee them. Thus, the Pattern 6 presents with an often-confusing spectrum of behaviors ranging from phobic avoidance of potential harm to counter phobic confronting it. Alternatingly meek or bold, cautious, or outrageous, cowardly or courageous, escaping or battling perennial dangers. Common to extremes or approaches is the attempt to reduce insecurity and uncertainty and hence quell the fear and doubt. If your flight or fight works well you might not even know you have fear.

[Source: Daniels, 1998, Type 6]

David would also explore defense mechanisms that "held each type together." These include processes from the psychoanalytic approach such as the following, in their order from Enneagram Type 1 to 9: reaction-formation, repression, identification, introjection, isolation, projection, rationalization, denial, and narcotization. There is a rich literature on defense mechanisms that could be applied to future explorations of the PDP view of personality and their potential overlap with these features of how our minds learn to cope with life (see Giuseppe & Perry, 2021). While we do not use the term defense mechanism in the PDP framework, it may fit well in the general notion of an adaptive strategy common to each pathway that "holds" the emotional, cognitive, and behavioral tendencies into a cohesive pattern in the moment and characterizes a pathway over time.

As we've seen, in the PDP framework, we see adaptive strategies as thought patterns and verbal narratives as well as emotional tone, drive, and reactivity, which are harnessed to attempt to handle the challenges of life. Here are some reflections from David about what the Enneagram of personality system meant for his own professional and personal development:

The Enneagram is a system that describes the human condition, as it's organized, from the inside out. It's far more than a simple "behavioral typology." It's a body of wisdom I stumbled on years ago of which I had no prior knowledge and one that profoundly changed my life once I understood it. At first it was difficult for me to publicly own this remarkable knowledge for understanding my self and that of others, because of its connections to spiritual life and paucity of research backing. Since I had come from a structured academic, medical background steeped in empirical science and its methodologies, I remained a "closet" follower for a good 18-months before "coming out." Besides this, the worlds of modern psychiatry and psychology can put people into rather negative, stereotypical personality groupings like paranoid, sociopathic, and narcissistic. I so disliked this way of categorizing people that I just refused to do it. Yet, because this Enneagram system is so powerful, so deep, so life enhancing, so LIBERATING, I finally could not do anything else but own it publicly. It is the most profound tool I've come across in my 50+ years as a doctor, therapist, professor, lecturer, teacher, and author. It helps us to better find, build, and sustain amazing, loving, intimate, and fulfilling relationships. As Helen Palmer (1998) so succinctly writes in her book, The Enneagram in Love and Work, *"Partnership demonstrates the differences between us. Each can be telling the truth, yet each can have a different story to tell." Those differences, when not understood, those stories of individual truth when not validated, can tear us apart. But when shared and held reverent, understood and not feared, those differences become an asset, not a detriment. Our differences are what allow us to live together far more effectively, productively, as well as, supportively, interestingly, and to a great extent, more joyfully. . . . There is nothing more important in our lives than to take "this" developmental journey. There is nothing more precious than to have developed our capacity to self-understand, to sustain relationships, to love, and to have done so with willingness, hope, compassion, and tenacity. May we all do this. Let's bring our love to ourselves and to one another—consciously, compassionately, and reverently. Let's bring our willingness to develop to our fullest, most-loving potential to our families, to our communities, to the world, and inevitably, to our planet.*

[Daniels & Dion, 2018, pp. xxviii–xxx]

David was a full-time, experienced psychotherapist who, in the maturity of his work, stayed open to new approaches. For the final 30 years of his working life, David found that the Enneagram approach transformed what he was able to offer to his clients, many of them as couples. For me personally, it was a deep honor to learn from David and to be inspired by his passion for this work and how it helped people find a new way of living. For the last dozen years of his life, David was a part of our PDP group, along with Laura Baker; his daughter, Denise Daniels; Jack Killen; and me—the coauthors of our journey with you here. We found our common science background an exciting starting place to address our challenging initial question: Is there a scientific framework that explains and perhaps expands the view of the Enneagram of personality? We hope this journey has been helping to open that question for further inquiry and application in your own life's work.

From a PDP perspective, this is a journey of a lifetime toward integration, one that is shaped in fascinating ways that are useful in our work as clinicians and helpful in cultivating deep psychospiritual growth. It is this integrative transformation that is at the heart of utilizing a PDP perspective in helping individuals in therapy to achieve more well-being, meaning, and connection in their lives. We wish you well on this journey toward wholeness in our lives!

References

Alexander, M., & Schnipke, B. (2020). The Enneagram: A primer for psychiatry residents. *The American Journal of Psychiatry*. https://doi.org/10.1176/appi.ajp-rj.2020.150301

Avinun, R., Israel, S., Knodt, A. R., & Hariri, A. R. (2020). Little evidence for associations between the big five personality traits and variability in brain gray or white matter. *NeuroImage, 220*, Article 117092. https://doi.org/10.1016/j.neuroimage.2020.117092

Baker, L. A., & Daniels, D. S. (1990). Nonshared environmental influences and personality differences in adult twins. *Journal of Personality and Social Psychology, 58*, 103–110.

Barrett, L. F. (2017). *How emotions are made: The secret life of the brain.* Mariner Books.

Barrett, L. F., Mesquita, B., Oschsner, K. N., & Gross, J. J. (2007). The experience of emotion. *Annual Review of Psychology, 58*, 373–403.

Bergeman, C. S., Chipuer, H. M., Plomin, R., Pedersen, N. L., McClearn, G. E., Nesselroade, J. R., Costa, P. T., Jr., & McCrae, R. R. (1993). Genetic and environmental effects on openness to experience, agreeableness, and conscientiousness: An adoption/twin study. *Journal of Personality, 61*(2), 159–179.

Blakemore, S. J. (2018). *Inventing ourselves: The secret life of the teenage brain.* Public Affairs.

Bland, A. (2010). The Enneagram: A review of the empirical and transformational literature. *The Journal of Humanistic Counseling, Education and Development, 49*(1), 16–31.

Bowlby, J. (1973) *Separation.* Pimlico.

Brazelton, T. B. (1983). *Infants and mothers: Differences in development.* Bantam.

Brazelton, T. B., & Greenspan, S. L. (2000). *The irreducible needs of children: What every child must have to grow, learn, and flourish.* Perseus Publishing.

Breger, L. (1974). *From instinct to identity: The development of personality.* Prentice Hall.

Briley, D. A., & Tucker-Drob, E. M. (2014). Genetic and environmental continuity in personality development: A meta-analysis. *Psychological Bulletin, 140*(5), 1303–1331.

Buss, A. H., & Plomin, R. (1975). *A temperament theory of personality development.* Wiley.

Buss, A. H., & Plomin, R. (1984). *Temperament: Early developing personality traits.* Erlbaum.

Callahan, W. (1992). *The Enneagram for youth: Counselor's manual.* Loyola University Press.

Caspi, A., Roberts, B. W., & Shiner, R. L. (2005). Personality development: Stability and change. *Annual Review of Psychology, 56*, 453–484.

Chestnut, B. (2013). *The complete Enneagram: 27 paths to greater self-knowledge.* She Writes Press.

Choi-Kain, L. W., Finch, E. F., Masland, S. R., Jenkins, J. A., & Unruh, B. T. (2017). What works in the treatment of borderline personality disorder. *Current Behavioral Neuroscience Reports, 4,* 21–30. https://doi.org/10.1007/s40473-017-0103-z

Christlieb, F. F. (2016). *Where (on earth) did the Enneagram come from?* Fatima Editores.

Damasio, A. (2010). *Self comes to mind: Constructing the conscious brain.* Pantheon.

Damasio, A. (2019). *The strange order of things: Life, feeling, and the making of cultures.* Vintage.

Daniels, D. (1994). Enneagram dynamics. Enneagram Handout Collection. *David N. Daniels Archives 1994.*

Daniels, D. (1998). Healing your habit of mind. David Daniels Enneagram Writings Collection. *David N. Daniels Archives 1998.*

Daniels, D. (2001). Nature and nurture. In C. Thompson & T. Condon (Eds.), *Enneagram Applications.* Metamorphous Press.

Daniels, D. (2004). The Enneagram basic propositions with personal reactivity. Enneagram Handout Collection. *David N. Daniels Archives.*

Daniels, D. (n.d.) *Integrating the higher qualities of our essence into our lives.* https://drdaviddaniels.com/integrating-essence-true-nature-lives/

Daniels, D. S. (1986). Differential experiences of siblings in the same family as predictors of adolescent sibling personality differences. *Journal of Personality and Social Psychology, 51,* 339–346.

Daniels, D., & Dion, S. (2018/2025). *The Enneagram, relationships, and intimacy: Understanding one another leads to loving better and living more fully.* (Independently published, 2018; forthcoming, New York: Morgan James Publishing.)

Daniels, D., & Price, V. (2009/2025). *The essential Enneagram: The definitive personality test and self-discovery guide.* Harper. (Original work published 2000)

Daniels, D., Saracino, T., Fraley, M., Christian, J., & Pardo, S. (2018). Advancing ego development in adulthood through study of the Enneagram system of personality. *Journal of Adult Development, 25,* 229–241.

Dass, R., & Bush, M. (2018). *Walking each other home: Conversations on loving and dying.* Sounds True.

Davis, K., & Panksepp, J. (2018). *The emotional foundations of personality: A neurobiological and evolutionary approach.* W. W. Norton.

Di Giuseppe, M., & Perry, J. C. (2021). The hierarchy of defense mechanisms: Assessing defensive functioning with the Defense Mechanisms Rating Scales Q-Sort. *Front Psychol.* 2021 Oct 15;12:718440. doi: 10.3389/fpsyg.2021.718440. PMID: 34721167; PMCID: PMC8555762.

Duschinsky, R. (2020). John Bowlby and the Tavistock separation research unit. In *Cornerstones of attachment research.* Oxford University Press. https://doi.org/10.1093/med-psych/9780198842064.003.0001

Dweck, C. (2006). *Mindset: The new psychology of success.* Random House.

Eysenck, H. J. (1952). Personality. *Annual Review of Psychology, 3,* 151–174.

Fox, N. A., Hane, A. A., & Pine, D. S. (2007). Plasticity for affective neurocircuitry: How the environment affects gene expression. *Current Directions in Psychological Science, 16,* 1–5.

Fox, N. A., Nichols, K. E., Henderson, H. A., Rubin, K., Schmidt, L., Hamer, D., Ernst, M., & Pine, D. S. (2005). Evidence for a gene–environment interaction in predicting behavioral inhibition in middle childhood. *Psychological Science, 16,* 921–926.

Galinksy, E. (2024). *The breakthrough years: A new scientific framework for raising thriving teens.* Flatiron Books.

Gilbert, P. (2010). *Compassion focused psychotherapy: Distinctive features.* Routledge.

Grant, A. (2021). *Think again: The power of knowing what you don't know.* Viking.

Graziano, W. G. (2003). Personality development: An introduction toward process approaches to long-term stability and change in persons. *Journal of Personality, 71,* 893–903.

Groh, A. M., Narayan, A. J., Bakermans-Kranenburg, M. J., Roisman, G. I., Vaughn, B. E., Pasco Fearon, R. M., & van IJzendoorn, M. H. (2017). Attachment and temperament in the early life course: A meta-analytic review. *Child Development, 88*(3), 770–795.

Gross, J. (2014). *The handbook of emotional regulation* (2nd ed.). Guilford Press.

Gurdjieff, G. I. (2012). *In Search of Being: The Fourth Way of Consciousness.* Boston: Shambhala Press.

Hall, C., & Lindzey, G. (1997). *Theories of personality* (4th ed.). John Wiley & Sons.

Heine, S. J., & Buchtel, E. E. (2009). Personality: The universal and the culturally specific. *Annual Review of Psychology, 60,* 369–394.

Hook, J., Hall, T., Davis, D., Tongeren, D., & Conner, M. (2020). The Enneagram: A systematic review of the literature and directions for future research. *Journal of Clinical Psychology, 76.* https://doi.org/10.1002/jclp.23097

Iacoboni, M. (2009). *Mirroring people: The science of empathy and how we connect with others.* Picador.

Ichazo, O. (1998). Foreword. In A. H. Almaas, *Facets of unity.* Diamond Books.

Immordino-Yang, M., Christodoulou, J., & Singh, V. (2012). Rest is not idleness: Implications of the brain's default mode for human development and education. *Perspectives on Psychological Science, 7*(4). https://doi.org/10.1177/1745691612447308

Izard, C., Stark, K., Trentacosta, C., & Schulz, D. (2008). Beyond emotion regulation: Emotion utilization and adaptive functioning. *Child Development Perspectives, 2,* 156–163.

James, W. (1902). *Varieties of religious experience: A study in human nature.* Longmans, Green and Co.

Jang, K. L., Livesley, W. J., & Vemon, P. A. (1996). Heritability of the big five personality dimensions and their facets: A twin study. *Journal of Personality, 64*(3), 577–592. https://doi.org/10.1111/j.1467-6494.1996.tb00522.x

Jayawickreme, E., Fleeson, W., Beck, E., Baumert, A., & Adler, J. (2021). Personality dynamics. *Personality Science, 2,* Article e6179. https://doi.org/10.5964/ps.6179

John, O. P., & Srivastava, S. (1999). The big five trait taxonomy: History, measurement, and theoretical perspectives. In L. A. Pervin & O. P. John (Eds.), *Handbook of Personality* (pp. 102–138). Guilford Press.

Kagan, J. (1997). *Galen's prophecy: Temperament in human nature.* Routledge.

Kahneman, D. (2011). *Thinking, fast and slow.* Farrar, Straus and Giroux.

Killen, J. (2009). Toward the neurobiology of the Enneagram. *The Enneagram Journal, 2*(1), 40–61.

Kubzansky, L. D., Martin, L. T., & Buka, S. L. (2009). Early manifestations of personality and adult health: A life course perspective. *Health Psychology, 28,* 364–372.

Kuper, N., Modersitzki, N., Phan, L., & Rauthmann, J. (2021). The dynamics, processes, mechanisms, and functioning of personality: An overview of the field. *British Journal of Psychology, 112*(1), 1–51.

Joyce, J. (2008). *Dubliners.* Oxford World's Classics. (Original work published 1914).

Lemery, K. S., Goldsmith, H. H., Klinnert, M. D., & Mrazek, D. A. (1999). Developmental models of infant and childhood temperament. *Developmental Psychology, 35,* 189–204.

Lengua, L. .J., & Gartstein, M. (2024). *Parenting with temperament in mind,* Washington, D.C.: American Psychological Association.

Loehlin, J. C. (1992). *Genes and environment in personality development.* Sage.

Loevinger, J. (1976). *Ego development.* Jossey-Bass.

Maxon, B., & Daniels, D. (2008). Personality differentiation of identical twins reared together. *The IEA Enneagram Journal, 1,* 1–12.

Mayer, J. D. (2005). A tale of two visions: Can a new view of personality help integrate psychology? *American Psychologist, 60,* 294–307.

McAdams, D. P. (1992). The five-factor model in personality: A critical appraisal. *Journal of Personality, 60,* 329–361.

McCrae, R. R., & Costa, P. T., Jr. (1994). The stability of personality: Observations and evaluations. *Current Directions in Psychological Science, 3,* 173–175.

Mesulam, M. M. (1998). From sensation to cognition. *Brain, 121,* 1013–1052.

Naranjo, C. (1990). *Ennea-type structures.* Gateways/IDHHB.

Naranjo, C. (1994). *Character and neurosis.* Gateways/IDHHB.

Narvaez, D., Bradshaw, G., & Mate, G. (2023). *The evolved nest: Nature's way of raising children and creating connected communities.* North Atlantic Books.

Palmer, H. (1988). *The Enneagram: Understanding yourself and the others in your life.* Harper Collins.

Palmer, H. (1993). *The Enneagram in love and work: Understanding your intimate and business relationships.* Chronicle.

Palmer, H., & Brown, P. (1998). *The Enneagram advantage: Putting the 9 personality types to work in the office.* Three Rivers Press.

Panksepp, J. (1998). *Affective neuroscience: The foundations of human and animal emotions.* Oxford University Press.

Panksepp, J., & Biven, L. (2012). *The archaeology of mind: Neuroevolutionary origins of the human mind.* W. W. Norton.

Plomin, R., & Daniels, D. (1987). Why are children in the same family so different from one another? *Behavioral and Brain Sciences, 10,* 1–60.

Porges, S. W. (2001). The polyvagal theory: Phylogenetic substrates of a social nervous system. *International Journal of Psychophysiology, 42,* 123–146.

Porges, S. W. (2011). *The Polyvagal Theory: Neurophysiological Foundations of Emotions, Attachment, Communication, and Self-regulation.* New York: W. W. Norton.

Porges, S. W. (2024). *Polyvagal Perspectives: Interventions, practices and strategies.* New York: W. W. Norton.

Posner, M. I., & Rothbart, M. K. (2018). Temperament and brain networks of attention. *Philosophical Transactions of the Royal Society B, 373,* Article 201720154. https://doi.org/10.1098/rstb.2017.0254

Riso, D. R., & Hudson, R. (1999). *The wisdom of the Enneagram: The complete guide to psychological and spiritual growth for the nine personality types.* Bantam Books.

Roberts, B. W., & DelVecchio, W. F. (2000). The rank-order consistency of personality traits from childhood to old age: A quantitative review of longitudinal studies. *Psychological Bulletin, 126,* 3–25.

Rothbart, M. K., Ahadi, S. A., & Evans, D. E. (2000). Temperament and personality: Origins and outcomes. *Journal of Personality and Social Psychology, 78,* 122–135.

Rothbart, M. K., & Bates, J. E. (1998). Temperament. In N. Eisenberg (Ed.), *Handbook of child psychology: Vol 3. Social, emotional and personality development* (5th ed., pp. 105–176). Wiley.

Rothbart, M. K., & Posner, M. I. (2022). Individual differences in temperament and the efficiency of brain networks. *Current Opinion in Behavioral Sciences, 43,* 242–248. https://doi.org/10.1016/j.cobeha.2021.11.001

Rumi, M. J. (1997). The Guest House. (C. Barks, Trans.). (Original work published 1436). Harper Collins.

Rutter, M. (2007). Gene-environment interdependence. *Developmental Science, 10,* 12–18.

Saudino, K. J. (2005). Behavioral genetics and child temperament. *Journal of Developmental and Behavioral Pediatrics, 26*(3), 214–223.

Schwartz, R. (2021). *No bad parts: How the internal family systems model changes everything.* Sounds True.

Segal, N. L. (2000). *Entwined lives: Twins and what they tell us about human behavior.* Plume.

Segal, N. L. (2017). *Twin mythconceptions: False beliefs, fables, and facts about twins.* Academic Press.

Shiner, R. L., & Caspi, A. (2003). Personality differences in childhood and adolescence: Measurement, development, and consequences. *Journal of Child Psychology and Psychiatry, 44,* 2–32.

Shneidman, E. S. (1993). *Suicide as psychache: A clinical approach to self-destructive behavior.* Jason Aronson.

Siegel, D. J. (2001a). Memory: An overview, with emphasis on the developmental, interpersonal, and neurobiological aspects. *Journal of the American Academy of Child and Adolescent Psychiatry, 40*, 997–1011.

Siegel, D. J. (2001b). Toward an interpersonal neurobiology of the developing mind: Attachment, "mindsight," and neural integration. *Infant Mental Health Journal, 22*, 67–94.

Siegel, D. J. (2010a). *The mindful therapist.* W. W. Norton.

Siegel, D. J. (2010b). *Mindsight: The science of personal transformation.* Bantam.

Siegel, D. J. (2017). *Mind: A journey to the heart of being human.* W. W. Norton.

Siegel, D. J. (2018). *Aware: The science and practice of presence.* Tarcher.

Siegel, D. J. (2020). *The developing mind* (3rd ed.). Guilford Press.

Siegel, D. J. (2023). *IntraConnected: MWe (me + we): As the integration of self, identity, and belonging.* W. W. Norton.

Siegel, D. J. (forthcoming). *The mindful therapist (2nd ed.): 4-D psychotherapy from the inside out.* W. W. Norton.

Skvortsova, K., Iovino, N., & Bogdanovic, O. (2018). Functions and mechanisms of epigenetic inheritance in animals. *Nature Reviews Molecular Cell Biology, 19.* https://doi.org/10.1038/s41580-018-0074-2

Sroufe, L. A., Egeland, B., Carlson, E., & Collins, W. A. (2005). *The development of the person.* Guilford Press.

The Narrative Enneagram. (2020). *The Enneagram for therapists, counselors, and coaches.* Original contributors: Palmer, Helen and Daniels, David, The Enneagram Professional Training Program (1988–2013). Additional contributors: Daniels, David, Saracino, Terry, Gilbert, Marion, and Rosario, Reneé (2014–2020).

Thomas, A., & Chess, S. (1977). *Temperament and development.* Brunner/Mazel.

Thomas, A., Chess, S., Birch, H., Hertzig, M., & Korn, S. (1963). *Behavioral individuality in early childhood.* New York University Press.

Thompson, R. A., Lewis, M. D., & Calkins, S. D. (2008). Reassessing emotion regulation. *Child Development Perspectives, 2*, 124–131.

Vaish, A., Grossmann, T., & Woodward, A. (2008). Not all emotions are created equal: The negativity bias in social-emotional development. *Psychological Bulletin, 134*(3), 383–403. https://doi.org/10.1037/0033-2909.134.3.383

Valiant, G. (1992). *The ego mechanisms of defense.* American Psychiatric Association Publishing.

van IJzendoorn, M., & Bakermans-Kranenburg, M. J. (2012). Integrating temperament and attachment. In M. Zentner & R. L. Shiner (Eds.), *Handbook of temperament* (pp. 403–424). Guilford Press.

Venkatraman, A., Edlow, B., & Immordino-Yang, M. (2017). The functional anatomy of the reticular formation. *Frontiers of Neuroanatomy, 11.* https://doi.org/10.3389/fnana.2017.00015

Vukasović, T., & Bratko, D. (2015). Heritability of personality: A meta-analysis of behavior genetic studies. *Psychological Bulletin, 141*(4), 769–785. https://doi.org/10.1037/bul0000017

Waddington, C. H. (1957). *The strategy of the genes.* Allen & Unwin.

Wertenbaker, C. (2017). *The Enneagram of G. I. Gurdjieff.* Codhill Press.

Wiltse, V., & Palmer, H. (2009). Hidden in plain sight: Observation on the origins of the Enneagram. *The Enneagram Journal, 2,* 104–137.

Wright, A. J., & Jackson, J. J. (2022). Childhood temperament and adulthood personality differentially predict life outcomes. *Scientific Reports, 12,* Article 10286. https://doi.org/10.1038/s41598-022-14666-0

Index

About the Authors

Laura A. Baker, PhD, is a professor of psychology at the University of Southern California, a certified Iyengar yoga teacher (CIYT), Enneagram consultant, and researcher and teacher in the emerging science of spirituality. She earned her BA in psychology from the University of Kansas and her MA and PhD from the University of Colorado, Boulder, where she trained in behavioral genetics and quantitative psychology. Her research involves the gene-environment interplay in human behavior. She directs the Southern California Twin Project at USC, a NIMH-funded longitudinal twin study of the effects of genes and environment on externalizing behavior problems and their social and biological risk factors from childhood to young adulthood. She has published over 125 scientific research articles and book chapters in behavioral genetics, and was the 2021 recipient of the Behavioral Genetics Association's Dobzhansky Award for lifetime achievement in behavioral genetics. Laura teaches courses in behavioral genetics, human sexuality, contemplative neuroscience, and the science of yoga and meditation.

Laura also teaches yoga and meditation to faculty, staff, and students at USC. As a student of ancient spiritual approaches to understanding the mind, she became interested in the Enneagram as a model of personality. She first encountered the Enneagram at the intensive workshops led by David Daniels in the narrative tradition, and became part of the Patterns of Developmental Pathways (PDP) group and their efforts to present a consilient model for understanding this system in the context of contemporary psychological science.

David N. Daniels, MD (August 30, 1934–May 26, 2017) was a world-renowned Enneagram teacher and therapist, clinical professor of psychiatry and behavioral sciences at Stanford University School of Medicine, the lead author of the best-selling *The Essential Enneagram: The Definitive Personality Test and Self-Discovery Guide* (2000/2009/2025 (25th anniversary edition, Harper Collins) and of *The Enneagram, Relationships, and Intimacy* with coauthor Suzanne Dion (2018/2025, forthcoming updated edition, Morgan James Publishing).

David was educated at Stanford University School of Medicine and completed his medical degree in 1958. He then served on the faculty in the Department of Psychiatry and Behavioral Sciences at the Stanford University School of Medicine until 1970, at which point he started a private psychiatry practice and remained on the clinical faculty. He discovered the Enneagram in 1984 and worked tirelessly for 33 years until his death in 2017 to teach the Enneagram as a psycho-spiritual system while also bringing rigor, scientific thinking, and credibility to it. He had a clear vision— the Enneagram was the very best tool available to relieve one's suffering, to understand each other, and to love and live more fully.

In private practice for over 40 years, David also taught the Enneagram system at Stanford University, in the community, and internationally for 33 years. Together with author and teacher Helen Palmer, he founded the Palmer-Daniels Enneagram Professional Training Program, now called The Narrative Enneagram, and was one of the founders of the International Enneagram Association (IEA) who led efforts to sponsor the first International Enneagram Association conference at Stanford University in 1994.

As one of the founding fathers of the modern Enneagram, he trained thousands of Enneagram teachers and therapists and helped to develop the Enneagram system for practical use in helping, healing, and self-actualization in therapeutic practice, couples and marriage counseling, parenting, the workplace, sports, prisons, and self-help for everyone. He was devoted to relieving suffering in people and their relationships.

David felt it was important to revere the spiritual origins and remarkable preciseness of the Enneagram and its cosmic laws. He was passionate about bridging the Enneagram to science and was excited to find consilience with affective neuroscience. David would be grateful to Dan, Laura, Denise, and Jack. His work is being carried on at drdaviddaniels.com.

Denise Daniels, PhD, is a developmental psychologist, Enneagram consultant, and Silicon Valley startup executive. Her work with the Enneagram began in 1984 shortly after her father, David Daniels, learned the Enneagram from Helen Palmer. Denise's Enneagram expertise includes consulting work with scientists seeking a better understanding of the Enneagram, use of the Enneagram in parenting and the understanding of child development, and workplace applications. She brings her 40-year study of the Enneagram system to consulting in the empirical sciences, the intersection of the Enneagram with formal, mathematical, and data sciences, and the ancient discovery, history, and cosmic laws of the Enneagram. As a certified teacher in The Narrative Enneagram, Daniels has taught and facilitated workshops on the Enneagram in both Silicon Valley companies and at Stanford University.

Daniels's psychology degrees include a BA from the University of California at Berkeley, and an MA and PhD from the University of Colorado at Boulder. She completed four years of postdoctoral work at Stanford University Medical Center. Daniels is the author of numerous articles, book chapters, and online publications.

Trained in personality, behavioral genetics, and developmental psychology research, Daniels brought her knowledge to the applied fields of educational and health technology. Some of her contributions include: the first K–12 education website on the internet, called edscape.com, in 1994; a child development and health website serving seven million parents a month, called education.com, in 2007; and the novel use of Zoom in online education of therapists in 2012. Today, her work in technology includes data science, responsible AI, and technical innovation that can transform the internet.

Daniels has deep personal and professional interests in the human growth potential and transpersonal psychology. The search for meaning in the mystery of being human, the exploration of consciousness and the cosmos, and understanding knowledge beyond what is visible are her current areas of study.

Jack Killen, MD, received his AB from Kenyon College in 1971 and his MD from Tufts University in 1975. After training and certification in internal medicine and medical oncology at Georgetown University, he began a 33-year career overseeing multidisciplinary clinical research programs at the National Institutes of Health (NIH). For 16 of those years, he was deputy director (1987–1993) and then director (1994–2001) of the Division of AIDS in the National Institute of Allergy and Infectious Diseases. There he played key leadership roles in the creation and evolution of many major NIH research programs on HIV/AIDS treatment and prevention around the world, and development of policy regarding ethics of clinical research in the developing world. In 2003 he brought that experience to what is now the NIH's National Center for Complementary and Integrative Health, becoming deputy director in 2007. He retired in 2015.

Jack first encountered the Enneagram in 1996 as another part of a personal journey that includes deep dives into 12-step work, psychotherapy, meditation, and somatic practices. He was certified as a narrative tradition Enneagram teacher in January 2004, when his interests in the intersections of science, contemplative spiritual practices, and the Enneagram were ignited in the endlessly fascinating PDP collaboration. He has also completed certification by The Enneagram in Business as a trainer and coach and is a member of The Narrative Enneagram and the International Enneagram Association. He and his husband, Fred Boykin, a psychotherapist who uses the Enneagram extensively in his work with clients, now live in Fort Lauderdale, Florida, where lately he has fallen down the genealogy rabbit hole, and has once again taken up the French horn, after 50 years away.

Daniel J. Siegel, MD, received his medical degree from Harvard University, did his postgraduate medical training at UCLA in pediatrics and then child, adolescent, and adult psychiatry, and served as a training director and then a clinical professor in UCLA's department of psychiatry for three decades. He served as a National Institute of Mental Health research fellow, studying attachment, memory, and narrative, and the impact of parental insight on child development outcomes. A fellow of the American Psychiatric Association and recipient of other honorary awards, Dan works at the interface of science, clinical practice, public policy, and mental health education. He is the founding codirector of the UCLA Mindful Awareness Research Center and founding co-principal investigator at the Center for Culture, Brain, and Development. He is currently the executive director of the Mindsight Institute in Santa Monica, California.

Dan is the founding editor of the Norton Professional Books Series on Interpersonal Neurobiology, which now includes over 100 books, this book being one. He is the author of numerous books, including five *New York Times* bestsellers: *Mind: A Journey to the Heart of Being Human*; *Aware: The Science and Practice of Presence*; *Brainstorm: The Power and Purpose of the Teenage Brain*; and with Tina Payne Bryson, *The Whole Brain Child* and *No Drama Discipline*. Dan continues to be active as a practicing psychotherapist harnessing the consilience of interpersonal neurobiology to apply transdisciplinary approaches in practical and innovative ways in psychotherapy. The Mindsight Institute is the brick-and-mortar home for interpersonal neurobiology and offers extensive immersive educational programs for professionals and the public interested in wholeness and mental health: see drdansiegel .com and mindsightinstitute.com.